MY TURF

MY TURF

HORSES, BOXERS, BLOOD MONEY, AND THE SPORTING LIFE

William Nack

DA CAPO PRESS
A MEMBER OF THE PERSEUS BOOKS GROUP

Cataloging-in-Publication data for this book is available from the Library of Congress.

ISBN 0–306–81250–9

All of the stories in this book, with the exception of "Dubai's Dream Team," were originally published in SPORTS ILLUSTRATED Magazine and are used with the permission of the publisher. Copyright © Time Inc. ALL RIGHTS RESERVED. "Dubai's Dream Team" first appeared in GQ October 2002.

The author would like to acknowledge the following contributions:
"Blood Money" and "Breakdowns" were written with Lester Munson
"Collision at Home" was written with special reporting by Mike Donovan
"The Muscle Murders" was written with special reporting by Don Yaeger and Teagan Clive.

Published by Da Capo Press
A Member of the Perseus Books Group
http://www.dacapopress.com

Da Capo Press books are available at special discounts for bulk purchases in the U.S. by corporations, institutions, and other organizations. For more information, please contact the Special Markets Department at the Perseus Books Group, 11 Cambridge Center, Cambridge, MA 02142, or call (800)255–1514 or (617)252–5298, or e-mail specialmarkets@perseusbooks.com.

1 2 3 4 5 6 7 8 9—07 06 05 04 03

To Abigail, Noah, and Ayla

CONTENTS

INTRODUCTION

In December of 1971, near the close of a particularly raucous Christmas party in the Suffolk County office of *Newsday*, the Long Island paper, I finally heeded the urgings of several of my fellow reporters on cityside and launched upon a favored soliloquy that suddenly, even magically, altered the whole direction of my life. To ribald cries of encouragement, with all of us well into the eggnog, I mounted a desk in the middle of the *Newsday* cityroom and there, from the mists of memory, summoned aloud the names of all the Kentucky Derby winners from 1875 to the then-present—all ninety-seven of them in a row, from Aristides, the little chestnut who won the inaugural running, right through to Cannonero II, the big bay from Caracas who had won it just seven months before.

I was a political/environmental writer at the time, a periodic scribbler on the evils of detergents in groundwater and on Long Island duck sludge in the Great South Bay, on the secondary and tertiary treatment of garden-variety sewage, on the incredibly shrinking fresh-water aquifers that underlie Long Island, and on the increasingly lugubrious state of the Blue Point oyster, the sweetest and most succulent of all the neighborhood mollusks. Covering such stories, of course, merely fell between the hours spent detailing the little dramas and madnesses that ruled the day, the spoils of the times—the body bags returning from Vietnam, the head-on collisions that wiped out entire families, the racial riots and arson fires and train wrecks, and the assorted gaucheries of Suffolk's reigning Gladstones and Disraelis, with enough political knifings and suicides to make any reporter's day. At the time, I figured I was on my way to cover national politics, with a foreign desk in Buenos Aires or Beijing thrown in later, and simply had never imagined myself as a writer of sports, a chronicler of races and games, though I was a daily reader of the sports page and a great admirer of its more estimable practitioners, from Red Smith and Jimmy Cannon to John

Lardner and W.C. Heinz. As I clambered down from that table, David Laventhol—then the editor of *Newsday* and a fiercely competitive closet horseplayer (he would later handicap the races for *Newsday* under the nom de plume of "Clocker Dave")—sidled up to me and asked, "Why do you know that?"

"I memorized them when I was a kid," I told him. "The week after Swaps won the Washington Park Handicap. Labor Day, 1956." That was back in the days when I was just beginning to inhabit the sunnier aprons of Chicago racetracks with my father, a $2 bettor, in the mid-1950s, back when I started prowling the grandstand at Arlington Park and first inhaled the scent and rhythms of the game, with its enchanting history and lore. Laventhol listened, fascinated, as I described my larval stages as a racetrack habitué—my youthful adventures at the 1958 and 1960 Kentucky Derbys, the summer as a hotwalker and groom at old Arlington—and the hours spent studying names and thoroughbred pedigrees.

"You're not happy covering politics or the environment, are you?" Laventhol said.

"Not particularly," I said. "There are some days at the county legislature when I'd rather be having a root canal."

"Would you like to cover horse racing for us?" David asked.

I thought that maybe I'd not heard him right. I leaned closer. "Seriously," he said. "We're adding a Sunday paper in the spring and we'll need someone to write about racing. It would be the perfect job for you. Let me know . . . "

Five minutes later, to my astonishment, I was a sportswriter. The only thing Laventhol asked was that I write him a note applying for the job and telling him why I wanted it. "I don't want people knocking on my door and asking why you're doing this," he said. "It *is* a little strange. So write me a note and I'll post it." I recall nothing of that memo to Clocker Dave but a single line: "After covering politicians for the last four years, I'd love the chance to cover the whole horse."

Seven years later, after more than three years as a *Newsday* turfwriter and almost four as a general sports columnist, I joined the staff of *Sports Illustrated*, and for nearly twenty-three years the magazine served me generously as a home port from which I could scour and trace the many rich and curlicue tapestries of sport. Except for the one about the Arabs in horse racing, which I wrote as a freelancer for GQ, all of the pieces contained in this volume first ran in *SI* between 1988 and 2001, and each in its way reflects my bias for covering sport beyond the games, outside of the arena and the box score.

Even as a columnist, I never had much patience chasing after events, covering the games and races and keeping the score, though I certainly did my share of U.S. Tennis Opens and World Series, of Indy 500s and Triple Crowns and Super Bowls. Many of my brethren, I cautiously suspect, went into the business of writing in order to attend games; like my favorite colleagues, Tom Callahan, John Schulian, and Red Smith, I went into the business of attending games in order to write. Not that daily journalism was without its sublime compensations. I once saw Reggie Jackson hit three home runs on three straight pitches to win the World Series for the Yankees, the last off a 55-mile-an-hour knuckle ball that flew 450 feet into the black at Yankee Stadium. Saw Roberto Duran quit on his feet against Sugar Ray Leonard in New Orleans, his scraped lips muttering "No mas . . . No more box." Saw the Russian weightlifter Vassily Alexyev, the strongest man in the world, on a summer night in Montreal, clean and jerk more iron over his head than any man ever in recorded history. Hell, I saw Secretariat win the Belmont by 31 lengths, his final strides as clean and pure as his first. I can hear yet the roar of all those crowds.

All that aside, however, I never felt more passionate than in pursuing the tales told herein—than in reporting and writing the story behind the leukemia death of Ernie Davis, the first black Heisman Trophy winner; or in exploring the long and unjust incarceration of Hurricane Carter, for three murders he did not commit; or in chasing the black ghosts of Sonny Liston and Big Daddy Lipscomb, both of whom died of suspiciously administered overdoses of heroin; or in searching months for the angry and tormented chess recluse, Bobby Fischer, the loneliest of all loners; or in sitting for hours with Robbie Davis, the jockey, talking about his life as a boy growing up with an evil stepfather in Pocatello, Idaho, and how that mean existence made him suicidal and many years later drove him in a panic from New York back to his roots; or in listening to A.J. Foyt and Keith Hernandez, their voices sometimes quavering, as they recalled their turbulent lives with father.

While most of my colleagues came to sportswriting right out of college, with no detours along the way, I slipped in through the back door of the cityroom, still hearing the wail of police sirens and the thump of gavels on political podiums. I never really left that world, and the stories here entombed more reflect the harsher lights of city streets, of the emergency rooms of the real world, than they do the softer hues that fall like twilight shadows on the playing fields. Not a few of my colleagues, stricken by the pangs of conscience that attend the belief that sports were not worthy of their toils, have fled to the metro or national desks. Alas, having already worked those asylums, I never suffered that delusion for an instant. Instead, in an odd kind of way, I brought the instincts of the cityroom with me, trying to balance one foot in the ball yard and the other in the world of larger human woes.

I've really had it both ways, and never more vividly than during that ten days in January of 1977 when I covered the Super Bowl in California, where John Madden and the Oakland Raiders stomped on the Minnesota Vikings and I kept writing Fred Baryshnikov when I was thinking Fred Biletnikoff; left there to watch Olympic gold medalists Howard Davis and Leon Spinks make their bows as professional boxers in Las Vegas; and, finally, flew into Salt Lake City to cover the execution of Gary Mark Gilmore. In that string of endless days, nothing was more dramatic than Gilmore's final utterance, "Let's do it!" and the muffled pop of rifle fire from the prison cannery. I sensed then that they were all somehow the same, all media happenings and photo ops, from the boisterous kick-off to the muted horn of Gilmore's death, each just another event in that increasingly weird, far gaudier show that was America of those times.

I missed absolutely nothing in that move from cityside. For me, as I hope these pieces suggest, sports turned out to be the whole horse.

PART 1

TURF WRITING

PURE HEART

*J*ust *before noon the horse was led haltingly into a van next to the stallion barn, and there a concentrated barbiturate was injected into his jugular. Forty-five seconds later there was a crash as the stallion collapsed. His body was trucked immediately to Lexington, Kentucky, where Dr. Thomas Swerczek, a professor of veterinary science at the University of Kentucky, performed the necropsy. All of the horse's vital organs were normal in size except for the heart.*

"We were all shocked," Swerczek said. "I've seen and done thousands of autopsies on horses, and nothing I'd ever seen compared to it. The heart of the average horse weighs about nine pounds. This was almost twice the average size, and a third larger than any equine heart I'd ever seen. And it wasn't pathologically enlarged. All the chambers and the valves were normal. It was just larger. I think it told us why he was able to do what he did."

In the late afternoon of Monday, October 2, 1989, as I headed my car from the driveway of Arthur Hancock's Stone Farm onto Winchester Road outside of Paris, Kentucky, I was seized by an impulse as beckoning as the wind that strums through the trees there, mingling the scents of new grass and old history.

For reasons as obscure to me then as now, I felt compelled to see Lawrence Robinson. For almost thirty years, until he suffered a stroke in March of 1983, Robinson was the head caretaker of stallions at Claiborne Farm. I had not seen him since his illness, but I knew he still lived on the farm, in a small white frame house set on a hill overlooking the lush stallion paddocks and the main stallion barn. In the first stall of that barn, in the same space that was once home to the great Bold Ruler, lived Secretariat, Bold Ruler's greatest son.

It was through Secretariat that I had met Robinson. On the bright, cold afternoon of November 12, 1973, he was one of several hundred people gathered at Blue Grass Airport in Lexington to greet the horse on his flight from New York into retirement in Kentucky. I flew with the colt that day, and as the plane banked over the field, a voice from the tower crackled over the airplane radio: "There's more people out here to meet Secretariat than there was to greet the governor."

"Well, he's won more races than the governor," pilot Dan Neff replied.

An hour later, after a van ride out the Paris Pike behind a police escort with blue lights flashing, Robinson led Secretariat onto a ramp at Claiborne and toward his sire's old stall—out of racing and into history. For me, that final walk beneath a grove of trees, with the colt slanting like a buck through the autumn gloaming, brought to a melancholy close the richest, grandest, damnedest, most exhilarating time of my life. For eight months, first as the racing writer for Long Island, New York's *Newsday* and then as the designated chronicler of the horse's career, I had a daily front-row seat to watch Secretariat. I was at the barn in the morning and the racetrack in the afternoon for what turned out to be the year's greatest show in sports, at the heart of which lay a Triple Crown performance unmatched in the history of American racing.

Sixteen years had come and gone since then, and I had never attended a Kentucky Derby or a yearling sale at Keeneland without driving out to Claiborne to visit Secretariat, often in the company of friends who had never seen him. On the long ride from Louisville, I would regale them with stories about the horse—how on that early morning in March of '73 he had materialized out of the quickening blue darkness in the upper stretch at Belmont Park, his ears pinned back, running as fast as horses run; how he had lost the Wood Memorial and won the Derby, and how he had been bothered by a pigeon feather at Pimlico on the eve of the Preakness (at the end of this tale I would pluck the delicate, mashed feather out of my wallet, like a picture of my kids, to pass around the car); how on the morning of the Belmont Stakes he had burst from the barn like a stud horse going to the breeding shed and had walked around the outdoor ring on his hind legs, pawing at the sky; how he had once grabbed my notebook and refused to give it back, and how he had seized a rake in his teeth and begun raking the shed; and, finally, I told about that magical, unforgettable instant, frozen now in time, when he had turned for home, appearing out of a dark drizzle at Woodbine, near Toronto, in the last race of his career, twelve in front and steam puffing from his nostrils as from a factory whistle, bounding like some mythical beast out of Greek lore.

Oh, I knew all the stories, knew them well, had crushed and rolled them in my hand, until their quaint musk lay in the saddle of my palm. Knew them as I knew the stories of my children. Knew them as I knew the stories of my own life. Told them at dinner parties, swapped them with horseplayers as if they were trading cards, argued over them with old men and blind fools who had seen the show but missed the message. Dreamed them and turned them over like pillows in my rubbery sleep. Woke up with them, brushed my aging teeth with them, grinned at them in the mirror. Horses have a way of getting inside of you, and so it was that Secretariat became like a fifth child in our house, the older boy who was off at school and never around but who was as loved and true a part of the family as Muffin, our shaggy, epileptic dog.

The story I now tell begins on that Monday afternoon last October on the macadam outside of Stone Farm. I had never been to Paris, Kentucky, in the early fall, and I only happened to be there that day to begin an article about the Hancock family, the owners of Claiborne and Stone farms. There wasn't a soul on the road to point the way to Robinson's place, so I swung in and out of several empty driveways until I saw a man on a tractor cutting the lawn in front of Marchmont, Dell Hancock's mansion. He yelled back to me: "Take a right out the drive. Go down to Claiborne House. Then a right at the driveway across the road. Go up a hill to the big black barn. Turn left and go down to the end. Lawrence had a stroke a few years back, y'know."

The house was right where he said. I knocked on the front door, then walked behind and knocked on the back, and called through a side window into a room where music was playing. No one answered. But I had time to kill, so I wandered over to the stallion paddock, just a few yards from the house. The stud Ogygian, a son of Damascus, lifted his head inquiringly. He started walking toward me, and I put my elbows on the top of the fence and looked down the gentle slope toward the stallion barn.

And suddenly there he was, Secretariat, standing outside the barn and grazing at the end of a lead shank held by groom Bobby Anderson, who was sitting on a bucket in the sun. Even from a hundred yards away, the horse appeared lighter than I had seen him in years. It struck me as curious that he was not running free in his paddock—why was Bobby grazing him?—but his bronze coat reflected the October light, and it never occurred to me that something might be wrong. But something was terribly wrong. On Labor Day, Secretariat had come down with laminitis, a life-threatening hoof disease, and here, a month later, he was still suffering from its aftershocks.

Secretariat was dying. In fact, he would be gone within forty-eight hours.

I briefly considered slipping around Ogygian's paddock and dropping down to visit, but I had never entered Claiborne through the back door, and so I thought better of it. Instead, for a full half hour, I stood by the paddock waiting for Robinson and gazing in the distance at Secretariat. The gift of reverie is a blessing divine, and it is conferred most abundantly on those who lie in hammocks or drive alone in cars. Or lean on hillside fences in Kentucky. The mind swims, binding itself to whatever flotsam comes along, to old driftwood faces and voices of the past, to places and scenes once visited, to things not seen or done but only dreamed.

It was July 4, 1972, and I was sitting in the press box at Aqueduct with Clem Florio, a former prizefighter turned Baltimore handicapper, when I glanced at the *Daily Racing Form*'s past performances for the second race, a 5 1/2-furlong buzz for maiden 2-year-olds. As I scanned the pedigrees, three names leaped out: by Bold Ruler–Somethingroyal, by Princequillo. Bold Ruler was the nation's preeminent sire, and Somethingroyal was the dam of several stakes winners, including the fleet Sir Gaylord. It was a match of royalty. Even the baby's name seemed faintly familiar: Secretariat. Where had I heard it before? But of course! Lucien Laurin was training the colt at Belmont Park for Penny Chenery Tweedy's Meadow Stable, making Secretariat a stablemate of that year's Kentucky Derby and Belmont Stakes winner, Riva Ridge.

I had seen Secretariat just a week before. I had been at the Meadow Stable barn one morning, checking on Riva, when exercise rider Jimmy Gaffney took me aside and said: "You wanna see the best-lookin' 2-year-old you've ever seen?"

We padded up the shed to the colt's stall. Gaffney stepped inside. "What do you think?" he asked. The horse looked magnificent, to be sure, a bright red chestnut with three white feet and a tapered white marking down his face. "He's gettin' ready," Gaffney said. "Don't forget the name: Secretariat. He can run." And then, conspiratorially, Gaffney whispered: "Don't quote me, but this horse will make them all forget Riva Ridge."

So that is where I had first seen him, and here he was in the second at Aqueduct. I rarely bet in those days, but Secretariat was 3–1, so I put $10 on his nose. Florio and I fixed our binoculars on him and watched it all. Watched him as he was shoved sideways at the break, dropping almost to his knees, when a colt named Quebec turned left out of the gate and crashed into him. Saw him blocked in traffic down the back side and shut off again on the turn for home. Saw him cut off a second time deep in the stretch as he was making a final run. Saw him finish fourth, obviously much the best horse, beaten by only $1^1/_4$ lengths after really running but an eighth of a mile.

You should have seen Clem. Smashing his binoculars down on his desk, he leaped to his feet, banged his chair against the wall behind him, threw a few punches in the air and bellowed: "Secretariat! That's my Derby horse for next year!"

Two weeks later, when the colt raced to his first victory by six, Florio announced to all the world, "Secretariat will win the Triple Crown next year." He nearly got into a fistfight in the Aqueduct press box that day when Mannie Kalish, a New York handicapper, chided him for making such an outrageously bold assertion: "Ah, you Maryland guys, you come to New York and see a horse break his maiden and think he's another Citation. We see horses like Secretariat all the time. I bet he don't even run in the Derby." Stung by the put-down "you Maryland guys," Florio came forward and stuck his finger into Kalish's chest, but two writers jumped between them and they never came to blows.

The Secretariat phenomenon, with all the theater and passion that would attend it, had begun. Florio was right, of course, and by the end of Secretariat's 2-year-old season, everyone else who had seen him perform knew it. All you had to do was watch the Hopeful Stakes at Saratoga. I was at the races that August afternoon with Arthur Kennedy, an old-time race-tracker and handicapper who had been around the horses since the 1920s, and even he had never seen anything quite like it. Dropping back to dead last out of the gate, Secretariat trailed eight horses into the far turn, where jockey Ron Turcotte swung him to the outside. Three jumps past the half-mile pole the colt exploded. "Now he's runnin'!" Kennedy said.

You could see the blue-and-white silks as they disappeared behind one horse, reappeared in a gap between horses, dropped out of sight again and finally reemerged as Secretariat powered to the lead off the turn. He dashed from last to first in 290 yards, blazing through a quarter in :22, and galloped home in a laugher to win by six. It was a performance with style, touched by art. "I've never seen a 2-year-old do that," Kennedy said quietly. "He looked like a 4-year-old out there."

So that was when I knew. The rest of Secretariat's 2-year-old campaign—in which he lost only once, in the Champagne Stakes when he was disqualified from first to second after bumping Stop the Music at the top of the stretch—was simply a mopping-up operation. At year's end, so dominant had he been that he became the first 2-year-old to be unanimously voted Horse of the Year.

Secretariat wintered at Hialeah, preparing for the Triple Crown, while I shoveled snow in Huntington, New York, waiting for him to race again. In February, 23-year-old Seth Hancock, the new president of Claiborne Farm, announced that he had syndicated the colt as a future breeding stallion for a then world record $6.08 million, in 32 shares at $190,000 a share, making the 1,154-pound horse worth more than three times his weight in gold. (Bullion was selling at the time for $90 an ounce.) Like everyone else, I thought Secretariat would surely begin his campaign in Florida, and I did not expect to see him again until the week before the Kentucky Derby. I was browsing through a newspaper over breakfast one day when I saw a news dispatch whose message went through me like a current. Secretariat would be arriving soon to begin his Triple Crown campaign by way of the three New York prep races: the Bay Shore, the Gotham and the Wood Memorial Stakes.

"Hot damn!" I blurted to my family. "Secretariat is coming to New York!"

At the time, I had in mind doing a diary about the horse, a chronicle of the adventures of a Triple Crown contender, which I thought might one day make a magazine piece. The colt arrived at Belmont Park on March 10, and the next day I was there at 7 A.M., scribbling notes in a pad. For the next forty days, in what became a routine, I would fall out of bed at 6 A.M., make a cup of instant coffee, climb into my rattling green Toyota and drive the twenty miles to Belmont Park. I had gotten to know the Meadow Stable family—Tweedy, Laurin, Gaffney, groom Eddie Sweat, assistant trainer Henny Hoeffner—in my tracking of Riva Ridge the year before, and I had come to feel at home around Belmont's Barn 5, particularly around stall 7, Secretariat's place. I took no days off, except one morning to hide Easter eggs, and I spent hours sitting on the dusty floor outside Secretariat's stall, talking to Sweat as he turned a rub rag on the colt, filled his water bucket, bedded his stall with straw, kept him in hay and oats. I took notes compulsively, endlessly, feeling for the texture of the life around the horse.

A typical page of scribblings went like this:

"Sweat talks to colt . . . easy, Red, I'm comin' in here now . . . stop it, Red! You behave now . . . Sweat moves around colt. Brush in hand. Flicks off dust. Secretariat sidesteps and pushes Sweat. Blue sky. Henny comes up. 'How's he doin', Eddie?' 'He's gettin' edgy.' . . . Easy Sunday morning."

Secretariat was an amiable, gentlemanly colt, with a poised and playful nature that at times made him seem as much a pet as was the stable dog . I was standing in front of his stall one morning, writing, when he reached out, grabbed my notebook in his teeth and sank back inside, looking to see what I would do. "Give the man his notebook back!" yelled Sweat. As the groom dipped under the webbing, Secretariat dropped the notebook on the bed of straw.

Another time, after raking the shed, Sweat leaned the handle of the rake against the stall webbing and turned to walk away. Secretariat seized the handle in his mouth and began pushing and pulling it across the floor. "Look at him rakin' the shed!" cried Sweat. All up and down the barn, laughter fluttered like the pigeons in the stable eaves, as the colt did a passable imitation of his own groom.

By his personality and temperament, Secretariat became the most engaging character in the barn. His own stable pony, a roan named Billy Silver, began an unrequited love affair with him. "He loves Secretariat, but Secretariat don't pay any attention to him," Sweat said one day. "If Billy sees you grazin' Secretariat, he'll go to hollerin' until you bring him out. Secretariat just ignores him. Kind of sad, really." One morning, I was walking beside Hoeffner through the shed, with Gaffney and Secretariat ahead of us, when Billy stuck his head out of his jerry-built stall and nuzzled the colt as he went by.

Hoeffner did a double take. "Jimmy!" he yelled. "Is that pony botherin' the big horse?"

"Nah," said Jimmy. "He's just smellin' him a little."

Hoeffner's eyes widened. Spinning around on his heels, jabbing a finger in the air, he bellowed: "Get the pony out of here! I don't want him smellin' the big horse."

Leaning on his rake, Sweat laughed softly: "Poor Billy Silver. He smelled the wrong horse!"

I remember wishing that those days could breeze on forever—the mornings over coffee and doughnuts at the truck outside the barn, the hours spent watching the red colt walk to the track and gallop once around, the days absorbing the rhythms of the life around the horse. I had been following racehorses since I was twelve, back in the days of Native Dancer, and now I was an observer on an odyssey, a quest for the Triple Crown. It had been twenty-five years since Citation had won racing's Holy Grail. For me, the adventure really began in the early morning of March 14, when Laurin lifted Turcotte aboard Secretariat and said: "Let him roll, Ronnie."

The colt had filled out substantially since I had last seen him under tack, in the fall, and he looked like some medieval charger—his thick neck bowed and his chin drawn up beneath its mass, his huge shoulders shifting as he strode, his coat radiant and his eyes darting left and right. He was walking to the track for his final workout, a three-eighths-of-a-mile drill designed to light the fire in him for the seven-furlong Bay Shore Stakes three days later. Laurin, Tweedy and I went to the clubhouse fence near the finish line, where we watched and waited as Turcotte headed toward the pole and let Secretariat rip. Laurin clicked his stopwatch.

The colt was all by himself through the lane, and the sight and sound of him racing toward us is etched forever in memory: Turcotte was bent over him, his coat blown up like a parachute, and the horse was reaching out with his forelegs in that distinctive way he had, raising them high and then, at the top of the lift, snapping them out straight and with tremendous force, the snapping hard as bone, the hooves striking the ground and folding it beneath him. Laurin clicked his watch as Secretariat raced under the wire. "Oh my god!" he cried. "Thirty-three and three fifths!" Horses rarely break 34 seconds in three-furlong moves.

Looking ashen, fearing the colt might have gone too fast, Laurin headed for the telephone under the clubhouse to call the upstairs clocker, Jules Watson. "Hello there, Jules. How fast did you get him?"

I watched Laurin's face grow longer as he listened, until he looked thunderstruck: *"Thirty-two and three fifths?"* A full second faster than Laurin's own clocking, it was the fastest three-furlong workout I had ever heard of. Tweedy smiled cheerily and said, "Well, that ought to open his pipes!"

Oh, it did that. Three days later, blocked by a wall of horses in the Bay Shore, Secretariat plunged through like a fullback, 220 yards from the wire, and bounded off to win the race by four and a half lengths. I could hear a man screaming behind me. I turned and saw Roger Laurin, Lucien's son, raising his arms in the air and shouting, "He's too much horse! They can't stop him. They can't even stop him with a wall of horses!"

I had ridden horses during my youth in Morton Grove, Illinois, and I remember one summer I took a little black bullet of a thoroughbred filly out of the barn and walked her to the track that rimmed the polo field across Golf Road. I had been to the races a few times, had seen the jockeys ride, and I wanted to feel what it was like. So I hitched up my stirrups and galloped her around the east turn, standing straight up. Coming off the turn, I dropped into a crouch and clucked to her. She took off like a sprinter leaving the blocks—swoooosh!—and the wind started whipping in my eyes. I could feel the tears streaming down my face, and then I looked down and saw her knees pumping like pistons. I didn't think she would make the second turn, the woods were looming ahead, big trees coming up, and so I leaned a little to the left and she made the turn before she started pulling up. No car ever took me on a ride like that. And no roller coaster, either. Running loose, without rails, she gave me the wildest, most thrilling ride I had ever had.

And there was nothing like the ride that Secretariat gave me in the twelve weeks from the Bay Shore through the Belmont Stakes. Three weeks after the Bay Shore, Turcotte sent the colt to the lead down the backstretch in the one-mile Gotham. It looked like they were going to get beat when Champagne Charlie drove to within a half length at the top of the stretch—I held my breath—but Turcotte sent Secretariat on, and the colt pulled away to win by three, tying the track record of 1:33 2/5.

By then I had begun visiting Charles Hatton, a columnist for the *Daily Racing Form*, who the previous summer had proclaimed Secretariat the finest physical specimen he had ever seen. At sixty-seven, Hatton had seen them all. After my morning work was over, I would trudge up to Hatton's private aerie at Belmont Park and tell him what I had learned. I was his backstretch eyes, he my personal guru. One morning, Hatton told me that Secretariat had galloped a quarter mile past the finish line at the Gotham, and the clockers had timed him pulling up at 1:59 2/5, three fifths of a second faster than Northern Dancer's Derby record for 1 1/4 miles.

"This sucker breaks records pulling up," Hatton said. "He might be the best racehorse I ever saw. Better than Man o' War."

Those were giddy, heady days coming to the nine-furlong Wood Memorial, the colt's last major prep before the Kentucky Derby. On the day of the Wood, I drove directly to Aqueduct and spent the hour before the race in the receiving barn with Sweat, exercise rider Charlie Davis and Secretariat. When the voice over the loudspeaker asked the grooms to ready their horses, Sweat approached the colt with the bridle. Secretariat always took the bit easily, opening his mouth when Sweat moved to fit it in, but that afternoon it took Sweat a full five minutes to bridle him. Secretariat threw his nose in the air, backed up, shook his head. After a few minutes passed, I asked, "What's wrong with him, Eddie?"

Sweat brushed it off: "He's just edgy."

In fact, just that morning, Dr. Manuel Gilman, the track veterinarian, had lifted the colt's upper lip to check his identity tattoo and had discovered a painful abscess about the size of a quarter. Laurin decided to run Secretariat anyway—the colt needed the race—but he never told anyone else about the boil. Worse than the abscess, though, was the fact that Secretariat had had the feeblest workout of his career four days earlier, when Turcotte, seeing a riderless horse on the track, had slowed the colt to protect him from a collision. Secretariat finished the mile that day in 1:42 $^2/_5$, five seconds slower than Laurin wanted him to go. Thus he came to the Wood doubly compromised.

The race was a disaster. Turcotte held the colt back early, but when he tried to get Secretariat to pick up the bit and run, he got no response. I could see at the far turn that the horse was dead. He never made a race of it, struggling to finish third, beaten by four lengths by his own stablemate, Angle Light, and by Sham. Standing near the owner's box, I saw Laurin turn to Tweedy and yell, "Who won it?"

"You won it!" Tweedy told him.

"Angle Light won it," I said to him.

"Angle Light?" he howled back. But of course! Laurin trained him, too, and so Laurin had just won the Wood, but with the wrong horse.

I was sick. All those hours at the barn, all those early mornings at the shed, all that time and energy for naught. And in the most important race of his career, Secretariat had come up as hollow as a gourd. The next two weeks were among the most agonizing of my life. As great a stallion as he was, Bold Ruler had been essentially a speed sire and had never produced a single winner of a Triple Crown race. I couldn't help but suspect that Secretariat was another Bold Ruler, who ran into walls beyond a mile. In the next two weeks, Churchill Downs became a nest of rumors that Secretariat was unsound. Jimmy (the Greek) Snyder caused an uproar when he said the colt had a bum knee that was being treated with ice packs. I knew that wasn't true. I had been around him all spring, and the most ice I had seen near him was in a glass of tea.

All I could hope for, in those final days before the Derby, was that the colt had been suffering from a bellyache on the day of the Wood and had not been up to it. I remained ignorant of the abscess for weeks, and I had not yet divined the truth about Secretariat's training: He needed hard, blistering workouts before he ran, and that slow mile before the Wood had been inadequate. The night before the Derby, I made my selections, and the next day, two hours before post time, I climbed the stairs to the Churchill Downs jockeys' room to see Turcotte. He greeted me in an anteroom, looking surprisingly relaxed. Gilman had taken him aside a few days earlier and told him of the abscess. Turcotte saw that the boil had been treated and had disappeared. The news had made him euphoric, telling him all he needed to know about the Wood.

"You nervous?" he asked.

I shrugged. "I don't think you'll win," I said. "I picked My Gallant and Sham one-two, and you third."

"I'll tell you something," Turcotte said. "He'll beat these horses if he runs his race."

"What about the Wood?" I asked.

He shook me off. "I don't believe the Wood," he said. "I'm telling you. Something was wrong. But he's O.K. now. That's all I can tell you."

I shook his hand, wished him luck and left. Despite what Turcotte had said, I was resigned to the worst, and Secretariat looked hopelessly beaten as the field of 13 dashed past the finish line the first time. He was dead last. Transfixed, I could not take my eyes off him. In the first turn, Turcotte swung him to the outside and Secretariat began passing horses, and down the back side I watched the jockey move him boldly from eighth to seventh to sixth. Secretariat was fifth around the far turn and gaining fast on the outside. I began chanting: "Ride him, Ronnie! Ride him!" Sham was in front, turning for home, but then there was Secretariat, joining him at the top of the stretch. Laffit Pincay, on Sham, glanced over and saw Secretariat and went to the whip. Turcotte lashed Secretariat. The two raced head and head for 100 yards, until gradually Secretariat pulled away. He won by $2\frac{1}{2}$ lengths. The crowd roared, and I glanced at the tote board: $1:59^2/5$! A new track and Derby record.

Throwing decorum to the wind, I vaulted from my seat and dashed madly through the press box, jubilantly throwing a fist in the air. Handicapper Steve Davidowitz came racing toward me from the other end. We clasped arms and spun a jig in front of the copy machine. "Unbelievable!" Davidowitz cried.

I bounded down a staircase, three steps at a time. Turcotte had dismounted and was crossing the racetrack when I reached him. "What a ride!" I yelled.

"What did I tell you, Mr. Bill?" he said.

I had just witnessed the greatest Kentucky Derby performance of all time. Secretariat's quarter-mile splits were unprecedented — $:25^1/5$, $:24$, $:23^4/5$, $:23^2/5$ and $:23$. He ran each quarter faster than the preceding one. Not even the most veteran racetracker could recall a horse who had done this in a mile-and-a-quarter race. As quickly as his legions (I among them) had abandoned him following the Wood, so did they now proclaim Secretariat a superhorse.

We all followed him to Pimlico for the Preakness two weeks later, and he trained as if he couldn't get enough of it. He thrived on work and the racetrack routine. Most every afternoon, long after the crowds of visitors had dispersed, Sweat would graze the colt on a patch of grass outside the shed, then lead him back into his stall and while away the hours doing chores. One afternoon I was folded in a chair outside the colt's stall when Secretariat came to the door shaking his head and stretching his neck, curling his upper lip like a camel does. "What's botherin' you, Red?" Sweat asked. The groom stepped forward, plucked something off the colt's whiskers and blew it in the air. "Just a pigeon feather itchin' him," said Sweat. The feather floated into the palm of my hand. So it ended up in my wallet, along with the $2 mutual ticket that I had on Secretariat to win the Preakness.

In its own way, Secretariat's performance in the 1 3/16-mile Preakness was even more brilliant than his race in the Derby. He dropped back to last out of the gate, but as the field dashed into the first turn, Turcotte nudged his right rein as subtly as a man adjusting his cuff, and the colt took off like a flushed deer. The turns at Pimlico are tight, and it had always been considered suicidal to take the first bend too fast, but Secretariat sprinted full-bore around it, and by the time he turned into the back side, he was racing to the lead. Here Turcotte hit the cruise control. Sham gave chase in vain, and Secretariat coasted home to win by 2 1/2. The electric timer malfunctioned, and Pimlico eventually settled on 1:54 2/5 as the official time, but two *Daily Racing Form* clockers caught Secretariat in 1:53 2/5, a track record by three fifths of a second.

I can still see Florio shaking his head in disbelief. He had seen thousands of Pimlico races and dozens of Preaknesses over the years, but never anything like this. "Horses don't *do* what he did here today," he kept saying. "They just don't *do* that and win."

Secretariat wasn't just winning. He was performing like an original, making it all up as he went along. And everything was moving so fast, so unexpectedly, that I was having trouble keeping a perspective on it. Not three months before, after less than a year of working as a turf writer, I had started driving to the racetrack to see this one horse. For weeks I was often the only visitor there, and on many afternoons it was just Sweat, the horse and me, in the fine dust with the pregnant stable cat. And then came the Derby and the Preakness, and two weeks later the colt was on the cover of *Time, Sports Illustrated,* and *Newsweek,* and he was a staple of the morning and evening news. Secretariat suddenly transcended being a racehorse and became a cultural phenomenon, a sort of undeclared national holiday from the tortures of Watergate and the Vietnam War.

I threw myself with a passion into that final week before the Belmont. Out to the barn every morning, home late at night, I became almost manic. The night before the race, I called Laurin at home and we talked for a long while about the horse and the Belmont. I kept wondering, What is Secretariat going to do for an encore? Laurin said, "I think he's going to win by more than he has ever won in his life. I think he'll win by 10."

I slept at the *Newsday* offices that night, and at 2 A.M. I drove to Belmont Park to begin my vigil at the barn. I circled around to the back of the shed, lay down against a tree and fell asleep. I awoke to the crowing of a cock and watched as the stable workers showed up. At 6:07, Hoeffner strode into the shed, looked at Secretariat, and called out to Sweat: "Get the big horse ready! Let's walk him about 15 minutes."

Sweat slipped into the stall, put the lead shank on Secretariat and handed it to Davis, who led the colt to the outdoor walking ring. In a small stable not 30 feet away, pony girl Robin Edelstein knocked a water bucket against the wall. Secretariat, normally a docile colt on a shank, rose up on his hind legs, pawing at the sky, and started walking in circles. Davis cowered below, as if beneath a thunderclap, snatching at the chain and begging the horse to come down. Secretariat floated back to earth. He danced around the ring as if on springs, his nostrils flared and snorting, his eyes rimmed in white.

Unaware of the scene she was causing, Edelstein rattled the bucket again, and Secretariat spun in a circle, bucked and leaped in the air, kicking and spraying cinders along the walls of the pony barn. In a panic, Davis tugged at the shank, and the horse went up again, higher and higher, and Davis bent back yelling, "Come on down! Come on down!"

I stood in awe. I had never seen a horse so fit. The Derby and Preakness had wound him as tight as a watch, and he seemed about to burst out of his coat. I had no idea what to expect that day in the Belmont, with him going a mile and a half, but I sensed we would see more of him than we had ever seen before.

Secretariat ran flat into legend, started running right out of the gate and never stopped, ran poor Sham into defeat around the first turn and down the backstretch and sprinted clear, opening two lengths, four, then five. He dashed to the three-quarter pole in 1:09^4/$_5$, the fastest six-furlong clocking in Belmont history. I dropped my head and cursed Turcotte: *What is he thinking about? Has he lost his mind?* The colt raced into the far turn, opening seven lengths past the half-mile pole. The timer flashed his astonishing mile mark: 1:34^1/$_5$!

I was seeing it but not believing it. Secretariat was still sprinting. The four horses behind him disappeared. He opened 10. Then 12. Halfway around the turn, he was 14 in front ... 15 ... 16 ... 17. Belmont Park began to shake. The whole place was on its feet. Turning for home, Secretariat was 20 in front, having run the mile and a quarter in 1:59 flat, faster than his Derby time.

He came home alone. He opened his lead to 25 . . . 26 . . . 27 . . . 28. As rhythmic as a rocking horse, he never missed a beat. I remember seeing Turcotte look over to the timer, and I looked over too. It was blinking 2:19, 2:20. The record was 2:26³/₅. Turcotte scrubbed on the colt, opening 30 lengths, finally 31. The clock flashed crazily: 2:22 . . . 2:23. The place was one long, deafening roar. The colt seemed to dive for the finish, snipping it clean at 2:24.

I bolted up the press box stairs with exultant shouts and there yielded a part of myself to that horse forever.

I didn't see Lawrence Robinson that day last October. The next morning, I returned to Claiborne to interview Seth Hancock. On my way through the farm's offices, I saw one of the employees crying at her desk. Treading lightly, I passed farm manager John Sosby's office. I stopped, and he called me in. He looked like a chaplain whose duty was to tell the news to the victim's family.

"Have you heard about Secretariat?" he asked quietly.

I felt the skin tighten on the back of my neck. "Heard what?" I asked. "Is he all right?"

"We might lose the horse," Sosby said. "He came down with laminitis last month. We thought we had it under control, but he took a bad turn this morning. He's a very sick horse. He may not make it.

"By the way, why are you here?"

I had thought I knew, but now I wasn't sure.

Down the hall, sitting at his desk, Hancock appeared tired, despairing and anxious, a man facing a decision he didn't want to make. What Sosby had told me was just beginning to sink in. "What's the prognosis?" I asked.

"Ten days to two weeks," Hancock said.

"Two weeks? Are you serious?" I blurted.

"You asked me the question," he said.

I sank back in my chair. "I'm not ready for this," I told him.

"How do you think I feel?" he said. "Ten thousand people come to this farm every year, and all they want to see is Secretariat. They don't give a hoot about the other studs. You want to know who Secretariat is in human terms? Just imagine the greatest athlete in the world. The greatest. Now make him six-foot-three, the perfect height. Make him real intelligent and kind. And on top of that, make him the best-lookin' guy ever to come down the pike. He was all those things as a horse. He isn't even a horse anymore. He's a legend. So how do you think I feel?"

Before I left, I asked Hancock to call me in Lexington if he decided to put the horse down. We agreed to meet at his mother's house the next morning. "By the way, can I see him?" I asked.

"I'd rather you not," he said. I told Hancock I had been to Robinson's house the day before and I had seen Secretariat from a distance, grazing. "That's fine," Hancock said. "Remember him how you saw him, that way. He doesn't look good."

I did not know it then, but Secretariat was suffering the intense pain in the hooves that is common to laminitis. That morning, Anderson had risen at dawn to check on the horse, and Secretariat had lifted his head and nickered very loudly. "It was like he was beggin' me for help," Anderson would later recall.

I left Claiborne stunned. That night, I made a dozen phone calls to friends, telling them the news, and I sat up late, dreading the next day. I woke up early and went to breakfast and came back to the room. The message light was dark. It was Wednesday, October 4. I drove out to Waddell Hancock's place in Paris. "It doesn't look good," she said. We had talked for more than an hour when Seth, looking shaken and pale, walked through the front door. "I'm afraid to ask," I said.

"It's very bad," he said. "We're going to have to put him down today."

"When?"

He did not answer. I left the house, and an hour later I was back in my room in Lexington. I had just taken off my coat when I turned and saw it, the red blinking light on my phone. I knew. I walked around the room. Out the door and down the hall. Back into the room. Out the door and around the block. Back into the room. Out the door and down to the lobby. Back into the room. I called sometime after noon. "Claiborne Farm called," said the message operator.

I phoned Annette Covault, an old friend who is the mare booker at Claiborne, and she was crying when she read the message: "Secretariat was euthanized at 11:45 A.M. today to prevent further suffering from an incurable condition. . . ."

The last time I remember really crying was on St. Valentine's Day of 1982, when my wife called to tell me that my father had died. At the moment she called, I was sitting in a purple room in Caesar's Palace, in Las Vegas, waiting for an interview with the heavyweight champion, Larry Holmes. Now here I was, in a different hotel room in a different town, suddenly feeling like a very old and tired man of 48, leaning with my back against a wall and sobbing for a long time with my face in my hands.

June 1990

Secretariat was survived by the four principal figures who shaped his fortunes on the racetrack. Owner/manager Penny Chenery ultimately became the First Lady of thoroughbred racing, an ambassador-at-large for the sport, and today remains a familiar presence at racing's major venues—from the Kentucky Derby to the Breeders' Cup. Jockey Ron Turcotte was paralyzed in a racing spill at Belmont Park on July 21, 1978, but in the company of his wife, Gaetane, he still can be seen wheeling around the major events, signing autographs and reminiscing about his days riding the colt. Lucien Laurin, who quit training horses in 1987, spent most of his retirement at his home in Key Largo, Florida, with his wife Juliette. He died in 2000, at age 88, at Miami's Baptist Hospital from complications following surgery to repair a broken hip. Sweat, whose handling of Secretariat had made him the most celebrated groom in America, died almost penniless in April 1998, after a long, twilight struggle with leukemia, in New York. He was 59.

SARATOGA

For 125 years, the crowds have flocked to Saratoga in August, drawn by the spring waters, the social whirl and, of course, the loveliest racetrack of them all

Major Odom was pacing. Arms akimbo and straw hat cocked, an unlit stogie stuck in a corner of his mouth, the 81-year-old trainer paced back and forth in the shadows of the elm trees in the Saratoga paddock. "Where the hell's my horse?" he said to no one in particular, his bushy gray eyebrows jumping up and down. Odom's given name is George, but no one ever calls him anything but Major. When he spoke, heads turned, looking for the missing filly. All the others had arrived in the saddling enclosure for the sixth race at Saratoga last Aug. 15, but there was no sign of Waggley. All at once, around a corner, she appeared, gliding across the paddock toward Odom, expanding in the light—a big, fine-boned gray filly with baby-seal eyes and a chorus girl's walk. Odom watched Waggley approach, then drew his hand across her back. "A little wet," he said. "Did she come over all right?"

"Didn't make a move," said her groom. Odom huddled with his jockey, Jean-Luc Samyn, reminding the rider that this race was a 6^1/$_2$-furlong sprint—half a furlong farther than Waggley really wanted to go—and that his filly would be breaking from the nine post, on the far outside: "She likes the outside, Jean, but you got a long way to go. But I think she's good, and she's training good. Just use your judgment."

Odom pushed through the shirt-sleeved crowd outside the paddock gate. A voice called out, "Good luck, Mr. Odom."

"That's what we need!" the old man said.

For folks born so blessed as Odom—and even for those with less luck—
Saratoga is as close to God's heaven as one can get in the horse racing game.

Santa Anita has its San Gabriel Mountains, Hialeah its flamingos and
palms, and Belmont Park its style and elegance, but only Saratoga offers the
19th century. On Aug. 3, 1863, a filly called Lizzie W. won the first horse
race ever run at Saratoga; this year, Aug. 3 was opening day for the track
and the 125th anniversary of Lizzie W.'s victory. Saratoga is not only the
oldest race meeting in the country but, after years of slumping handle and
attendance, it has emerged as one of the most prosperous and popular venues in American racing—rich in tradition, money and history.

Red Smith's standard directions for getting to the track still work: From
New York City, you drive north on the Thruway for about 175 miles, turn
off at Exit 14, take Union Avenue heading west—and go back about 100
years. The racetrack is right there on the left, just beyond the old wrought-
iron fence, past the picnic tables and the white-fenced paddock, just
beyond the high wooden beams and peppermint-striped awnings that
adorn the clubhouse and grandstand. Last summer, no one fit more com-
fortably into the old-time decor than Major Odom.

Odom first came to Saratoga Springs way back in '08, when he was two
years old. His dad, George Sr., was a Hall of Fame rider who turned to training when he quit the saddle. As a boy, the Major rode his father's stable
pony around town over rutted dusty streets on blazing August days. He
would gallop the pony in and out among the tasseled surreys and parasols,
the plumed hats and the derbies that paraded the streets. He would ride up
past the two big hotels, the Grand Union and the United States, in the
middle of town; down past the big Victorian houses that squatted along
Union Avenue and North Broadway.

Odom could hear the train whistles in the night. He saw the arrival of
the racehorses at the Spa, watched men opening the sliding boxcar doors
and unloading the animals, one by one. He watched as the horses walked
the mile to the track, manes blowing, while grooms held fast to the shanks
tethered to the halter rings. All the big horses came to Saratoga that way,
heels clicking down the boxcar ramps and stepping off through town: Man
o' War and Exterminator, Gallant Fox and Discovery, Top Flight and
Equipoise. He saw Upset beat Man o' War, Jim Dandy whip Gallant Fox;
he saw the birth of the Graveyard of Favorites, which is what horsemen
still call Saratoga.

"I saw 'em," Major Odom said. Saw 'em all at Saratoga, saw all the big
guns that came through town; heard the whips snapping and the irons

clanging and the distant pounding of hooves: Native Dancer and Nashua, Kelso and Forego, Ruffian, Secretariat, Damascus and Buckpasser, Alydar and Affirmed, Ridan and Jaipur. Trained a lot of winners at Saratoga himself, Major Odom did, back in the glory days.

"I won the Spinaway Stakes three years in a row," he said of the streak he put together from 1945 to '47 in Saratoga's premier race for 2-year-old fillies. "And I won a Travers here [in 1947] with Young Peter, but that was way back. . . . I like the old days, but then, I'm old myself. I still miss the casinos. In the 1930s and '40s, people would watch the races here and then go home, rest up, put on a tuxedo and go to the casinos down by the lake to gamble. Play roulette and dice and dance all night! The horses always liked it up here, too. They perked right up; it's the air and the water. The water's just as cold and clear as it can be. Delicious! The horses are happier here. So are the people. Lots of good times. Yeah, I used to win a lot of races here."

Waggley was the Major's final hope to win one more, the only horse he had in training last August. Long gone were the days when he trained 40 horses out of two barns at the Spa. Now he was up at 6 A.M., trudging to the track to care for one—he and his wife, Mary, bred and owned the filly, so she was family—but soon there would be none.

"This is my last year training at Saratoga," he said. "It's my last year training, period. I'll sell her in the fall. This is it for me. I'm not as frisky as I used to be. I've been coming up here for almost 80 years. Hey, 60 years I was trainin' those animals! Awful long time. Long enough."

Waggley stepped into the starting gate. Mary and the Major turned to the track. As the gates burst open, Waggley bobbled, her head dipping down. "She stumbled coming out!" cried Mary. The filly regained her footing, and Samyn set sail for the lead down the backside. Lying third, she raced to the throat of Rally For Justice, shot past her, and quickly ran down Wan'a Fella on the far turn. Major shook his head. "I wish he'd save her a little bit," he said.

Waggley turned for home in front by two, after running a half in :45^1/$_5$. Key Bid took out after her, slowly cutting into Waggley's lead. Inside the 16th pole, Key Bid caught her and drove on past to win by a neck. The race was just a tad too far for Waggley.

Odom grimaced. "Sonofabitch!" he growled. "If she hadn't stumbled, she'd have won."

Mary's voice sang out above the din: "They'll never beat her at six furlongs!"

"Next time," the Major said. "We'll run her one more time up here. She'll be ready."

Trainers have been saying that at Saratoga for years, of course, since that day four weeks after the Battle of Gettysburg, in 1863, when a one-eyed black jockey named Sewell—his given name was not recorded—rode Lizzie W. to victory in that first race here. Sewell and the filly soon disappeared, but Saratoga Springs has never been the same. By that time, the town was already known as America's Queen of the Spas, a resort town, a watering hole and a gambling hell that was beginning to attract the rich from New York City.

All of this happened, not incidentally, as the result of a series of geological changes that occurred some 300 million years ago, when a thin crust of shale still lay intact just under the land that is now Saratoga Springs. Beneath that crust was a deposit of limestone. Over millions of years, rainwater percolated through the shale, growing acidic as it picked up iron sulfate and other minerals from the rock. When the acidic water reached the limestone and mixed with it, the water, in chemical reaction, became naturally carbonated. For untold years the shale crust acted as a kind of giant cap covering the bubbling water.

Kenneth Johnson, the chairman of the geology department at Skidmore College in Saratoga Springs, says that no one is certain precisely when or why—perhaps it was the same stresses that forced the emergence of the Adirondack Mountains—but at some point that layer of shale ruptured, forming a fault line. The carbonated waters began oozing up through the crack in the shale, hissing through punctures all along the fault line, and it was thus that a series of natural events led to the birth of the springs.

The Iroquois called this land Saraghoga, "place of the swift water," and it was around the sparkling mineral springs that the destiny of the town was ultimately shaped. In the 19th century the springs brought lame and dyspeptic tourists "looking for the cure" to Saratoga to drink the water and to bathe in it. To accommodate them, the big hotels arose, and to keep and entertain them, the gamblers came, men like the legendary John Morrissey, a dark-eyed, bare-knuckled, Tammany Hall politician and roughneck who had reigned for five years (1853–58) as the American heavyweight boxing champion. Morrissey built the first Saratoga racetrack, and after the Civil War he built and ran the town's first big casino.

Thus the Spa began selling more than the baths that sparkled and the water that tasted kind of funny. Indeed, in the 65 years that followed the end of the Civil War—except for two years, 1911 and 1912, when a moral fervor gripped New York and the state passed a law banning horse racing—Saratoga Springs was the biggest gambling resort in America. By the Gay Nineties it had become a summer mecca for rich planters from Georgia and the Carolinas and for bankers and brokers from New York.

One of them, the sportsman William Collins Whitney, helped make the town a playground for the Social Register set and for the idle rich, and for those who came floating in their wake—the big gamblers and the assorted brigands, the prostitutes and the pimps. Indeed, Saratoga may have been the place, in America at least, where simple extravagance first grew into wretched excess.

This is the Saratoga where James Todhunter Sloan, the American-born jockey who had gone to England in 1897 to ride for royalty—he was the Steve Cauthen of his day—returned to Saratoga to ride a Whitney horse and pulled up to the door of the United States Hotel with 10 trunks and two English valets. This is the town where Diamond Jim Brady, who wore diamond buttons even on his underwear, came every summer, squiring Lillian Russell to the racetrack and casinos. And this is where the newly renovated Grand Union, then the largest hotel in the world (824 rooms), reopened in 1874 with a dining hall so vast that it seated 1,400 people at a time. "The waiters had to run from the kitchen to the far end with the scrambled eggs or else they'd be cold when they got there," says Saratoga native George Bolster.

This is the town where men came to play the horses by day and the tables by night. Gambling was against state law, but the gamblers took care of the cops and the pols, and the track and casinos grew fatter. Now and then there was an outbreak of moral outrage among the bluenoses of Saratoga, but the flow of gambling gold into the town every August was so rich and so steady that the work of the devil was usually happily condoned. Reggie Halpern, 82, a bookmaker in the '30s, still talks about the days when he used to travel to Saratoga on the Cavanagh Special, a train from Grand Central Station that was ridden almost exclusively by bookmakers.

When the train pulled into the old Saratoga station, hundreds of local citizens met the bookies as though they were conquering soldiers coming home from war. Speaking of another age, at times nostalgically, Halpern says, "We were greeted by the natives waving handkerchiefs; they held up boards that said: SINGLE ROOM $25 A MONTH. I stayed at the Grand Union—three dollars a night; lunch, 50 cents; dinner, a dollar—and we all walked to the racetrack in the afternoon. Al Jolson was always there, but he never performed at the clubs. He loved to gamble. Jack Benny used to like to sit on the porch of the Grand Union. Bing Crosby came up with

Don Ameche. I remember Harry Richman, with his tails, cane and top hat, singing Puttin' On the Ritz. Sophie Tucker and Joe E. Lewis played the Piping Rock Club."

Lewis, a nightclub comedian, was a legendary gambler known more for losing than for winning. A notorious horseplayer, he was fond of saying of Saratoga, "I like to come here every year to visit my money." They still tell the story of the morning when Lewis, who was staying in the United States Hotel in a room overlooking the railroad tracks, woke up early because a train groaned past his window, spouting steam and rattling the walls. Groggy, Lewis called the front desk and asked, "What time does this room leave for Chicago?"

Most of Saratoga's regular summer guests still come back each year to visit their money. Though the casinos have been closed since 1951, when state and federal probes revealed their ties to racketeers, they were not the only game in town when the last race was over. Fasig-Tipton, the thoroughbred auction house, has been selling yearlings at Saratoga since 1917, in what the firm's president, John M.S. Finney, once called "the world's biggest crapshoot." In this game, however, the shooter did not always crap out. In 1918, Sam Riddle gave $5,000 at Saratoga—a sizable sum for a yearling in those days—for an electrifying chestnut son of Fair Play. Riddle named the colt Man o' War. Today, in the course of a three-day select sale at its pavilion across from the racetrack, Fasig-Tipton continues to sell some of the most royally bred babies in America.

Last Aug. 11, the first night of the sale, 49-year-old Marvin Little Jr. waited through the final minutes of the biggest night of his life. Little had come to this sale every year since 1962, first as a groom mucking stalls for $7 a day, later as the manager of Newstead Farm in northern Virginia, long one of the leading consignors at Saratoga. Little had never brought a horse of his own to a Saratoga auction—the blood ran too rich for his income—but he had gambled and obviously scored the year before.

At a sale in Keeneland in January 1986, Little had stretched his resources and paid $58,000 for a 13-year-old broodmare named Fearless Queen. She was in foal to an untested stallion prospect, Dixieland Band, a stakes-winning son of the great Northern Dancer. "You know, $58,000 is a big hunk of money for somebody like me," Little says. "But I'm a gambler. The mare could have died at birth. The foal could have been crooked. But you have to take a shot. Life is a gamble."

On Feb. 21, 1986, Fearless Queen gave birth to a daughter. The mare did not die, and the baby was not crooked. In fact, she was a beauty, and she started Little to dreaming. For 19 years he had brought those royally bred

Newstead yearlings to Saratoga, which was fine enough, but he had always wanted to fetch a yearling of his own to the Spa. Now was his chance. If the filly was relatively weak on pedigree, she more than made up for it in looks, and so he entered her in the Saratoga sale. When Fasig-Tipton selected her—not just any thoroughbred yearling can be entered in the sale—Little started shining up his filly for the big night.

Many prospective buyers came by to see her, among them D. Wayne Lukas, whose eye for yearlings had already helped make him the most successful horse trainer in the country. After looking her over on the morning of the sale, Lukas said to Little, quietly, "A beautiful filly."

Little did not know what to expect when she walked into the ring. Standing in front of her stall, with a chaw of Red Man in his mouth, the man was dreaming again. "She could bring $100,000," Little said. "Then again, she could bring $25,000. Or $150,000. You never know till you sell 'em. No matter what she sells for, I've still got the mare. And she's back in foal to Dixieland Band."

Marvin Little laughed thinking about it. "I'm an old hillbilly from the back hills of Kentucky," he said. "You better believe I'm the poorest man selling a horse in this sale. But that's what made America great. I paid $58,000 for the mare in foal. I think this filly's gonna bring what I paid for the mare carrying her." He paused. "I hope," he said.

The handler led the chestnut filly into the sales ring, and the bidding rose up like a child's balloon into the night sky—beginning at $20,000, slowly, and then rising higher and faster, past $50,000 and $100,000 and $125,000, then over $150,000 and $160,000. Little held his breath; his eyes were popping. Lukas made the final bid: The auctioneer brought the hammer down at $185,000.

"What do ya think of that?" Little crowed back at the barn. "A hundred and eighty-five thousand dollars! That's makin' money, ain't it? And I still got the mare! I don't know what I'll do with all that money. I'll probably take some of it and buy another mare."

Of course, the nature of the gambling beast changes dramatically as you move from the sales ring at Fasig-Tipton to the betting windows of the racetrack across the street. Because of the illustrious names of the high rollers who have played the horses here, Saratoga has spawned more tales of truly epic gambling than any racetrack in America.

One afternoon 86 years ago, before the advent of income tax, John (Bet-a-Million) Gates, the barbed-wire baron, lost a staggering $400,000 playing the horses at Saratoga. On another day, according to Saratoga historian George Waller, Gates won so much money on a single bet that he used a grocery basket to carry his cash away. Old-time gamblers still recall the day in the late 1930s when Art Rooney, the founder of the Pittsburgh Steelers, all but swept the card at Saratoga and took a fortune from the track. Over the years, whenever he has been asked about that day, Rooney has steadfastly refused to discuss it.

"Art Rooney won six straight races here and walked out of the betting ring with $105,000," says Halpern, who made book at Saratoga at the time. "I know. I took some of the action."

And then there was Subway Sam Rosoff, the builder of much of the New York City subway system, who played the horses and the bon vivant with equal passion at Saratoga. "Rosoff always rented a house with an open porch on Union Avenue across from the racetrack," says Halpern. "He would leave the track after the fifth race. When the public walked by his house after the races, there was Subway Sam on his porch, with half a dozen beautiful showgirls, having cocktails served by a butler. A lot of people copied that scene on Union Avenue over the years. That's what made Saratoga such a memorable place."

If the gamblers today are no longer flamboyant high rollers in the tradition of Gates and Rosoff, they are more observant and methodical in their approach to the game. As in the past, they are not known by the names their mothers gave them. At Saratoga last summer, there were Al the Wise Guy and Ronnie the School Teacher, Big Stewie and Big Richie and Handsome Jimmy, with his custom-tailored suits. And there was Paul Cornman, also known as the Source, a 35-year-old former clocker whose celebrity as a horseplayer had become such that bettors accosted him for his opinions and often followed him to the windows to eavesdrop on his bets.

Four years before, Cornman was earning $50 a day as a handicapping teacher at the track and making occasional appearances on New York television programs to analyze the day's races. He was scratching and scuffling to make a living. "I was basically a degenerate horseplayer," Cornman says. "I would go on TV once a week and talk like I knew what was going on, then pull out of the parking lot in a 1968 Impala."

That summer at Saratoga he made the pivotal decision of his life. A run of good fortune at the windows had fattened his bankroll to $20,000, and he had had his eye on a horse named Win, an unknown gelding who ran as common as a goat on the dirt but who fought like a ferret on the turf. Midway through the Saratoga meeting in 1983, Cornman approached Win's owner-trainer, Sally Bailie, and told her he wanted to buy the horse. Bailie's price was $60,000. Unable to afford the whole horse, he bought one third of him for his $20,000. Most horseplayers confine themselves to expressing their opinions at the betting windows. Not Cornman. Very boldly he had invested virtually all he had in the horse. "It was the first time I was at peace with myself as a horseplayer," he says. "Things were finally coming around. I had never, never, never thought about buying a horse."

Suddenly he owned a third of one. Win ended up taking two consecutive runnings of the $75,000 Bernard Baruch Handicap, the premier grass race at Saratoga, in 1984 and '85. With his winnings, Cornman bought a majority interest in another horse, Exclusive Partner, who also appeared to be more ambitious on the turf than on the dirt. Cornman and his half-dozen fellow investors bought Exclusive Partner for $80,000, and in 1986 the 4-year-old colt won the majority owner his third consecutive Bernard Baruch Handicap. By the time Win was laid up with an injury in 1985, he had earned almost $1.5 million, of which Cornman took home almost $500,000. And Exclusive Partner had won $325,000 before Cornman and his group sold him in 1986 for $400,000.

Voila! The Source was suddenly rich and respectable—and compellingly enigmatic. More a horseplayer than a handicapper, he does not rely so much on speed figures or other state-of-the-art gambling angles as he does on an animal's appearance, which he scrutinizes in the paddock or the post parade.

Last summer Cornman was as reliable as a watch, materializing at the south end of the paddock fence, appearing out of nowhere to watch how the horses moved, to check their odds, to measure post positions against any track bias.

Late in the meeting, on Aug. 26, Cornman was suffering damnably. He was betting a lot of exactas and was hitting his share of winners, but the horses he picked to finish second were running like dogs. He began playing it safe. "When I used to go to baseball camp," he said, "and I'd get into a slump, the coaches used to say, 'Just hit everything up the middle.' That's all I'm trying to do now."

He was down $800 after the fifth race that day, and in the sixth he bet $900, including a $150 exacta—no, he could not resist—that would turn out to pay $48.40 for a $2 bet. The sixth turned him around, giving him a profit of $1,930 going into the seventh. That was a race on which Cornman had a definite opinion, but he was playing cautiously, still trying to stroke it up the middle. "I'll bet $500 on this," Cornman said. "If I blow it, I'm still up $1,400."

The seventh was a nine-furlong race on the grass, and he liked two horses, including a 15–1 shot named Dawn o' The Dance. "He's coming into form and looks good," said Cornman. Arguing against his own better judgment, he also liked El Jefe, a front-runner who had shown a disconcerting tendency to quit or tire—to hang, as they say—in the last part of a race. Nonetheless, Cornman bet $400 on El Jefe to win, at $3.50 to $1, another $80 on an El Jefe–Dawn o' The Dance exacta, and $20 on that exacta reversed.

It was painful to watch. El Jefe dashed to the lead out of the gate, with Dawn o' The Dance racing last until the turn for home. Watching El Jefe come off the final turn in front, Cornman said, "If he ever gets a mile and an eighth, it will be now."

But no. Deep in the stretch, tiring, El Jefe shortened stride. Cornman saw it coming and cried: "What did I tell you? El Jefe's a hangin' bum!" In the final strides, Dawn o' The Dance came roaring past them all to win it by almost two lengths. El Jefe finished second. Cornman scolded himself loudly: "I knew he couldn't win. Everything on paper tells you he's going to win, but you know he's going to lose because he's El Jefe and he's a hangin' bum!"

So Cornman lost his $400 win bet and the $80 exacta, but the Dawn o' The Dance–El Jefe exacta paid $192.40. His $20 bet on that earned him $1,924—considerably less than he would have pocketed had El Jefe won— giving him a profit for the day of $3,354. "At least he hung on for second," Cornman said. "I should be glad for small favors."

Moments later Cornman was back at the paddock to watch the horses saddle for the eighth.

Saratoga was never a place of leisure for Cornman—never a place to have an early dinner and relax, to kick back and swill cocktails like Subway Sam, watching the late people stroll by and in turn being watched by them. Indeed, there has always been a touch of the surreal about that twilight scene in Saratoga, with the crowds pouring out of the track at 6 P.M. and disappearing into the quaint 19th-century houses that they rent for the racing season—houses with spacious porches and columns, high-pitched roofs and ornamental gables, places that have balustrades and dormers and stained-glass windows.

"They are all like dollhouses," says trainer LeRoy Jolley. "You sit home and watch television and expect a big hand to come in the back door and start rearranging the furniture."

Liz Tippett lived in such homes in town for years, in one place or another, but last summer she divided time between her little farm east of Saratoga and her 70-foot boat, The Adventurer, on which she had arrived at a nearby Hudson River port after a sentimental journey from New York.

Mary Elizabeth Altemus Whitney Tippett was 81 last summer, and though she was mostly confined to a wheelchair, she made all the major balls and parties and even showed up one night at the yearling sales, wearing a fur coat. She also went to the track to watch her horses run. Sixty years before, she had been the belle of the ball in American high society, reputedly one of the most beautiful women in the land. "Smashing" is how an old acquaintance, Alfred Gwynne Vanderbilt, 75, described her.

Payne Whitney, one of New York's most prominent sportsmen, saw her one afternoon in a paddock at Saratoga and told his son, John Hay (Jock) Whitney, "That's the girl I want you to marry." They were wed on Sept. 5, 1930, and during most of the ensuing decade they spent August in Saratoga. In fact, they finally moved into one of the most spectacular estates in town—a big white wedding cake of a mansion with columns in front, broad lawns all around and its own private stables and training track adjoining the grounds of Saratoga race course. Living there, Liz Whitney came to represent, more than anyone else, the mystique of money and glamour that has surrounded Saratoga since the rich took over soon after the Civil War.

She did things with style and flair. Early one morning she showed up at the racetrack to watch the Whitney horses work, still dressed in the evening gown she had worn the night before and accompanied by a small kennel of dogs. "Why not?" she said last year. "We were out at the night-clubs till three or four in the morning. You'd go home, put a coat on, and go see your horses work."

That is not what she remembers best about her years at the Spa, however. For all the memories of childhood and horses and nights on the town, she recalls most vividly the day she walked out on her husband there. "He was too much a ladies' man for me, I'll tell you that," she said. "It was so stupid! But when you're young and you're sort of crazy about somebody and you see him out with Tallulah Bankhead and all those bums, I . . . I couldn't take it anymore, that's all. He brought Loretta Young to the house one weekend! But Tallulah was the worst. I just got tired of it. That's when I decided that Reno was the place for me."

Not knowing what to do or where to go, she took the advice of Harry Hopkins, one of Franklin Roosevelt's advisers, and sailed down the Hudson to see the president at Hyde Park. "I took a boat down there," she said. "That was a vivid day, going down there and talking to Franklin for all that time. He knew what was going on with Jock. He told me, 'Don't worry. I'll get you a lawyer.' Franklin was so nice. There are a lot of memories for me up here, some painful, quite a bit. But you have to do the best you can with what you've got left."

Which is exactly what Marvin Little and Major Odom did. With the proceeds of last year's yearling sale, Little bought himself a farm in Paris, Kentucky, and a young $33,000 broodmare by Roberto out of Kelly's Day. A week later the mare's full brother—an unraced 2-year-old named Brian's Time—broke his maiden en route to a Florida Derby victory and a fine showing in the Triple Crown. Little had struck gold again.

And on Aug. 23, in the fifth race at Saratoga, a six-furlong sprint for fillies and mares, the Major saddled Waggley for the last time. This was it for him, and what an ending it was. The gray bullet chased another speedball, Al's Helen, for a quarter mile, then bounded past her to open two lengths, which is what she won by as she drove across the finish. After all those years and all those winners, the Major had a final victory with his final starter. The old man smiled, lit up his cigar and snugged his hat down on his head.

"A good way to wind it up and get out, isn't it?" he said.

August 1988

THE LONGEST RIDE

In October, Mike Venezia was killed when he fell from a horse at Belmont Park, but fellow jockey Robbie Davis, whose colt trampled Venezia, was a victim too

It happened so fast that even today Robbie Davis has trouble sorting out the whole haunting nightmare: the terrible fall and the vision of the silks flashing beneath him, the sound like a water balloon bursting at his horse's feet, his own screaming voice, the sight of the dead jockey, and then his hiding like a child in the darkened broom closet in the first-aid room at Belmont Park.

On the afternoon of Oct. 13, 1988, in the fifth race at Belmont Park, Davis, atop Drums in the Night, was moving down the backstretch of the turf course and sensing in the hollow of his bones that he could not have been in a sweeter spot on this great green earth. "It was a beautiful, gorgeous, perfect day," Davis says. "There's nothing like a fall day in New York, you know, and I had won with my horse the time before and I had all sorts of horse under me."

Davis had never been riding better. With almost three months left in the year, his mounts had won 231 races and $7,154,435. He was the sixth-leading jockey in the nation in money won and was, at that moment, sitting just where he wanted to be. Drums in the Night was trailing the leaders but running strong against the bit in the $1^1/_{16}$-mile allowance race. "I was next to last," says Davis. "I was staying down on the inside, saving ground and waiting for some running room. I was waiting for the real running to start. Then all of a sudden. . . ."

Davis saw the horse directly in front of him—Mr. Walter K., with veteran jockey Mike Venezia up—stumble suddenly and veer to the right, out of Drums in the Night's path. Instinctively, Davis took hold of his horse, waiting to see what would happen in front of him. "All of a sudden I seen the jockey pop up right in front of me," he says, "and I took straight back to see which way he would go, so I could miss him. I didn't want to move until he committed himself in one direction or the other. All of a sudden he lost his balance—it happened so fast, I didn't know who it was—and he kicked off the left side of his horse, and he went under my horse. My horse tried to jump, but it was too late. He clipped him and stumbled. The jockey's head was right in the path of my horse, right underneath! I looked down and seen him under me, and my horse scissored his head with his back feet. Shattered his skull."

Davis screamed, "Oh, my God!" He looked back and saw the body lying on the grass, motionless in the sun. Caught in the hot whips of panic, Davis came undone. He looked over to his left and saw jockey Nick Santagata, and he hollered, "Nickie! Who was that? I just killed him! I just run over him. Who was that?"

Santagata glanced at Davis over his shoulder. "Venezia!" he shouted.

The two men raced together for the far turn. Davis screamed again to Santagata: "I killed him! I *swear* I killed him. What do I do? Do I ride? I can't believe it. Nickie! What do I do?"

Santagata never answered, and together the two men drove their horses home. Drums in the Night finished fourth, and as Davis pulled him up at the clubhouse turn, he looked over his left shoulder and saw the ambulance already out on the backstretch. Venezia had been killed instantly, the blow from Drums in the Night's hooves having struck his head so sharply that it dislodged his right eye. But as Davis slowly walked his horse back to the unsaddling area, he didn't know that. He prayed, "God, I know I busted something, but I just hope he's O.K."

Davis dismounted and took the saddle off Drums in the Night and studied the horse's feet. "They were beautiful horse feet, so dainty," says Davis, "and he stood there so kind, the horse did, and there were no marks on him, and he was just a beautiful black horse with nice perfect feet, and I'm looking down and saying, 'These are the feet. Why these feet? Why this horse? Why this?'"

Davis walked slowly back through the passage under the grandstand and down the stairs to the underground maze that leads to the jockeys' room. When he got below, he saw the ambulance sitting in the service tunnel, Pinkerton guards all around it, and he began hollering at the driver and the guards, "What the hell are you doing here? Get him to the hospital! What are you waiting for? Why are you leaving him here? Get him out of here! Out! Now!"

In a daze, Davis walked toward the ambulance, but someone stepped in front of him. "Don't look," the man told him. "Please, Robbie. Don't look."

Suddenly there was a commotion on the other side of the ambulance, and Davis saw jockey Angel Cordero Jr. arguing with the guards. Cordero's voice was resounding in the subterranean tombs of Belmont Park: "Hey! Mike was my friend. You can't tell me I can't look in there. You can't tell me what to do!" The guards let Cordero approach the vehicle. All his life Davis will remember the moment, that singular look on Cordero's face as he peered inside the ambulance. "He looked ghostly, pale and white, like he'd aged five years all at once," Davis says.

Davis had to see for himself. He pushed past the guards and looked in the back window of the ambulance. The horror was entire. "He's lying in there on a board," Davis says. "With his head turned away from me. I peeked in. All I could see was blood so thick on his face, and he was lying there motionless. I thought, Oh, no. It can't be!"

Davis bolted for the first-aid room, opened the door of the broom closet and closed it behind him, leaving himself alone in the sudden dark. He fell to his knees. His whole life flashed past him, as though it was *he* who was dying, and in a way he was. "It was flashing and flashing and flashing," Davis says. "If it wasn't one thing flashing, it was something else. All the violent things in my life came back to me. I was on my knees, and I was gripping my fists and saying, 'God, why me? Why does this happen to me all the time? Why do I have to take the pain all the time? Why so much pain?' My whole life was flashing."

Flashing back to those afternoons, so rich in an oily aroma that he can smell them now. Back to when he was four and was sitting on the gasoline tank of his Uncle Tim's dirt bike, holding on to the handlebars as he and his uncle roared along at 60 miles an hour among the rock-encrusted hills outside Pocatello, Idaho. Back to the day he got the call at Eddy's Bakery, where he was stacking bread, and found when he got home that Uncle Tim, who had been like a father to him, had died of carbon monoxide poisoning in a mining accident. Back to the night that his best friend plunged to his death when the friend's truck rolled off a 60-foot cliff into a cemetery on the east side of Pocatello. Back to his own aborted suicide attempt, when at three one morning he screeched his light-blue 1968 El Camino to a stop just shy of the tree he had been aiming for at the end of Kinghorn Road. Back to the fights at home between his mother and his stepfather Thomas William Darner, the sound of the ashtray smashing through the television screen, and the nights he hid in the closet or under the bed or covered his head with a pillow and screamed to muffle the noise of the violence. Back to his terrorized childhood and the sexual abuse he suffered at the hands of his stepfather. Back to all those years of biting anger, self-loathing and shame that had sprung from that abuse, the dark little secret of his life.

After Davis had spent a few agonizing minutes wrapped in the blanket of darkness within that closet, there was a knock on the door. Davis saw a man step forward in the ray of light. Davis was weeping. The voice said, "It's O.K., Robbie. It's O.K. There's nothing you could have done. We just watched the films. There's no way you could have avoided it."

Davis was inconsolable, and in a state nearing shock. "He was white," says his valet, John Mallano, who had opened the closet door. Almost immediately, Davis began to shear himself of his past. After undressing in the jockeys' room, he told Mallano, "Throw everything away. Throw my boots away, my pants, my T-shirt. Everything I was wearing. I don't want these clothes around me ever again."

The next day, after a memorial service for Venezia at Belmont Park—at which Davis fell sobbing to his knees—he quietly told his wife, Marguerite, "Let's go get my hair cut. Maybe I'll feel better." So he had the barber "cut all that old stuff off," he says. "And I cut all my nails down."

His moods swung between sorrow, depression and remorse, and at times he appeared as frail and helpless as one of his three children—Kristen, 3, Jacqueline, 2, and Robbie Jr., then an infant of two months. He refused to attend Venezia's wake—"I can't do it," he told Marguerite—and so she went in his place. "When I left the house, he was sitting in the rocking chair in the bedroom, clutching the baby's blanket," she says.

All that week Davis brushed off repeated entreaties that he ride again, refused to talk to most of those who called and at night swam in and out of turbulent sleep. One night Marguerite awoke to find him mumbling and sweating next to her. The nightmare played and replayed like an old black-and-white movie. "I kept seeing it over and over," Davis says. "Mike kept falling off in front of me. Then the other riders started falling off in front of me, and I started getting paranoid in my dreams."

After Venezia's funeral, in Westbury, New York, on Oct. 17, which Davis did attend, he finally settled on what he had to do. His former agent, Lenny Goodman, had been begging him to keep riding. "It's like falling off a horse," Goodman had told him. "You got to get back up and ride right away. You've got to put this behind you!" But Davis wasn't buying that. He had another agenda, the hidden one that had been haunting him. And so, a week after the accident, Marguerite found him frantically packing all their belongings—winter and summer clothes, books, tapes, pictures, VCRs, golf clubs, dirt bike. "I knew exactly what I wanted," Davis says. "But I was in a frenzy, I was hysterical."

"What are you doing?" Marguerite asked.

"I just want to get out of here!" Robbie said. "I want to escape for a while. Take a vacation. I want to go home. I want to get back to myself. To my roots."

So, at age 27, riding high in his prime as one of the leading jockeys in one of the richest venues of American racing, Davis packed his family and their belongings, aimed his Suburban truck west and hit the gas. Until last week, to the dismay and confusion of all his friends, Davis did not ride in another horse race. True to his word, too, he did go home again.

Pocatello lies in the fertile Snake River Valley in the foothills of the Rocky Mountains in southeastern Idaho, just above the western wing of the Caribou National Forest. It was there, in that one-time railroad tent town that's now a trade and industrial hub of 46,340 people, that Davis was born and raised. He barely knew his natural father, who left his family to get a job and never came back. "He hitchhiked and ended up in Oregon," says Jana McOsker, Robbie's mother. "He just left me there"—with Robbie, then 2, and his sister, Jodi, an infant.

Theirs was a hardscrabble existence. McOsker went on welfare and worked around town as a bartender, a waitress and a cook. The kids lived itinerant childhoods, moving from one place to another, and Robbie attended practically every grade school in Pocatello at least twice. "I'd show up, and they'd say, 'Hey, he's back again!'" he says. McOsker says they usually packed up and moved when the rent came due. "I'd move in with my brother until I got another check, and then I'd move into an apartment," she says.

At an early age Robbie began making money. When Jodi lost two fingers in a washing machine wringer, Robbie went to work at a gasoline station next to their house, cleaning out the bathroom and putting the oil cans away at closing. He was five years old and earning 50 cents a night. "He earned 12 dollars and bought her a tricycle when she was in the hospital," McOsker says. At other times he sold Kool-Aid on street corners, and he spent his summers pushing a power lawn mower, the gasoline can swinging from the handlebar, around Pocatello. He washed dishes and bussed tables at a restaurant after school. He hawked the *Idaho State Journal* on the street. He gave his mother money for gas and groceries. "He once had a garage sale and sold all of his toys so we'd have money," she says. "You wouldn't believe this boy. He was special."

His teachers remember him as a sensitive, polite, hardworking lad who was particularly devoted to his sister. "A real likable kid, the kind you just like to be around," says Del Hildreth, Robbie's homeroom teacher at Irving Junior High School.

Hildreth had no idea what Robbie had endured: the unspeakable instances of sexual abuse he had suffered for four years in the 1970s at the hands of Darner. In 1976 Darner was convicted of sexual assault and served three years in the New Mexico State Penitentiary at Santa Fe. McOsker says today that she didn't know what had been going on in her house until she found photographic evidence of it and brought charges against Darner. Today, she lives with the remorse. "I am very ashamed and don't know what to say," she says. For years Davis told no one about the abuse and it became the central, gnawing secret of his life, until it ultimately surfaced as a primary force that drove him from New York.

By the time he reached the end of the 10th grade at Pocatello Senior High, Davis was entertaining thoughts of suicide. As with many abused children, his sense of self-worth had broken down, and with that came the onset of his chronic depression, his anger turned inside out. "You're made to feel like the lowest thing on earth," he says. "I've been so low at times that I've sat on a curb and felt that was where I belonged. I felt like a bad person. That's the way you feel." His best friend, Jeff Lindauer, had just died when his truck dropped off that cliff. Davis was stung by guilt over that, too. "Just a month before, I had showed him how to get up there," he says.

He started drinking vodka and dropped out of school, in which he saw no future. "A kind of waste," he says. "I had already grown up a long time ago. I hated myself for whatever happened in the old time. I just didn't have no use in life anymore."

One evening, in aimless despair—"I was so depressed, you know," he says—he backed up the El Camino on Kinghorn Road, dropped it into gear and set sail for that big tree. Headlights on, he barreled toward it through the darkness. He doesn't know why he hit the brakes, but he did, locking the drums with a screech. "I slid to a stop about a foot away," he says. "Something touched me. I didn't want to die, and I hit the brakes and I set there, it was three o'clock in the morning, looking at the tree, just crying. I didn't have a dad. . . ."

McOsker has known a lot of men in her life—she has been married eight times, twice to the same man—but none of the men she brought home became a father to the boy. Instead, Davis found his surrogate in Tim Lords, his mother's brother. Uncle Tim was his mentor, his teacher. "The father that I never had," Davis says. "He taught me everything."

Uncle Tim's death in a freak mining accident in 1979 left Davis grieving as he never had. "That was devastating," he says. "It was so unbelievable. I would throw rocks at trees for hours. I was crazed." But Uncle Tim had left him far more than grief and summer memories, as things turned out, and the most valuable gift of all was an abounding love of racing and speed—those hair-blowing, rock-climbing, wind-in-your-face ascents up mountain trails to a freedom Davis had never before known. He vividly remembers when he was four and Uncle Tim would take him riding on the dirt bike. "He went so fast I couldn't breathe," Davis says. "Took my breath away. Sixty miles an hour. We'd fly over jumps, climb mountains. We'd hit something and he'd hang on to me. I wasn't afraid of anything."

At 15 Davis got his first dirt bike—he had saved the money while working at a pizzeria—and he rode it every day. For the deeply scarred young man, that dirt bike meant escape, a way to get away. "I could ride up to 40, 50 miles a day," Davis says. "I loved it. It was my first love. The wind and the mountains and the freedom! I was so comfortable with it." He dreamed of one day being a professional dirt-bike racer, and he began entering small events in and around Pocatello. He won a few races, he says, just amateur stuff: "All I got was trophies."

The 5' 1" Davis soon found that he could race for more than that at Pocatello Downs, the local racetrack that was part of a county fair circuit for quarter horses and thoroughbreds. He was almost 19, working at Eddy's Bakery, when a coworker and part-time horse trainer, John Dalkey, urged him to come out to the Downs and learn to be a rider.

"I thought, Hey, I can do that!" says Davis. Soon he had quit his $250-a-week bakery job and hired on as a groom at $65 a week, first with Dalkey and then with veteran trainer Marv Whitworth, who became the surrogate father he had been looking for since Lords had died. That summer, 1979, Davis mucked stalls and slipped into the game as easily as a pitchfork into a bed of straw. He quickly learned how to ride and then really went to the races in 1980, when he rode his first winner, in a 220-yard dash for Appaloosas at the fairgrounds in Burley, Idaho. He still gets a rush, recalling the race.

"Oh, God," Davis says. "Out of the gate it was like a dirt bike coming out of the hills off a jump—voom! Like a dragster coming off the line, with the front wheels coming off the ground. He was really a fast horse. God, what a blast!"

Davis loved his work and threw himself into it, wanting to be a jockey more than anything he had ever wanted in his life. "You'd tell him to be at the barn at four o'clock in the morning, and he was there at four, waiting for you," says trainer Lynn Bowman, who employed Davis then.

"You could set your watch by him," Whitworth says. "I never had a boy so dedicated or want anything as bad. He had ambition. You had to be around him to see the intensity. And what an athlete! A natural—his balance, his coordination on a horse, and real fine hands—and he never, never abused his mount in any way."

Whitworth and Davis grew so close that until very recently Whitworth was the only person with whom Davis had shared the secret of his past. "It makes your gut crawl," Whitworth says.

That fall Davis packed off to a quarter-horse and thoroughbred ranch in Southern California. He got his seasoning there, riding and exercising 22 horses a day all winter, but what he really learned was what he wanted to do with his life. The inspiration dawned on him the day he visited Santa Anita Park, the Taj Mahal of California racing. In the spring, with the Idaho racing season coming up, Davis announced he was going to ride in California. Whitworth told him to stay one more summer in Idaho. "You're not ready for California," Whitworth said.

Of course, Davis stayed in Idaho. He was the leading rider that summer on the fair circuit—at bull-rings in such places as Idaho Falls and Blackfoot—but when the fall came, there was no keeping him in the bushes. In fact, he was gone for good, heading for the thoroughbreds, the big time. He tried his hand with a trainer at Turf Paradise in Phoenix and won four races there, and followed the trainer when he moved to Louisiana Downs. But he languished there for months, unable to get mounts. He had begun his one-year apprenticeship in May of '82, after he had won the fifth race of his career, but he went nowhere with the "bug"—the weight allowance granted to apprentices—in so provincial an outpost as Shreveport. One afternoon, jockey Sam Maple told him that he ought to go to New York. "They'll ride you with the bug in New York," Maple told him. "You might not stay when your bug is over, but you can make $100,000 there as an apprentice."

That's all Davis had to hear. A few days later he was edging his El Camino across the East River and onto Long Island. He hired himself a hustling agent, Steve Adika, and together they lit up the tote boards. The very sight of mammoth Belmont Park, with its sweeping grandstand and infield and its $1^{1}/_{2}$-mile oval, left him in awe. He climbed on his first mount in New York, Commanche Brave, on Sept. 2, 1982. "I walked out of that paddock to the track and it took my breath away," Davis says. "I thought, I'm here. This is it."

Commanche Brave, a 20–1 shot, won that race, and it was not long before Davis was the hottest bug boy in New York. At Aqueduct that winter, he was the leading rider in races won, with 51. He won his first stakes race, the Lucky Draw, on Rock Lives, in February of 1983. He won some 170 races as a bug, all but 17 of them in New York and New Jersey, and made more money than he had ever dreamed of seeing. When he lost his bug on May 28, 1983, he found that Maple had been right. "I had $100,000 in the bank," Davis says. "Cash! I was ready to come right back to Pocatello. I was going to be the King of Pocatello! I was going to have the nice car and the boat and take all my friends fishing."

He did nothing of the sort. Instead, he went back to work. There was the inevitable lull in his action after he had lost his weight allowance, but Adika pestered trainers to give Davis a break. Six weeks later, sure enough, they started lifting his leg again. "Steve pushed and pushed us to ride him," says trainer H. Allen Jerkens. So, unlike most hot apprentices who lose their bugs and disappear, Davis stuck in New York. Of course, it was more than just Adika who did it. "Robbie learned as an apprentice how to rate horses," Jerkens says. "Through the years, guys who learn to rate horses keep going. Guys who don't learn, don't do anything after they lose the bug."

His early triumphs notwithstanding, Davis lived a difficult life in New York. He usually kept to himself. "God, it was lonely," he says. "I'd win a $75,000 stake and come home to an empty house. What a cold feeling. You tend to be a loner when you have such shame. There was so much shame there. When I skated, I always skated alone."

Davis roller-skated often in New York, as he had as a kid in Pocatello, and on one Friday night in the spring of 1984, at the Roller Castle in Elmont, New York, a pixieish blonde introduced herself to him. They skated couples. He had always been afraid to date, insecure and wary as he was, and there was an awkward moment when he took her hand and said, in his first words to her, "Boy, you got rough hands! Been digging ditches or something?" Marguerite Hoveling, who did a lot of yard work, liked him anyway. "He was shy and polite," she says. They have been together ever since. They got married the next February—they had their kids one-two-three—and shared the months during which Davis moved in among the leaders of his profession. He made money whip over stirrup in New York and earned the same kind of reputation among horsemen there as he had in Idaho—as a friendly, polite, personable young man with a quick, pearly smile and no apparent demons driving him. "I put on a good front," Davis says. "I didn't want anybody to see through me."

What they would have seen last summer, had they been able to see through him, was a man increasingly in turmoil. "I was like a time bomb," he says. "I was very, very depressed. I kept all my anger in. You build up a lot of anger. You can be in a great mood and all of a sudden you think of something that happened, and it just turns everything. Then you're mad at everything. . . . I hated myself. I could never do enough or accomplish what I wanted. I was always mad at myself and at other people. I used to build up a big hate for people, and it hurt inside."

And it was all a secret, down at the deep root of the rage, a secret unshared for years even with his wife. "It was always there," he says. "It was just grinding at me: 'You've got to tell her, you've got to tell her,' I'd say to myself. 'No, she doesn't have to know this. It'll hurt her too much.'" He envisioned her leaving him if he told her of his past, running to her mother's Long Island house with the kids, telling her mother, Hey, this guy was sexually abused, he's a complete wacko!

He didn't know how to handle his turbulent emotions. Last summer he felt them mounting. "It was getting worse and worse," he says. "I was getting meaner and meaner, angrier and angrier. For no reason whatsoever, I'd fly off the handle. I was a real crybaby in the jocks' room; things would happen to me in a race and I'd scream and holler at the other riders. I was getting scared of myself."

Davis was carrying all that unchecked baggage from his childhood when, on that fine October afternoon, Venezia fell in front of him, Davis peered into the ambulance and then ran off to hide. As his life flickered before him in that closet, the scenes of violence and abuse, something in him seemed to die. A kind of serenity came over him, as if the accident, in catharsis, had suddenly slain all the old torments in his life. "It pulled a trigger," he says. "It shot off inside me and went through me. I never loved people more in my life than that moment right there. All the hate I had for everybody, it just all went away."

With that began the craving to head home. Davis says, "It's hard to explain, but there was something pulling me back to Pocatello—to my values. I was packing too heavy a load. There was too much I had to get off my mind."

There was also that delicate matter of unburdening himself to his wife. They drove to Edwardsville, Kansas, and spent two months, off and on, with his mother and sister. They spent $85,000 on a huge motor home.

They took a skiing trip to Colorado before Christmas, and then one night, after all those years of keeping it in, Davis finally let it out, first telling Marguerite of the deaths of Lindauer and Lords and how hard it had been growing up and how low he had been at times.

"I took a lot of abuse when I was young," he said.

"What kind?" she asked.

"Sexual. I was sexually abused by a man my mother was married to. . . ."

It was easier than he had thought it would be. They talked about it into the night. "It just flowed out," Davis says. "We were both crying. She was so understanding. We tied the knot that much tighter. She held me all night and we went to sleep. It was such a relief. It was like a new beginning."

On Christmas Day, Davis talked to Lenny Goodman by telephone—he had taken over the rider's book early last year—and Goodman reminded him that Gulfstream Park was opening soon. Davis was not ready. "Only millionaires take off like this," Goodman said. "You're taking the longest vacation in history!"

Speaking to one of America's leading riders, a 27-year-old whose mounts had amassed lifetime earnings of $37,382,325, Goodman may have been right. But Davis was still too involved in sorting things out and looking for answers, unfolding his childhood bit by bit to his wife, and just being with his family and wheeling around the West. They finally came to Pocatello on Jan. 10, hooked up at Sullivan's motor park and lived there for nearly two months. They never connected their telephone—a blessing, what with all the people looking to talk to Davis—but you could reach them here and there if you tried. At the laundromat on Fifth Avenue. At the home of Bonnie Lords, Tim's widow. At the Whitworth home in Inkom. At the ski lodge at Pebble Creek. At the home of Buddy Jones, an old pal from the days when he and Davis worked at the bakery. At the skating rink. At the Downs for the races on weekends.

The Davises remained in Idaho until one snowy morning in early March, when he and Marguerite suddenly decided to leave. They drove west, through Las Vegas and into Southern California. Robbie was itching to ride again.

The old nightmares were gone. Davis still occasionally thought about Venezia, a gentle, soft-spoken man who, like Davis, had been an apprentice sensation in New York, in 1964. Davis recalls spending hours with Venezia after the races, talking about life and their kids. Venezia left a wife and two children when he died, at age 43—a son, Michael Edward, 15, and a daughter, Alison, 8. "I think about him, not every day, but every once in a while," Davis says. "I don't dwell on it. I still feel a little hurt over it, but there ain't nobody on earth who can change it. I think about his kids, his son and daughter, and I feel that they were lucky they got to know him."

Nor do the memories of the accident haunt Davis as they did immediately after the mishap, when he blamed himself "totally." Totally? Oh yes. After all, Davis says, Drums in the Night had natural early speed, but he had chosen to take him back, leaving him behind Venezia and Mr. Walter K. down the backstretch. If *only* he had sent Drums in the Night to the lead. . . . If *only* he hadn't shown Lindauer how to get to the top of the cliff. . . . And if *only* he had been bigger and stronger he might have been able to strike back at his stepfather. . . .

Which is what he thinks he may have finally done, symbolically, on that day last October. "That makes sense to me," he says. And sense is what Davis is still trying to make of what happened to him five months ago. It was a confusing, chaotic, desperate time in his life, and he has not yet fitted all the pieces together. Clearly he had passed through a purging experience that frightened and humbled him, but ultimately lifted him.

And where he found himself on the hazy, sunny afternoon of March 8 was in the jockeys' quarters at Santa Anita racetrack. It was nearly three o'clock. He had just slipped into red-white-and-blue silks and was waiting for the fifth race. He would ride a 15–1 shot, Hickory Crest—his first mount since the accident and his first for his new agent, Jeff Franklin, whom he had hired only five hours earlier. (During Davis's months of inactivity, Goodman didn't take on a new client.) Davis had been touched by the warmth of his welcome in the jockeys' room at Santa Anita—the home of such riders as Chris McCarron, Laffit Pincay Jr. and fellow Idahoan Gary Stevens, who won the Kentucky Derby last year on Winning Colors. "They came over and shook my hand and gave me a hug. Chris was very comforting," said Davis as he sat and felt the anxiety mounting.

"Boy, I have butterflies like crazy, but it feels good to put the silks back on," he said. "It's like I've got the bug again, and this is my first mount."

He rode Hickory Crest like a jittery young apprentice too. Heading into the far turn, lying fourth, the filly suddenly kicked into gear and took off, nearly running up the heels of the horse in front of her. Davis, noted for his silky hands, snatched Hickory Crest back too hard, causing her to throw her head in the air. To make matters worse, just after they straightened out for home, he dropped his whip. They finished fourth. "Whew!" he said. "Old fumble-fingers. I'm a little embarrassed. My hands got all tangled up. I felt like a bug boy again. But everything will come back to me."

It began coming back in the next race, in which he finished a solid third aboard Swifterthanthewind, at 8–1, in his only other race of the day. "My hands were normal," he said. Davis appeared tired but relieved as he emerged from the jockeys' room at the end of that first day back, to find Marguerite and the kids waiting to greet him. Even the fans were glad to see him. "Welcome to Santa Anita," one horseplayer said, reaching to shake Davis's hand.

So it was here, at the foot of the San Gabriel Mountains, that Robbie Davis ended up—after fleeing New York, after weeks of traveling the Northwest, after months of tortuous journeying through his conscience and his past. There he was after his two rides, standing near the paddock in blue jeans, as the bugle sounded the call to post for the eighth race and the horses strode through the sunshine onto the track. This was his world, a world of silks and starting gates and powerful thoroughbreds pounding for home.

"It's been a long, long road back," Davis said. "Longer than anyone can imagine."

March 1989

Fourteen years after that tragic accident at Belmont Park, Robbie Davis is still a factor in the hotly competitive jockey colony of New York. After a less than memorable career in California—though he was the leading stakes rider at Del Mar in 1990—Davis returned to New York in 1992, where he regained his form of the mid-1980s and became a regular among the leading jockeys, winning riding titles at Belmont Park and Aqueduct. As of August 2002, at age 41, Davis had already won 3,383 races in his career, from 24,240 mounts, and more than $115.5 million in purses. He has homes on Long Island and outside Saratoga, where he and Marguerite are raising their children, three sons and three daughters.

THE SHOE

At 3 A.M. on Aug. 19, 1931, in a two-room adobe shack in the West Texas farm town of Fabens, Ruby Shoemaker had already been in labor some six hours. At first she had thought the pains were caused by the cantaloupe she had eaten for dessert the night before. She was only 17, and eight months pregnant. Her husband, B.B., who clerked in the feed store down the street, was out celebrating his birthday. Ruby figured he had gone to Juarez. Brother Phillips of the Fabens Baptist Church had come by to see what he could do, and his wife had come, too, and heated up some water on the four-burner kerosene stove. Brother Phillips had fetched Ruby's mother, Maudie Harris, because Ruby had asked for her. Then Doc McClain came by to handle the delivery. The boy, who was born at three, weighed one pound, 13 ounces. He had a full head of black hair, and when Doc McClain held him up, Ruby thought he looked like a drowned rat. The Doc spanked him on the rear but couldn't get a sound from him; he was silent even then. Despairing, the Doc put the baby at the foot of the bed and declared, "That will never live."

"Well, I don't care what you say," said Maudie Harris. "He's cold." She picked up the baby from the foot of the bed and carried him to the sink across the room and got a rag and some soap and washed him off in the water that Brother Phillips' wife had heated. Then she wrapped the baby in a doll's blanket and opened up the oven door and lit the stove. She turned the heat to low and put the baby on a pillow in a shoe box on the oven door. Then she pulled a chair up to the oven and sat there. The baby had his eyes open and he moved now and again but made no sound for two hours. Ruby drowsed on the bed, awoke, drowsed some more. At about five, Ruby heard what she thought was a field mouse crying, a tiny screeching sound. It was the boy. "Ruby, I think he's hungry," Maudie said, and brought him over to the bed. Ruby couldn't get over his hands, how small they were, so small they looked like little claws. The boy was simply too weak to suckle, so they got a breast pump and eyedropper and fed him. Then they

43

tried to fit him with a regular diaper, but he got lost in the huge folds, so they cut the diaper into quarters which fit just right. "He'll live, Ruby, he'll live," Maudie said. "He's a little fighter."

Today, at age 48, William Lee Shoemaker has been born anew. He is riding into his fourth decade in the saddle as if it were his second. Horses and racing have been in this man's life for as long as he can remember—manes blown back against his hands, the roar of the crowd at the turn for home, two on top, the sound of hoofbeats in his ears. And surely, whatever he does and sees and feels today he has done and seen and felt before. But no longer is he the despairing Shoe of a few years ago, the tired Shoe who had a little potbelly and wondered if his career was at an end.

"It's been like a rejuvenation, a new beginning," he says. "I wish I could go on forever. I enjoy it. I enjoy riding today more than ever before. Because of the situation, partly, the way it changed. But also because of the knowledge—what I know in bringing horses up to different races, what I've been through all these years. *I know how to do it.* It's here that counts. Right now. Today. For me. I know my business. I know my game. And I love it."

The art was always in the hands, of course, instruments as fine and delicate as any rider ever had, and in his 31-year career Shoemaker has shaped the most impressive record of any jockey in the history of the sport. As of last Thursday, Shoemaker had ridden more horses (33,650), won more races (7,841), more stakes races (796), more $100,000 races (155) and more money ($77,275,929) than any man who ever looked between the ears of a horse. He has won virtually every stakes race in America, including three Kentucky Derbies, two Preaknesses and five Belmonts. California has been his base, and there were years when he owned the West Coast. Through 1967, when he was topped by Jerry Lambert at Santa Anita, Shoemaker had won 17 straight riding titles there. He has won the Santa Anita Handicap, for years the Coast's most important race for older horses, nine times. Ten times he has led the nation's riders in money won. He has ridden most of the very best horses to perform on the American turf in his three decades, a roll call of champions good enough to rate a wing in the Racing Hall of Fame: Coaltown, Swaps, Gallant Man, Round Table, Intentionally, Sword Dancer, Cicada, Crimson Satan, Jaipur, Kelso, Northern Dancer, Tom Rolfe, Buckpasser, Damascus, Arts and Letters, Dr. Fager, Vitriolic, Ack Ack, Dahlia and Forego. And last year he got the mount on Spectacular Bid after Ronnie Franklin was replaced following his poorly executed ride in the Belmont Stakes.

"I think he's the best horse I've ever ridden," says the Shoe. "Each time I ride him, he convinces me more. He does everything like a great horse should do it. He won on every kind of track you can imagine. Carried his weight and won. He's so versatile you can move any time you want and then move again if you have to. And the horse is maturing, getting better, I think. We haven't seen the best of him yet." The man is sitting in the living room of his San Marino, California, house, sipping a vodka and tonic and puffing on a thin cigar. It is growing late. A fire is burning in the fireplace. He removes the cigar from his lips and leans slightly forward, the smoke lifting a question in the air. "Who ever in their life has been able to do that?" he says. "Oh, I'm a good rider. Can ride. I know that. But who has ever been able to do that? At 48 years old, to get on a horse like that?"

Despite all the riding championships, all the notable horses he has ridden, all the years of celebrity, there is in Shoemaker a quality of solitariness, not surprising perhaps in a man from the wide spaces of Texas. Shoemaker spent his youth there, and when he moved to California at the age of 10, he left with more than its dust in his hair. His parents were divorced when he was four. Ruby took the child to live with her in Winters, in central Texas. She and her parents, Ed and Maudie, sharecropped a ranch. They picked cotton. They grew alfalfa. They spent much of their time in the fields with burlap bags slung over their shoulders, chopping cotton or cutting corn. "Work, work, work," Ruby says. "It was a rough life in the Depression, I'll tell you, and little old Bill knows it."

Recollections of his enterprise and self-sufficiency still draw howls of laughter from Ruby and her cousin, Dorothy Abbott. One day, while working in a field in the hot sun, Bill threw his hoe at Grandpa Harris' feet and walked off toward the house. "Grandpa," he said. "I'll never pick up another hoe. There's gotta be a better way to make a living, and I'm gonna find it." He was eight years old.

Another time, he and his younger brother, Lonnie, were visiting Dorothy Abbott on her ranch and playing with Dorothy's 4-year-old son, Dick. Dorothy looked out the window, wondering what the boys were doing, and saw Dick lying under the water pump, about 100 yards away, with Bill standing over him working the handle. In a panic, she dashed across the yard. "There was my boy Dick," she says, "out colder than a mackerel, and there was little Bill, this little bitty thing, pumping water on him, just as calm as a cucumber. I said, 'What happened?' And Bill said, 'The horse kicked Dick in the chest. We drug him over here. He'll be all right.' He was just as nonchalant as he could be."

Bill was six years old. He had been around horses from his earliest years, and he actually drew his first mount when he was five, in 1936, the year Bold Venture won the Kentucky Derby. Ruby and Ed Harris were leaving the ranch house for the fields when Ruby heard her father say, "Look! Look!" She turned to the corral just in time to see Bill climbing up on the top rung of the wooden fence. The family stable pony was alongside. Ruby screamed, "My Gawd! He's gonna get killed."

"Shhhh," said Ed. "You're gonna scare the horse." Bill reached over, grabbed the pony's mane and jumped, pulling himself aboard. "I liked to have a fit." Ruby says. "So I just froze there and watched him. He grabbed the mane and kicked his little legs, and the horse just walked around the corral with him. He was holdin' on to that horse and grinnin' like I don't know what. He just wasn't afraid of anything."

Certainly not Tommy Campbell, an uncle who made a kind of career of harassing the boy. Campbell locked him in the tool shed one day. He had just told Ruby about it, rather smugly, when she saw Bill turning the corner behind the shed. "He only thought he locked me in there," said Bill. "I dug my way out." He had burrowed out beneath the back wall. "He dug himself out like a dog," she says.

Shoemaker brought that unflappable calm—and that knack for getting out of trouble—to every racetrack he rode on. Few jockeys, if any, have ridden neater on a horse—hands back with a long hold, sitting ever so still. And few have had his ability to keep a horse out of trouble, to find the surest way home, to rate a horse, to control him with the subtlest flick of his wrist and hands, to slip-slide out of traffic and hold a horse together in a drive. Eddie Arcaro used to say that Shoemaker could ride a horse with silken threads for reins.

Shoemaker was a sensation almost from the start—his first win came on Shafter V at Golden Gate Fields on April 20, 1949—the heir apparent to Arcaro among the sport's legends, but he had his share of adversity. One episode is legend by now. In the 1957 Kentucky Derby, riding Gallant Man, Shoemaker was locked in a struggle with Iron Liege and Bill Hartack, when he stood up briefly, mistaking the 16th pole for the finish line. Gallant Man never really lost a beat, but he may have hesitated an instant at a moment when he couldn't afford to. Iron Liege won it by a whisker.

A rider of less resilience might not have survived the gaffe, but Shoemaker did, coming back to win the Belmont on Gallant Man. In the ensuing years he was preeminent, taking the money-winning title in 1958 for the fourth time in his career, and then every year thereafter through 1964, when young Braulio Baeza came along.

As Shoemaker neared the '70s, though riding as well as ever on both coasts, a malaise set in. In 1967, the year he rode Damascus to the Horse of the Year title, the first year in Shoe's career in which his mounts earned more than $3 million, for the first time in his life he felt his enthusiasm waning. Ever since he had ridden Swaps to record-smashing victories in 1956, his mounts had earned at least $2 million annually, but there had been a certain evenness to his career. "Maybe it was getting boring to me," he says. "I'd been doing it so long by then, riding all kinds of races all the time. It wasn't that I was up and down. I was like on an even keel all the time. If maybe I'd had some variety in there, maybe if I'd done bad in there and couldn't get things going, it might not have happened."

But 1968, the year he approached with a yawn, brought more variety than he had reckoned for. All through his career, despite occasional mishaps and spills, Shoemaker had never had a serious injury. In January at Santa Anita he suffered a badly broken femur when his horse, Bel Bush, fell and accidentally kicked him. Doctors inserted a rod in his leg to keep it together. "We couldn't get a rod small enough at our hospital," one of the surgeons, Dr. Robert Kerlan, says. "We had to get one from Children's Hospital." The 13-month convalescence was a kind of agony that Shoemaker had never before had to endure. "I just went crazy," he says. "I realized how much I enjoyed riding because I couldn't do it. I'd been taking it for granted. Anytime I wanted to do it, I could do it: anytime I didn't want to, I didn't have to. But when I couldn't do it, that put a different light on the whole picture. It made me realize what an idiot I was, thinking the way I did. That broken leg turned out to be good for me."

He came back in February of 1969, but not for long. On April 30, a filly flipped over backward in the paddock at Hollywood Park, throwing him and pinning him against a hedge. The accident crushed his pelvis, tore his bladder and damaged nerves in his leg. "It was what we call a Humpty-Dumpty injury," Kerlan says. "You know, 'All the King's horses and all the King's men couldn't. . . .' His pelvis was like a large dinner plate that had been broken in a lot of pieces. There wasn't much to set. There was no way to open this up and put it back together. He was put in traction until it showed some evidence of healing. It was a tough injury."

Shoemaker was out another three months and though horsemen wondered whether he would ever ride again, "There was never any doubt in my mind that I would come back," he says. "I accepted it. I know a lot of people thought that that would be the end of me and my career. But I never had that feeling."

In 1970, to much hoopla, he won his 6,033rd horse race, passing Johnny Longden as the winningest rider in the history of the sport. Shoemaker stands 4' 11" and wears a 2D shoe—and for all his career his weight has hovered around 95 pounds. He has never had to do battle with his weight, as Longden did in the last years of his career, never had to face the problem that seems to consume so many riders as they near 40, heading for the sweatbox at noon with towels wrapped around their necks. So, as Shoemaker turned the corner of his third decade as a rider, there was reason to believe, barring injuries, that he could go on almost indefinitely—for as long as he wanted to ride, for as long as the reflexes remained, for as long as he stayed fit.

He had always taken care of himself. Then in the early '70s he found himself in a kind of trap, a blind switch from which he couldn't escape. He was married to a woman he no longer loved and didn't want to live with anymore—a woman, he says, whose social aspirations, outlook and interests were incompatible with his. He says this not to condemn but to explain what happened to him in the early '70s, when he lost his desire to ride, began declining to work horses in the morning, at times called in sick to the jocks' room and began to think he had had it as a rider.

Shoemaker was first married in 1950, when he was only 18 and in his second year as a rider, to Virginia McLaughlin, whom he had met through a fellow jockey. The marriage lasted for 11 years, and they had two adopted children. They were divorced in 1961. "We were too young," says Shoemaker.

Then Shoemaker married Babbs Bayer of Texas, whom he had met a few years before. "Bright, pretty and clever," Shoemaker says. Bill and Babbs lived first in Pasadena, then San Marino, a fashionable, conservative community not far from Santa Anita. In the mid-'60s they made a big move socially, going to live on the 31st floor of a high-rise in Beverly Hills.

Bill Shoemaker was a celebrity. In his soft-spoken, easygoing kind of way, he had emerged as the embodiment of thoroughbred racing on the Coast, as recognizable in Southern California as any movie star. Racetrackers admired him to the point of reverence. Horse players called him "The Shoe" and bet him with both hands. Latin bettors took to calling him "El Zapatero," The Shoemaker, and also "El Maestro," The Teacher. And as the years went by they spoke of him as "El Viejo," The Old One, but always respectfully.

In Beverly Hills, of course, the Shoemakers were on all the invitation lists. Babbs was stunning in fur coats and expensive clothes and beautiful jewelry. She and Bill were seen at the right places. Babbs got into charity work, which is the thing to do in Beverly Hills, and the couple was frequently mentioned in society columns.

Shoemaker, however, had always thought of himself as a simple, uncomplicated man of simple, uncomplicated tastes. He was, after all, the shy little son of a former sharecropper who had grown up poor in the Depression in Texas and made it rich in the Golden Land. Now here he was in Beverly Hills in the social whirl. Unremembered hosts introduced him to unremembered guests whom he did not particularly want to know. "I want to introduce you to Bill Shoemaker," the hosts would say. Shoemaker remembers the refrain. "I've heard that a trillion times," he says. "I never really wanted to know them. I went to their houses and I couldn't remember them now if I tried because I want to put it out of my mind. I remember going to the parties. But I can't remember whose parties they were, or why they were."

In 1973, out of fear for their lives, the Shoemakers moved from their 31st-floor apartment—"We had an earthquake at six o'clock one morning," says the Shoe, "and the building was going around and you could hear the girders squeaking"—to a home in Beverly Hills that Babbs had redesigned. Instead of snugging the bar into a corner, which she thought would reinforce Bill's disposition to withdraw, she had the bar built so it jutted out into the living room area, to bring him into the center of things. Though the disposition to be so never left him, he was no longer the retiring youngster of the '50s. At the party Babbs threw at Chasen's to introduce her plastic surgeon to 300 or so friends and acquaintances, Bill met the guests at the door. Babbs Bayer Shoemaker says she doesn't believe she overdid the social side. She says she understood his needs as a rider and an athlete and didn't know he didn't like the kind of life they were leading. But Shoemaker says that these were among the important reasons why he slipped as a jockey in the early '70s, why he periodically failed to fulfill his responsibilities as a rider, why he considered retirement in 1974 and why, ultimately, he sought the divorce that Babbs wound up granting him.

"You can't be a leading rider and make the society columns at the same time," says Trainer Charles Whittingham, one of Shoemaker's oldest friends in racing. "I got off the beaten track," says Shoe.

Shoemaker remained among the leading riders of stakes horses, but in the early years of the decade he was riding progressively less. Worse, he wasn't riding with the aggressiveness and command that had marked him in his heyday. He was, to be sure, still a star, and he never became less than the No. 1 rider for Whittingham, who stuck by him when the slip began.

This is not to say he rode poorly, for he never lost his touch, his feel, his sense of pace and rhythm. "It's a touch, a feel you have with your hands, like a golfer," says Shoemaker. "They are there all the time, your feel, your touch. You *learn* the craft and you might *improve* on the technique, but the touch and feel are there. Your legs and other parts of your body go, but your touch . . . no."

What went was the desire. He won 195 races on 881 mounts in 1971, the first year, except for the times when he was injured, he had taken fewer than 900 mounts. In 1973, the nadir of his career, he accepted only 639 mounts and won 139 races; the next year his 17% winning percentage was the lowest in a career that had averaged about 24%. "He didn't really care that much in those years," says Laffit Pincay Jr., one of Shoemaker's closest friends. "I could tell just watching him. Not taking too many chances. He didn't ride aggressively on young horses. I know when a rider's really trying. I know when a rider's going out of his way to win. I looked at him one day in the jocks' room and he looked like a little fat man."

One of his oldest friends in the jockeys' room, Don Pierce, figured that Shoemaker would announce his retirement. "I thought it was only a matter of time," says Pierce. "I've known him a long time, and he was depressed. Bill's always kibitzing in the jocks' room. Touching you with a hot coffee spoon. Stealing someone's cuff links. Hitting your funny bone." He pauses. "It came on so slow it never really hit me; I just occasionally missed the kibitzing. It got to the point where he'd walk into the jocks' room, not say much to anyone, ride and leave. But he never complained."

"I guess I'm the type who holds all that in and keeps it to himself," Shoemaker says. "I always thought I could handle my own problems, but apparently I couldn't." He didn't even complain to the man he had known the longest, the man with whose family he had lived in his early days on the track, his surrogate father and agent from the beginning, Harry Silbert. Silbert is the only agent Shoemaker has ever had, and is as protective of his rider as any man who ever scrawled a horse's name in a condition book. Back in 1950, when Shoemaker was about to lose the apprentice bug and with it many mounts, he said to Harry, "Maybe you should try to get another rider; you got a family to support." Harry scoffed. "Don't worry about it, Bill," he said. "You're going to make it."

The early 1970s were especially trying for Silbert, an avuncular, soft-spoken former Brooklynite who is almost as unobtrusive as the Shoe. Silbert would get him the mounts, but whether Shoemaker would actually show up to ride them became problematical. "I never knew from one day to another," Silbert says. Late in the morning Shoemaker might call Dean

Scarborough, the clerk of the scales at Santa Anita, and take himself off his mounts for the day. "He'd call and say he didn't feel too good," Scarborough says. "Touch of the flu." Silbert would call Scarborough, who would pass on the news. "If he wasn't there, I'd go home," Harry says. "I'd have to face the trainers in the morning. I'd say Bill got sick; but how many excuses can you make? I had an idea what was wrong, but I just couldn't talk about it with him."

"Tell me what's wrong," Harry would say.

"Nothing wrong," the Shoe would reply.

"I *know* something's wrong. You can't keep it in you. You have to talk to people. You're going to blow up."

"No problem with you," the Shoe would say. "Problems at home."

"I met a lot of nice people in Beverly Hills, but it wasn't my style," Shoemaker says. "An athlete's supposed to be doing a job the next day, and those people don't have anything to do. They can sleep all day. It affected my riding. It affected my attitude about it a lot. You get up the next day and don't feel any good. It doesn't help you none getting home at midnight or one in the morning. It wasn't good. You don't really give a damn. You're on a horse and you do something, and if it works, fine; if it doesn't, who cares? That sort of thing."

Pincay was right. The old fire was gone. Some horsemen saw uncharacteristic mental lapses in Shoemaker's riding. Longden, now a trainer, saw a man who had lost his sharpness. "He had to have something on his mind," Longden says. "Something was bothering him. Oh, I could tell. He wasn't riding like he should've been riding. He was making wrong moves. It wasn't Shoemaker. He was making decisions in a race that weren't his. Shoemaker is the best rider I ever saw. There has never been any better rider. I don't think so. No sir. When Shoe is right, he's right there—Johnny-on-the-spot. He takes over when another rider is there just thinking about it. He's thinking about it and Shoe's done it. Shoe wasn't thinking."

Shoemaker didn't want to confront his problems, to admit his marriage was a failure, so he told people he was tired. "I feel like I've had it," Shoemaker told Silbert in the Santa Anita parking lot one day in 1974. "I'm tired." It was the first time he had ever said such a thing to Silbert. "What do you mean you're tired and you don't feel like riding?" Harry demanded. "I don't want you to go out this way." Looking back on it now, Shoemaker says he probably rationalized his loss of interest and desire by telling himself that he was getting older and that he should be riding less.

As he cut back on his mounts, Babbs recalls saying to him, "'Either you have to announce your retirement or you have to stay with it and ride.' We had just bought a home in Beverly Hills. The notes come due at the bank and life goes on. To cut his riding in half made a difference in our lifestyle, a life-style I was never aware he didn't enjoy. I enjoyed my life with William very much and I think I did understand that he had to stay in shape. I think he's wrong when he says I didn't understand his career."

Shoemaker's return to top form came in stages. It began when he decided to ride as he knew he could ride—or get out. This was no act of survival. Hollywood Park offered him an executive job in 1973, but he turned it down; he knew he could always train horses. Now he ran to get in shape. He watched his diet. And, finally, he went through a rigorous testing program at the National Athletic Health Institute in Inglewood, California, to find out exactly what kind of condition he was in. "It turned out he was in the top 10% of all the athletes that we did," Kerlan says. "It was very stimulating for him."

So he was back, and now without the potbelly. He had always ridden his share of stakes winners, even when he was slipping, but in 1976 he got an unexpected lift when his old friend Frank Whiteley chose him to ride Forego. In the fall of that year he patiently fashioned out of certain defeat one of the most exquisite finishes in the history of racing. Hopelessly out of it turning for home in the Marlboro Cup at Belmont Park, letting the huge gelding drift toward the middle of the track, never snatching him off balance to alter his course, Shoemaker pushed and sweet-talked Forego home, just getting up to win by a snip over Honest Pleasure. The old horse had never run better, but he needed the old man that day.

By then things had begun to resolve themselves in Bill Shoemaker's life. He and Babbs separated on Feb. 14, 1977, St. Valentine's Day; she sued for divorce the following day, citing "irreconcilable differences" by which she says she meant, "Well, quite frankly, he was in love with another woman." If he wasn't then, he was soon enough.

Babbs moved to Palm Springs, leaving Bill their five toy poodles, Misshoe, Tuffy, Tissue, Missy and Bruiser. "I was happy and relieved when she drove out of the driveway," he says. "I could play with the dogs and enjoy life."

On July 24 Shoemaker became engaged to Cindy Barnes, a 27-year-old sportswoman who shared his interest in racing and preference in life-style—and used to beat him in tennis. They had met 10 years earlier at Del Mar and had been casual friends ever since. "The real turning point with me, in my mind, was when I started dating Cindy," Shoemaker says. "I've often thought how strange life is. Unbelievable. When I met her, she was just a young girl, about 20. She rode horses, hunters and jumpers.

She played tennis. Who in the hell would ever think I'd wind up marrying her? Never ever crossed my mind." And then, with his marriage on the rocks, it suddenly did. On their second date after the divorce, he made what was less a proposal than a proclamation. "You know," he said, "you're going to marry me." To which she replied, "I am?" "She liked the things I liked, the life that I liked, the kind of life I lived," says Shoemaker. "She was into it."

The divorce was granted at 4 P.M. on March 6, 1978, and at 4 P.M. on March 7 Cindy and Bill were married in the backyard of her parents' home in Cardiff-by-the-Sea, outside San Diego. They settled into a small house in Beverly Hills with the five poodles and a barbecue, on which he liked to broil chicken for dinner, and they played backgammon in the evenings. "The past was gone," Cindy Shoemaker says. "It was our own life now."

And things were breaking for them. In 1978 Shoemaker's mounts earned $5,231,390, a personal high, and this year they could exceed even that, largely because he is riding Spectacular Bid. When trainer Bud Delp and owners Harry, Tom and Teresa Meyerhoff decided to take Ronnie Franklin off the horse, Delp gave the Meyerhoffs the names of a few jockeys to consider: Chris McCarron, Darrel McHargue, Jacinto Vasquez and Shoemaker. After Franklin's near-disastrous ride on Spectacular Bid in the Florida Derby in March, an angry Delp had said, "Shoemaker's only a phone call away," and Silbert had offered a pocketful of change. "Anytime you need me," he said.

Delp finally decided to replace Franklin when the horses were going down the backstretch in the Belmont. He believed Franklin was riding scared, evading a jockey with whom he was feuding, Angel Cordero Jr., and chasing an 80–1 shot. "That's when it first hit my mind," Delp says. "We knew we had to come back to New York for the Marlboro Cup and the Jockey Club Gold Cup—and Cordero. It was a decision that had to be made for the best interests of Bid." Delp favored Shoe. Besides Shoemaker's experience and style and the extraordinary gift of his hands, to whose touch Delp felt Bid would respond like Pegasus, there was one more important factor.

"How do you feel about it?" Harry Meyerhoff asked.

"I'd love to meet that rider," Bud said. "You know, I never met him."

"I haven't either," said Harry. "That would be nice."

It did not take the Meyerhoffs long to decide. "We're going with the heel-and-toe man," said Harry Meyerhoff. The only reservation he and his trainer had about Shoemaker was his age. "Not so much his physical reactions as his mental attitude," Meyerhoff says. "At his age. . . ."

Actually, Meyerhoff couldn't have entertained an emptier fear. For already this was a more buoyant Shoemaker, and with every gust of wind at his back he was feeling even more exhilarated. Since he had left one life and begun another, he was a different person. And he was up to his old tricks, back to doing things he had stopped doing, back to the hot-spoon trick and hiding the cuff links. Doc Kerlan, who owns horses, stopped in the jockeys' room at Hollywood Park one day last summer, draped his $375 sports coat over a chair and sat down to play cards. When the card game was over, Kerlan left and went to his box seat and sat down. He reached into his right pocket for a mint. And then he leaped from his seat, yelling, "That little son of a—" To this day the coat still smells of chili sauce. "I knew absolutely without doubt who it was," Kerlan says. "There isn't anyone as diabolical when it comes to practical jokes. But I got him. I waited several weeks. I made a special mixture of slime, the kind that you can buy, and I mixed it with butyric acid, which is the stinkingest stuff in the world, and I mixed it into one of the most horrible mixtures that ever existed, and one day he had his little boots set out and I filled the shoe part with it and he put his foot in it."

Last fall Shoemaker won the Marlboro Cup with Spectacular Bid, on a day on which the man could apparently do no wrong. Counting back on her fingers, Cindy figures that that was the day she got pregnant. For the first time in a long while, at age 48, Shoemaker was going to be a father. "He was in a state of shock," she says, "ecstatic shock. For a while Bill was driving me crazy: 'Don't lift this, don't lift that. Don't eat this, don't eat that. Don't do this, don't do that.'" At the year's end Shoemaker's mounts had earned $4,427,860, sixth best in the country.

In April the Shoemakers moved from Beverly Hills to San Marino, a change not without symbolic meaning. "There was nothing to keep me in Beverly Hills anymore," Shoemaker says.

Now racetrackers fairly marvel at a man renewed. "He's a great rider, he always was, but I see a new vitality, a new energy about him," says Trainer John Russell.

"Through all this rain and mud and bad days we've been having, Shoe's the first one on the scale," says Scarborough, who once took the messages when Shoe called in with the flu. "He's sort of the leader, by example. Jockeys complain about the rain and cold, and Shoe listens and laughs at them."

"I have never seen Shoemaker so happy in the 25 years I've known him," says Laz Barrera, who trained the Triple Crown winner Affirmed. "He is riding as good as he ever has at any time in his life."

Shoemaker is riding like a bug boy again, as a matter of fact, working horses in the morning, hustling them home in the afternoon. Silbert turned the corner of a shed recently and, to his amazement, saw Shoemaker down on his knees stripping bandages off a horse he had just worked. "I'm like a little kid again, you know?" Shoe says. "I want to get out there and see how a horse feels and try to work him the right way and not work him too hard or too easy, just enough to help him get ready for his next race.

"I like to be around the horses in the morning—the atmosphere, it's what I enjoy in life. That's my lifestyle. That other thing is for somebody in the movies, not me. My lifestyle is early in the morning. The sun's coming up. The air's fresh. See the horses breathing, the steam coming out of their noses, having a feel for it, enjoying it. They have different personalities. A good trainer can watch his horse walk to the track and almost know how good his horse feels. That comes from a lot of years being around them. That's what you call having a 'feel' for the game. That's the good part, the morning. You feel the difference from one work to the next and see how they develop, *feel* how they develop. I feel it. I know it. They're communicating with you—if you only know what to look for and how to read it."

"I'm so darn happy for him," says Arcaro. "But he's still 48 going on 49, and nothing saves you there. Time rolls by, and those kids are going to come up and chop on him." Well, they've been chopping on El Viejo for years, and they haven't cut the mainspring yet.

Shoe puffs on his cigar and taps his forehead. "I'm not as good now as I was when I was 25, 30 years old, physically, but mentally I'm better," he says. "If somebody had told me when I was 28 that I would still be riding when I was 48, I'd have said, 'You've got to be crazy.' Whatever happened to me in life, I tried to keep everything on an even keel and think right about it. I never got silly about it. Even when I wasn't thinking good. I always had a little stability to me that kept me in there going. You know what I mean? That probably saved me. I never got silly."

Whatever it was, it got him to 1980, to here, to right now, as rich as any rider in the game, richer in a way. His is an old American story—the story of the Texas boy too tough to die at birth, who threw down the hoe and climbed on the horse and dug his way out of the tool shed and came West and made his fortune and his name and who got lost and was found again.

It is growing dark and El Viejo is driving home from Santa Anita, down Laurel Canyon Boulevard. He is silent. Then he slips the car over to the curb, where Laurel Canyon meets Moorpark Street, and cuts the engine of his BMW in front of Flowersville, a florist. "I'm going to make Cindy happy," he says. "She loves flowers. Just be a minute." He chooses a freshly cut old-fashioned bouquet of carnations and chrysanthemums, sweet william and baby's breath. "Thank you," he says to the cashier. "Very pretty."

The lady is breathless. "Do you know who that is?" she says as he leaves. "That's Bill Shoemaker. He's the sweetest man in the world."

June 1980

On Feb. 3, 1990, at age 58 and with 42 years in the saddle, Shoemaker retired as the leading rider of all time with 8,833 winners from 40,352 mounts, purse earnings of more than $123 million, 11 victories in Triple Crown races (including four in the Kentucky Derby, the last as a geezer of 55 in 1986, aboard Ferdinand) and 1,009 stakes wins. On April 8, 1991, at the start of an extremely promising career as a trainer, Shoemaker was paralyzed from the neck down when the Ford Bronco he was driving veered off the road and plunged down a 50-foot embankment in San Dimas, California. When he arrived at the hospital an hour later, his blood-alcohol level was .19, more than twice the legal limit. After almost six months of convalescence, The Shoe resumed work as a trainer, but his career eventually stalled. He retired from training on Nov. 3, 1997, after saddling only 90 winners in 713 starts. He and Cindy divorced in 1994, after 16 years of marriage. Shoemaker died in October 2003.

BLOOD BROTHERS
AND BLUEGRASS

*When Sunday Silence meets Easy Goer in the
Breeders' Cup Classic, the pride of two sons of
Kentucky's Hancock family will be at stake*

He left Claiborne Farm that day in a rush, bursting out the front door of
the farm's office and heading toward the Chevy station wagon. He
could taste the salt in his tears.

Even today, Arthur Boyd Hancock III remembers that cold December
afternoon in 1972 as vividly as he remembers the pain and turmoil that
tracked his life and led him inevitably out that front door: the drinking and
the car wrecks, the bar fights and the nights in jail, the long years of conflict and rejection that marked life with father. He can still recall the sound
of his father's foghorn voice berating him, the angry threats and impreca-
tions. He can remember the occasional whuppings his father delivered—
that coldcocking right to the jaw and the kick to the belly when he was
down. But that was over now, and all that remained for Arthur to face were
the consequences of his improvident youth.

Three months earlier, on Sept. 14, Arthur's father, A.B. Hancock Jr.,
had died of cancer, leaving his wife, Waddell, and four children: daughters
Clay, 27 years old, and Dell, 19, and sons Arthur III, 29, and Seth, 23. In
the 25 years before his death, the 62-year-old Kentuckian, who was known
to all as Bull Hancock, had emerged as the godfather of American thoroughbred breeding, the single most influential force in making the U.S. the
international leader of both the blood-stock business and the sport of racing. In Claiborne Farm, Bull had left behind the preeminent thoroughbred

breeding farm in the world—a 4,570-acre Bluegrass showplace outside Paris, Kentucky, that was home to royally bred mares and to the most formidable assembly of stallions in the world.

Many rich men trusted Bull with their money, and they spent millions gambling on his advice. His nickname suited him. He was a large man, 6' 2" and 230 pounds, a bourbon-sipping raconteur with a deep, reverberating voice, an enormous sense of presence and a temper that was as quick as it was legendary. He missed a crucial putt one day while playing golf and became so enraged that he heaved his putter into a nearby creek. Still frothing, he grabbed his golf bag out of his caddie's hands and threw *it* into the creek. At that moment, his caddie started laughing, and so Bull picked up the caddie and threw *him* in after the putter and the bag.

Bull was competitive in the extreme, and it was his enduring frustration that he spent his adult life in futile pursuit of his most fervent dream. As big as he was in the breeding game, with access to all those stallions and with his celebrated insight into pedigrees, Bull never owned a Kentucky Derby winner. Claiborne had bred some Derby champs for other owners, but no Hancock had ever *owned* a Derby winner, and the Hancocks had been breeding horses at Claiborne since Bull's father, Arthur I, founded the place in 1910.

Bull's quest to breed and own that one big 3-year-old colt was the consuming passion of his life. Most of the best horses he raised for himself happened to be fillies, and raising fillies was just not the way to win the Derby. One spring day in 1970, one of Bull's finest mares, Continue, went into labor. She was carrying a foal by the Argentine champion Forli. "This could be my Derby horse," Bull told the 27-year-old Arthur as they drove to the foaling barn to watch the birth.

Bull paced nervously outside the stall as the farmhands helped Continue in the delivery. The moment the whole foal emerged, Bull peeked inside the stall and asked, "Well, what is it?"

"It's a filly, Mistah Hancock," said farmhand James Christopher.

Bull wheeled around and bellowed, "Sonofabitch, another filly!" He kicked the wall, booted over a filled water bucket, then began walking in circles, muttering in anguish: "What is it I've done? Why do I deserve this?" Calming down, he finally asked, "Is she all right?" Just then Christopher turned the foal over, and where her left eye should have been there was an empty socket.

"She only has one eye," Christopher said.

Bull jumped as though he had been electrocuted, then kicked a feed tub six feet into the air, sending it crashing out the barn door. "Goddam it!" he hollered. "Not only a filly, but a *one-eyed* filly!"

He named her Tuerta. Little did he know it at the time but, true to the curious twists and turns of the breeding business, that one-eyed filly would one day help fulfill Bull's ultimate quest.

When Bull died in 1972, Arthur III figured that Claiborne Farm would be his to run. He was, after all, the oldest son and had worked at all levels on the farm. Seth had just graduated from the University of Kentucky and had begun to work at Claiborne full-time. "I wanted to carry on my father's name," Arthur says. "It was what I had been programmed to do."

And, indeed, an executor of Bull's will says Arthur probably would have gotten the job had it not been for Ogden Phipps. Phipps, one of Bull's closest friends and most important clients, had been named by Bull as an adviser to the estate on matters relating to the horses. According to the executor, when Arthur was suggested as the logical candidate, Phipps objected, saying Arthur got drunk and into fights all the time. Phipps denies this.

But there was no denying Arthur's history as the family rebel or his reputation as a carouser and womanizer. "I was a freewheelin', hard-drinkin', guitar-pickin', bar-brawlin', skirt-chasin' fool," he says. And Arthur did little to endear himself to his father's friends. A couple of months after Bull's death, on the day the farm dispersed some of Bull's racehorses in New York, Arthur showed up at the sale with eyes red from a night of heroic drinking. Already he had sensed a coolness from Phipps, and now there was a distinct chill. Arthur began to suspect that his fate had been determined.

In the executors' meeting at Claiborne that December, he learned that the advisers wanted Seth as president of Claiborne, with Arthur in a subordinate role. Arthur knew instantly what he had to do; there was no chance that Arthur Boyd Hancock III would work for his younger brother.

Arthur stood up, all 6' 4" of him, and said, "Y'all run it like you want to. You don't need me anymore. I'm out."

Out the door, that is, and into the Chevy. He hit the gas pedal and fled down the driveway. It was the most crushing moment of his life. Claiborne had been his home, his birthright. Feeling alone and suddenly lost, cut from his roots and his heritage, he was scared, facing things on his own for the first time in his life. "When I was young, I once thought that I wanted to be an explorer," Arthur says. "Well, I was exploring now. It was like crossing the sea from England to America. I thought, You'll find out at least what you're going to do in life and at least you'll do it yourself. If they don't want me, fine. Screw'em. I'm not gonna hang around if I'm not wanted.

"It's like a song I once wrote: *If it's all the same to you, I'll be leavin' in the mornin'*. But at the same time I was torn all to pieces."

He felt resentment toward Seth and was filled with bitterness toward Phipps, whom he perceived as the architect of his removal. Arthur stopped in Paris to call his best friend, Paul Sullivan, at a pay phone.

"I just dropped out of Claiborne," he said.

"Oh, my God!" said Sullivan. "You gotta be joking."

True to form, Arthur got into his cups that night, drinking until the wee hours with Sullivan. Sometime past midnight, Arthur began plotting his return. He was living alone at the time, a few miles down the road from Claiborne, on a little 100-acre spread that Bull had leased him to run on his own. It was called Stone Farm. Arthur vowed he would build it into a showplace and one day would show Phipps and all the rest that he was his father's son.

"Someday I'm gonna win the Kentucky Derby," he told Sullivan, "and someday I'll be *bigger* than Claiborne."

Sullivan said, "Bring this fool another Budweiser!"

Almost 17 years after washing down his promises with yet another beer, Arthur Hancock III steers his black Mercedes between two wide fields of grass. It is a fine autumn day in the countryside northeast of Paris. He pulls over to the side of the road and points: "That field over there, where that big tree is growing, is where I raised Sunday Silence as a yearling on Stone Farm. Back over yonder"—he gestures to another field a quarter mile away, in the direction of Claiborne—"is where Easy Goer grew up as yearling at the same time. Ain't life strange? When they were yearlings, they could have looked over their fences and seen one another. Probably did. Now they're running for Horse of the Year."

On Nov. 4, Hancock will be sitting in an owner's box at Gulfstream Park in Florida, nervously awaiting the start of the $3 million Breeders' Cup Classic and the season's final performance by his fast and gutsy 3-year-old, Sunday Silence. In a nearby box will sit Ogden Phipps, now 80 and the owner of Easy Goer, the dazzling chestnut who has already had three memorable Triple Crown duels with Sunday Silence. And somewhere nearby will be Seth Hancock, who watched Easy Goer grow up at Claiborne.

In what is now as much a clash of owners and farms as a rivalry of horses, these two colts will meet one last time to determine who is the best horse in the U.S. In the contests of owner versus owner and brother versus brother, it will be impossible to measure the pride at stake. And it seems fitting that on Breeders' Cup day the spotlight will fall on two horses who were born and raised on neighboring pastures once walked by America's most important breeder of thoroughbreds. Somewhere, Bull Hancock will be smiling.

Bull was born in 1910, the same year his father founded Claiborne Farm on 1,300 acres of land in Bourbon County, 16 miles northeast of Lexington. Claiborne flourished as a stud farm through the 1920s, and by the 1930s, Arthur Hancock was widely acknowledged to be one of the finest horsemen of his day.

Bull Hancock was his father's creation, the son raised to run the empire after he was gone. "I started with my dad, riding out with him to open gates," Bull once said. "He paid me a nickel a day. After that I went to sweeping sheds and shaking empty stalls. It was tough work, but it was for me. I never wanted to be anything but a horseman."

Bull attended Princeton (class of '33), where he played football and baseball and studied eugenics and genetics. But when he returned to Claiborne in 1945, after serving in the Army Air Corps during World War II, the farm had a twilight presence to it. "It had sunk to a very low place," says Waddell. "The mares had all gotten old. The stallions were not fashionable. The farm had fallen into disarray."

Bull gradually took over the running of Claiborne from his ailing father and began to look for that big stallion who would lead Claiborne to a post-war resurgence. He found him in Ireland. Of Hancock's many contributions to breeding and racing in America, none remotely approaches his purchase, in 1949, of the Irish horse Nasrullah, son of the brilliant Nearco.

As a student of genetics at Princeton, Bull had bred fruit flies. Says Arthur, "He used to say that among the fruit flies, the complete outcrosses were the ones that had the energy and vigor. He called that 'hybrid vigor.'" In thoroughbred breeding, a horse is a complete outcross if no name appears more than once in the first four generations of his family tree. With Nasrullah, Bull undertook the application of his hybrid-vigor theory and infused American bloodlines with the Nearco fire, bringing a whole new pedigree to Kentucky mares.

After the war, Bull purchased the stakes-winning Miss Disco, whose pedigree was old American domestic. He was going to add her to his own broodmare band when Mrs. Henry Carnegie Phipps, Ogden's mother and one of the farm's best clients, expressed an interest in owning her. Reluctantly, Bull sold her. In 1953, Mrs. Phipps bred Nasrullah to Miss Disco, and on the night of April 6, 1954—one of the most historic moments in American horseracing—Miss Disco gave birth to her complete outcross, a bay that Mrs. Phipps named Bold Ruler.

After being voted Horse of the Year in 1957, Bold Ruler became a phenomenon as a stallion at Claiborne. From 1963 to 1969, he was America's leading sire, probably the greatest that this country has ever produced. He crowned his incredible career as a stallion when, in 1969, he was bred to Somethingroyal. The next spring, she foaled Secretariat.

Behind Nasrullah, Bold Ruler and a host of other stallions, Claiborne became a repository of the most vigorous bloodlines in the world, and Bull became the most powerful man in the breeding business. It was into this tradition of success, in the shadow of this imposing man, that Arthur and Seth were born. All Bull ever wanted, of course, was for his boys to grow up as he had grown up, working to one day replace their father. "His dream was for Seth and me to run the farm," says Arthur. "That's what he always talked about. For us to carry on when he died."

But when Arthur came of age, he did not know what he wanted to do. "I always loved the horses and the farm," he says, "but I didn't think I could ever equal anything my daddy or granddaddy had done. I saw myself living a life of raisin' horses and probably never havin' any good ones. I sort of wanted to break away and do something on my own."

Much to Bull's dismay, Arthur began veering off on his own at an early age. He loved music, and his grandmother bought him a ukelele when he was seven. The opening lyrics to the first song he ever learned sound like an omen of his hell-raising future:

> I went home the other night
> Drunk as I could be
> Found a head, in my bed
> Where my head ought to be

Bull did not want his son playing music, and the boy first felt the sting of his father's disapproval one night at a family dinner. Arthur was 10, fascinated by the shining trumpets that the kids played in the school band.

"Can I get a trumpet for Christmas?" Arthur asked. "If I learn to play it well enough, I might be able to get in the band."

His father threw down his napkin and glared at the boy across the table. Biting off each word, Bull said, "When we were at Princeton, my football friends and I always wondered who'd have the goddam kid who played in the band!"

Arthur didn't get the trumpet, but instead graduated from the ukelele to the guitar, which became his emblem of rebellion. In 1956, when he was 13, he dyed his hair black, swept it back and donned a black leather jacket. His friends called him Elvis, and he learned to play well enough to sing a few songs one day on a Paris radio station. All full of himself, he strutted in the front door of Claiborne House, the white-columned family manse, and saw his father sitting there reading the *Daily Racing Form*.

"Well, well, well," said Bull. "If it isn't the canary comin' home to roost."

"It nearly killed me when Bull would say things like that to Arthur," says Waddell. "That absolutely cut me to the quick. I loved Bull, I adored him. But they were fightin' words. I tried to control myself. I'd say, 'Please try to be a little more considerate of the boy's feelin's.'"

That was not easy. Bull's favorite saying was, "The only real happiness in life is a job well done." He expected Arthur to take as much interest in Claiborne as he did. Arthur was picking his guitar in the house one afternoon, trying to learn how to play Ricky Nelson's "Hello Mary Lou," when Bull asked if he wanted to see some of the new foals.

"Thanks, Daddy, but I want to finish this song," he said.

"You know what you remind me of?" asked Bull.

"No, sir," said Arthur.

"The goddam court jester."

One night, when Arthur was 17, Bull told him to be home at 11:00. At 10:50, Arthur called from a hamburger joint in Paris to say that he would be 15 minutes late. Bull hung up on him. Instead of coming straight home, Arthur waited for his cheeseburger. When he walked in the front door at 11:15, Bull was standing behind it. The first right to the jaw dropped Arthur to the floor, and then Bull started kicking him. Arthur scrambled to his feet, but Bull knocked him down again. Leaning over his son, Bull said, "I tell you to be in at 11 o'clock, you goddam be in at 11 o'clock. Understand?"

Such episodes of physical violence were infrequent, and Arthur admits to provoking his father's anger. "I was scared of Daddy, but I admired him tremendously, and I loved him," he says. "But I was just an arrogant, cocky little sucker. You're Bull Hancock and your son gets up at Joyland Park in Lexington and plays rock 'n' roll with Little Enis and the Tabletoppers. Wild and crazy hair. They write in the Lexington papers the next day that Bull Hancock's son was singin' 'Johnny B. Goode' and doin' the duckwalk across the Joyland stage. I think a lot of that caused the clash."

Seth never stirred his father's ire as Arthur did. "I saw the problems Arthur had and what I viewed as his mistakes," says Seth. "I thought, I ain't comin' in late, I ain't gonna argue with him. You couldn't win. I could see that. I just stayed away from those types of things, and we got along fine."

Arthur's errant ways continued in college, at Vanderbilt. As a sophomore, a week after swimming to the Southeastern Conference championship in the 100-meter freestyle, he was still celebrating his victory. He left a party and was driving about 100 mph down a Nashville road, his radio blaring, when three police cars pulled him over. A policeman jerked him out of the car. Arthur started laughing and dancing the monkey in the road. They slammed him against the hood, handcuffed him and took him to the station. When they tried to give him a Breathalyzer test, he drew in all the air he could—"I was really fit from swimmin'," he says—and exhaled so hard that the balloon exploded.

He laughed in their faces and spent the night in a dim cell that reeked of vomit, lying on a cot, facing the wall. "Oh, Lord," he moaned. It was not the last night he would spend in a drunk tank.

He graduated from Vanderbilt in 1966, worked a year as a groom at Belmont Park for the Phipps family's trainer, Eddie Neloy, and then headed back to Claiborne to resume his apprenticeship under his father. The end nearly came in 1969. Arthur was attending a wedding reception, and drinking too much, when a group of men began goading him with an unseemly suggestion regarding one of his sisters. He punched one of them so hard in the face that the fellow left a bloody trail as he skidded across the floor. It took four men, including the bride's father, to get Arthur out the door. The next morning, Arthur was visited by his old drinking nemesis, "Mr. R.E. Morse," as he calls him. The bride's family were old friends of the Hancocks, and Bull was mortified.

"Pack your bags and get out," Bull told him.

Arthur did some of the fanciest talking of his life, pleading with his father to forgive him. Bull grew quiet. He looked at Arthur sadly. "I was like you once," he said. "Get a grip on it, Bud. Be a man."

So Arthur stayed. A year later, Bull sent him to Stone Farm, to learn the business for himself. He was doing just that when Bull died and his executors gave Claiborne to Seth. When Arthur attended the January sales at Keeneland in 1973, men who had backslapped him two months before— "Hey, Ahhthur, how ya doin'?"—now dropped their heads when they saw him.

"They figured I was useless," he says. "They figured, here's a sonofabitch who can't follow Claiborne tradition."

While Arthur slipped off to Stone Farm to rebuild his life, Seth rose to assume his father's place—a 23-year-old college graduate suddenly thrust to the top of the greatest breeding establishment in the world, in charge of a farm worth tens of millions in livestock. Says Seth, "Arthur had the burden to bear on his shoulders of bein' turned out in the cold, and I had the burden to bear on my shoulders, like some young basketball coach, of following in the footsteps of John Wooden or Adolph Rupp. So, you know, everybody's got to carry their own bag of rocks. Carry them and do the best you can."

Seth carried his triumphantly in February of 1973. In his first major job as head of Claiborne, he syndicated Secretariat, in 32 shares, for a then world-record $6.08 million, convincing breeders to shell out $190,000 a share 10 weeks before the horse would run in the Kentucky Derby. Now all he had to do was wait for the race, and while Seth and Claiborne didn't own Secretariat, Seth now had a reputation at stake. "What would have happened if the horse had failed?" he asks. "I might have gone down with him."

Instead, Secretariat won the most spectacular Kentucky Derby in history, and Seth was feted as a chip off the old block, Bull's son, the bearer of the torch. Arthur was at the Derby, and that night he went home to Stone Farm. "I went back to the little house," he says. "Seth had won the Kentucky Derby. My little brother! I felt terrible."

In the years after Arthur left Claiborne—while he was scuffling around Bourbon County fitting parcels of land together, gathering clients and looking for stallions and mares—hundreds of people would see him and mistakenly call out, "Hi, there, Seth." Arthur Hancock had almost evaporated. "It was strange," he says. "Seth was the man."

At times Arthur drank as if to self-destruct, getting tanked in town and then driving home too fast. In 1975 he saw a pretty blonde named Staci Worthington working at a sale, and his first thought was, she looks like an angel, but I don't deserve her—wasted rogue that I am. He finally did ask her out, and they eloped in 1977. But Arthur was still the invisible man. Staci would introduce herself to people and they would say, "Are you related to Seth Hancock?"

By the time Arthur married Staci, he had purchased Stone Farm from Bull's estate and added a few other parcels of land, for a total of 844 acres. The vow he made to Sullivan that night in 1972 was no empty one. He talked about it all the time to Staci. "He wanted to win the Kentucky Derby, and he wanted to be bigger than Claiborne," she says. "He was trying to prove something to his father. It really didn't matter if his father was here or not. And he had to prove something to himself."

He worked tirelessly building up Stone Farm. In 1977 he purchased another 1,500 acres, and he was on his tractor or bulldozer all day, pulling up old wire fences, clearing trees, filling washes, mowing pastures. He built miles of fencing and collected clients to board their mares at Stone. "Seven days a week, from six in the morning to six at night," he says. "Year after year."

He began standing some unfashionable stallions, such as Cougar II, at Stone Farm, and he bought relatively inexpensive mares, such as Peacefully, to breed to them. He mated those two in 1978, and the following spring Peacefully foaled a horse at Stone that Hancock named Gato Del Sol. Why did he decide to breed Peacefully to Cougar II? "A complete outcross," he says. "Hybrid vigor!"

In partnership with Leone Peters, he entered Gato Del Sol in the 1982 Kentucky Derby. The big gray was 21–1, and Arthur stood numbly, in disbelief, as his horse came from dead last in a field of 19, charged to the lead nearing the eighth pole and won by 2^1/$_2$ lengths. And when the OFFICIAL sign flashed, he and Staci took off for the winner's circle. A Hancock had finally bred and *owned* a Kentucky Derby winner. "I felt like I could float right over that infield," Arthur says. "I thought, 'Now I know what is meant by walking on air.' I did something that Daddy tried to do all his life and couldn't. I was overwhelmed. I did it all myself! I said, 'I'm not such a stupid, worthless bastard after all.'"

Using Gato as collateral for a bank loan, Arthur quickly bought another 1,200-acre tract of land, making Stone larger than Claiborne. To Sam Ransom, one of Claiborne's old farmhands, now working for Stone, Arthur said, "Just think, we've won the Derby and now we're bigger than Claiborne." To which Sam, who often speaks in rhymes, replied, "We might be bigger in size, but Claiborne's bigger otherwise."

Indeed, Arthur and Stone Farm had still not achieved anything near the stature of Claiborne. Seth had done a splendid job of keeping the Claiborne barns filled with some of the best prospects in racing and developing such leading sires as Mr. Prospector and Danzig. In 1979, Claiborne won an Eclipse Award for breeding.

In 1984, a bay colt named Swale became the first Kentucky Derby winner owned by Claiborne; Seth, at last, had fulfilled his father's fondest dream. Swale, unlike Gato Del Sol and much in the Claiborne tradition, was regally bred, a son of 1977 Triple Crown winner Seattle Slew. And the dam? None other than the one-eyed Tuerta, at whose birth Bull had kicked the feed tub out of the barn.

Despite his success with Stone Farm, Arthur still had problems; his new work ethic was tainted by his old play ethic. Although he had become a family man with four children and had begun to build a grand stone house on a hilltop, a place suitable for a successful Kentucky breeder, he still suffered bouts of self-destruction. "I always felt like John Wayne, the rancher, going into town for a drink after the cattle drive, shootin' it up in the saloon with the boys. I went into Paris to drink. But one night I landed in the police station for four hours and I was thinkin' about my children and my wife at home, and tears ran down my cheeks. I thought, Ain't this something? Would they be proud of Daddy? That day changed my life. I've hardly had a drink since. That day in the police station was really the bottom for me."

Arthur started climbing toward the top in 1984, when Halo, an expensive stallion, began stud duties at Stone Farm. When one of Halo's sons, Sunday Silence, won this year's Kentucky Derby, Arthur found himself, along with his two co-owners, floating to the winner's circle for the second time in seven years.

Arthur has made a kind of peace with Seth—he was best man at Seth's wedding two years ago, and they have a cordial, if not affectionate, relationship. But Arthur's hostility toward Phipps, while diminished, has not disappeared. Phipps, for all his success in breeding and racing, has never had a Derby winner. When Sunday Silence won the Derby, he beat the odds-on favorite Easy Goer, Phipps's horse. For Arthur the vengeance was sweet. "It was poetic justice," he says. "He once prevented me from having what I most wanted in life, and in the Derby I prevented him from having what he wanted too. I hope he wins the Derby next year—unless I'm in it."

If Sunday Silence should win the Breeders' Cup, it will crown the long comeback for Arthur. At times he wonders how he ever got where he is. "You look back and say, 'How did you do that?' I could have been a half-assed songwriter out in L.A., pickin' a guitar, gettin' drunk a couple of times a week, writin' songs. It's amazing I ended up where I am."

He certainly has left his old lifestyle. He has had four brief slips in four years. "I can't drink," he says. "Each time I did, it was the same thing. I got a visit from R.E. Morse. And then the depression, guilt, sadness. It's like I'm not even the same person when I drink. Know what I mean? Who *was* the bad one, anyway, Jekyll or Hyde?"

He looks out the window of his study, past the shelves of gleaming trophies and out across the rolling fields of soft grass. "I think it worked out well for me *and* for Claiborne," he says. "I'm sure Daddy would be proud of me."

October 1989

In their climactic battle of 1989, Sunday Silence snatched the lead from Blushing John with 200 yards to go, then held off a charging Easy Goer to win the Breeders' Cup Classic—and the title of U.S. Horse of the Year—by a neck. Seth is still the president of Claiborne Farm, but it is Arthur who has left the larger postscript. After twice nearly winning the Derby a third time—with second-place finishers Strodes Creek in 1994, beaten by two lengths, and Menifee in 1999, beaten a diminishing neck by long-shot Charismatic—Arthur had the goods again in 1998, when he and Houston sportsman Bob McNair bred and sold a stylish-looking yearling for $4 million to Japanese businessman Fusao Sekiguchi. Named Fusaichi Pegasus, the colt won the Derby two years later by 1 1/2 lengths. Sekiguchi later sold him as a breeding stallion for a world-record $62 million. Arthur Hancock sold Sunday Silence to Japanese breeders in 1990 for $11 million, and the horse quickly emerged as the dominant stallion over there, the leading sire year after year. He died in 2002, at age 16, from complications brought on by foundering. Easy Goer died at Claiborne in 1994, at the young age of 8, of anaphylactic shock.

BREAKDOWNS

On this early Sunday afternoon, along a narrow path of dirt over which Man o' War and Secretariat had once swept in flight to historic victories in the Preakness Stakes, a dainty chestnut filly named So Sly stood frozen in her final autumn light, nervously balancing herself on three legs.

Her 20-year-old groom, Mike Murphy, looked at her for a moment and averted his eyes, his face ashen. He had just run the 700 yards from where he'd been watching the race, in front of the Pimlico grandstand, and he was still carrying the halter and the lead shank on which he had led her to the races that day.

"Oh, jeez," he said.

Murphy knew what had to be done. The distal end of the filly's cannon bone in her left foreleg, just above the ankle, had snapped in half, and the shaft of it was white and bare and jutting, like a peg leg, from a thin brown stocking of skin. Below it the hoof and the lower pastern and ankle bones hung loosely on the ground, tethered to the leg by a single swath of hide and ligament. It was 1:38 P.M. on Oct. 3, and only the bleeding had stopped. Now a fate and a world not of the filly's making was closing in around her—the horse ambulance waiting there to take her away, the pinched expressions of the groom and the pony girl, and the track veterinarian moving toward her with his needles. Five minutes earlier, in the second race at Pimlico, a $1^1/_{16}$-mile claiming event for cheap fillies and mares worth \$8,000–\$8,500, So Sly and jockey Frank Douglas were racing sixth in a field of nine, moving three wide as they charged around the far turn. Russian Vixon was running right next to her when suddenly Freddy Castillo, Russian Vixon's jockey, heard the sound that riders have come to know and fear as no other.

"The crack of a baseball off a wooden bat," as Castillo puts it.

Half-ton racehorses, traveling at 36 miles per hour, strike the ground with splintering force, exerting a 12,000-pound load on the cannon bone alone, and in that instant, on this day, the one in So Sly's left leg blew violently apart. The scene that followed looked like something out of Pickett's Charge. Caving left, So Sly pitched Douglas forward, in somersaults, and on her way down she chop-blocked Russian Vixon, sending her sprawling. Castillo tumbled into the dirt. "She snapped her leg off," Castillo says. "It all happened so quick."

Falling left, Russian Vixon slammed into the horse on the rail, Kels Clever Choice, who crashed to the earth and catapulted her jockey, Joe Rocco, through the air. Rocco had taken a terrible spill two weeks before when a horse had broken down beneath him on the turf course and a passing horse had kicked him in the head. Now as he lay on the dirt he was thinking, Not again. For an instant there were bodies everywhere. And barely had the other horses hit the wire when one of the oldest and most poignant of racetrack rituals began to be played out near the 3/8 pole.

None of the jockeys was seriously hurt. The two inside horses scrambled to their feet and bounded away. Then there was So Sly. She managed to get up but went down, then rose and hobbled in circles, leg dangling, until the pony girl and the ambulance rushed to her side. Jamie Richardson, an ambulance worker, took the reins of her bridle in his left hand and pushed gently against the horse's neck, trying to steady her on three legs. "Whoa now," Richardson said. "Whoa. . . ."

Murphy stepped forward and kissed her on the nose. The filly dropped her head. Then Murphy turned and walked up the racetrack, holding the halter and shank. He did not want to see what was coming now. Nothing at a racetrack stirs chaos and confusion like a loose, catastrophically injured horse—they are often in a state of panic—and by the time Dr. David Zipf, the track veterinarian, arrived on the scene, Richardson had spent several anxious minutes trying to keep the filly steady and calm. As Zipf climbed from his car, Richardson yelled, "You got a radio? I've been standing here with her like this for five minutes!"

"They were saying all the horses were up and running around," Zipf said. "I don't know. . . ."

The vet was bearing large hypodermic syringes—one with 100cc's of a purple solution, a potent barbiturate to euthanize her, and one with barbiturate mixed with succinylcholine, a drug that would force her to the ground while the barbiturate did its work. "Get the tarp up over here," a voice yelled. Two men, standing behind the rail, raised a turquoise screen to block the view of distant spectators and so protect them from their feelings. "Come on, hold her here," Zipf said to Richardson.

So Sly stood facing the turn for home, her eyes wide and her ears working, as Zipf moved to her left side. Twenty yards down the racetrack Murphy was leaning with his back against the fence, his head down. Zipf emptied the syringes into the jugular. So Sly collapsed almost at once on her left side and died moments later in the sun. Murphy did not stay to watch the rest. He took her bridle and turned to leave. "You work with them seven days a week, and then this happens," he said. "I don't know. . . ." The ambulance was backed to where So Sly was lying. The third race was only 20 minutes away, and she had to be removed so the show could go on. They wrapped a length of wire cable three times around her neck—"All right, take it in!" someone shouted—and then dragged her aboard with a winch. And hauled her away.

There is much uncertainty about why so many racehorses end up dead on American tracks every year; but the figures are appalling and unacceptable by any humane standard. In a paper she will present this December to the American Association of Equine Practitioners, researcher Julie Wilson of the University of Minnesota will show for the first time just how bad the numbers are. In 1992, Wilson has found, 840 horses suffered fatal racing breakdowns on American tracks. That is one fatality for every 92 races, or more than one percent. And that does not reflect the number of horses fatally injured in morning workouts. "I think more horses break down in the morning than in the afternoon," says New York trainer Howard Tesher. Wilson's figures also show that a far larger number—3,566 horses—broke down so severely last year that they could not finish the races in which they were hurt. That is one in every 22 races.

"That's way too many," says Dr. Gregory L. Ferraro, a widely respected veterinary surgeon who, disillusioned with what he calls the "rampant" use of drugs on the backstretch, walked away three years ago from perhaps the most lucrative private practice at Southern California tracks, which are among the most prosperous in the world. He sees a strong connection between drug use and breakdowns, and Ferraro does not mean only illegal medications, which veterinarians are under increasing pressure to use, but also the widespread use of legal corticosteroids, as well as the two most prominent legitimate drugs: the diuretic Lasix, which supposedly suppresses bleeding from the lungs, and phenylbutazone, or "bute," an analgesic that reduces inflammation in the joints.

"I stood up for the horsemen the first time 60 Minutes came around," Ferraro says of a segment that aired on the news program more than a decade ago. "I said, 'Don't take the bute away. Don't take the Lasix away.'

And now I feel I was wrong, because I see what's happened 15 years later. It led us down the wrong path. It opened the gate. One little step at a time, it takes you out there. Somewhere you've got to draw the line, and the easiest place to draw the line and *protect* the horse is to say, 'None.' It's not like a guy who's playing football, who has the option to say, 'You can inject that if you want, but I'm not goin' out there. I'm not gonna take the risk.' Those horses don't have that option."

In a 1992 article in the *North American Review* entitled "The Corruption of Nobility: The Rise & Fall of Thoroughbred Racing in America," Ferraro penned a stinging rebuke against drug abuse on the backstretch, saying, "In general, treatments designed to repair a horse's injuries and to alleviate its suffering are now often used to get the animal out onto the track to compete—to force the animal, like some punch-drunk fighter, to make just one more round. Equine veterinary medicine has been misdirected from the art of healing to the craft of portfolio management, and the business of horse racing is in the process of killing its goose with the golden eggs."

There is no grander and gaudier goose than the annual Breeders' Cup; and a week from Saturday at Santa Anita Park, when the finest equine athletes in the game do battle in seven races for $10 million in purses, thousands of racing's patrons and habitués will be engaged in hand-wringing unprecedented in the sport's long history. Its economic woes aside, the horse racing industry has reached a critical state in regard to public confidence—that is, among the millions who watch it more for pleasure than for profit—and it has reached that point over the last few years because of the near carnage that has been taking place during some of the game's most celebrated events, most notably in the nationally televised Breeders' Cup itself and the Triple Crown. But the breakdown and death of So Sly at Pimlico a month ago is far more typical than Union City's more widely publicized crippling and ensuing destruction in the Preakness last spring. Aside from the emotional connections of Murphy and a few others, So Sly was just another largely anonymous horse who broke a bone in just another race on yet another forgettable card. The regularity of such events has benumbed even those whose lives are most at risk—the jockeys.

"It's happened so many times to me, I can't keep track of it," said jockey Douglas after So Sly's fall, "It's the name of the game. Nothing we can do about it."

But the nonchalant shrug will no longer suffice. If Secretariat's spectacular triumph in the 1973 Belmont Stakes took the sport to a new level of popularity, the breakdown and death of Ruffian two years later did more to besmirch racing than anything that had ever happened in the game. Race-horses had been breaking down for centuries, but never before in an event so widely seen as the great match race between Ruffian and Foolish Plea-sure at Belmont Park. And never a horse with so vast and passionate a fol-lowing as the flying black filly who had never been headed and had never known defeat. Even today the images in black and white swim powerfully through memory: of Ruffian battling the colt head-and-head as they sailed down the backstretch, of the pigeon flying up in front of her, of Ruffian bobbling horribly and limping to a stop, and then Manny Gilman, the track veterinarian, fitting the shattered ankle with an inflatable cast and rising and walking away, both hands bloody.

For many who turned off their TV sets that day, thoroughbred racing has had blood on its hands ever since. And in the last three years, of course, the situation has gotten worse. In a sense the shocking breakdown of Go for Wand in the 1990 Breeders' Cup Distaff at Belmont, as she and Bayakoa went hammer and tongs 100 yards from the wire, poisoned the well even more deeply than Ruffian's demise, since Go for Wand went down deep in the stretch, in full view of everyone, and then tried to stand on a foot that flapped around grotesquely as she bounded in a panic in front of the horri-fied crowds that filled the grandstand.

This was no isolated occurrence in the Breeders' Cup. Since the event's inaugural running in 1984, there has been an injury, breakdown or fatality in virtually every Cup renewal. Last year Mr. Brooks broke down turning for home in the Breeders' Cup Sprint, dashing English riding legend Lester Piggott into the upper stretch; and while Piggott survived, with minor injuries, the horse had to be destroyed. And this spring, with the sport increasingly under attack from animal rights groups, Union City never even made it to the far turn at Pimlico, again focusing public attention on the issue of death on the race-track. No sooner had that unseemly mess subsided than Prairie Bayou, the Preakness winner himself, was galloping quietly down the backstretch in the Belmont Stakes when he broke down so completely that his left foreleg was a ruin—a broken cannon bone, a ruptured suspensory ligament and fractured sesamoid in his ankle, and a pastern bone so devastated, as an autopsy would reveal, that it looked like a building shattered by an earthquake.

All levels of the racing business—breeders, owners, trainers and, partic-ularly, veterinarians and equine scientists—are still feeling the aftershocks of Prairie Bayou's death. The fatality caused a huge public outcry, and the results of the horse's autopsy promise to put racing further on the defensive and give new leverage to those convinced that drugs are destroying the game. The little gelding's death has focused debate more than ever on the causes of racetrack breakdowns and on what, if anything, can be done to prevent them. And on how to treat them once they do occur, short of emptying the syringe into the jugular.

"It is urgent," says breeder Arthur Hancock III, who raised two Kentucky Derby winners, Gato Del Sol and Sunday Silence. "When you see Lester Piggott, one of the world's greatest jockeys, going down in the Breeders' Cup and lying there motionless, it puts the fear of God into you. We can't stand too much of that anymore. You get to the proverbial straw that broke the camel's back. No pun intended."

No one can say with precision why so many horses break down on the racetrack. The reasons advanced range from improper shoeing to undetected stress fractures, from the proverbial "bad step" to the escalating use of painkillers. And there are those who strongly suggest that horses are being inbred too closely or raised too softly. In any case there is one point on which many horsemen do agree: The American thoroughbred is not as tough and sturdy as he used to be. He's a far more fragile animal than the raw-boned beasts of yore. Consider such old-fashioned stars as the 1918 Kentucky Derby winner, Exterminator, who won 50 of 100 races; or Discovery, who won 27 of 63 and carried as much as 143 pounds; or Citation, who won 19 of 20 races in 1948, tossing in the Triple Crown along the way.

There have been modern-day exceptions, of course, including the great geldings Forego (won 34 of 57 starts) and John Henry (won 39 of 83 starts), but they were athletes rare among their pampered peers. Young horsemen like trainer Shug McGaughey (whose five stakes wins at Belmont Park on Oct. 16 represent the most notable training feat of the decade) look upon the records of past thoroughbreds with something close to awe. "I've read in books about the training schedules of horses who ran from the 1930s through the middle of the 1960s, and there is no way these horses today could take that," McGaughey says. "I mean, running them in the Derby Trial at a mile on Tuesday, blowing 'em out a mile two days later, on Thursday, and then running 'em back in the Kentucky Derby on Saturday! Those long, hard mile works they used to do, most of the horses couldn't take that today—not only physically but mentally, too. With them being more inbred, we've weakened the race, and the more fragile they're gonna be."

One of the most remarkable changes that has occurred in racing over the last 30 years, outside the advent of the use of corticosteroids, is the rise of the commercial yearling market and the breeding of horses solely for the marketplace. Back in the old days, when the Whitneys and the Guggenheims and the Vanderbilts ruled the game, they looked beyond mere pedigree in breeding horses and actively sought to produce the soundest as well as the fastest horse, mating stallions to mares with the view toward canceling out each other's physical defects. As these families' influence diminished in racing, the commercial breeders bought their mares and took to breeding them not for stoutness nor soundness but for how the mating looked on paper. Hall of Fame trainer John Nerud says that the game today is suffering the consequences of this vast myopia. "They didn't pay attention to the soundness of horses," Nerud says. "And why should they? They didn't breed to race. They bred for the sales catalog, hoping they would interest the Europeans and Arabs for a $13 million price."

On top of that, says trainer P.G. Johnson, the many horses raised for the sales ring are far softer than those raised by the breeder to race. Those who bred their horses to run would turn out their yearling herds in great fields and, from the time they were weaned until they were broken under tack, the young horses would spend months fighting and playing and bloodying each other's noses. "The horses got tough," Johnson says. "Tough and competitive. They roughhoused it. When we started to get more horses sold at yearling sales, they got softer. In April the sales breeder takes them out of the fields and separates the colts in individual pens. There's a softening that goes on. They don't want them coming into the sales ring all scratched and cut up from running loose and kicking each other. They want them to look like show horses. They want them fatter. And they just aren't as tough. We're not *breeding* a softer horse, but we're *raising* one."

And, in many cases, sending them out on the track with dangerous infirmities masked by narcotics and painkillers. "I've been on the racetrack since 1972, and I think drug abuse on the backside is more rampant than it ever was," says Ferraro, the California vet. "With the Ruffian breakdown in '75, the sympathies generated within the industry gave an immediate impetus to protecting horses from breakdowns. From 1976 through 1986 we came a long way. People were making an effort to protect horses, like building the hospitals at Santa Anita and Hollywood Park." And then the recession struck, along with the tax-law changes that removed horses from the roster of depreciable assets, and money grew as tight as the blue jeans on the backstretch. The biggest money-earner of all at the track, the noble running horse, became the asset most expendable—another piece of inventory to be turned over and over in the increasingly furious human scramble to survive.

"From 1989 to the present, it has gotten worse," says Ferraro, whose racetrack practice is now limited to surgery and treating the sick. "This isn't going to make me very popular, but racing should be held account-able for this. I had the biggest practice and the best stables. I could see what was happening and where it was going, and I said, 'I'm getting out. I've had enough.' It makes me sick. . . . There's a lot of pressure involved. The horse owner is pressing the trainer to win at any cost. The trainer's trying to do everything he can. The veterinarian's the only one who has the knowledge, and *should* have the judgment, to say, 'This is enough. Don't go any further. We're crossing the line with this animal.' He's got to have enough gumption to stand up and say, 'No!' But they don't. They're under economic pressure themselves. . . . You've got people who have one or two horses, more than they can afford, and you have owners coming up with the drugs *themselves* and saying, 'Hey, my physician told me about this. You should try this.' The problem is now, for every guy [veterinarian] that stands up and says no, there's three other guys that'll say, 'I'll do it for ya.' I feel sorry for the young vet that comes on now, because he's almost obligated to cheat if he wants to earn a living. I don't see how he can with-stand the pressure."

After 21 years of experience working the Southern California race-tracks, Ferraro sees an unmistakable link between many catastrophic break-downs and the abuse of drugs. Asked how many were related to the mask-ing of pain with drugs, legally or otherwise, Ferraro said. "More than half."

Much of the pervasive drug use at the racetrack is officially condoned. Only New York, among all the nation's racing jurisdictions, forbids the use of bute or Lasix on horses while racing. Elsewhere, these medications are so routinely administered that the official program published at many tracks is required to list which horses are running with the aid of which medication.

In this atmosphere in which sanctioned drug use has become the norm, perhaps the most abused drugs of all are the corticosteroids, which kill pain by reducing inflammation in the joints (bute, by contrast, is a *nons-*teroidal anti-inflammatory). Serial injections can seriously weaken the soft tissue in the joints of an actively campaigning horse. Ferraro estimates that close to 70% of racehorses have, at some point in their careers, been "tapped," as these steroidal injections are called on the backstretch. "Pharmacologists will tell you that corticosteroids are not damaging to the joint if they're given with rest," he says. "But when you give them with exercise, when you give them and *then* compete, they are deleterious. The other thing about cortisone is that with multiple use, its good effects tend to decrease and its bad effects tend to increase. It's the multiple injections that really nail you. It's like diminishing returns—more is not better with cortisone."

New York trainer John Veitch agrees that economic conditions have forced horsemen to rely on such painkillers to keep unsound horses competing. As the backstretch economy has deteriorated, so have horses' joints. "Corticosteroids are very prominent," says Veitch. "I'm sure they have contributed to some of the catastrophic breakdowns that we've seen. The horse is compromised."

This is particularly so, says Ferraro, among the armies of cheaper horses who make up the bulk of the racing population. "Obviously, with the horse in the upper class, trainers and vets are using it sparingly," he says. "Those horses that are running every week for a ham sandwich, a lot of them get popped every time they go." A classic abuse of the drug, Ferraro says, occurs with the trainer of a cheap claimer suffering from an inflamed tendon. The trainer wants to get rid of the horse, but knows no one will claim him if he shows up in the paddock with the telltale bulge in his lower leg. So the trainer snuggles up to the vet, asking him to inject a tad of the elixir to reduce the swelling.

"So the cortisone gets injected," says Ferraro. "The guy puts the horse in the race, some other guy claims him, and the horse pulls up at the half-mile pole with a ruptured tendon. Perfect example of what goes on. Nobody's the wiser. Too many horses are being trained by veterinarians and not by trainers."

In the search for ways to prevent catastrophic injuries, nothing has buoyed the industry's scientists more than the mammoth, open-ended research project in California that has gathered revealing data from the autopsies performed on every horse that has died at the state's five thoroughbred tracks over the last four years (nearly 900 so far). The California Necropsy Project at the University of California, Davis, has involved an unlikely amalgam of politicos, professors, veterinarians, and trainers looking for the causes of crippling injuries on the racetrack. Budgeted at

$500,000 a year, with most of the money taken out of the state's simul-
cast handle, it represents the first concerted effort to probe the breakdown phenomenon.

Dr. Sue Stover, one of the researchers, has already made several findings
involving "microfractures" in various types of bones in which it was
thought such fractures did not occur. Microfractures, too small to be
detected by the conventional X-rays that most track vets use, can lead to
unexplained soreness in an animal and to breakdowns. "These microfractures can become a large fracture," Stover says. "I call it the postage stamp
effect. Just as a stamp tears cleanly along the line of perforated holes, the
larger fracture can occur along a line of microfractures." So breakdowns,
she concluded, do not occur randomly in normal bone; they are ordinarily
and tragically caused by horses taking the inexplicable "bad step." Veterinary scientists believe they are onto something significant.

In its efforts to diagnose microfractures and abnormal bone that would
predispose a horse to a full-blown fracture, researchers at the Equine
Sports Medicine Program at Tufts School of Veterinary Medicine have
been using scintigraphy, a technique in which a horse is injected with a
radioactive isotope that isolates skeletal "hot spots"—places where injured
bone is rebuilding itself. Scintigraphy, which has been used for years in
treating humans, reveals more accurately than any other diagnostic tool
the precise location and extent of the abnormal activity. The technique
has gained such acceptance that a machine has recently been installed at
Santa Anita—the first such device ever installed at an American track—
and trainers are just beginning to bring their horses by to get their hot
spots read.

"I had a filly that was sore all over, and I had no idea what was going on,"
says trainer Richard Mandella, who has 32 horses at Santa Anita. "Scintigraphy found stress microfractures in the hind legs, and now I know what to
do to help the horse get back into training. The machine finds the needle
in the haystack."

It is in that kind of learning process that researchers like Howard See-
herman of Tufts see the best chance for heading off racetrack breakdowns.
"We must conform the training process to the healing and remodeling
processes of the bone," he says. "The industry must realize this. It is not
enough to talk about the infamous bad step."

But even if such advanced techniques succeed in warning horsemen of
impending disasters by detecting the earliest stress fractures, the racing
industry will always be faced with the unavoidable and inevitable acci-

dent—the dead-game horse who pushes too hard on the fragile envelope and falls, the horse who gets tangled in traffic while switching leads, the horse who does, in fact, take that bad step. However they go down, injuries of the kind that doomed Go For Wand—ruptured suspensory ligaments and blood vessels and a dislocated ankle—present a daunting medical problem. Horses are born with limited circulation to the lower leg, and when the few blood vessels to the area are gone, there is no delivery system for antibiotics to fight infection or for oxygen to prevent gangrene.

"Repairing is not possible when they do that much soft-tissue damage," Larry Bramlage, a noted Kentucky equine surgeon, says. "That's akin to amputation in people. Our size problems are bigger. They weigh a thousand pounds. The ability to reason with the patient is not there. A horse sleeps standing up, not lying down, and it's impossible to give the injured tissue some relief from bearing weight. The horse has to have four legs to walk on, or the opposite leg becomes overloaded and it starts to fail, bringing on laminitis. All of those things make it very difficult to save them."

But not impossible. Dr. Ric Redden, a prominent Kentucky veterinarian, has kept some horses alive for years by amputating wounded limbs and fitting them with prosthetic devices. And Bramlage is saving horses today who would have had little chance 15 years ago. He has surgically repaired a number of badly injured horses so that they are able to carry on with stud duty, including such popular stallions as Saratoga Six and Noble Dancer, using a procedure that involves fusing the bones in the horse's ankle joint. While the joint is forever fixed and immobile, it is strong enough to allow the horse to stand and bear his weight. Such surgery, he says, might have worked on the kind of injury suffered by Ruffian.

Whatever the encouraging indicators provided by medical research, those signs of progress are of minor import compared with the elephant in racing's living room, around which most everyone steps gingerly in various states of denial: drugs at the track. "I mean, get the drugs out of racing, man," says Ferraro. "The incentive now in racing is to use medication improperly. We've got to make it cost too much to cheat, make the incentive to race clean. . . . We had an excuse in the '50s and '60s and '70s because we didn't know any better about medication. But we know better now. We don't have an excuse anymore. We *know* what it does."

The incentive to diminish the incidence of breakdowns will come not only from a beleaguered industry pressured by a public increasingly disillusioned about the treatment of horses, but also from racing's other endangered species, the jockeys. On Feb. 23, 1990, in the sixth race at Tampa Bay Downs, a 27-year-old apprentice jockey named Benny Narvaez was riding a horse named That a Boy Girl on the turn for home when a mare named Dance Appeal, racing in front of him, went down with a fractured leg. Her breakdown triggered a spectacular four-horse spill in which Narvaez, a father of four who had just won his first race the day before, somersaulted over his mount's head when she tried to jump the horse sprawled in front of her. "I went over and onto my back," he recalls. "I hit hard. I knew I was hurt bad right away. I could not feel anything."

Two years later, in a court case that stunned the industry, a jury of five men and a woman awarded Narvaez $4.4 million in damages after finding that the racetrack was solely responsible for Narvaez's crippling injury—he is paralyzed from the chest down—on the grounds that the track veterinarian failed to perform an adequate exam on Dance Appeal before the race. Dance Appeal, trial testimony revealed, had a medical history involving an ankle injury that her trainer had treated with a corticosteroid a few days before the race. Sitting in his living room last week, Narvaez played a tape of the race several times over—"I have watched it maybe 500 times," he says. "There was nothing I could do"—and reflected on the perils that face his fellow riders every day.

"It is a dangerous sport, *the* most dangerous," he says. "In car racing the drivers have cages and seat belts. In football, equipment. Us, nothing. And we have to depend on the vets and the trainers and tracks to be sure we are racing on and against sound horses. We proved we are not. But, in a big way, it was too late for me. My accident could have been prevented, and so can others."

November 1993

This story caused a furor in the racing industry when it ran on the eve of the 1993 Breeders' Cup at Santa Anita, and no one took a harder hit than Dr. Greg Ferraro, who had spoken so candidly about the obvious link between catastrophic breakdowns and the abuse of drugs, particularly the corticosteroids. Shamefully ostracized by all but two of his veterinary peers, who saw him as a threat to their business, and shunned by horsemen who otherwise admired his manifest veterinary skills, Ferraro suffered damnably for a year, his business falling off to almost nothing, but he gradually brought his practice back. He ultimately got his just reward. In 1997, Ferraro was appointed director of the Center for Equine Health at the University of California at Davis, a major research facility that he described as "dedicated to relieving the ills of the horse."

DUBAI'S DREAM TEAM

*I*t was a moment that joined two worlds, one in which the very old really began to understand the very new. It was 5:40 P.M. on Saturday, May 1, 1999, ten minutes after a horse named Charismatic—yet another male-line descendant of the immortal Eclipse—had won the 125th running of the Kentucky Derby, and they were leading the chestnut colt into the winner's circle at Churchill Downs. The fourth-largest crowd in Derby history, some 150,000 strong, were on their feet in a thunderous salute, pumping fists and cheering through the vaulting grandstand tiers. And then, suddenly, down on the racetrack—among the dazed trainers and dirt-spattered jockeys, among the beaten horses and their muttering grooms—the most influential figure in the modern history of the sport, Sheik Mohammed bin Rashid al-Maktoum, materialized along the outside rail near midstretch. Sheik Mohammed, the crown prince of the oil-rich emirate of Dubai, the brains and energizing force behind the global racing empire known as Godolphin Stables, had descended from his clubhouse box to check on his horse, Worldly Manner, who had faded to seventh after menacing for the lead on the turn for home.

His Highness reportedly had paid $5 million for Worldly Manner the autumn before, with the calculated purpose of winning this Kentucky Derby, but that the colt had failed him here did not seem to pain him. Standing by that fence, his back to the stands, he watched quietly as Charismatic, his nostrils hotly flared, strode in triumph toward the blanket of red roses. No man alive has had more experience in such jubilant settings. From Ascot to Epsom in England, from Longchamp in Paris to the Curragh in Ireland, from Italy to Melbourne to Hong Kong, Sheik Mohammed has followed his horses into charmed circles everywhere. Now, in the gloaming of a late Kentucky afternoon, he seemed to have found his most passionate love anew. Only one reporter, a scribe from the Thoroughbred Times, *was there to record his thoughts as he leaned against the fence and sighed. "You can't find this anywhere except here." he said. "This is fabulous. We'll be back. Within the next four years, we will win it."*

Three years later, that moment in Louisville remained among his most vivid memories, that and the long walk down the homestretch to the barns, with fans lining the fence and yelling to him. "I remember I was walking to the stables from the racetrack," he was saying now, in the glow of the fire, "and people who did not know me were saying, 'Sheik, come back! Come back and see us again!' That gave me a great feeling. They love racing there. They like to win. In America they like the competition. They like someone to come and challenge!"

Late of a cool evening in the desert outside Dubai, some thirty kilometers east of the hard lights of the city and the Persian Gulf, a wood bonfire was blazing in a pit of sand, its sparks licking upward in gentle gusts of wind toward the breast of a cloudless sky. A crescent moon, appearing as though ordered by the sheik himself, hung in the heavens like a silver pendant on a chain of stars, and a few dunes away you could almost smell the roasting lamb and hear the music from his party, Arabian Nights, wafting through the desert air. It was two days before the running of the sport's most lucrative card—seven races worth more than $15 million in purses, crowned by the $6 million Dubai World Cup—and the sheik was holding a soiree under tents for some 2,000 revelers who sipped wine, nibbled kebabs and rode his camels. He would arrive late, as usual, with his entourage in tow.

Sheik Mohammed had spent most of the day in the desert, riding in a 130-kilometer championship endurance race in which his mount, a 7-year-old Arabian gelding named King of the Wind, so weakened in the heat that the sheik decided not to persevere with him. "He is young and got a bit tired," he said on dismounting. "He does not have the experience." Undeterred, Sheik Mohammed then mounted his Land Rover and took off in a billow of sand to chase and cheer on three of his racing sons, one of whom, 18-year-old Sheik Hamdan bin Mohammed al-Maktoum, would win the event in 5:24:57. (In Arabic names, the word *bin* means "son of"; *al-Maktoum*, in this case, means "of the family of Maktoum.") His eyes alight, a broad grin breaking the dark contours of his neatly trimmed mustache and beard, the father greeted the victorious son as though he had just won the Derby.

It was almost nine o'clock by the time Sheik Mohammed arrived at the campfire outside his desert retreat. Horses may be a passion—he was married on horseback, in front of 20,000 people, in a ceremony that cost $44 million—but they consume only a slice of his jam-packed schedule. A onetime jet-fighter pilot, he is the defense minister of the United Arab Emirates. His cell phone chimes almost constantly. A half-dozen solemn-faced Bedouin guards, sitting motionless on rugs and pillows in the bowl of light, sprang to their feet at his approach. At age 52, dressed in sandals and a simple black robe (a kandora) and wearing a black-corded headdress, he looked trim and fit.

"What you saw today is my heritage," Sheik Mohammed said. "No thoroughbred could run an endurance race with these horses. What you saw today were Arab horses."

Over the past twenty-five years, the sheik has been reclaiming his Arab history in lush places far removed from the deserts of Dubai, and that pursuit has made him the most dominating force ever involved in the thoroughbred game. Together with his two older brothers—Sheik Maktoum bin Rashid al-Maktoum, the ruler of Dubai and prime minister of the UAE, and Sheik Hamdan bin Rashid al-Maktoum, Dubai's deputy ruler and the UAE's minister of finance and industry—Sheik Mohammed has spent more than $2 billion on the sport, most of it in extraordinary raids on the world's thoroughbred gene pool. Grateful breeders in Lexington, Kentucky, refer to the three Maktoums, affectionately, as the Doobie Brothers and wait for their private 747, nicknamed the Magic Carpet, to roll to a stop on the runway at Blue Grass Airport—directly across Versailles Pike from the blue-ribbon-yearling sales at Keeneland Race Course.

No thoroughbred owner in history has come close to matching the size and scope of the Maktoums' racing empire. Between 1980 and 1993, the period of its most feverish growth, they spent $477 million on 1,000 yearlings, according to *The Blood-Horse*, the industry's leading trade publication. That does not include the money they shelled out privately for yearlings and weanlings and for stallion shares and broodmares. Nor do those numbers reflect the staggering sums they have spent on the vast tracts of farmland from Great Britain to central Kentucky, nearly 17,000 neatly manicured acres. The Maktoums have seventy-one stallions working at their various studs, most of them at Sheik Mohammed's place in England; a veritable buffalo herd of the bluest-blooded broodmares in the world, almost 1,000 strong; and around 1,200 horses in training around the globe.

Sheik Mohammed has been the inspiration behind this growth—the point man for the family, its sheiker and mover. In 1993, in a move unprecedented for the sport, he created the Godolphin Stables. Named after the Godolphin Arabian, one of the thoroughbred breed's three foundation sires, it is no less than an equine all-star team—a stable of some 250 racehorses selected each year from among the most talented in the brothers' possession.

Far more than a sporting enterprise, Godolphin is designed to advertise Dubai to the world. Faced with a diminishing supply of oil, the Maktoum family has been working for years to unleash the economy from black gold, to build on the emirate's tradition as a tax-free, duty-clean entrepôt where capital flows relatively unhassled. So far the brothers have succeeded. Last year revenues from oil contributed only 6 percent of Dubai's gross domestic product. Tourism and trade, banking and the Internet—plus alcohol and hookers, many from Russia with love—have made the bustling burg the most wide-open city in the Middle East. A Singapore in the sand, a Hong Kong without Beijing. Home to major tournaments in golf, tennis and motorboat racing. Godolphin was enlisted to spread the word.

"Godolphin is Dubai," says the sheik. "Everything is for Dubai."

And what better way to bear the emirate's message, given its culture and history, than on the back of a very fast horse?

Reclining on a rug by the fire, his elbow resting on a pillow, Sheik Mohammed began fingering his cultural pulse, feeling for his Bedouin tradition, for the lore and legend he had learned as a boy growing up in Dubai. "In Arabia the family would have a horse, a falcon and a dog," he said, "and the Arab would treat them like they were family. When they had no food, the very last food they had would be offered to the dog or the falcon or horse—before they offered food to their children. The horse was the meaning of life. They attacked on the horse. They ran away on the horse. And that is why Arabian horses were bred for thousands of years. That is why they bred the good female to the good male. The Arabs would travel a long distance with a mare to be bred to a good stallion. It was life and death for them."

From these ancient tribal roots, enriched by centuries of breeding, the swiftest of the species would emerge—an amalgam of the fine-boned Arab and the heavier English-warrior stock. "The thoroughbred is a magnificent horse," he said. "But remember: He descended from the three Arab horses—the Darley Arabian, the Godolphin Arabian, the Byerley Turk."

Of the three, the most important was the Darley Arabian, who was purchased as a 4-year-old in 1704 in the Syrian city of Aleppo by the British merchant Thomas Darley, who then shipped him home to his father, Richard. The Godolphin Arabian, foaled in 1724, also went through Syria on his way to England, where his blood mixed like an elixir with the Darley

Arabian's. Standing in Yorkshire, the Darley simply launched the most prolific of all thoroughbred sire lines, one that today accounts for 90 percent of all racehorses. In short, the Darley begat a horse named Bartlett's Childers, who begat Squirt, who in turn begat Marske. In 1763, ten years after the Godolphin Arabian died of remorse after accidentally stepping on his favorite cat, Marske consorted with a mare named Spiletta, a granddaughter of the mighty Godolphin himself. From that union, in 1764, fell a small roasted chestnut named Eclipse, so named in honor of a total eclipse of the sun that had occurred that year.

Undefeated on the courses, where he turned his races into bloodless exhibitions, Eclipse retired as a towering giant of the turf, prompting racing historian Theodore Cook to write, "He never had a whip flourished over him, or felt the rubbing of a spur, outfooting, outstriding and outlasting every horse that started against him." At the stud, Eclipse became the golden whirlwind. Virtually all the Kentucky Derby winners of the past fifty years, including the three American Triple Crown winners of the 1970s—Secretariat, Seattle Slew and Affirmed—trace in a direct and unbroken male line, through sire and grandsire and great-grandsire and beyond, to the Darley Arabian by way of Eclipse.

Sheik Mohammed understood this passing of the blood as a young man at Cambridge, where he used to attend the races at nearby Newmarket. This was during that electric era when the great Nijinsky II—the 1970 English Triple Crown winner, another tail-male descendant of the Darley Arabian—was bounding like a wild stag around the heath. "I would go to Newmarket and sometimes watch by the fence," the sheik said. "Many times I wasn't allowed to go in. My allowance was £3 a week, and I could not afford it."

Never lost upon him was the ancient tale of those three desert stallions. The sheik glanced off into the night now, the faintest smile on his face, as though the three were still out there, not far from where they'd gamboled from wadi to dune 300 years before.

"These three stallions went to England," he said quietly, "and when I went there as a student, the ordinary English people could trace the thoroughbred up to Eclipse, but beyond that they did not know where the thoroughbred came from. And they pretend to say, 'These are our horses!' In 1976 I went to the yearling sales in England for the first time and I bought three horses, and one of them was Hatta, who won the Molecomb Stakes at Goodwood. An important race! And the people said, 'Hey, where'd you come from? Who are you?' And I said to them, 'I come following my dream's blood, because all these horses running were descended from my horses.' It took some time for them to understand."

The seminal event in the emergence of modern Dubai was announced on June 6, 1966, though it attracted but mild notice. In the next day's issue of the *New York Times*, tucked in a small corner of the paper, on page 74, was a three-paragraph story that began, "The Continental Oil Company announced yesterday that a subsidiary, the Dubai Petroleum Company—also the operator for a group of companies of a concession in the Persian Gulf off the coast of Dubai—had found oil, apparently in commercial quantities. It is the first oil to be found in an area controlled by that sheikdom."

That discovery of oil off the coast of Dubai ultimately led to a rebirth of the thoroughbred sport across the Atlantic and to a period of unprecedented prosperity in the Bluegrass region of central Kentucky. As Europe had suffered through two world wars and the shambles they left behind, American breeders had hungrily imported the best of the European bloodstock. By the latter half of the twentieth century, U.S. racing was the strongest in the world, culminating in the 1970s with those three magnificent Triple Crown winners and those soaring flights of Ruffian, the fastest American filly of modern times; the unfortunate Alydar; the mighty geldings Forego and John Henry; and Kentucky Derby winners Riva Ridge, Foolish Pleasure and Spectacular Bid.

The Irish and English had arrived at the Kentucky sales in force by then—most notably in the figure of Robert Sangster, the heir to an English soccer-pools fortune—but in 1980 there followed Sheik Mohammed, his dreams newly fueled by some 350,000 barrels of oil a day.

His Highness slipped into Lexington, inauspiciously, just to scout the terrain. He stayed at a small motel in town, at one point ordering coffee for his room, only to be told, "You'll have to get your own coffee, sir." When he returned the following year, leading a retinue of attendants, he sought to rent a few hotel rooms—presumably ones with room service—and to open a line of credit at Keeneland. The requests raised eyebrows on Versailles Pike. The rooms at the Hyatt had been reserved a year in advance, and lines of credit were not handed out like parking stickers. "We did not know who they were," recalls James "Ted" Bassett III, then the president of Keeneland. "We were not familiar with the emirate. But Hyatt had just built a hotel in Dubai. And, mysteriously, things happened. I'm not aware of the machinations in the reservation department, but they got their rooms."

And very quickly, their line of credit. In fact, just before the sale at Keeneland, Sheik Mohammed had made his presence felt at the nearby Fasig-Tipton venue. He was there to inspect a yearling for his eldest brother, Sheik Maktoum, when another swam into his field of vision. "Suddenly, I saw this filly coming toward the ring," he recalled. "And I said, 'Look at her!' She was so beautiful. I said, 'That's an Arab!' The way she looks. The way she moves. So they led her to the ring, and I went back by myself to bid for her. No vet had looked at her for me. I had not inspected her. I just saw her! And I got her!"

He bought her that day for $325,000, his first yearling purchase in Kentucky, and it turned out to be among the most important of his life. He called her Awaasif, which means "tempest" in Arabic, and two years later, after winning the Yorkshire Oaks in England, a major stake, she was named that country's champion 3-year-old filly. Sheik Mohammed would spend $2.4 million at Keeneland that July, but none of his eight yearlings would match what Awaasif did for him on the track—and as a grandam in retirement.

Sheik Mohammed showed up at Keeneland again, in 1981, when Sangster and the Greek shipping tycoon Stavros Niarchos were keen to buy an attractive son of Northern Dancer, the 1964 Kentucky Derby and Preakness winner who had become the most prepotent sire of grass horses in the world. The sheik left Niarchos behind at $3 million and forced Sangster to bid $3.5 million before he let go of his neck. The sheik then went to $3.3 million for another son of Northern Dancer, out of Sweet Alliance. Alas, he got the best of it that day. The Sweet Alliance colt, named Shareef Dancer, ended up winning the Irish Sweeps Derby on the way to being syndicated as a stallion for $40 million.

In the years to come, no one dominated the sales like the Maktoums. Rich as Sangster and Niarchos were, they were no match for a family whose income now approached $10 million a day. And never was this clearer than on the night of July 19, 1983, when the sheik and the Brits, again led by Sangster, came to Keeneland intent on buying another strapping son of Northern Dancer. At the time, the world-record price for a yearling was $4.25 million, and as the bidding rose in the night like a boardwalk balloon, all eyes in the pavilion stared in wonder at the seven-digit electronic board above the sales ring. When it flashed $4.5 million, breaking the record, the crowd erupted in cheers.

And it wasn't over yet. The bidding climbed, the two groups leapfrogging each other, to $5 million, to $5.5 . . . $5.6 . . . $5.7 . . . $5.9 . . . $6 million! It continued rising. Sangster bid $6.9 million, reported the *Lexington Herald-Leader*, and then Sheik Mohammed's special adviser, Colonel

Dick Warden, looked over to John Leat, the sheik's personal assistant, for a sign of what to do. His Highness continued staring impassively ahead, his eyes never leaving the sales ring. Leat nodded. Warden bid $7 million. The crowd cheered again.

The war went on. The bidding climbed to $8 million, to $8.6. . . $8.9. . . $9 million. The Sangster group went to $9.5 million. Here Warden, bidding $9.6, looked up and mouthed, "Jesus Christ." The board would soon run out of digits. Bassett sat stunned. "We all held our breath," he says. "Who would have thought, in our wildest dreams, that we would ever sell a horse for $10 million?"

Then Sangster took it there. Briefly, the board flashed seven zeros, starting all over again, as auctioneer Scott Caldwell announced the bid. And then Warden nodded again and the board lit up: $200,000. The Brits at last said no. The sheik swept from the room to wild applause. The colt, named Snaafi Dancer, turned out to be a bust; he developed a lung infection early and never raced. At stud he proved virtually impotent, siring only one foal, but that hardly mattered.

What did matter, in the end, was the nature of the Maktoums' commitment. With money of no concern, the brothers kept buying, pouring all those millions into their racing and breeding operations, and they saved the sport in Britain even as they rose to rule it. Once the influx of cash and racing stock had reinvigorated the game, though, their success at the track set the horsemen to grumbling. Even the late Queen Mother was said to have muttered about "all that Arab gold."

And yet, Sheik Mohammed, the man at the center of this whirl, barely flinched. Much like his father—Sheik Rashid bin Said al-Maktoum, who first led Dubai away from a dependence on oil—he makes decisions quickly and has a restless energy in carrying them out. Also like his father, who died in 1990, he likes to rule and is far more amiable and outgoing than either of his elder brothers. Those who know him, who have spent time around him, speak of the man in tones of reverence, even awe. "He's got an aura around him, a light, a presence," says jockey Frankie Dettori. "And he has the stamina of King Kong. He doesn't sleep. He rides 120 kilometers on a horse. He's opening this and doing that. He's out looking at his racehorses. He's flying here and there, talking on his cell phones. He's got six. I don't know how he does it."

The sheik has embraced falconry and the racing and breeding of camels. He is also a poet, who pens his verse in Arabic (his friends refer to him as Sheikspeare), which is all one journalist needed to know to win an audience with him. Carol Flake was in Dubai to do a magazine story on camel racing in the Middle East. In time Sheik Mohammed came to know who she was—he would wave to her from afar as she mixed among the Bedouins—but despite her oft-repeated pleas to one of his closest aides, he put off granting her an interview. Flake had learned that the sheik's favorite racing camel was a female named Mahna—a Ruffian in his herd of drome-daries—and the night before Mahna was to race, she composed a poem to her, writing it in the Arabic form known as the kaseeda, a kind of ode. (A published poet herself, Flake had written her doctoral thesis in English on the poet Wallace Stevens.)

Fortunately for the journalist, Mahna ran brilliantly and won. Immediately afterward Flake approached one of the sheik's guards and told him she had written a poem about Mahna and wanted to show it to the sheik. Looking incredulous, the guard duly relayed the message. His Highness, who was out in his Land Rover watching the races, responded by asking her to read it on national television. And so she read her ode, "For Mahna":

A ship that rides the wind-driven waves,
The camel, the dhow of the desert,
Rocks up and down the dunes,
Lending life and form to shifting sands.

Out of the desert she sails,
Rhythmic as a lullaby,
Fast as a falcon,
Enduring as stone.

In her stride are eons of journeys,
From oasis to wadi, camp to camp.
Where her forerunners roamed without roads,
She must race to prove her worth anew.

In this, she shares with her master
Not just the way to survive but the will to win.

Two days later, Flake was summoned to an audience with Sheik Mohammed. "I have observed how you have related to the Bedouins, my people," he told her. "I appreciate that." He also thanked her for the poem, reciting for her the last two lines. "Yes, that is the way of the camel," he told her. The audience lasted two hours, and she came away from it with the powerful sense that his love for animals expressed a deeply felt wish, even a need, to stay in touch with his people and their shared roots—indeed, to keep the Bedouins themselves connected to their vanishing past. "He told me, 'It is a way of being able to relate to my people. It is something we will always have in common,'" she says.

And then, with a wave of his hand, the sheik summoned an attendant, who appeared as if from nowhere, bearing a gift the sheik had clearly ordered for the occasion—a one-inch medallion cut from mother-of-pearl with a gold figure of a camel embossed on the front. The words for mahna were inscribed on the back. "It is still the most beautiful thing I own," Flake says.

The Sheik's equine all-star team grew not from a noble wish to save his heritage but, rather, from a desperate need to preserve his sanity. By the early 1990s, the man had so many thoroughbreds in Great Britain and France that he was employing thirty-six trainers. Unlike most owners, he was an accomplished horseman, and he often found himself at loggerheads with conditioners who did what they wanted, arguing with him over decisions or ignoring his wishes to point for a certain race. According to an old saw, it is common for trainers to treat owners like mushrooms: keep them in the dark and cover them with manure. Sheik Mohammed bristled at that notion. He had no interest in simply writing the checks and posing for pictures in the winner's circle.

"I am a difficult owner because I want to be hands-on," he said. "I want to be there. I want to see what is happening. I want to know what's going on."

American jockey Steve Cauthen, who began riding in Britain not long after he won the Triple Crown on Affirmed, ended up as the sheik's main rider in the early '90s, and he could understand the man's displeasure. "It was frustration over not feeling as involved as he wanted to be," says Cauthen. "The fact was, he got too big too quickly and had too many trainers. As a jockey, you didn't know which horse was best, because all his trainers were sneaking around trying to beat one another. It was hard for Sheik Mohammed. It got out of control."

From this chaos, Godolphin was born, what the *Sunday Times of London* would call Dubai's "miracle in the desert." As conceived, it gave Sheik Mohammed control over the family's finest horses and a state-of-the-art training base in Dubai to which this crème de la crème could be brought every winter to prepare in the sun for the next year's campaign. When the sheik revealed his plan in Britain, most trainers resisted it, scoffing at the very idea. In fact, he brought four of his English trainers to Dubai and took them straight to his training facility, with its new dirt surface.

"We were standing against the fence," recalls the sheik, "and I said, 'Gentlemen, would this racetrack produce me a classic winner?' Now, they are top trainers, and they looked at the track and they looked at me, and one of them said, 'What are you going to feed them, sand?' I made a hard decision, but that is how Godolphin was formed. You can't just sit back. You have to have an aim. You have to lead!"

In one stroke, the sheik had created his own racing ship. His fingerprints were everywhere, on everything. Godolphin has always had a trainer of record—Saeed bin Suroor, a former Dubai policeman, has held the job since 1995—but it's the sheik who does the navigating. In the first year, 1994, he sent the filly Balanchine off from the Dubai desert and witnessed his own vindication. After winning the Epsom Oaks, one of England's five classic races, she pulverized the colts in the Irish Derby. The next year, in a training feat that stunned the racing establishment, the sheik sent Lammtarra from Dubai and, in only the second start of the colt's career and without the benefit of a single prep race, he won England's most important race, the Epsom Derby; what made the victory sweeter still was that Lammtarra's maternal grandam was old Awaasif.

The Dubai operation was perceived from the start as a global gateway for Godolphin, a springboard from which the stable could bound in all directions, and that year it served as precisely that. Godolphin scored significant victories, from Japan and Hong Kong in the East to France, Britain and the United States in the West. For all the stable's success, though, what is missing today is that one triumph Sheik Mohammed has sought more passionately than any other, the one he began coveting that afternoon in 1999, when he leaned on the rail at Churchill Downs and saw the magic of the crowds. With a win in America's most famous horse race, he could at least take hold of the exposure he so dearly desires. Three years ago, at Keeneland, the sheik approached trainer Bob Baffert, who had won the Derby in 1997 with Silver Charm and in 1998 with Real Quiet. The sheik explained to Baffert his strategy for winning the Derby. He told him about Godolphin's winter workouts in Dubai. "Am I doing it the right way?" he asked.

"No," Baffert said bluntly. "The horses need to run in America."

In 2000 the sheik began fielding a division of well-bred Godolphin 2-year-olds in California. He hired a notable Baffert assistant, Eoin (pronounced owen) Harty, to get them accustomed to racing here in America.

The best colt Harty has trained so far, Street Cry, missed the 2001 Derby with an injury, but he exploded as a 4-year-old. To date he has won the Dubai World Cup and the Stephen Foster Handicap at Churchill Downs, both in smashing style, and he is an early favorite to win the Breeders' Cup Classic at Arlington Park and the Eclipse Award as America's Horse of the Year. There's no telling what kind of talent Harty will find among the fifty hotbloods he now has in training.

Godolphin may be O for 4 in the Derby, not even close to winning with any of its starters, but Sheik Mohammed has been spending large sums of money at the sales—more than $40 million in three years at the Keeneland summer venue alone—much of it aimed at buying pedigrees more suited to running on the dirt. Designer genes aside, the question is whether the sheik's approach to training them is prudent: The Kentucky Derby is the hardest race to win in America, if not the world, and shipping horses to Dubai and back only makes the challenge that much harder. Lammtarra's victory in the Epsom Derby, off no prep races, was possible only because the Epsom is a twelve-furlong turf race in which the pace is usually soft through the early stages. Trainers say it does not require the rigorous conditioning of the Kentucky Derby—a ten-furlong cavalry charge on the dirt in which the horses often fly full bore from the outset and for which they are routinely toughened through a series of rough-and-tumble prep races. Epsom is Leisure World compared to Churchill Downs.

Until this year, one of Sheik Mohammed's unspoken goals was to be the first Arab to win the roses. To that end, he shelled out $2.3 million for a yearling son of Pulpit at the Keeneland sale in September 2000. He names his most promising horses after the emirate, and he called this colt Essence of Dubai. The horse won the United Emirates Derby last March, and many immediately saw him as a contender in Kentucky. Alas, in one of the diabolical vagaries of this game, a Saudi Arabian prince named Ahmed bin Salman—a joke-swapping, party-going media baron out of Riyadh—paid $990,000 for a colt named War Emblem a mere three weeks before the Churchill classic. Bob Baffert saddled him, Victor Espinoza rode him, but the colt did all the work. Sailing on his own to the lead, unpressured, he turned for home and repulsed all challengers through the stretch, bounding off to win the Kentucky Derby by four lengths. War Emblem had raced four times prior to that, twice tiring in stakes races in New Orleans before finally coming to hand, and those preps on the dirt had clearly left him lean and wired. Essence of Dubai, who had run two prep races in the emirate, was never in the hunt and finished ninth, beaten by thirteen lengths.

The Arabs are hotly competitive with one another, and the prince, who would die of a heart attack eleven weeks later, could not resist sticking it to his Bedouin cousins in Dubai. "I am the first Arab to win it," he gloated to the press.

Just thirty days earlier, while perched beneath the desert stars, Sheik Mohammed had waved off all suggestion that he needed to prep his horses in America. "Everyone is entitled to their own opinion," he said. "Maybe they are right. Maybe I am right. But if I am sure about something, I don't stop because someone else is doubting me."

Bolting straight up on his rug, he denounced the very thought that he might need to hire a proven Derby trainer like Baffert, spelling out his response with two letters: "N-O. No! Then Bob wins the Derby, not me! If I win the Derby, I don't want somebody else getting credit. What would I achieve in that? Many people wanted me to hire Bob Baffert. He is a very good trainer. If he wins it, then everybody says Bob Baffert won it. Not the Dubai team—the team that lived in the desert during the winter."

The Godolphin team could win it from Dubai, to be sure, but they may need another Secretariat or Seattle Slew to pull it off. And yet somehow it seemed perfectly fitting that after rising to leave, Sheik Mohammed should draw the evening to a close with a parable about two animals. "When the gazelle wakes up in Africa," he said, "he must make sure he outruns the fastest lion, or he will be killed. When the lion wakes up in Africa, he must make sure he outruns the slowest gazelle, or he will starve. I don't care if you are a lion or a gazelle. When you wake up, you better start running!"

Was there a lesson hidden in the fire? Ah, but of course—might just one of his Kentucky Derby horses be as tough and battle hardened as that lion? As lean and fit as that gazelle?

October 2002

PART 2

BOXING

THE ROCK

Former heavyweight champion Rocky Marciano
was a tough-fisted brawler in the ring and a
tightfisted mystery out of it

"I DON'T KNOW WHAT I'M DOING HERE. I CAN'T SING.
AND I CAN'T DANCE. BUT JUST TO BE SOCIABLE,
I'LL FIGHT THE BEST MAN IN THE HOUSE."

—*Rocky Marciano, addressing patrons of*
The Rifle, a London pub, circa 1967

She sensed what had happened the instant that she heard her mother scream. Sat frozen for a moment in her bedroom at the top of the stairs. Knew for sure what she had lost out there, someplace in the Midwest, out there among the cornfields in the dark.

Mary Anne was only 16 then, but old enough to know the chances that her father had been taking, day after day, as he crisscrossed America in all those storm-whipped, wind-sheared private planes, often holding in his ample lap a grocery bag filled with $100 bills, as much as $40,000 a bag, looking like some pug-nosed desperado who had just knocked over a savings and loan. By then, by that late evening of Aug. 31, 1969, Rocky Marciano was just a few hours shy of his 46th birthday; it had been 13 years and four months since the April day in 1956 when he had finally risen from the crouch and retired, at 49–0, as the only undefeated heavyweight champion in history. He had moved through those years as he had once moved in the ring, in a relentless, unremitting pursuit of what he desired—

money and women, celebrity and respect, all that he ever wanted as the poor son of a shoe-factory worker growing up in Brockton, Massachusetts, during the Depression.

By that August night Marciano had become his own savings and loan, rich beyond his most extravagant boyhood dreams, a kind of wandering minstrel of money, in fact, dispensing cash loans with the careless facility of song. Indeed, he had accumulated vast stores of cash since he had quit the ring, mostly through personal appearances, and by 1969 he had at least $750,000 in loans on the street, not including the $100,000-plus he had lent to a loan shark linked to the Cleveland mob whose business he was helping to finance. He had even more money squirreled away in assorted hiding places—stuffed in pipes, in safe deposit boxes, in curtain rods, in all his favorite places—from Cuba to Florida to upstate New York to Alaska. He never paid for anything if he could help it; he could, for example, beat the telephone company by using slugs or a tripping wire to get his money back from coin-operated phones. Even if he had a round-trip commercial airline ticket, usually part of the deal when an appearance called him out of town, he would try to scrounge a freebie lift to his destination, often by calling on a network of private pilots who were willing, for the pleasure of his company, to bear him where he wanted to go. Back home in Fort Lauderdale, of course, he would hustle off to the airport to exchange the ticket for cash.

Mary Anne knew well the perilous edge on which he lived. In 1965, on a trip from Los Angeles to Honolulu, Rocky had hitched a ride on a cargo plane and loaded Mary Anne and a friend of hers in the hold in back. "They put little jump seats in for my friend and me, and my father and his friend were sitting on the top of the luggage," Mary Anne recalls. "A window blew in and we went into a nosedive and a red light came on and I thought, I'm 12 and I'm going to die. My father kept saying, 'Don't worry. You're gonna be O.K.'" He had escaped serious injury in a light-plane accident a year or two earlier, and for a long time his family and his friends had been importuning him to fly on commercial jets. "You are trying to save money in the wrong places," one of his closest friends and fellow skirt chasers, couch designer Bernie Castro, used to scold him. "You are risking everything. . . ."

On Sunday, Aug. 31, Marciano was in Chicago with one of his oldest pals, Dominic Santarelli, and handling the logistics of his life as recklessly as ever. His wife, Barbara, had turned 40 on Aug. 30, two days before Rocky's 46th, and he had promised her that he would be home to celebrate their birthdays on the day that fell in between, Aug. 31, a family tradition.

In fact, that afternoon, in the Marcianos' oceanfront home in Fort Lauderdale, the gifts had all been wrapped and the guests had already arrived. The sweetest gift of all was waiting there unwrapped. Unbeknownst to his father, the Marcianos' 17-month-old adopted son, Rocco Kevin, had learned how to walk while his father was gone, and Barbara had arranged a welcoming scenario that had the toddler carrying Rocky's presents to him when he walked in the door.

"We were all waiting with the birthday cake," recalls one of the friends, June Benson. "Then Rocky called from Chicago. He said, 'I'm gonna make an appearance in Des Moines, and then I'll fly right back. Hold everything.'"

That was the last his family ever heard from him. Frankie Farrell, the nephew of Marciano's pal, Chicago mobster Frankie (One Ear) Fratto, was opening an insurance brokerage in Des Moines, and he had convinced Marciano to fly there with him from Chicago to make an appearance. Farrell had hired Glenn Belz, who had not been cleared to fly by instruments and had logged only 35 hours of flying at night, to pilot the single-engine Cessna 172 from Midway Airport to Des Moines. They took off at 6 P.M., despite warnings of a storm front billowing in front of them, and three hours later had made it as far as Newton, Iowa, when their plane was seen flying barely 100 feet off the ground, into a roiling bank of clouds. Reappearing once, it rose and disappeared again. In his laudable 1977 study, *Rocky Marciano: Biography of a First Son,* author Everett M. Skehan wrote: "The plane crashed into a lone oak tree in the middle of a cornfield. It was totally demolished by the impact, which killed all three passengers. A wing was sheared off and landed 15 feet from the tree; the battered hull skidded on and came to rest in a drainage ditch 236 feet away. Rocky's shattered body was found braced firmly in the seat of the wrecked Cessna. . . . Belz and Farrell had been thrown clear. . . ."

It was late evening in Fort Lauderdale when the doorbell rang on North Atlantic Boulevard. Mary Anne heard her mother answer the door. She bolted to the staircase after she heard the scream. Jack Sherlock, the Fort Lauderdale police chief and an old friend of the family, was standing just inside the door. "Are you sure it's him? Are you sure it's not Rocky *Graziano?*" Barbara was saying, referring to the former middleweight champion of the world with whom her husband was often confused. "It can't be. Are you sure?"

Mary Anne started down the stairs. "Is my dad dead?" she asked.

"I'm sorry," Sherlock said.

Rocco Francis Marchegiano would have turned 70 years old on Sept. 1, and by the time he died, almost a quarter of a century ago, the life he had created for himself outside the ring was quite as large and unlikely as the figure he had once cut inside it. Of course, Lord only knows what he might be doing today had he somehow survived his endless peregrinations; how many sacks of cash he might have wadded up and squireled away in his far-flung caches; how big his lending business might have become; or how long he could have avoided arousing the serious curiosity of IRS agents, not only over his out-of-pocket lending business, for which he kept no books or paperwork, but also over his travels around the banquet circuit, where he insisted on payment in cash only. It was a strange, fantastic world he had built for himself, one shaped in considerable part by the obsessive, relentless quest for $100 bills, for cash to feed his lending business, for cash to buy his way into multitudes of deals, for cash to toss onto Pasqualena Marchegiano's dining room table.

"He'd come home sometimes with two bags of money, and he'd give his mother one," Marciano's longtime accountant and traveling companion, Frank Saccone, recalls. "Five or six thousand dollars in each bag. His mother would count it, all over the table." She would then stack it neatly in piles.

"What do you want me to do with it, Rocky?"

"Keep it, Ma, for spending money."

His idiosyncrasies were often so irrational as to drive Saccone to teary despair. One evening in the mid–1960s, Saccone recalls, Marciano had just delivered a speech at a large function in Montreal, when one of the organizers approached him and Saccone in the lobby of the hotel where they were staying. Thanking Marciano profusely, he handed him an envelope containing a check for $5,000. The Rock shook his head. "Can you cash the check for me?" he asked.

That would not be possible; the banks were closed. "I'll guarantee it," the man said.

"That's not it," Rocky said. "I don't take checks. I'd rather have the cash."

It was an awkward moment. "Look," Rocky said, "do you have $2,500 in cash? I'll take that. You keep the check."

Saccone took Rocky aside. "Why don't you let *me* take the check, and *I'll* cash it," Saccone said. "Then I'll give you the cash."

Rocky insisted. "I want the cash, right now!"

"But, Rocky, you're throwing $2,500 away!" said Saccone. "I know these people. I know this check is good. It's a cashier's check. *It is cash in the form of a check.* Try to imagine that."

There was no trying. "These are my deals," Rocky said. "If I want cash, it's my business. Don't interfere."

Marciano turned to the organizer. "Can you get me $2,500 in an hour?" he asked. An hour later the man was back with the money, as bemused as Saccone at Marciano's thinking. "Is this really what you want?" Saccone asked.

"That's great," said Rocky, happily handing the organizer the check.

Saccone traveled the world with Marciano, on hundreds of trips, and he never knew the man to want it any other way. "He had this crazy, crazy need for cash," Saccone says. "He loved the sight of cash. A check was just a little piece of paper. I remember times he'd get a check and lose it. He'd put it somewhere and forget about it. He'd reach in his pocket and pull out checks that were all tattered. I've seen him give away checks for $50,000, $100,000. I'm talking big money. He didn't even associate that with money. To him a check was just a piece of paper. But if he had $40,000 in $10 bills, there was no way he'd give any of that away. He *believed* in green stuff."

There was always plenty of it flowing his way and far more abundantly in the days after his retirement than during his years in the ring. Marciano was an enormously popular champion, and more than his complexion lay at the source of the appeal. The archetypal working-class stiff from blue-collar Brockton, he brought to the lights a boxing style edited down to its barest essentials, an unearthly power of will and tolerance for punishment, particularly around the chin; and he had what columnist Red Smith called "a right hand that registered nine on the Richter scale," and a left hook that trembled the upright like an aftershock. Stir into this mix an incomparable appetite for work, a quality of meekness and humility that was often affecting—after knocking out his boyhood idol, Joe Louis, in the eighth round of their 1951 fight in New York, Marciano wept openly in Louis's locker room—and that crooked smile on a darkly handsome mug, and what you had was the ideal composite for the central character in a cartoonlike Hollywood movie.

None of this was even remotely foreseeable in the beginning, back in the days he spent at the James Edgar Playground, in the rough-and-tumble Irish-Italian streets of central Brockton, where he dreamed of escaping the want of his childhood by making it as a catcher in the big leagues. Slow afoot, without a major league catcher's arm, he worked hours on his short, powerful stroke. "There were 40 or 50 of us shagging balls for Rocky," says Nicky Sylvester, a boyhood friend and later the court jester in his entourage. "He wouldn't give anyone else a chance. Two hours of hitting!" Marciano used to run lunch down to his father, Pierino, a laster at a nearby shoe factory, and the sight of his father standing at his machine, his undershirt drenched, both legs and arms moving at once, a dozen tacks held in his lips, spoke to him of a life he did not want to lead. "I'll *never* work in a shoe factory," he told his family, according to his brother Sonny. "I have to find a way out."

Climbing out of Brockton and leaving the dread privations of his boyhood behind was the theme with variations that ruled him the rest of his life. "He was deathly afraid of being broke," says former world featherweight champion Willie Pep, one of Marciano's best friends. "He used to say to me, 'I'll never be broke again.' He was a tough guy with a buck, Rocky. He was afraid."

Marciano was drafted in 1943 and began boxing in the Army, chiefly as a way to avoid KP and other schlock details. He devoted all his considerable energies to it only after his discharge from the service, in 1946, and an abortive tryout with a Chicago Cub farm team in North Carolina in the spring of 1947. By then, fighting under an assumed name, Rocky Mack, to protect his amateur status, he had knocked out one Lee Epperson in the third round of a bout in Holyoke, Massachusetts, and earned $35. He fought as an amateur the rest of that year and into the next, and at 5' 10" and less than 190 pounds, with only a 68-inch reach, shorter than that of any other heavyweight champion who ever lived, he appeared on his way to Palookaville. One afternoon in '48, Goody Petronelli, who would one day train Marvin Hagler to the world middleweight championship, was leaving the gym on Center Street in Brockton when he ran into Marciano. Goody had seen him in the amateurs and was surprised when Marciano told him that he was turning pro.

"I never thought he'd make it," Petronelli says. "He was too old, almost 25. He was too short, he was too light. He had no reach. Rough and tough, but no finesse."

But he had that hammer, that Cro-Magnon chin and that fearless, unbridled instinct for the attack. He turned pro on July 12, 1948, when he scored a first-round knockout over Harry Bilazarian in Providence, and then fought 10 more times before Christmas, all the matches ending in knockouts, seven in the first round. Brockton is only 25 miles from Providence, where he fought 15 of his first 17 fights, and a Brockton cheering section soon began showing up to witness the mayhem. Recalls Sylvester: "When Rocky had a guy in trouble in Providence, all the Italians from Brockton would stand up and yell, 'Timmmmmmberrr!'"

They were shows bereft of art. Trainer Lou Duva, who would take Evander Holyfield to the heavyweight title some 40 years later, recalls driving with Vic Marsillo, the manager of Sugar Ray Robinson, to see an early Marciano brawl in New England. The word *footwork* does not make it in describing what Duva saw that night. "Rocky kept falling down," he recalls. "He kept missing and going through the ropes. I said to Vic, 'He's as strong as a bull.' Vic said, 'Are you kidding? He can't fight at all.' It was Charley Goldman who straightened him out."

Charley trained fighters for Al Weill, the New York manager and promoter, and that fall he had Marciano and his Brockton trainer, Allie Colombo, begin working with him in Manhattan. Goldman was the training guru for a young Angelo Dundee, later the trainer of Muhammad Ali and Ray Leonard, and Goldman seemed apologetic about how the young man looked. Says Dundee, "So Charley told me, 'Ange, I gotta guy who's short, stoop-shouldered, balding, got two left feet and, God, how he can punch!' I remember going on the subway to the CYO gym, and in walks Rocky with a pair of coveralls and a little canvas bag." Goldman knew that Marciano had trained hours as a baseball catcher, and he taught him to swarm and slide and throw from a crouch, rising as though he were pegging to second base.

"Charley taught the technique that if you're tall, you stand taller," Dundee recalls. "If you are shorter, you make yourself smaller. Charley let him bend his knees completely to a deep knee squat. He was able to punch from that position, come straight up from the bag and hit a heck of a shot. . . . It was just *bang-bang-bang-bang-BANG* and get him outta there. And he was the best-conditioned athlete out there."

No one understood his limitations better than Marciano himself, and his whole monkish existence in the gym and on the road was geared to making up for them, to developing what gifts he had. He thought nothing of walking the 75 blocks from his room to the gym to train. A health buff long before it became the fashion, he ate veggies, sipped only an occasional glass of Lancer's rosé, always with dinner, and carried a jar of honey in his pocket to sweeten his coffee. He chewed but never swallowed his steak, and left the ruminated chaws in a bowl next to his plate. And Marciano may be the only fighter in history who exercised his eyeballs, obtaining for this purpose a pendulum that he rigged above his bed. Lying flat on his back, with his head still, he would follow the pendulum back and forth with his eyes—convinced, of course, that stronger eyeballs did a better fighter make. More than once he sparred 250 rounds for a single fight, 100 rounds more than normal, and there was never anything in his ring work to suggest a hesitation waltz.

Marciano never met an opponent, particularly among the 43 he knocked out, who did not leave the ring with a fairly intimate knowledge of that fact. Even long after Goldman had straightened out his feet and taught him how to slip a punch and make a weapon of his left, there was a merry unpredictability about what would happen next when Marciano was in the ring. He threw punches from every conceivable point on the compass, and the legal ones landed everywhere from the navel to the top of the head. Some even found the chin.

But it was in the fights in which Marciano was in trouble, behind in points or cut and bleeding, that he created the persona he would carry with him all the way to that fatal field in Newton. And his signature moment in the ring, the instant when the myth was born, came at the single most dramatic turning point of his life. It was the night of Sept. 23, 1952, in Philadelphia, in the 13th round of his 15-round title fight against the world heavyweight champion, Jersey Joe Walcott, and the time was growing short for an increasingly desperate Marciano. A beautiful boxer, clever and resourceful, Walcott had built up an easy lead in points, and all he had to do was keep Marciano away. Marciano had chased but not quite found, had thrown but not quite landed, had struck but not quite hard enough. By the 13th round he knew there was only one way to win it. He waded in yet again. And then, as Walcott feinted back toward the ropes, Marciano suddenly stepped in and threw a short, overhand right that struck Walcott on the jaw with such force that it distorted his face, dropped him to one knee and left him slumped forward, kneeling unconscious, with his left arm slung through the ropes.

So Marciano's long journey out of Brockton was finally over, and the belief in his indomitability became a kind of article of shared faith among his ardent followers. Marciano defended his title only six times in the $3^1/2$ years that he held it, but he did nothing to discourage the belief that he was invincible and much to embellish it. In fact, in his second fight against Ezzard Charles, in New York, on Sept. 17, 1954, he once again turned imminent defeat into sudden, stunning triumph. Like one of those Benihana chefs butterflying a jumbo shrimp, Charles hit Marciano with a blow in the sixth round that split his left nostril down the middle; blood spurted everywhere. At the end of the round no amount of work could stanch the bleeding. Marciano's corner was in a panic. The ring doctor let it go through the seventh, with Marciano bleeding heavily, but by the eighth round the corner sensed that time was short. They were all screaming at the champion to press the attack. Marciano fought with a fury. A right hand floored Charles. Glassy-eyed, he climbed back slowly to his feet. Marciano rushed back at him, landing thumping lefts and rights, until Charles at last fell for the count.

No matter what happened, in the end the Rock would find a way.

When Marciano retired on that April day in 1956, seven months after knocking out Archie Moore in nine, he had not only fulfilled his father's most oft-expressed wishes—"Don't do anything to disgrace the family name. Don't do anything I'll be ashamed of"—but he had also brought honor to it beyond the old man's unlikeliest hope. More than undefeated, he left the ring utterly untainted, and this despite one underworld figure's efforts to coax him to hit the water in his May 16, 1955, defense against Don Cockell, an Englishman, in San Francisco. One of Marciano's closest California friends, Ed Napoli, recalls the day he sat with Marciano in a hotel room in that state and listened as a gangster made him an offer to throw the fight. Cockell was a long shot, at 10–1, and Marciano could always win back the title in a rematch.

"Rocky, you can be set the rest of your life if you throw this fight," the mobster told him.

At which point Marciano got angry, Napoli says, and ordered the mobster out. "You disgust me," the fighter told him. "I'm ashamed that you're Italian. Get outta here and don't come back." The fight ended in the ninth round with Cockell, out on his feet, sagging in the arms of referee Frankie Brown.

As celebrated and mythic a folk hero as he became to the workaday Italian-American across the land, Marciano found himself to be an even larger, more respected figure among members of the underworld, a life-sized icon whose company and favor were sought by hoodlums wherever he went. Over the years, with all the running around he did, Marciano kissed the cheeks of many of the major crime-family bosses—Raymond Patriarca, Carlo Gambino, Frank Costello and Vito Genovese, who when he was dying put out the word that he wanted Marciano to visit him in prison. Rocky paid the call. "Rocky went to Leavenworth to show Genovese films of his fights," says Richie Paterniti, one of Marciano's best friends during the last 12 years of his life. "Wherever we went there were mob guys. They loved him because he represented what mob guys really want to be, the toughest guy in the world, right? A macho guy. They all had respect for him. They all wanted to be with him. They kissed his ass. Every mob guy. He was an Italian, and he beat up every guy he faced. He exuded power, an air of authority. That's why they wanted to bask in his sunshine."

They could not indulge him enough. They bought him dinner and gave him money and set him up with their tailors. When Saccone first went to New York with Marciano, he found himself among all these shiny suits. "We'd go to these elaborate restaurants and sit with 15, 20 underworld characters, but I didn't know it," he says. "I was a naive accountant from Brockton. I thought they were just friends of Rocky's and they liked him. Rocky finally told me who they were. They couldn't do enough for him. They'd say to him, 'I got a beautiful tailor. Let me take you down there and get you some suits.' They'd buy him six suits, three dozen shirts. He loved it and *they* loved it."

In spite of the casual social contact he had with hoodlums, he feared the violence and notoriety of the underworld, and he made it a point not to get involved in their businesses. "Let's keep our distance," Marciano used to tell Paterniti. In fact, according to an underworld source, one of the most feared hoodlums in the history of organized crime, Felix (Milwaukee Phil) Alderisio, saw Marciano not only as a venerated Italian-American folk hero whose reputation had to be protected, but also as a kind of naive, innocent bumpkin from Brockton who had to be watched, lest he stumble blindly into trouble. "He was an Italian champ, and they wanted him to be clean," the source said. "All the boys. That came out of Chicago. Milwaukee Phil said, 'Keep him clean. Don't get him dirty. Protect him at all costs. He's a goofball; he doesn't know what he's doing.' Chicago had an umbrella over him."

The only time Marciano ever faced serious trouble with the law was after he began quietly investing vast sums of cash, $100,000 at a crack, in the loan-sharking business of Pete DiGravio, with whom he often stayed in Cleveland. "If you've got some cash and want to make some money on it," DiGravio told Rocky, "I've got the outlet. Guaranteed. No bad debts in my place." The Rock was in. Marciano never felt that he was involved in anything illegal, says Saccone, and justified his investments on the grounds that he was merely lending to the shark and not involved in the dirty end of the business, on the street itself.

Of course, there was never anything in writing, since the Rock did not believe in paper. "All unsecured loans," says Saccone. "Never secured. Never-never. No piece of paper. No note. Nothing signed. All in his head. I can recall him saying to me, 'Jeez, I know I loaned somebody $5,000 in New York, and I can't remember who it was. But I'll remember it.' He never did. It was gone. Rocky was a very articulate, intelligent man, but when it came to business, he was so, so stupid."

This nearly got him into trouble in Cleveland when the Internal Revenue Service started looking into DiGravio's affairs. When the IRS asked him where he had obtained some large sums of money, DiGravio told investigators, "Rocky Marciano loaned it to me." And when they asked to see the contracts, DiGravio told them, "We don't have contracts. He just gave me the cash." With nothing on paper, Marciano grew anxious when the Cleveland IRS office invited him in for a visit to explain his ties to DiGravio. Marciano was an extravagant evader of taxes, never declaring any income unless it left a paper trail, but until the Cleveland inquiry, Saccone had finessed all IRS queries by having them transferred to the Brockton office, where "they loved Rocky," says Saccone. "It wasn't difficult to get rid of the cases. He was a great charmer, Rocky. We'd spend two minutes discussing the case, and the rest of the time Rocky would tell stories about his first fight with Walcott. The IRS guys would eat it up."

Cleveland was another matter. Marciano and Saccone made the trip together to Ohio, and the morning they arrived they called the IRS office to tell investigators that they were in town. "Forget about it," the agent told Saccone. "Pete DiGravio just got killed." DiGravio had been cut down by rifle fire on the 16th hole of a golf course outside Cleveland. Marciano, Saccone says, never saw a dime of the thousands that he had given the shark—fearing that word of his loan might leak out, he never made a claim on the estate—and this was not the first time that one of his investments had evaporated. Marciano raced around the country looking for deals to sink his money in, and he lost hundreds of thousands in ill-chosen ventures. Taken in by the hoariest of scams imaginable, he once actually bought swampland in Florida. He lost nearly $250,000 on some coal company in Pittsburgh, even more than that investing in component parts for telephones, and once confided to a Florida friend, Jim Navilio, that he had found an investment that couldn't miss: "I got a guy who can cure arthritis," said the Rock.

When he wasn't chasing after these and other phantoms, he was spending an inordinate amount of time trying to collect bad debts. At times he enlisted in this enterprise his wide variety of friends, from a law-abiding New York State judge, John Lomenzo, to his old Chicago pal Frankie Fratto, a reputed syndicate terrorist. In the early '60s, when Marciano grew tired of waiting for repayment of a $75,000 loan to a Toronto businessman, he appealed to Judge Lomenzo, who shed his robes and headed north with Marciano to Canada. A distinguished jurist who would later serve as New York's secretary of state, Lomenzo made a plea for mercy and compassion on behalf of his poor client, Marciano. "Rocky is having hard times, and he loaned you the money," said the judge. The businessman wrote out a check immediately. Waiving his own private rules, Marciano took the paper and cashed it.

Fratto was persuasive in his own quiet way when Marciano sent him collecting. "If people did not pay Rocky back, I would help him," he says. It was all very simple: "I went to them and told them, 'You owe my friend some money. I suggest you pay it back.' They did not give me a hard time."

Mostly, though, Marciano did his own enforcing. Saccone remembers the time he and Marciano were strolling through Brockton when Rocky, pleading business, excused himself and ducked into Brockton Eddie Massod's pool room and gambling hell on Center Street. Massod owed Marciano $5,000, and he hadn't made a payment in months. Worse, he had been hiding from him, a no-no at the Marciano savings and loan. "If you couldn't pay it back, be a man and face it," Saccone says. "You could never hide on him." The Rock found him on the third floor, from where Saccone, standing on the sidewalk below, could hear the rising shouts. Glancing up, he saw Brockton Eddie hanging halfway out the window and the former heavyweight champion of the world leaning over him, a hand clutched around Eddie's throat.

"I've waited long enough!" Marciano screamed. "No more stalling. I want my money. Now. . . . Now!"

"I need a little more time," gurgled Eddie.

"No more time. . . . No more time!"

A few minutes later Marciano stepped from the door counting a sheaf of $20 bills, the first of dozens of installments that Saccone would be in charge of collecting monthly from Massod. The CPA was only one in a vast and intricate mesh of people, friends and followers of unusual ardency, who worked what lives they had of their own around the odd, often nocturnal, unpredictable movements of the Rock. Marciano had been married to the same woman, the former Barbara Cousins, the daughter of a Brockton cop, since Dec. 31, 1950, but the union unraveled long before the decade was done. Barbara tended to obesity, had a serious drinking problem and smoked heavily—she would die of lung cancer in 1974—whereas her husband's tastes ran more to svelte, statuesque blondes, that single glass of wine and smokeless rooms. "He couldn't stand his married life," says Saccone. "He loved his daughter, and she loved him, but he had no relationship with his wife. There was nothing compatible between them. He wanted to do things, and she didn't."

So the mesh included people, such as the late Lindy Ciardelli on the West Coast and Paterniti on the East Coast, whose job was to help feed

Marciano's prodigious sexual appetite. "Rock liked girls, know what I mean?" Paterniti says. "Nobody wants me to tell you about it, but Rock was insane about girls—all the time. Rocky was the heavyweight champion of girls. Forget about the fights. He was crazy about the girls; that's all he wanted to do. Rocky constantly had orgies and parties, night and day. . . . A friend of mine in New York got me and Rocky thousands of girls. Honestly, literally a thousand girls. We had girls every single day and night. I carried a suitcase full of vibrators. I mean, we used to call Rocky the vibrator king. I had a suitcase that I took all over, filled with vibrators and electric massagers and emotion lotion and all kinds of creams and oils. . . . We went to Pennsylvania and we were with these mob guys and they were bringing us girls and Rocky said, 'Don't let 'em know we got all that stuff. They'll think that we're weird or somethin'.'"

There were women for Marciano everywhere he went in those days after his retirement. That a woman be waiting for him was as requisite for his appearance as the folded $100 bills. "He never had an affair," says Santarelli, his Chicago underworld pal, who booked him to make appearances and advertisements all over. "I don't think he had sex with the same girl twice. Never, that I know, and I knew him a long time. Any girls he had sex with, you couldn't bring her to dinner no more. That's it. Get rid of her. He never wanted to see her again. For dinner, or even a cup of coffee. If he ever went to some place and there was not a girl waiting for him, he'd never come back."

So it was this lust for women and the hunger for making deals and the quest for cash that drove the Rock to the road. He had the whole mesh linked together perfectly, his life and travels so arranged that he never had a need for anything. There was the network of pilots, of course, and then all those eager aides-de-camp awaiting him with cars and limos at whatever airport he was headed for. He was, by consensus, the world's worst driver.

On one of his occasional sojourns to the family home in Fort Lauderdale, he did a commercial for a car dealership and for his fee asked for a gold Firebird 400. He gave it to Mary Anne so she could pick him up at the airport. She remembers a comic interlude of her youth when a motorcycle cop pulled her over one day and discovered she not only did not have a driver's license but also was only 13. She told the cop who her father was and where she lived. The cop roared off to fetch Rocky. "I waited until they came roaring back," Mary Anne says. "My father in his Bermuda shorts, no shirt, bare feet, baseball cap, black hair blowing, with his arms around the cop, holding on. The cop asked my father for his autograph and drove off."

The cop no doubt left thinking he had saved Fort Lauderdale from this adolescent menace. "The world's worst driver drove me home," she says. "My dad did not even have a license."

So he had all his chauffeurs in place. He had rooms and places to stay all across America—at Ed Napoli's in Los Angeles, at Lindy Ciardelli's in Santa Clara, California, at Ben Danzi's 12-room apartment in New York, at Bernie Castro's estates on Long Island and in Florida, at Santarelli's in Chicago, at any hotel he chose in Las Vegas and at scores of homes all over Providence and Brockton, Buffalo and Boston. Santarelli recalls one night in Las Vegas when they were watching Jimmy Durante on stage and Durante announced, "Ladies and gentlemen, in our audience tonight we have the undefeated heavyweight champion of the world—and *America's guest*—Rocky Marciano." Touchy on the nerve of his parsimony, the Rock got all indignant. "Can you imagine this guy?" he said to Santarelli. "He ties a rope around his suitcase so his clothes don't fall out, and he says that about me?"

But that was what he was, America's guest. In all the years, going back to the championship days, there was never a single reported sighting of Marciano picking up a check. One evening, at a table of 12 in a Chicago restaurant, the waitress passed by the seat of businessman Andy Granatelli, the manufacturer of STP motor oil additive, and unknowingly gave the check to the Rock. In a hot panic he tossed it over his shoulder, onto the floor, and demanded of Santarelli, "How could she bring me the check with Andy Granatelli sitting here? Who owns this place? He's trying to be a smart guy." Marciano never ate there again. He knew all the restaurants where he did not have to pay—dozens of restaurateurs sought him out to decorate their tables—and when he was dining with any of his innumerable fat-cat associates, which was quite often, his immediate entourage of traveling friends was under orders never to buy as much as a round of drinks. Just about every such friend suffered Marciano's rebuke for offering to pay for something.

One night, after watching Castro pick up the umpteenth straight dinner check at an expensive New York restaurant, Saccone asked for the tab. Marciano grabbed him and took him aside. "Don't ever, *ever* do that!" Marciano scolded. "When you're with me, you don't pay a nickel. When you're with me, and you're my friend, you don't touch anything: never, never, never." Saccone protested that he felt uncomfortable freeloading all the time. "I'm capable of paying my own way," he said.

"Doncha understand?" said Marciano. "These people *wanna* be around me. Let them pick up the tab. They enjoy it. They wanna do it."

The freebies, as Marciano saw it, were among the benefits a man received for being part of the entourage, for being there when Rocky needed him. In all the hours in all the years he worked for Marciano, Saccone never dared send him a bill, never received a dollar for his services. The adventures were the payment, and the bonus was all the business that Marciano nudged his way. "He introduced me to people who were very substantial in my getting work," Saccone says. So it was for all the professionals, the lawyers and bookkeepers alike, who served Marciano's needs.

"Rocky was a door-opener, the greatest door-opener in the world," says Santarelli. "I'm an Italian guy from the old neighborhood in Chicago. I'd go to parties with Rocky and meet nice people, business people. 'How you doin', Mr. Santarelli?' Business people would contact me to get ahold of him. Many people called me: 'Do me a favor. Set up Rocky for me.' Rocky was a great guy, everybody loved him—if a favor was needed, Rocky would be there—but he was being used all the time. In every walk of life, every friend. Everybody used him. Even the priests used him, restaurant owners used him, women used him, movie stars used him, mob guys used him. . . ."

Knowing this, of course, Marciano refused to go anywhere for free, and the only exception involved the occasional favor for a friend, as when he showed up one day in Michigan to referee some fights, at no charge, for Goody Petronelli, when Goody was running a boxing program in the U.S. Navy.

"You had to pay him to show up for fights," says Santarelli. "He got $250 just to step in the ring to be introduced as the former heavyweight champion. If you wanted Rocky, you had to pay for it. In cash."

If Marciano thus beat the IRS out of some taxes, Santarelli says, that was not the only reason he insisted on payments in cash. On numerous occasions, he says, Marciano complained to him that, under his contract with Al Weill, his former manager, he had to pay Weill 50% of all his earnings—not only from his days as a fighter but also from his years in retirement. "He took 50 percent of Rocky in and out of the ring," says Santarelli. "That's the reason Rocky retired. That was the conflict. He didn't want to pay Al Weill any more money. Even for a personal appearance, Weill wanted 50 percent of it. He wanted cash because he didn't want Weill to get a dime."

The whole object of Marciano's daily existence, the reason for the network that moved and sustained him from place to place, was to get him from one sunset to the next without spending a dime. "There wasn't anything he ever needed that he couldn't get with just a phone call," says his brother Sonny.

On occasions it was only the phone company that stood between Rocky getting through a day in which he got away free and a day in which he was forced to spring for a coin. Marciano worked on correcting that nettlesome problem by using those slugs to make calls, or by feeding that wire contraption into the coin deposit in an apparent attempt to lobotomize the system. He had an unfathomable hostility toward phone companies, and more than once he was observed hammering a phone cradle as though it were Jersey Joe Walcott's nose in the 13th round at Philadelphia. On one occasion, says Napoli, Marciano lost a dime and went berserk, pounding on the phone with the receiver.

"It took my dime," he cried.

At New York's La Guardia Airport one day a phone did not return his dime after he got a busy signal. He screamed at the operator, "You sonuvabitch! I want my dime back!" When that failed, he ripped the receiver out of the phone, threw it on the floor and then began walking past the bank of pay phones along the wall, pressing the coin-return buttons, then fingering the empty coin slots and then ripping all the receivers out of the machines.

"I thought, My God, what is he doing?" says Saccone.

For as much as he coveted the cash, of course, the paradox is that he did not need it, never used it to buy himself anything, never put all but a small part of it to any other use but in the service of his own dark, meretricious underground of unsecured loans and fanciful investments. In fact, it is difficult to imagine anyone handling money more cavalierly or treating it with such unconscious contempt, dating back to the days when, according to his biographer, Skehan, he used to stuff it in plastic bags and tape it inside the water tanks above the toilet bowls in his hotel rooms; or when, one night, he took off and left $27,520 in a plastic bag among clothes mildewing in a suitcase in Napoli's care; or when, too impatient to sit through a stage performance of The Great White Hope, he told his daughter, who was sitting next to him, that he would meet her for dinner later at La Scala and then bolted out of the theater, leaving a brown paper bag mashed in his seat. Mary Anne happened to notice it and stuck it in her purse before she left. They had just settled in for dinner when Marciano said, "Oh, God, I'll be right back. . . ."

"You left something?" she asked, removing the bag.

It contained $40,000.

This was Marciano, impulsive and restless, distracted and eccentric, who climbed into the Cessna that night at Midway Airport, and it was fitting that he left for Des Moines with a paid Chicago-to-Fort Lauderdale airline ticket tucked in his pocket. When he called home to say he was heading west to make that appearance, his family life had become a lie, and his life had more hiding places than his money and more secrets than hiding places. When Santarelli and Benny Trotta, the Baltimore mob associate, saw him off at the Butler Aviation terminal that day, Marciano had no intention of returning to Fort Lauderdale anytime soon. "I'll see you in the morning," Santarelli recalls Rocky telling them. All Farrell needed to do, to get him on that plane, was play on his weaknesses for cash, in the form of a $500 fee, and women. "They promised Rocky a young broad, 17 or 18 years old, to help little Frankie Farrell," Santarelli says.

That was all it took to lift him off toward the distant storm.

No one knows what eventually happened to the $40,000 that Mary Anne recovered from the theater seat that night in New York, just as it is hard to imagine what might have happened to all the rest of the cash, perhaps more than $2 million, he loaned out and stashed away. Most of Marciano's friends and family believe that the bulk of his savings ended up in the bomb shelter on the Ocala, Florida, estate of Bernie Castro, who died two years ago. Mary Anne used to go there with her father, and she vividly recalls him placing his hand on a pipe that ran through the shelter: "He told me, 'Remember this spot, Mary Anne. A great place to hide money. Remember this pipe.'"

A year after the accident, Mary Anne says, she and her mother went to Castro's estate to ask him if they could search the shelter. "He told us, 'Don't be silly,'" she says. They never got inside. Mary Anne figured that some of the money was in safe deposit boxes, under assumed names, and she found doodlings of Rocky's that suggested he might have used two names: Mr. Rocco and Mr. March. She tried to make sense of code words he used to write down, such as *powerless* and *insecure*, but got nowhere. "For many years I tried to put it together," she says. "I even had a CIA friend who helped me search Swiss bank accounts. Nothing."

Believing himself to be immortal, Marciano had no use for life insurance, and wills were only for people who foresaw an end he simply could not imagine. He died intestate, and his family had a terrible struggle at first. The taxes and expenses to maintain the oceanfront house were "so astronomical," Mary Anne says, that the family had to move two miles inland in Fort Lauderdale, to a more modest, four-bedroom ranch house. "It was rough," Mary Anne says. "My mother sold her diamonds for us to live. There were all sorts of liens on the estate; it wasn't settled for five years."

Mary Anne lives in the ranch house with her grandmother Betty Cousins, whom she calls Nana, and Rocco Kevin, 25, who goes by Rocky Jr. An electrical engineering student at Florida Atlantic University, in Boca Raton, Rocky Jr. bears a resemblance to his father, and Mary Anne thinks that he was born out of a relationship that her father had with a Florida woman. Barbara had had five miscarriages after having Mary Anne, and she had become "desperate to adopt." Magically, a lawyer who was close to Marciano found a mother willing to give her child up for adoption.

"I think it was all arranged," Mary Anne says.

"I have my suspicions," Rocky Jr. says. "My one regret in life is that I didn't get to know my father."

Mary Anne has nothing but fond memories of him and the time they spent together. "To me he was gentle and caring," she says. "He'd pick me up and spin me on his knee. He'd come in off trips and he'd yell. 'Barb, can you get me a glass of water?' And then he'd walk into little Rocco's room and pick him up and say, 'My son! My son!'" His death shattered the family. "When he died, a piece of my mother died," Mary Anne says. In her last days Barbara lay in bed and hallucinated, seeing her husband beckoning to her. "Rocky, I'm not ready to go yet," she would say. "I have to take care of Mary Anne and Rocky." Barbara died in 1974 and was entombed next to her husband in a Fort Lauderdale mausoleum.

Mary Anne is sitting at the kitchen counter in her home, sipping iced tea and smoking a cigarette. She has not had an easy few years. On Aug. 4, 1992, she was released from the Broward Correctional Institution after serving eight months of a 22-month sentence for her part in a robbery at a club in Fort Lauderdale. "I made a few mistakes," she says. "I just got mixed up with the wrong people. It's been rough for me, very rough. I never hurt anybody. The only people I ever hurt were myself and my family. I was brought up very well. I had a good family background. The mistakes I made are my own. I went the easy way instead of toughing it out. I felt so bad when those articles came out about me. I didn't want his name to be tarnished: Rocky's daughter. What a nightmare. I'm still on probation, but I've come a long way. I was made to look at myself and make some serious changes."

Marciano left a large and lasting legacy as a prizefighter, as a historic force and presence in the game, but that was not all he left in Fort Lauderdale. Nana Cousins, 89, feels angry and bitter toward him for the kind of life he lived, for his long absences as a husband and father, for what he put his family through. In a living room scattered with photographs, in a house where his son and daughter live, there are no photos of the former undefeated heavyweight champion of the world. Twenty-four years after his death, he is still old business, unresolved. Mary Anne is telling that story about how Rocky loaded her and her friend into that freebie cargo plane bound for Hawaii when she was 12, and how the window blew in and the plane went into a dive. Mary Anne laughs.

"You should *never* have got on that plane," Nana scolds. She is standing with her back to the kitchen window, facing her granddaughter. "God, he was tight!"

Mary Anne tosses back her hair and turns to smile sweetly at her. "But, Nana, I could get anything I wanted out of him."

"And me?" Nana says. "I even bought my own ticket to see him fight Joe Louis. And he lived with us! Everything I say is true. We could write a book. Too bad. We really did like him in those days. . . ."

"I loved him and I always did," says Mary Anne.

"You should. He was your father. But he wasn't a good father."

Mary Anne shakes her head. "He was a wonderful father."

"O.K.," says Nana. "All right, have it your way."

"I think he *was* wonderful. I only had him 16 years."

"Did you have a father, Mary Anne?" Nana says, softly.

"Yes, I did."

"He was gone!"

"So what? We went everywhere together, and we spent quality time, and we did, so, I mean, yes, we did," says Mary Anne. "Some people can live a life-time and not have what I've had. They don't communicate. I was very lucky. My mother and father were two wonderful people, and I was very fortunate."

"Say it your way," Nana says.

"That's the way I remember it."

Nana drifts toward the door. "Barbara should have gone through with her divorce."

Mary Anne looks down, shaking her head. "Oh, brother," she says. "Would you let out the dog, please? She's locked in my room."

"You're just trying to get rid of me."

"No, I'm not."

Nana starts out the kitchen door. "It's all coming out in a book some day."

"Fine, write a book."

"Maybe I'll be six foot under, but . . . when I get to the other side, I'll tell loverboy a thing or two."

August 1993

O UNLUCKY MAN

Fortune never smiled on Sonny Liston,
even when he was champ

"SOMEDAY THEY'RE GONNA WRITE A BLUES SONG JUST FOR FIGHTERS.
IT'LL BE FOR SLOW GUITAR, SOFT TRUMPET AND A BELL."

—*Charles (Sonny) Liston*

It was already dark when she stepped from the car in front of her house on Ottawa Drive, but she could see her pink Cadillac convertible and Sonny's new black Fleetwood under the carport in the Las Vegas night.

Where could Charles be? Geraldine Liston was thinking.

All through the house the lamps were lit, even around the swimming pool out back. The windows were open too, and the doors were unlocked. It was quiet except for the television playing in the room at the top of the stairs.

By 9:30 P.M. on Jan. 5, 1971, Geraldine had not spoken to her husband for 12 days. On Christmas Eve she had called him from St. Louis after flying there with the couple's seven-year-old son, Danielle, to spend the holidays with her mother. Geraldine had tried to phone him a number of times, but no one had answered at the house. At first she figured he must be off roistering in Los Angeles, and so she didn't pay his absence any mind until the evening of Dec. 28. That night, in a fitful sleep, she had a vision so unsettling that it awakened her and sent her to her mother's room.

"I had the worst dream," Geraldine says. "He was falling in the shower and calling my name, 'Gerry, Gerry!' I can still see it. So I got real nervous.

I told my mother, 'I think something's wrong.' But my mother said, 'Oh, don't think that. He's all right.'"

In fact, Sonny Liston had not been right for a long time, and not only for the strangely dual life he had been leading—spells of choirboy abstinence squeezed between binges of drinking and drugs—but also for the rudderless, unfocused existence he had been reduced to. Jobless and nearly broke, Liston had been moving through the murkier waters of Las Vegas's drug culture. "I knew he was hanging around with the wrong people," one of his closest friends, gambler Lem Banker, says. "And I knew he was in desperate need of cash."

So, as the end of 1970 neared, Liston had reached that final twist in the cord. Eight years earlier he was the undisputed heavyweight champion of the world—a 6' 1½", 215-pound hulk with upper arms like picnic roasts, two magnificent, 14-inch fists and a scowl that he mounted for display on a round, otherwise impassive face. He had won the title by flattening Floyd Patterson with two punches, left hooks down and up, in the first round of their fight on Sept. 25, 1962; 10 months later he had beaten Patterson again in one round.

Liston did not sidestep his way to the title; the pirouette was not among his moves. He reached Patterson by walking through the entire heavyweight division, leaving large bodies sprawled behind him: Wayne Bethea, Mike DeJohn, Cleveland Williams, Nino Valdes, Roy Harris, Zora Folley et al. Finally, a terrified Patterson waited for him, already fumbling with his getaway disguise, dark glasses and a beard.

Before the referee could count to 10 in that first fight, Liston had become a mural-sized American myth, a larger-than-life John Henry with two hammers, an 84-inch reach, 23 knockouts (in 34 bouts) and 19 arrests. Tales of his exploits spun well with the fight crowd over beers in dark-wood bars. There was the one about how he used to lift up the front end of automobiles. And one about how he caught birds with his bare hands. And another about how he hit speed bags so hard that he tore them from their hinges, and ripped into heavy bags until they burst, spilling their stuffing.

"Nobody hit those bags like Sonny," says 80-year-old Johnny Tocco, one of Liston's first and last trainers. "He tore bags up. He could turn that hook, put everything behind it. Turn and snap. Bam! Why, he could knock you across the room with a jab. I saw him knock guys out with a straight jab. Bam! In the ring, Sonny was a killing machine."

Perhaps no fighter had ever brought to the ring so palpable an aura of menace. Liston hammered out danger, he hammered out a warning. There was his fearsome physical presence; then there was his heavy psychic baggage, his prison record and assorted shadows from the underworld. Police in three cities virtually drove him out of town; in one of them, St. Louis, a captain warned Liston that he would wind up dead in an alley if he stayed.

In public Liston was often surly, hostile, and uncommunicative, and so he fed one of the most disconcerting of white stereotypes, that of the ignorant, angry, morally reckless black roaming loose, with bad intentions, in white society. He became a target for racial typing in days when white commentators could still utter undisguised slurs without Ted Koppel asking them to, please, explain themselves. In the papers Liston was referred to as "a gorilla," "a latter day caveman" and "a jungle beast." His fights against Patterson were seen as morality plays. Patterson was Good, Liston was Evil.

On July 24, 1963, two days after the second Patterson fight, *Los Angeles Times* columnist Jim Murray wrote: "The central fact . . . is that the world of sport now realizes it has gotten Charles (Sonny) Liston to keep. It is like finding a live bat on a string under your Christmas tree."

The NAACP had pleaded with Patterson not to fight Liston. Indeed, many blacks watched Liston's spectacular rise with something approaching horror, as if he were climbing the Empire State Building with Fay Wray in his hands. Here suddenly was a baleful black felon holding the most prestigious title in sports. This was at the precise moment in history when a young civil rights movement was emerging, a movement searching for role models. Television was showing freedom marchers being swept by fire hoses and attacked by police dogs. Yet, untouched by image makers, Liston steadfastly refused to speak any mind but his own. Asked by a young white reporter why *he* wasn't fighting for freedom in the South, Liston deadpanned, "I ain't got no dog-proof ass."

Four months after Liston won the title, *Esquire* thumbed its nose at its white readers with an unforgettable cover. On the front of its December 1963 issue, there was Liston glowering out from under a tasseled red-and-white Santa Claus hat, looking like the last man on earth America wanted to see coming down its chimney.

Now, at the end of the Christmas holiday of 1970, that old black Santa was still missing in Las Vegas. Geraldine crossed through the carport of the Listons' split-level and headed for the patio out back. Danielle was at her side. Copies of the *Las Vegas Sun* had been gathering in the carport since Dec. 29. Geraldine opened the back door and stepped into the den. A foul odor hung in the air, permeating the house, and so she headed up the three steps toward the kitchen. "I thought he had left some food out and it had spoiled," she says. "But I didn't see anything."

Leaving the kitchen, she walked toward the staircase. She could hear the television from the master bedroom. Geraldine and Danielle climbed the stairs and looked through the bedroom door, to the smashed bench at the foot of the bed and the stone-cold figure lying with his back up against it, blood caked on the front of his swollen shirt and his head canted to one side. She gasped and said, "Sonny's dead."

"What's wrong?" Danielle asked.

She led the boy quickly down the stairs. "Come on, baby," she said.

On the afternoon of Sept. 27, 1962, Liston boarded a flight from Chicago to Philadelphia. He settled into a seat next to his friend Jack McKinney, an amateur fighter who was then a sportwriter for the *Philadelphia Daily News*. This was the day Liston had been waiting for ever since he first laced on boxing gloves, at the Missouri State Penitentiary a decade earlier. Forty-eight hours before, he had bludgeoned Patterson to become heavyweight champion. Denied a title fight for years, barred from New York City rings as an undesirable, largely ignored in his adopted Philadelphia, Liston suddenly felt vindicated, redeemed. In fact, before leaving the Sheraton Hotel in Chicago, he had received word from friends that the people of Philadelphia were awaiting his triumphant return with a ticker-tape parade.

The only disquieting tremor had been some other news out of Philadelphia, relayed to him by telephone from friends back home, that *Daily News* sports editor Larry Merchant had written a column confirming Liston's worst fears about how his triumph might be received. Those fears were based upon the ruckus that had preceded the fight. The *New York Times*'s Arthur Daley had led the way: "Whether Patterson likes it or not, he's stuck with it. He's the knight in shining armor battling the forces of evil."

Now wrote Merchant: "So it is true—in a fair fight between good and evil, evil must win. . . . A celebration for Philadelphia's first heavyweight champ is now in order. Emily Post probably would recommend a ticker-tape parade. For confetti we can use shredded warrants of arrest."

The darkest corner of Liston's personality was his lack of a sense of self. All the signs from his past pointed the same way and said the same thing: dead end. He was the 24th of the 25 children fathered by Tobey Liston, a tenant cotton farmer who lived outside Forrest City, Arkansas. Tobey had two families, one with 15 children and the other with 10; Charles was born ninth to his mother, Helen. Outside the ring, he battled his whole life against writers who suggested that he was older than he claimed he was.

"Maybe they think I'm so old because I never was really young," he said. Usually he would insist he was born on May 8, 1932, in the belly of the Great Depression, and he growled at reporters who dared to doubt him on this: "Anybody who says I'm not 30 is callin' my momma a liar."

"Sonny was so sensitive on the issue of his age because he did not really *know* how old he was," says McKinney. "When guys would write that he was 32 going on 50, it had more of an impact on him than anybody realized. Sonny didn't know *who* he was. He was looking for an identity, and he thought that being the champion would give him one."

Now that moment had arrived. During the flight home, McKinney says, Liston practiced the speech he was going to give when the crowds greeted him at the airport. Says McKinney, who took notes during the flight, "He used me as sort of a test auditor, dryrunning his ideas by me."

Liston was excited, emotional, eager to begin his reign. "There's a lot of things I'm gonna do," he told McKinney. "But one thing's very important: *I want to reach my people.* I want to reach them and tell them, 'You don't have to worry about me disgracin' you. You won't have to worry about me stoppin' your progress.' I want to go to colored churches and colored neighborhoods. I know it was in the papers that the better class of colored people were hopin' I'd lose, even prayin' I'd lose, because they was afraid I wouldn't know how to act. . . . I remember one thing so clear about listening to Joe Louis fight on the radio when I was a kid. I never remember a fight the announcer didn't say about Louis, 'A great fighter and a credit to his race.' Remember? That used to make me feel real proud inside.

"I don't mean to be sayin' I'm just gonna be the champion of my own people," Liston continued. "It says now I'm the world's champion, and that's just the way it's gonna be. I want to go to a lot of places—like orphan homes and reform schools. I'll be able to say, 'Kid, I know it's tough for you and it might even get tougher. But don't give up on the world. Good things can happen if you let them.'"

Liston was ready. As the plane rolled to a stop, he rose and walked to the door. McKinney was next to him. The staircase was wheeled to the door. Liston straightened his tie and his fedora. The door opened, and he stepped outside. There was no one there except for airline workers, a few reporters and photographers and a handful of P.R. men. "Other than those, no one," recalls McKinney. "I watched Sonny. His eyes swept the whole scene. He was extremely intelligent, and he understood immediately what it meant. His Adam's apple moved slightly. You could feel the deflation, see the look of hurt in his eyes. It was almost like a silent shudder went through him. He'd been deliberately snubbed.

"Philadelphia wanted nothing to do with him. Sonny felt, after he won the title, that the past was forgiven. It was going to be a whole new world. What happened in Philadelphia that day was a turning point in his life. He was still the bad guy. He was the personification of evil. And that's the way it was going to remain. He was devastated. I knew from that point on that the world would never get to know the Sonny that I knew."

On the way out of the airport, after a brief press conference, Sonny turned to McKinney and said, "I think I'll get out tomorrow and do all the things I've always done. Walk down the block and buy the papers, stop in the drugstore, talk to the neighbors. Then I'll see how the *real peoples* feel. Maybe then I'll start to feelin' like a champion. You know, it's really a lot like an election, only in reverse. Here I'm already in office, but now I have to go out and start campaignin'."

That was a campaign that Liston could never win. He was to be forever cast in the role of devil's agent, and never more so than in his two stunning, ignominious losses to Cassius Clay, then beginning to be known as Muhammad Ali. In the history of boxing's heavyweight division, never has a fighter fallen faster, and farther, than did Liston in the 15 months it took Ali to reduce him from being the man known as the fiercest alive to being the butt of jokes on TV talk shows.

"I think he died the day he was born," wrote Harold Conrad, who did publicity for four of Liston's fights. By the nearest reckoning, that birth would have been in a tenant's shack, 17 miles northwest of Forrest City and about 60 west of Memphis. Helen had met Tobey in Mississippi and had gone with him to Arkansas around the time of World War I. Young Charles grew up lost among all the callused hands and bare feet of innumerable siblings. "I had nothing when I was a kid but a lot of brothers and sisters, a helpless mother and a father who didn't care about any of us," Liston said. "We grew up with few clothes, no shoes, little to eat. My father worked me hard and whupped me hard."

Helen moved to St. Louis during World War II, and Charles, who was living with his father, set out north to find her when he was 13. Three years later he weighed 200 pounds, and he ruled his St. Louis neighborhood by force. At 18, he had already served time in a house of detention and was graduating to armed robbery. On Jan. 15, 1950, Liston was found guilty of two counts of larceny from a person and two counts of first-degree robbery. He served more than two years in the Missouri state pen in Jefferson City.

The prison's athletic director, Father Alois Stevens, a Catholic priest, first saw Liston when he came by the gym to join the boxing program. To

Stevens, Liston looked like something out of *Jane's Fighting Ships*. "He was the most perfect specimen of manhood I had ever seen," Stevens recalls. "Powerful arms, big shoulders. Pretty soon he was knocking out everybody in the gym. His hands were so large! I couldn't believe it. They always had trouble with his gloves, trouble getting them on when his hands were wrapped."

In 1952 Liston was released on parole, and he turned pro on Sept. 2, 1953, leveling Don Smith in the first round in St. Louis. Tocco met Liston when the fighter strolled into Tocco's gym in St. Louis. The trainer's first memory of Liston is fixed, mostly for the way he came in—slow and deliberate and alone, feeling his way along the edges of the gym, keeping to himself, saying nothing. That was classic Liston, casing every joint he walked into, checking for exits. As Liston began to work, Tocco saw the bird tracks up and down Liston's back, the enduring message from Tobey Liston.

"What are all those welts from?" Tocco asked him.

Said Liston, "I had bad dealin's with my father."

"He was a loner," Tocco says. "He wouldn't talk to nobody. He wouldn't go with nobody. He always came to the gym by himself. He always left by himself. The police knew he'd been in prison, and he'd be walking along and they'd always stop him and search him. So he went through alleys all the time. *He always went around things.* I can still see him, either coming out of an alley or walking into one."

Nothing was simpler for Liston to fathom than the world between the ropes—step, jab, hook—and nothing more unyielding than the secrets of living outside them. He was a mob fighter right out of prison. One of his managers, Frank Mitchell, the publisher of the *St. Louis Argus*—who had been arrested numerous times on suspicion of gambling—was a known front for John Vitale, St. Louis's reigning hoodlum. Vitale had ties to organized crime's two most notorious boxing manipulators: Frankie Carbo and Carbo's lieutenant, Frank (Blinky) Palermo, who controlled mob fighters out of Philadelphia. Vitale was in the construction business (among others), and when Liston wasn't fighting, one of his jobs was cracking heads and keeping black laborers in line. Liston always publicly denied this, but years later he confided his role to one of his closest Las Vegas friends, Davey Pearl, a boxing referee. "He told me that when he was in St. Louis, he worked as a labor goon," says Pearl, "breaking up strikes."

Not pleased with the company Liston was keeping—one of his pals was 385-pound Barney Baker, a reputed head-cracker for the Teamsters—the St. Louis police kept stopping Liston, on sight and without cause, until, on May 5, 1956, 3$^1/_2$ years after his release from prison, Liston assaulted a St.

Louis policeman, took his gun, left the cop lying in an alley and hid the weapon at a sister's house. The officer suffered a broken knee and gashed face. The following December, Liston began serving nine months in the city workhouse.

Soon after his release Liston had his second run-in with a St. Louis cop. The officer had creased Liston's skull with a nightstick, and two weeks later the fighter returned the favor by depositing the fellow headfirst in a trash can. Liston then fled St. Louis for Philadelphia, where Palermo installed one of his pals, Joseph (Pep) Barone, as Liston's manager, and Liston at once began fighting the biggest toughs in the division. He stopped Bethea, who spit out seven teeth, in the first round. Valdes fell in three, and so did Williams. Harris swooned in one, and Folley fell like a tree in three. Eddie Machen ran for 12 rounds but lost the decision. Albert Westphal keeled in one. Now Liston had one final fight to win. Only Patterson stood between him and the title.

Whether or not Patterson should deign to fight the ex-con led, at the time, to a weighty moral debate among the nation's reigning sages of sport. What sharpened the lines were Liston's recurring problems with the law in Philadelphia, including a variety of charges stemming from a June 1961 incident in Fairmount Park. Liston and a companion had been arrested for stopping a female motorist after dark and shining a light in her car. All charges, including impersonating a police officer, were eventually dropped. A month before, Liston had been brought in for loitering on a street corner. That charge, too, was dropped. More damaging were revelations that he was, indeed, a mob fighter, with a labor goon's history. In 1960, when Liston was the No. 1 heavyweight contender, testimony before a U.S. Senate subcommittee probing underworld control of boxing had revealed that Carbo and Palermo together owned a majority interest in him. Of this, Liston said, he knew nothing. "Pep Barone handles me," he said.

"Do you think that people like [Carbo and Palermo] ought to remain in the sport of boxing?" asked the committee chairman, Tennessee Senator Estes Kefauver.

"I wouldn't pass judgment on no one," Liston replied. "I haven't been perfect myself."

In an act of public cleansing after the Fairmount Park incident, Liston spent three months living in a house belonging to the Loyola Catholic Church in Denver, where he had met Father Edward Murphy, a Jesuit priest, while training to fight Folley in 1960. Murphy, who died in 1975, became Liston's spiritual counselor and teacher. "Murph gave him a house to live in and tried to get him to stop drinking," Father Thomas Kelly, one of Murphy's closest friends, recalls. "That was his biggest problem. You could smell him in the mornings. Oh, poor Sonny. He was just an accident waiting to happen. Murph used to say, 'Pray for the poor bastard.'"

But even Liston's sojourn in Denver didn't still the debate over his worthiness to fight for the title. In this bout between good and evil, the clearest voice belonged to *New York Herald-Tribune* columnist Red Smith: "Should a man with a record of violent crime be given a chance to become champion of the world? Is America less sinful today than in 1853 when John Morrissey, a saloon brawler and political headbreaker out of Troy, N.Y., fought Yankee Sullivan, lammister from the Australian penal colony in Botany Bay? In our time, hoodlums have held championships with distinction. Boxing may be purer since their departure; it is not healthier."

Since he could not read, Liston missed many pearls, but friends read scores of columns to him. When Barone was under fire for his mob ties, Liston quipped, "I got to get me a manager that's not hot—like Estes Kefauver." Instead, he got George Katz, who quickly came to appreciate Liston's droll sense of humor. Katz managed Liston for 10% of his purses, and as the two sat in court at Liston's hearing for the Fairmount Park incident, Liston leaned over to Katz and said, "If I get time, you're entitled to 10 percent of it."

Liston was far from the sullen, insensitive brute of the popular imagination. Liston and McKinney would take long walks between workouts, and during them Liston would recite the complete dialogue and sound effects of the comedy routines of black comedians like Pigmeat Markham and Redd Foxx. "He could imitate what he heard down to creaking doors and women's voices," says McKinney. "It was hilarious hearing him do falsetto."

Liston also fabricated quaint metaphors to describe phenomena ranging from brain damage to the effects of his jab: "The middle of a fighter's forehead is like a dog's tail. Cut off the tail and the dog goes all whichway 'cause he ain't got no more balance. It's the same with a fighter's forehead."

He lectured occasionally on the unconscious, though not in the Freudian sense. Setting the knuckles of one fist into the grooves between the knuckles of the other fist, he would explain: "See, the different parts of the brain set in little cups like this. When you get hit a terrible shot—*pop!*—the brain flops out of them cups and you're knocked out. Then the brain settles back in the cups and you come to. But after this happens enough times, or sometimes even once if the shot's hard enough, the brain don't settle back right in them cups, and that's when you start needing other people to help you get around."

So it was that Liston vowed to hit Patterson on the dog's tail until his brain flopped out of its cups. Actually, he missed the tail and hit the chin.

Patterson was gone. Liston had trained to the minute, and he would never again be as good a fighter as he was that night. For what? Obviously, nothing in his life had changed. He left Philadelphia after he won the title, because he believed he was being harassed by the police of Fairmount Park, through which he had to drive to get from the gym to his home. At one point he was stopped for "driving too slow" through the park. That did it. In 1963 he moved to Denver, where he announced, "I'd rather be a lamppost in Denver than the mayor of Philadelphia."

At times, in fact, things were not much better in the Rockies. "For a while the Denver police pulled him over every day," says Ray Schoeninger, a former Liston sparring partner. "They must have stopped him 100 times outside City Park. He'd run on the golf course, and as he left in his car, they'd stop him. Twenty-five days in a row. Same two cops. They thought it was a big joke. It made me ashamed of being a Denver native. Sad they never let him live in peace."

Liston's disputes were not always with the police. After he had won the title, he walked into the dining room of the Beverly Rodeo Hotel in Hollywood and approached the table at which former rum-runner Moe Dalitz, head of the Desert Inn in Las Vegas and a boss of the old Cleveland mob, was eating. The two men spoke. Liston made a fist and cocked it. Speaking very distinctly, Dalitz said, "If you hit me, nigger, you'd better kill me. Because if you don't, I'll make one telephone call, and you'll be dead in 24 hours." Liston wheeled and left.

The police and Dalitz were hardly Liston's only tormentors. There was a new and even more inescapable disturber of his peace: the boisterous Clay. Not that Liston at first took notice. After clubbing Patterson, he took no one seriously. He hardly trained for the rematch in Las Vegas. Clay, who hung around Liston's gym while the champion went through the motions of preparing for Patterson, heckled him relentlessly. Already a minor poet, Clay would yell at Liston: "Sonny is a fatty. I'm gonna whip him like his daddy!" One afternoon he rushed up to Liston, pointed to him and shouted: "He ain't whipped nobody! Who's he whipped?" Liston, sitting down, patted a leg and said, "Little boy, come sit in my lap." But Clay wouldn't sit; he was too busy running around and bellowing, "The beast is on the run!"

Liston spotted Clay one day in the Thunderbird Casino, walked up behind him and tapped him on the shoulder. Clay turned, and Liston cuffed him hard with the back of his hand. The place went silent. Young Clay looked frightened. "What you do that for?" he said.

"'Cause you're too fucking fresh," Liston said. As he headed out of the casino, he said, "I got the punk's heart now."

That incident would be decisive in determining the outcome of the first Liston-Clay fight, seven months later. "Sonny had no respect for Clay after that," McKinney says. "Sonny thought all he had to do was take off his robe and Clay would faint. He made this colossal misjudgment. He didn't train at all."

If he had no respect for Clay, Liston was like a child around the radio hero of his boyhood, Joe Louis. When George Lois, then an art director at *Esquire*, decided to try the black-Santa cover, he asked his friend Louis to approach Liston. Liston grudgingly agreed to do the shoot in Las Vegas. Photographer Carl Fischer snapped one photograph, whereupon Liston rose, took off the cap and said, "That's it." He started out the door. Lois grabbed Liston's arm. The fighter stopped and stared at the art director. "I let his arm go," Lois recalls.

While Liston returned to the craps tables, Lois was in a panic. "One picture!" Lois says. "You need to take 50, 100 pictures to make sure you get it right." He ran to Louis, who understood Lois's dilemma. Louis found Liston shooting craps, walked up behind him, reached up, grabbed him by an ear and marched him out of the casino. Bent over like a puppy on a leash, Liston followed Louis to the elevator, with Louis muttering, "Come on, git!" The cover shoot resumed.

A few months later, of course, Clay handled Liston almost as easily. Liston stalked and chased, but Clay was too quick and too fit for him. By the end of the third round Liston knew that his title was in peril, and he grew desperate. One of Liston's trainers, Joe Pollino, confessed to McKinney years later that Liston ordered him to rub an astringent compound on his gloves before the fourth round. Pollino complied. Liston shoved his gloves into Clay's face in the fourth, and the challenger's eyes began burning and tearing so severely that he could not see. In his corner, before the fifth round, Clay told his handlers that he could not go on. His trainer, Angelo Dundee, had to literally push him into the ring. Moving backward faster than Liston moved forward, Clay ducked and dodged as Liston lunged after him. He survived the round.

By the sixth, Clay could see clearly again, and as he danced and jabbed, hitting Liston at will, the champion appeared to age three years in three minutes. At the end of that round, bleeding and exhausted, he could foresee his humiliating end. His left shoulder had been injured—he could no longer throw an effective punch with it—and so he stayed on his stool, just sat there at the bell to start Round 7.

There were cries that Liston had thrown the fight. That night Conrad, Liston's publicist, went to see him in his room, where Liston was sitting in bed, drinking.

"What are they sayin' about the fight?" Liston asked.

"That you took a dive," said Conrad.

Liston raged. "Me? Sell my title? Those dirty bastards!" He threw his glass and shattered it against the wall.

The charges of a fix in that fight were nothing compared with what would be said about the rematch, in Lewiston, Maine, during which Liston solidified his place in boxing history. Ali, as the young champion was now widely called, threw one blow, an overhand right so dubious that it became known as the Phantom Punch, and suddenly Liston was on his back. The crowd came to its feet in anger, yelling, "Fake! Fake!"

Ali looked down at the fallen Liston, cocked a fist and screamed, "Get up and fight, sucker! Get up and fight!"

There was chaos. Referee Joe Walcott, having vainly tried to push Ali to a neutral corner, did not start a count, and Liston lay there unwilling to rise. "Clay caught me cold," Liston would recall. "Anybody can get caught in the first round, before you work up a sweat. Clay stood over me. I never blacked out. But I wasn't gonna get up, either, not with him standin' over me. See, you can't get up without puttin' one hand on the floor, and so I couldn't protect myself."

The finish was as ugly as a Maine lobster. Walcott finally moved Ali back, and as Liston rose, Walcott wiped off his gloves and stepped away. Ali and Liston resumed fighting. Immediately, Nat Fleischer, editor of *The Ring* magazine, who was sitting next to the official timer, began shouting for Walcott to stop the fight. Liston had been down for 17 seconds, and Fleischer, who had no actual authority at ringside, thought the fight should have been declared over. Walcott left the two men fighting and walked over to confer with Fleischer. Though he had never even started a count, Walcott then turned back to the fighters and, incredibly, stepped between them to end the fight. "I was never counted out," Liston said later. "I coulda got up *right* after I was hit."

No one believed him, of course, and even Geraldine had her doubts about her husband's efforts. Ted King, one of Liston's seconds, recalls her angrily accusing Sonny later that night of going in the water.

"You could have gotten up and you stayed down!" she cried.

Liston looked pleadingly at King. "Tell her, Teddy," he said. "Tell her I got hit."

Some who were at ringside that night, and others who have studied the films, insist that Ali indeed connected with a shattering right. But Liston's performance in Lewiston has long been perceived as a tank job, and not a convincing one at that. One of Liston's assistant trainers claims that Liston threw the fight for fear of being murdered. King now says that two well-dressed Black Muslims showed up in Maine before the fight—Ali had just become a Muslim—and warned Liston, "You get killed if you win." So, according to King, Liston chose a safer ending. It seems fitting somehow that Liston should spend the last moments of the best years of his life on his back while the crowd showered him with howls of execration. Liston's two losses to Ali ended the short, unhappy reign of the most feared—and the most relentlessly hounded—prizefighter of his time.

Liston never really retired from the ring. After two years of fighting pushovers in Europe, he returned to the U.S. and began a comeback of sorts in 1968. He knocked out all seven of his opponents that year and won three more matches in 1969 before an old sparring partner, Leotis Martin, stopped him in the ninth round of a bout on Dec. 6. That killed any chance at a title shot. On June 29, 1970, he fought Chuck Wepner in Jersey City. Tocco, Liston's old trainer from the early St. Louis days, prepared him for the fight against the man known as the Bayonne Bleeder. Liston hammered Wepner with jabs, and in the sixth round Tocco began pleading with the referee to stop the fight. "It was like blood was coming out of a hydrant," says Tocco. The referee stopped the bout in the 10th; Wepner needed 57 stitches to close his face.

That was Liston's last fight. He earned $13,000 for it, but he wound up broke nonetheless. Several weeks earlier, Liston had asked Banker to place a $10,000 bet for him on undefeated heavyweight contender Mac Foster to whip veteran Jerry Quarry. Quarry stopped Foster in the sixth round, and Liston promised Banker he would pay him back after the Wepner fight. When Liston and Banker boarded the flight back to Las Vegas, Liston opened a brown paper bag, carefully counted out $10,000 in small bills and handed the wad to Banker. "He gave the other $3,000 to guys in his corner," Banker said. "That left him with nothing."

In the last weeks of his life Liston was moving with a fast crowd. At one point, a Las Vegas sheriff warned Banker, through a mutual friend, to stay away from Liston. "We're looking into a drug deal." said the sheriff. "Liston is getting involved with the wrong people." At about the same time two

Las Vegas policemen stopped by the gym and told Tocco that Liston had recently turned up at a house that would be the target of a drug raid. Says Tocco, "For a week the police were parked in a lot across the street, watching when Sonny came and who he left with."

On the night Geraldine found his body. Liston had been dead at least six days, and an autopsy revealed traces of morphine and codeine of a type produced by the breakdown of heroin in the body. His body was so decomposed that tests were inconclusive—officially, he died of lung congestion and heart failure—but circumstantial evidence suggests that he died of a heroin overdose. Though there were fresh needle marks on one of his arms, close friends insist that he was too terrified of needles to have injected himself with anything. An investigating officer, Sergeant Gary Beckwith, found a small amount of marijuana along with heroin and a syringe in the house.

Geraldine, Banker, and Pearl all say that they had no knowledge of Liston's involvement with drugs, but law enforcement officials say they have reason to believe that Liston was a regular heroin user. It is possible that those closest to him may not have known of his alleged drug use. Liston may have lived two lives for years.

Pearl was always hearing reports of Liston's drinking binges, but Liston was a teetotaler around Pearl. "I never saw Sonny take a drink." says Pearl. "Ever. And I was with him hundreds of times over the last five years of his life. He'd leave me at night, and the next morning someone would say to me, 'You should have seen your boy, Liston, last night. Was he ever drunk!' I once asked him. 'What is this? You leave me at night and go out and get drunk?' He just looked at me. I never, ever suspected him of doing dope. I'm telling you, I don't think he did. He was scared to death of needles."

Some police officials and not a few old friends think that Liston may have been murdered, though they have no way of proving it now. Conrad believes that Liston became deeply involved in a loan-sharking ring in Las Vegas, as a bill collector, and that he tried to muscle in for a bigger share of the action. His employers got him drunk, Conrad surmises, took him home and stuck him with a needle. There are police in Las Vegas who say they believe—but are unable to prove—that Liston was the target of a hit ordered by Ash Resnick, an old associate of Liston's with whom the former champion was having a dispute over money. Resnick died two years ago.

Geraldine has trouble comprehending all that talk about heroin or murder. "If he was killed, I don't know who would do it." she says. "If he was doing drugs, he didn't act like he was drugged. Sonny wasn't on dope. He had high blood pressure, and he had been out drinking in late December. As far as I'm concerned, he had a heart attack. Case closed."

There is no persuasive explanation of how Liston died, so the speculation continues, perhaps to go on forever.

Liston is buried in Paradise Memorial Gardens, in Las Vegas, directly under the flight path for planes approaching McCarran International Airport. The brass plate on the grave is tarnished now, but the epitaph is clear under his name and the years of his life. It reads simply: A MAN. Twenty years ago Father Murphy flew in from Denver to give the eulogy, then went home and wept for an hour before he could compose himself enough to tell Father Kelly about the funeral. "They had the funeral procession down the Strip," Murphy said. "Can you imagine that? People came out of the hotels to watch him pass. They stopped everything. They used him all his life. They were still using him on the way to the cemetery. There he was, another Las Vegas show. God help us."

In the end, it seemed fitting that the exact date of Liston's death should remain as obscured as the exact day of his birth, and that, after all those years he should finally play to a friendly crowd on the way to his own burial—with a police escort, the most ironic touch of all.

Geraldine remained in Las Vegas for nine years after Sonny died—she was a casino hostess—then returned to St. Louis, where she had met Sonny after his parole, when he was working in a munitions factory. She has never remarried, and today works as a medical technician. "He was a great guy, great with me, great with kids, a gentle man," says Geraldine.

With Geraldine gone from Las Vegas, few visit Sonny's grave anymore. Every couple of minutes a plane roars over, shaking the earth and rattling the broken plastic flowers that someone placed in the metal urn atop his headstone. "Every once in a while someone comes by and asks to see where he's buried," says a cemetery worker. "But not many anymore. Not often."

February 1991

TRUE TO HIS WORDS

Hurricane Carter, a top middleweight who spent 18 years in prison for murder, was exonerated with the help of a boy from Brooklyn and some resourceful Canadians inspired by his autobiography

L ate of an April evening in 1974, Rubin Carter was sitting at the small desk in his five- by seven-foot cell in Rahway (New Jersey) State Prison, reading the manuscript of his autobiography, when he picked up that faint, metallic scent of menace in the incarcerated air. The man had spent nearly half of his 37 years behind bars—the past seven for a triple murder that he vehemently insisted he had not committed—and in the course of time he had learned to read, like a second language, the quietest shifts in mood and rhythm inside prison walls.

Carter looked at his watch. It was past 10. He went to the door of his cell. Outside, the lights were still on in his wing. Rahway ran like a time-piece, and one of the things a man could always count on was the dimming of the houselights at 10. In the second language, lights off beyond that hour was good: lights on bad. "It meant that something extraordinary was going on," he says.

Carter was the leader of the Rahway Inmates Council, a group of jail-house rockers working for prison reform. That very day Carter had presided over a peaceful, if unauthorized, meeting in the prison rec hall, urging inmates to air their grievances through the council. He sensed he was in trouble for that. Indeed. Rahway was preparing to ship him back to Tren-ton State—the maximum-security prison where he had previously done time—on charges of inciting a riot.

"I *knew* they were coming to get me." he says. "I didn't have to hear rumors."

That left him but one thing to do.

Quietly he picked up his footlocker, his standing locker, his desk—every movable object in his room except his bed—and stacked them against the door of his cell. He then stripped off his shirt and denims and pulled on his sweatpants and sweat-shirt, the one with the hood to cover his shaved head. Fearing an attack of Mace, he uncapped a jar of Vaseline and swabbed his neck and face with jelly, spreading it in thick gobs around his nose and eyes. He was ready.

It was surely no wonder, in this hour of maximum danger, that he should choose to face the enemy on the terms he understood best, gleaming and hooded in a very small space. Back in the mid-1960s, Rubin (Hurricane) Carter had been the No. 1-ranked middleweight fighter in the world—a fierce, unembraceable attacker with a hard body, a mastiff's courage and a left hook that whistled as it worked.

Carter lost his only shot at the middleweight title on Dec. 14, 1964—a 15-round unanimous decision to champion Joey Giardello. Nearly two years later he was training for his second chance, against champion Dick Tiger, when he and a former high school track star named John Artis, a college-bound 19-year-old who had never been in trouble with the law, were arrested in Paterson, New Jersey, for the June 17, 1966, slaying of three whites in Paterson's Lafayette Bar & Grill.

For all the years that Carter would spend in prison for that crime—from 1967 to '85, from the first day of his confinement at Trenton State through his extraordinary metamorphosis at Rahway, through two demonstrably tainted trials to his final vindication and walk to freedom—he would proclaim his innocence by living in contempt and defiance of his keepers. On first entering Trenton he refused to surrender his wristwatch and ring; to shave his goatee, as prison rules required: to work at any of the prison jobs. As punishment he spent three months in The Hole, his first of many descents into that airless, sepulchral dungeon. When they finally raised him up out of The Hole, he refused to wear prison clothes. He refused to undergo psychiatric evaluations. An angry recluse, he ate his meals alone in his cell, heating up cans of soup with a small copper coil. Late into the night prisoners could hear him tapping at his antediluvian typewriter, a manual Underwood left to him by a parolee, pecking out his story in the long, impassioned cadences of his rage.

Now, on this April night in 1974, he sat on his bed, looking like some deranged warrior peering out from the hollow of his cowl, his black face smeared with translucent war paint, listening for the sound of boots marching along the tier. They came at about three o'clock. "With Mace and chains and shackles," Carter recalls. "Fifty of them, all lined up out there. Guards in their full riot gear."

Carter froze. From inside a helmet, a muffled voice boomed: "Come out, Carter! Come out!"

"I mean this." Carter warned them. "I ain't going with you. If anybody comes in here to get me, God forbid. You'll need 20 men! First come, first served."

At that moment Bobby Martin, a sergeant of the guards, arrived on the scene. He had just rushed back to Rahway from his house and was on a mission to save a man he regarded as a friend. "I never met anybody like him," says Martin, a captain now in the New Jersey prison system. "I used to go in the cell and talk to him during lunch. You're not supposed to do that, but I'd do it." Martin owed Carter one, too. One day, when Martin was a rookie, he had found himself trapped by two thugs on the tier in Four Up Wing. Carter came to Martin's rescue, knocking out the assailants.

Martin came to the door and looked inside. "Ever see Rubin's eyes when he's mad?" says Martin. "His eyes get real small—like a mad cat's eyes. I looked at him and said, 'Good Lord. Help me now.' He was going to war."

Martin asked Carter to let him in. Carter removed the barricade and opened the door. Inside, the two men huddled quietly. Martin told Carter that they were taking him to Trenton State. He assured Carter that nothing bad would happen to him. "Let me hook you up, and I'll take you down to Trenton," Martin said. "Eventually you're going to have to go, whether you beat 15 of us. Or 20 of us. There'll be a hundred more."

The promise of Martin's escort was all Carter needed. "I'll go," he said, and he rose to leave. Before he left, though, Carter scooped up the manuscript of his book and stuffed it into his sweatpants. Holding the sheaves of paper to his body, Carter left Rahway in the dead of that terrifying night. "If they had stripped me naked," he says, "I would have taken that manuscript. It was a little thread of hope. The hope that somebody, someday, would read it and understand what had happened to me. What *was* happening to me. It was my lifeline—my message beyond the walls."

Six years later, one September day in 1980, a 16-year-old black youth named Lesra Martin arrived at a used-book fair being held in a warehouse in Toronto. Lesra was accompanied by what he would call "my new Canadian family"—eight white entrepreneurs who had plucked him out of the Bushwick ghetto of Brooklyn the year before and brought him north to live and study in their tree-shaded house in Toronto. Lesra was extremely bright, and the Canadians had taken him to the fair to feed his increasing appetite for books, encouraging him to find works by black writers as a way of learning about the culture and history of his people. While roaming the warehouse, Lesra saw a black face on the cover of a hardback. He picked up the book—*The 16th Round: From Number 1 Contender to Number 45472* by Rubin (Hurricane) Carter.

Lesra paid a dollar for it.

That afternoon in his room, Lesra curled up with the book. *The 16th Round*, published to general acclaim in the fall of 1974, was an angry, eloquent indictment of growing up black in America, of the New Jersey judicial system that had arrested Carter and locked him up and of the medieval prisons that had so long confined him. Lesra became engrossed in Carter's tale of his life: his youthful days as a gang leader in New Jersey and his arrest at age 12 for attacking, with his Boy Scout knife, a man he accused of sexually assaulting him; Carter's six years in the Jamesburg (New Jersey) State Home for Boys, his escape from there and his enlistment in the Army in '54; his discharge from the Army and his quick arrest for the Jamesburg escape, for which he spent 10 months in the Annandale (New Jersey) Reformatory; his arrest in '57 for purse snatching ("the most dastardly thing I've ever done," Carter would say) and the four years he served in Trenton State for that crime; his release from Trenton; and his rise to fame as a prizefighter.

Early in the book, where Carter described how a policeman had hassled him as a boy, Lesra—who had experienced the same thing in Brooklyn—so identified with the story that he started reading it out loud to his Canadian friends. They too got caught up in the tale, and for the next few nights they took turns reading it to each other.

They learned, among other things, that at 2:30 in the morning of June 17, 1966, two black men walked into the Lafayette Bar in Paterson, opened fire with a shotgun and a pistol and instantly killed two people: the bartender, James Oliver, and a patron, Fred Nauyaks. A second patron, Hazel Tanis, died of her wounds a month later. A third customer, William Marins, suffered a head wound that partially blinded him. That night Carter and Artis were drinking and dancing in a local club, and, accompanied by a third black man, John Royster, they left the club and went driving in Carter's white Dodge Polaris about the time of the Lafayette Bar shootings. Carter let Artis drive.

At one point a policeman stopped the three men, but when he saw Carter in the backseat—Carter was probably the most recognizable citizen of Paterson, a nationally known fighter with a signature shaved head—he waved them on, telling them that the police were looking for "two Negroes in a white car." After Artis dropped off Royster, he and Carter suddenly fit the police description, and they were stopped again. The police whisked them off to the scene of the crime and then to a hospital, where Carter and Artis were placed before the wounded Marins. Asked by police if these were the men who had shot him, Marins shook his head no. Marins and Tanis agreed that the killers were light-skinned blacks, about six feet tall, and that the man with the shotgun, whom the state would later claim was Carter, had a pencil mustache. Carter was 5' 7", very dark, with a thick mustache and goatee; Artis was light-skinned and 6' 1".

Carter and Artis were given lie-detector tests, and each passed. The police then released them. Two weeks later, during a grand-jury hearing at which both Carter and Artis testified, the city's investigator in charge of the case, Vincent DeSimone, testified that "the physical description of the two holdup men is not even close [to that of Carter and Artis]." Furthermore, DeSimone said, both killers had worn "dark clothing." Carter had worn a white jacket, Artis a light-blue V-neck sweater. The grand jury returned no indictment.

Carter and Artis were arrested four months later, on Oct. 14, for the Lafayette Bar murders. What had happened during the interval to turn Carter into a light-skinned, six-foot black with a pencil mustache? The state had produced two eye-witnesses, Alfred Bello and Arthur Dexter Bradley, who would testify that Carter was one of the gunmen; Bello would also identify Artis. Both witnesses were repeat offenders, but their testimony was the key to convicting Carter and Artis, even though the state suggested no motive for the crime. Bello testified under oath that the state had offered him nothing for his testimony but protection. On June 29, 1967, Carter was given one concurrent and two consecutive life sentences, Artis three concurrent life terms.

While in prison Carter focused all his energy on resisting his jailers and fighting for his freedom. "I don't belong here," he told members of the prison board. "I am *not* a criminal. You are not going to treat me like you treat other people here." In prison he lost his right eye in what he called a "botched operation" to correct a detached retina. (It was to seek improved medical treatment for inmates that he then joined the Inmates Council.) Though his schooling was limited, he read Plato and imagined himself communing with Socrates. He was respected by fellow prisoners because he was a man of his word. "When he said he would do something," says Bobby Martin, "he did it."

When Lesra and his Canadian friends finished *The 16th Round*, they were convinced of Carter's innocence and curious about his fate. They searched through newspaper files at the Toronto Reference Library for information on him.

What they learned stunned them: Late in 1974, just weeks before the publication of Carter's book, Bello and Bradley recanted their testimony identifying Carter and Artis as the Lafayette Bar killers. They told both a public defender and reporter Selwyn Raab of the *New York Times* that Paterson police had pressured them into lying in exchange for reward money and lenient treatment for crimes they had committed.

"I was 23 years old and facing 80 to 90 years in jail [for robbery]," Bradley told Raab. "There's no doubt Carter was framed. . . . I lied to save myself."

Carter's case became a cause célèbre among civil libertarians and the political left, new and old. In the autumn of 1975, radio stations across the nation began playing Bob Dylan's new song, *Hurricane*. One of the verses went like this:

> Now all the criminals in their coats and their ties
> Are free to drink martinis and watch the sun rise
> While Rubin sits like Buddha in a ten-foot cell
> An innocent man in a living hell.

During the recantation furor of 1974, a tape recording surfaced of a De-Simone interview with Bello on Oct. 11, 1966. The New Jersey Supreme Court, to which Carter and Artis had appealed their convictions, listened to the tape. The transcript, the court stated, "shows that in the beginning Bello was unable to identify Artis as one of the two men and was not sure of Carter. He was also uncertain of the make of the white car used by the gunmen, which he had seen driving slowly through the area and later parked on the street. However, as the interview progressed, and after De-Simone had given assurances that Bello would receive favorable or sympathetic treatment, Bello became positive in his identification of Carter and Artis and the car in which they had been riding."

Not only had the defendants not known about such inducements, which they could have used to discredit Bello's testimony during their trial, but also Bello had not disclosed the fact that he had been offered more than protection. The New Jersey Supreme Court, in a 7–0 decision, overturned the 1967 verdict on the grounds that the state had violated the U.S.

Supreme Court's Brady rule, which requires prosecutors to give exculpatory evidence to the defense.

Carter and Artis got a second trial, in the fall of 1976. By then, however, Bello had reversed himself again. He testified once more that he had seen Carter and Artis leaving the murder scene carrying guns. This time, with an admitted perjurer as its key witness, the state offered a motive for the Lafayette Bar killings, portraying them as an act of "racial revenge." The alleged motive, presented at a time of widespread racial tension and fear of urban riots, was baseless in fact and prejudicial in nature, but the jury did not see it that way. On Dec. 22, Carter and Artis were convicted a second time of the Lafayette Bar murders. Their prison sentences from the first trial were reinstated.

Once the Canadians had caught up with all these developments, they were more intrigued than ever. They tracked down Carter by telephoning Trenton State, and then Lesra composed the first letter he had ever written. It began "Dear Mr. Carter" and ended with "Please write back. It will mean a lot." The letter described how a kid from one of the meanest ghettos in New York had ended up reading *The 16th Round* with a "family" of white folks in Toronto.

This is, in its fashion, a tale of two cities. Most of Lesra's Canadian friends had first met in the 1960s as students at the University of Toronto, where some were involved in social work and in helping expatriate Americans dodge the draft during the Vietnam War. The Canadians came from a salad of backgrounds. Sam Chaiton, who studied modern languages and literature, was the son of Jews who had immigrated to Canada after surviving the German death camp at Bergen-Belsen. Terry Swinton and his sister Kathy were the children of a wealthy Toronto business executive. Lisa Peters, divorced and with a young son, Marty, had emerged from a life of poverty to study psychology at the university. She would later become involved in drug rehabilitation work.

They and a few others eventually went into business together, importing batiks from Malaysia, and in 1976 they bought a house to share in Toronto. In '79, weary of long trips to the Orient, they began looking for something else to do with their restless energy. Chaiton and Terry Swinton went to work testing a device intended to reduce pollution in automobile engines. Their experiments took them that summer to Brooklyn, where the U.S. Environmental Protection Agency had a lab. It was there that they met Lesra, who had a summer job at the lab. Fascinated with these foreigners—"Dere go Canada!" he would say when they passed him—he started hanging around them.

"We responded to his spark and light and curiosity," says Chaiton. "He responded to us, and we became very friendly. We loved him right off the bat."

"They trusted me," Lesra says. "That meant a lot."

The boy lived with his parents, Alma and Earl, and five of his seven siblings in a fourth-story apartment with no railing on the top staircase and no knob on the door. They were churned in poverty. Earl had once been the lead singer in a popular doo-wop group, the Del Vikings, but the group had long ago disbanded, and he had been disabled since falling in a factory accident. Lesra's oldest brother, Earl Jr., was in prison for breaking and entering, and Lesra earned money for the family by bagging and delivering groceries and working at the lab.

When Chaiton and Terry Swinton returned to Toronto, they invited Lesra and a friend to visit them there. The boys spent three days playing in Toronto's parks and gamboling about town, and when the Canadians invited Lesra back a few weeks later, he fairly leaped into their arms. By the end of his second visit, the Canadians had grown so fond of him that they offered to make a home for him in Toronto and send him to school there. "We want to give you a chance to have a good education," Chaiton told Lesra. Lesra was eager to join them.

The Canadians approached Alma and Earl with their plan, and Earl flew to Canada to see where his 15-year-old son would live. It did not take him long to decide. Bushwick was a war zone. Lesra "didn't stand a chance if he stayed in Brooklyn," says Chaiton. "There was no way he would get anywhere."

When Lesra moved to Toronto in the fall of 1979, the effects of his ghetto life were manifest. He was malnourished and suffering a chronic infection that made his nose run and his eyes bloodshot. Antibiotics cured the infection; the Canadians' plump refrigerator, the malnutrition. But nothing would touch Lesra more deeply than being taken to an ophthalmologist and being fitted for eyeglasses. "I was blind," Lesra says, "and I didn't even know it. I had nothing to compare it to. The world was a blur."

His poor eyesight mirrored the state of his education. It was apparent that he could not attend public schools in Canada. "He was almost illiterate," says Chaiton. So he began tutoring Lesra at home. Since black ghetto English was Lesra's primary tongue, Chaiton says, he began teaching Lesra the King's English as if it were a second language. "I got a textbook instructing how to teach English to a foreigner," he says.

The Canadians read to Lesra from books such as Claude Brown's *Manchild in the Promised Land*, about the author's life in Harlem, and within a year they began urging him to read, on his own, the autobiography of Frederick Douglass. Lesra literally cried in fear of that book, with its long words and serpentine prose, but the Canadians kept after him until, in the summer of 1980, he managed to finish reading it. "The problem we had was not one of his intelligence but of the overwhelming feeling of inferiority he had," says Chaiton. "Overcoming those psychological barriers was awful."

Down in Trenton, meanwhile, Carter had been going through a sea change of his own. After his second conviction, he says, "I wanted to die." He had turned his face to the wall and withdrawn even further into himself. "I was looking down a long, dark tunnel," he says.

Carter saw and talked to almost no one, in prison or out. At his insistence, his wife, Mae Thelma, had stopped coming to see him. (They were divorced in 1984.) Carter hibernated with his books for three years. Then, on a sweltering afternoon in 1979, the summer that Lesra met the Canadians, Carter did something that he hadn't done in years. He went outside, to the yard, to escape the prison heat. "I was looking at the big wall, 30 feet high, with gun towers, and suddenly a light lit up, and I could see through the wall," he says. "No, it was not a hallucination! I was amazed. As suddenly as it appeared, it disappeared. I had heard about these things. So I began reading about Eastern religions. And I began growing my hair, something I hadn't done in 20 years. And I cut off my beard."

That was the Carter, softened around the edges, to whom Lesra wrote his letter in 1980. "I was leaving me, and I didn't even know it," Carter says. "I was opening up. And suddenly this letter came. How could I not respond? His letter had so much energy! There was a feeling there. . . . I typed a reply."

Thus began a relationship tying the man to the boy and the Canadians, a relationship that would ultimately change Carter's life. He and Lesra exchanged several letters that fall, and Lesra suggested visiting Carter when he was home in Brooklyn over Christmas. Carter hesitated; at Trenton visitors met prisoners in the abandoned cells of the former death row, next to the execution chamber where Bruno Hauptmann had died after being convicted of killing the Lindbergh baby, and Carter did not want to expose Lesra to its unearthly grimness. "This face is *trying* to get *there* and not bring another face here," he wrote to the family. "So if Lesra wishes to come—he will."

For Lesra it was haunting to step inside that tomb. He had a powerful sense that this was the world he had escaped when he went to Canada. "When I heard those steel gates closing behind me," he says, "I thought, I could be in here." Carter could feel him trembling when they embraced. The boy told the man about his family in Brooklyn and his new life in Canada, about his studies and the books he was reading. He was working on weekends, sending money home to his relatives, but he felt guilty for leaving them and accepting the chance he had been offered. "How did I deserve escaping that?" he asked Carter. "Why me?"

"You never deserved to be there in the first place," Carter told him, "so you don't have to feel guilty about getting out."

The two connected. Carter heard a boy's laughter that he had not heard in years. "Lesra was in a state of joy," Carter says. "You could feel it. It was like a son coming to see me. He was just so effervescent, and I loved the way he spoke, so precisely, and the way he laughed, even in this death house. The way Lesra was gave a lot of credibility to the Canadian family. I knew then that this was not a hoax. These were not people playing with our lives. It made me listen to them, and at that time I wasn't listening to anybody."

Early in 1981, at the Canadians' urging, Carter began calling them collect, and that February, Chaiton, Peters, and Terry Swinton drove to Trenton to see him. No one knew it at the time, of course, but the freeing of Hurricane Carter had begun. The Canadians were shocked at Carter's appearance. "He looked almost fragile." Swinton says. "A hundred and thirty-five pounds. He wasn't eating. A can or two of soup a day. He looked to us like a really gentle person, more like a writer than a prizefighter."

They teased Carter at once about his soft demeanor. "We don't believe you were ever the Number One contender," Chaiton said. "Come on!"

Carter turned on his "baleful stare," the one he had learned from hanging around and sparring with Sonny Liston, but the Canadians laughed at him. Peters's father had been an amateur fighter, and whether it was because of that or the poverty she and Carter had both experienced when they were young, the two began forming a strong attachment.

Over the next few months, in visits, phone calls and letters, the Canadians learned a lot about Carter's life in prison. "Don't you go to parole meetings?" Terry Swinton once asked.

"You have to admit guilt and be remorseful." Carter said. "How can I do that? I don't want a parole. I want to be exonerated."

"Do you need anything?" asked Swinton.

"I've got everything I need in my cell," Carter said. "Jesus, Socrates, and Buddha. I fill the voids in my life with figures in history. I don't need anything else."

"Man, that's a shame," Chaiton said. "If you've got everything you need, then it's not too bad a place."

Carter snapped off his words: "If you need anything, if you want anything, then this place has a hold over you because they can deny you that. The least painful thing is not to want anything. All I want is my freedom, and they deny me that every day, every hour that I am here. Do you understand?"

They soon understood a lot of things, and they liked what they saw of Carter. Indeed, Carter quickly became another member of their family, one who happened to be living far from home. The Canadians began by visiting him once a month for long weekends, staying in cheap motels near Trenton, and by the spring Carter was calling them collect several times a week. He wrote them a letter in which he said, "For the first time in my life . . . I can truly say that I trust somebody. I trust you. And without reservations."

That letter deepened the Canadians' resolve to help Carter find his way out. "If you had a brother in jail for something he didn't do," Terry Swinton says, "wouldn't you do everything possible to help him?"

For the next 4½ years, that is precisely what the Canadians did. At the end of 1981, using money they had made selling batiks, they turned their business efforts to renovating houses in Toronto. They also began spending 10 days a month in New Jersey, visiting Carter and becoming immersed in the history of the Lafayette Bar case. On Dec. 5, just before Artis was released on parole after serving 15 years, Carter was exiled to Trenton State's dreaded Vroom Readjustment Unit for the system's incorrigibles. Artis, a model prisoner, had attended Glassboro (New Jersey) State College while doing his time, leaving prison unguarded in the morning and returning at night, and had taught adult-education courses for inmates; Carter, meanwhile, was sent to Vroom for 90 days for refusing to stand up in his cell for a head count.

He spent the first 15 days in The Hole, "where you are like dead," he says. "No air, no ventilation. They turned on the heat in the summer and turned it off in the winter. Do you know what it's like to be powerless? Totally and utterly powerless? I never knew a prisoner who did not go to his cell at night and cry. Not every night, but every prisoner. You could hear them. You could hear everything. I still hear everything. Only this time I had Lisa, Lesra, Terry, and Sam to hold on to. They were my anchors."

In January 1982, with Carter calling Toronto for several hours a day, the Canadians' long-distance telephone charges were $4,238.39. By then the Canadians had broken Carter's resistance to accepting their gifts of food, clothing and appliances. Peters had argued, "You are denying yourself stuff before [the guards] have a chance to take it away. You are helping them keep you kept. If they want to take it, let them."

Now Carter was walking around in a pair of sheepskin slippers, wearing a velvet robe and watching television in his cell. Moreover, every month the Canadians sent him a 25-pound box of his favorite canned foods, chiefly exotic nuts and date breads. The only time the Canadian anchors were not there for him was when he quietly cut them loose in the fall of 1982, a few months after the New Jersey Supreme Court, by a 4–3 decision, rejected his appeal for a third trial on the grounds that the defense had not adequately demonstrated that suppressed evidence might have affected the outcome of the second trial. "It was just crushing," Terry Swinton says. Carter was inconsolable over the decision, despite a stinging dissent by Justice Robert Clifford, who wrote that the prosecution's chief witness, Bello, was "a complete, unvarnished liar, utterly incapable of speaking the truth."

Retreating into his carapace, Carter did not call his friends for nearly eight months. The house in Canada went into mourning. "I was getting ready to settle back into prison—absent good food, absent love and companionship," Carter says. "Lisa used to send me great big novelty cards. I had those pasted on those walls. I used to look at them. I felt helpless." He finally called the Canadians late in the summer of 1983. "I need you guys," he told them.

A few weeks later the Canadians decided to make one final push. They put their house on the market, and three of them—Chaiton, Terry Swinton and Peters—moved to New Jersey. The others moved into a smaller house in Toronto, where Lesra had graduated that year from high school with straight A's. He had just enrolled at the University of Toronto, where he would major in anthropology. The Canadians' commitment staggered Carter. "I was astounded," he says. "They set up house!"

Carter asked for, and received, a transfer from Trenton to Rahway, and the Canadians took an apartment near the prison, which was closer than was Trenton State to the New York offices of Carter's and Artis's lawyers, Myron Beldock and Lewis Steel, and to those of Leon Friedman, a renowned constitutional scholar who was assisting them with the case. For nearly two years the Canadians scoured New Jersey searching for new evidence and witnesses to exonerate Carter and Artis. They set up shop in Beldock's law firm at 46th Street and Fifth Avenue.

"The Canadians did the one thing that impresses me," says Beldock. "They did their homework." They had sent ahead a black case containing a three-by-nine-foot chart in which they had painstakingly detailed how the testimony of various state witnesses had changed over the years. "It was like a jump-start," says Beldock. "Very exciting."

Chaiton and Terry Swinton sat in the office surrounded by documents, and they pored through papers and folders. "It was like there were two law firms up there," Steel says. "One was Beldock's and the other was This Thing, across the hall, with the Canadians. You could go in there and ask one of these guys, 'We think in such and such a hearing that such and such was said. Do you know what I mean?' Twenty minutes later, they would come across the hall with a transcript open to the page: 'Is this what you're looking for?'"

The Canadians "heightened our awareness and our ability to handle even small issues, which all got woven into these briefs," Beldock says. Friedman was in charge of writing the legal sections of the briefs, and he recalls one day when he saw an unfamiliar statement in the draft of a brief. "Where did this come from?" Friedman asked Ed Graves, another attorney working on the case.

"The Canadians put it in," said Graves.

"Are you *sure* it's right?"

"Leon," said Graves, "if the Canadians say it's right, it's right."

What all the parties remember, as they were preparing the papers seeking a writ of habeas corpus from U.S. District Court Judge H. Lee Sarokin, was the crackling energy that went into the work—and the panicky sense that this was Carter's last chance to be freed from prison.

By the fall of 1985, Carter's transformation was so dramatic that he was almost unrecognizable. His cell looked like a yuppie pad. He was growing an amaryllis bulb in a pot, padding around on a Persian rug, listening to Otis Redding on his tape deck, hanging Manet prints on the walls, drying his hands on monogrammed towels and eating everything from crab béchamel to beef Wellington—all offerings from the Canadians, who were determined to grease his transition from prison to the outside world. He was greeting fellow prisoners with a smile and a nod and giving fatherly advice to rookie guards.

Two weeks before Sarokin's decision, convinced he would soon be free, Carter started giving away all of his belongings—his typewriter and clothes, his 125 books, his prints and his copper coil. Terry Swinton visited him in prison and asked him where he had gotten his raggedy haircut. "My hair's falling out in clumps," Carter said. "The tension, I guess."

On Nov. 6, 1985, Beldock called the Canadians' apartment to tell them that Sarokin's decision was coming down the next day. The veteran judge had studied voluminous files—by his own reckoning, Carter's is the most important case he has ever decided. "I have seen some very good briefs," Sarokin recalls, "but this was about the best set of briefs I've ever seen. A remarkably good job."

The next day the Swintons went to Sarokin's chambers and waited; Peters stayed at the New Jersey apartment, waiting for Terry Swinton to call, while she talked by phone with Carter. Chaiton, Lesra and the others were at home in Canada, sitting in silence. At about 11 o'clock, Graves walked out of Sarokin's chambers holding the opinion over his head, a smile wreathing his face. Swinton grabbed the papers and read:

"The extensive record clearly demonstrates that [the] petitioners' convictions were predicated upon an appeal to racism rather than reason, and concealment rather than disclosure. . . . To permit convictions to stand which have as their foundation appeals to racial prejudice and the withholding of evidence critical to the defense, is to commit a violation of the Constitution as heinous as the crimes for which these petitioners were tried and convicted."

Terry Swinton called Peters. She and Carter heard the click of call waiting. Peters hit the button. "We did it!" screamed Swinton. She hit the button again. "We won!" she told Carter.

Stunned, Carter raised his eyes. Then he shouted: "We won! We won!"

Paulene McLean, a friend of Lesra's, called Canada. "A complete silence fell over the house," says Lesra. "We were stunned. It was as if, after holding our breaths all those years, we finally could exhale."

In minutes, word had swept around the prison, and then radios were carrying the news. Prisoners flocked around Carter, patting him on the back, while others came running.

"Rube, you've won!"

"Rube, you're on the radio!"

"Way to go, Rube!"

Sarokin ordered Carter released the next day. The state appealed the judge's decision for 26 long months, right up to the U.S. Supreme Court, but it lost at every level. Finally, on Feb. 26, 1988, a Passaic County judge formally dismissed the 1966 indictments. The 22-year odyssey of Rubin Carter and John Artis had ended. It had touched many people in many ways; and it had left the two defendants changed beyond their memories.

For Artis, an only child raised by doting parents to be respectful and live responsibly, prison was a long nightmare that robbed him of his freedom, his wish to raise a family, his dreams of a career as a professional football player. He says it is not easy to confront a prospective employer, who always gets around to asking him what crime he was convicted of. "Ah, triple murder. But. . . ." It's a stigma to this day. And given the tortuous history of the case, it's difficult to explain away.

The state had tried hard to get Artis to testify against Carter. Officials took Artis to his father's house at Christmastime in 1974 and promised him freedom the next day if he fingered Rubin. He refused. "It would have been a lie," Artis says. "I wasn't brought up like that."

He could not help himself one day in 1973 when he was out on furlough. He was in Paterson, and he had to see the bar where the three people were murdered. He had never been in there. "It was no different than any other bar I'd ever seen," he says. "People kept lookin' at me. I stood inside the door and just looked around. I was trying to place what happened there, from the testimony in the trial . . . and then I left."

Artis lives in Portsmouth, Virginia, and works with troubled youths. "Being in prison is like being dead, and I want these kids to know that," he says. "And you know what? When we were cleared, no one even apologized."

Lesra Martin still goes back to Bushwick to visit his siblings and see the old friends who have escaped the usual traps. There are not many left. "I will never forget where I came from," he says. "Ghetto life will always be a part of me. I do not want that feeling to go away." He is further away from it today than ever. After graduating with honors from the University of Toronto, he went to graduate school in sociology at Dalhousie University in Halifax, Nova Scotia—a last stop on the Underground Railroad, which spirited slaves out of the South. He was drawn to the black community there. Last year, after getting his master's degree, Lesra entered the law school at Dalhousie. He is interested in constitutional law.

"I enjoy where I am now," Lesra says. "It's frightening that there are still hundreds of thousands of people in the ghettos who can't read or write. I'm no genius. I was just given access and resources. When you're going through what I went through, you don't realize how miraculous it is. But it *is* miraculous."

And Carter is where he is because Lesra was where he was. The former inmate No. 45472 moved to Canada in 1988, after the state dismissed the charges against him, and for the last four years he has spent much of his time reading, writing, and lecturing. He also got married. Lisa Peters is Lisa Carter now.

"I love it up here," says Carter, who intends to remain a U.S. citizen but has applied for landed immigrant status in Canada. He helped Chaiton and Terry Swinton write a book about their shared experience, called *Lazarus and the Hurricane*, using Lesra's Biblical name. Now, having also written a screenplay based on the book—it has been making the rounds in Hollywood—Carter and the Canadians are doing research on a proposed book about the kidnapping and murder of the Lindbergh baby in 1932.

They work out of a six-bedroom, half-timbered house on 10 acres of land, about 20 miles north of Toronto. They leased the house in a state of disrepair three years ago and converted it into the European hunting lodge that it resembles today. Carter also helped build the two-stall barn behind the house, and in fair weather he likes to spend his leisure riding his horse, Red Cloud, along the trails that wind through the woods and fields for miles around. "I always loved to ride horses, even back in my days as a fighter," Carter says. Horses certainly suit his new lifestyle. Carter has been given the name Badger Star by a medicine man in the Lakota Indian nation, whose culture and traditions Carter regularly studies. He has also been adopted into the family of a local Cree elder, Vern Harper.

Carter has been a willing speaker at colleges and law firms, and he was recently asked to deliver a lecture next fall at Harvard Law School before a student conference on the writ of habeas corpus. Says Judge Sarokin, "I can't think of anybody, with all the opposition now to habeas corpus, who better symbolizes the need for it than Hurricane Carter."

The Great Writ, as legal scholars call it, has been coming under heightened attack from the political right, and civil libertarians view it today as a kind of endangered species, particularly given the ultraconservative cast of the U.S. Supreme Court. Leslie Harris, chief legislative counsel of the American Civil Liberties Union in Washington, D.C., says that the Bush Administration has made elimination of habeas corpus the centerpiece of its efforts to look tough on crime. The writ is the only instrument by which the federal judiciary can correct abuses of the Bill of Rights at the state court level, according to Harris, and the Carter-Artis case shows how vital an instrument it can be.

It is now more than 25 years since Carter was arrested in Paterson, yet wherever he speaks, he tells a tale of a past that will not let him go. "It is not finished," he says. "I still feel the loneliness. I still feel the pain. I feel it now. I feel *everything*. The day you get out of prison is the day your sentence begins."

April 1992

THE LONG COUNT

Seventy years ago, in a heavyweight title bout in Chicago, Jack Dempsey knocked Gene Tunney to the canvas. What happened next made this the most famous fight in the Golden Age of Sports

"THE CROWD STRETCHED AWAY . . . SO FAR THAT SITTING IN THE HEAT AND GLARE OF THE CONE LIGHTS JUST UNDER THE RING YOU COULDN'T SEE THE LAST ROWS OF CUSTOMERS. YOU COULD ONLY SENSE THAT THEY WERE THERE FROM THE COMBERS OF SOUND THAT CAME BOOMING DOWN THE SLOPE OF THE STADIUM OUT OF THE DARKNESS."
—*Westbrook Pegler,* Chicago Daily Tribune, *Sept. 23, 1927*

The sudden and furious sequence of punches grew out of nowhere, without warning, in the center of the ring. It began when the heavyweight champion of the world, Gene Tunney, threw a long left jab at Jack Dempsey's two-day stubble. Aged and finished as a fighter though Dempsey was, he saw it coming, canted his head slightly to the left, slipping the punch, and countered with a looping right that struck Tunney on the left side of his face.

Dempsey's right forced Tunney back. The challenger did not hesitate. He moved forward, looking as though he'd picked up an old, familiar scent from his days as a saloon fighter, a kind of psychic blood trail leading to a kill, and as he closed on Tunney, he suddenly planted his right foot and, in a single rolling motion of his shoulders, lowered himself into a crouch and then sprang out of it, throwing a left hook as he rose. The blow caught the champion going back, driving him even farther toward the ropes, and at once Dempsey was all over him. He cocked Iron Mike, the name to which his right hand answered, and fired.

Nine rows back, a 20-year-old racehorse trainer named H.A. (Jimmy) Jones, later famed for training Triple Crown winner Citation, leaped to his feet when he saw Dempsey wading in to strike. "Dempsey was like a cat—just like a cat!—the way he pounced," Jones, 90, recalls. "After chasing Tunney all night, Dempsey finally got a whack at him. And he whacked him good!"

Up at ringside, in the press rows, the newly appointed sports editor of the *Washington Post*, 22-year-old Shirley Povich, had never seen or heard a crowd like this nor ever would. "Most thought Dempsey was in for the kill," says Povich, 92. "They had been waiting for it from the start. It was a Dempsey crowd, and everything he did brought a roar."

More than 145,000 souls had collected that night in Chicago's Soldier Field, the largest crowd ever to witness a prizefight, and for nearly 30 minutes the show had been a monotonous parody of the first Dempsey-Tunney fight, a year earlier at Philadelphia's Sesquicentennial Stadium, where the quicker, fitter Tunney, 28 years old and boxing masterfully, won all 10 rounds against an aging, awkward champion who, at 31, appeared to have nothing left after three years of ring idleness. It was the first time in history that the heavyweight title had changed hands on a decision, and the public resented Tunney for dethroning the revered Dempsey in such unworthy fashion. "A lousy 10-round decision," says Povich. Now here they were again, and after 6½ rounds of Tunney's sticking and moving, beating Dempsey to the punch, Dempsey whacked him with the hook and, uncorking Iron Mike, smashed him back against the ropes.

Tunney flailed weakly with a right, exposing his head, and for the first time in almost 17 rounds of fighting—in what had been for Dempsey, who had more one-round knockouts than any other heavyweight in history, the maddening pursuit of a ghost—Dempsey finally had the target before him, stunned and stationary. So he stepped inside and ripped a short, jolting left to the side of Tunney's jaw. It was a nearly perfect hook; had it landed another inch or two forward, on the point of the chin, Tunney's cornermen would have been reaching for the smelling salts to wake their fighter up. His knees buckling, the champion began to sink along the ropes. In a rush to finish him, Dempsey grazed Tunney's face with a poorly thrown right, then lashed another hook to his head. Tunney was pitching backward—his right leg, bent awkwardly, was caught under him—when

Dempsey, looming like a thunderhead, drove him down into the deck with a hard right to the face.

Tunney landed with a thud that no one heard. Pandemonium had descended on the place.

"Dempsey was hitting him as he went down," recalls Jones. "Bang! Bang! Bang! Bang! I'll never forget it. I could see the glaze in Tunney's eyes as he got hit. A right and a left and a right! Four or five times, real quick. Hard, hard punches! His mouth opened up, and then he went down on his back."

From the press rows Paul Gallico of the New York *Daily News* was heard yelling in a high-pitched voice into a phone to his editors, "Tunney is down from a series of blows!" Nearby, sitting right behind Damon Runyon, Povich could hear voices around him screaming at the fighter still standing in the ring, "Come on, Jack!"

Povich sees it yet today: "Tunney is going down, and my memory is sharp of Dempsey pummeling him on the head as he sags. And I can still see Tunney's hand, a vivid memory, reaching for the [middle] rope and finally grabbing it."

Beyond Soldier Field, 50 million people gathered by their home radios as announcer Graham McNamee, speaking to more people at one time than any man ever had, blurted out the news in his cracked, quavering voice: "And then Dempsey comes back, and Tunney is down! Tunney is down from a barrage of lefts and rights to the face!" Nine people died of heart attacks listening to that broadcast, three of them during McNamee's blow-by-blow of the seventh round.

Eleven-year-old Dan Satenstein was at home in Chicago sharing the earphones of a crystal set with his 20-year-old brother, Charlie, when Dempsey pounced. "I started to scream, 'Tunney is down! He knocked him down!'" Dan, 81, recalls. "My [two] brothers started screaming and jumping up and down. But then there was such bedlam and noise at Soldier Field that we lost the audio. 'I can't hear,' I kept saying. 'Everything is drowned out.'"

The voice of McNamee was lost in those great combers of sound that boomed out of the Chicago night. In Hell's Kitchen, on Manhattan's tough West Side, another 11-year-old boy had been leaning far out the window of his tenement flat and listening, across a 10-foot gangway, to a neighbor's radio describing the fight. "I'd never seen or heard anything like it before," says 81-year-old Harold Robbins, author of *The Carpetbaggers* and other popular novels. "I was hanging there, from my waist out. I could hear the voice, but then there was all the excitement and noise, and I couldn't tell who was down or what was going on."

It was precisely 10:34 p.m. on Sept. 22, 1927, 70 years ago this week, and what was going on in the middle of Soldier Field was the most dramatic, memorable sporting event of its era, the so-called Golden Age of Sports. Even today, seen in the silvery flicker of old films, the aftermath of the knockdown bedevils the eye and haunts the memory of that night.

The knockdown rule decreed by the Illinois State Athletic Commission was plain enough: *When a knockdown occurs the timekeeper shall immediately arise and announce the seconds audibly as they elapse. The referee shall first see that the opponent retires to the farthest corner and then, turning to the timekeeper, shall pick up the count in unison with the timekeeper, announcing the seconds to the boxer on the floor. Should the boxer on his feet fail to stay in the corner, the referee and timekeeper shall cease counting until he has so retired.*

A dazed Tunney is sitting on the floor, and Dempsey skips around him, heading toward his own corner, directly behind Tunney, while timekeeper Paul Beeler, at ringside, counts. . . .

One!

Now Dave Barry, the referee, is touching Dempsey's chest and pointing to a neutral corner to his left, ordering Dempsey there, but the fighter ignores him and steps into his own corner, about five feet behind Tunney, who has just uncrooked his twisted right leg. . . .

Two!

Barry follows Dempsey, standing between him and the fallen fighter, and he again points to the neutral corner, yelling at Dempsey to leave. . . .

Three!

Only now does Dempsey move, sliding his hand along the top rope as he lumbers away from his corner. . . .

Four!

Here Barry finally turns toward Beeler and hears the count. . . .

Five!

But instead of picking up that count in unison with his timekeeper, Barry calls out, "*One!*"

The Long Count, the name by which this fight forever will be known, has begun.

Of all the major sports figures of the 1920s—from Red Grange in football to Bill Tilden in tennis, Bobby Jones in golf and Man o' War in racing—none cut a swath as wide as the two largest figures of all: Jack Dempsey and Babe Ruth. Born less than five months apart in 1895, they arrived at the dawning of the Golden Age of Sports as rising folk heroes: Dempsey as the new heavyweight champion of the world, Ruth as the emerging home run king.

Just hours before the Long Count, with a man on base in the bottom of the ninth inning and the New York Yankees losing to the Detroit Tigers 7–6, Ruth struck a towering two-run, game-winning homer that landed five rows from the top of Yankee Stadium's rightfield stands. He carried the bat in his hand around the bases. The home run was his 56th of the season. Eight days later, on Sept. 30, he would hit number 60. The Yankees would never again be quite the team they were that year—perhaps the greatest baseball team that ever played—and Ruth would never have a season like that again. Indeed, between Soldier Field and Yankee Stadium, those closing days of September 1927 would be the zenith of that era in sports.

And so, in the end, there was a sense of symmetry in what was happening in those frantic days surrounding the Long Count, with Ruth circling the bases as Dempsey ascended as a martyr into myth.

Never in the history of American sports had there been a scene like the one at Soldier Field. For hours through the early evening, as American flags fluttered on the rim of the stadium and a light rain came and went, thousands of people swarmed across Michigan Avenue and filed through the gates. "Along the upper sweeps of the stadium, 500 and 600 feet away, it looked like a flow of army ants through the dim, hazy light," wrote Grantland Rice in the *New York Herald Tribune*.

The day before, as the gate swelled toward a record $2,658,660—about $22 million in today's dollars and thus the largest gate, by far, in the history of boxing—the promoter of the fight, Tex Rickard, called the event "the crowning achievement of my life." Rickard has been called the greatest boxing promoter of all time, and he was certainly among the most flamboyant showmen of his era. He was born in a dusty roadside hovel in Missouri, and on his way to Soldier Field he prospected for gold in the Yukon, was a faro dealer in the Klondike, ran saloon gambling halls in gold-rush towns in Alaska and Nevada, served as the marshal of Henrietta, Texas, owned a cattle ranch in Paraguay and was a soldier of fortune in South Africa.

Along that path, he began promoting fights. In 1906, in Goldfield, Nevada, Rickard put up $30,000 in cash as the guaranteed purse for the lightweight championship bout between Joe Gans and Battling Nelson. It was twice the largest purse ever before offered for a lightweight fight, and Rickard caused a local sensation by putting the money on display, in stacks of gleaming, newly minted $20 gold pieces, at a Goldfield bank.

Rickard thus launched himself as a seller of fights. By 1927 he was at the apex of his powers. He had first promoted Dempsey in 1919, when the fighter took the heavyweight title from Jess Willard, and together they had grown rich beyond any contemporary measure in sports. There were five million-dollar gates during the '20s, and Dempsey and Rickard figured in all of them. Indeed, with Rickard at the till, Dempsey became sports' fattest cash cow. In the first four of those million-dollar gates, he attracted customers who paid nearly $6 million, and the Long Count would bring that sum to nearly $9 million.

"Who can tie that for five appearances?" wrote Rice. "Who can come within $5,000,000 of [Dempsey's] mark? . . . He is the greatest drawing card in sport."

And Chicago, to be sure, was Rickard's piéce de résistance. Sitting at ringside, he presided over the richest, gaudiest assembly of people that any sporting event had ever drawn. For days, trains pulling private and Pullman cars had converged on Chicago from every point of the compass—*The Broadway Limited* from New York, the Illinois Central from the South, the Santa Fe from out West—in what one railroad worker described as "the greatest troop movement since the war." When a train chartered by James J. Corbett, the former heavyweight champion, arrived at the LaSalle Street Station, half the talent of Broadway stepped off, including George M. Cohan and Irving Berlin.

Rickard had the audacity to offer 42,000 *ringside* seats, at $40 apiece. Some of those seats were 137 rows back from the ring, but Rickard sold them all—to Hollywood entertainers such as Al Jolson and Charlie Chaplin; to European royalty, including Princess Xenia of Greece; to all those Eastern swells, the Astors and the Harrimans and the Whitneys, who had arrived by private railroad cars; and to thousands of bankers, mobsters, industrialists, lawyers, and politicians. "Plutocrats rubbed elbows with pickpockets," the *Herald Tribune* reported. They had occupied the swankiest hotel rooms in town, and now they hovered like moths around the brightly lit ring—Rickard's personal signature on the night, with its gilded posts and the gilded water buckets hanging from them.

"Everybody was there," recalls Povich, one of 1,200 newsmen at the fight. "If you were a celebrity, you *had* to be there. It was the place to be. It was being whispered that some ringside seats were selling for a *hundred* dollars. My, my!"

Pridefully beholding his grandest creation, Rickard turned to the man sitting next to him, Hype Igoe of the *New York World*, and said, "Kid, if the earth came up and the sky came down and wiped out my first 10 rows, it would be the end of everything. Because I've got in those 10 rows all the world's wealth, all the world's big men, all the world's brains and production talent. Just in them 10 rows, kid. And you and me never seen nothing like it."

The fight had everything a showman could want in a promotion. It had the smell of money and the taste of blood, as all fights did when Dempsey was involved; a sense of intrigue born of persistent rumors that the fix was in for Dempsey; and a powerful current of history and romance. (No heavyweight champion who had lost the title had ever won it back.) Could the old Manassa Mauler come back and reclaim his crown from this dancing, counterpunching pretender? Most of all, in the national psyche, the fight offered two men as contrasting in their styles outside the ring as in. It was in this contrast that Rickard found the promotional hook he had also used in his other most celebrated bouts: the pitting of a hero against a villain.

Dempsey had played the villain in his day. Unfairly accused of being a draft dodger in World War I—he was exempted on grounds that he was the sole support of a half dozen relatives—Dempsey was widely perceived as a slacker when he defended his title against the French war hero Georges Carpentier on July 2, 1921. He was cast as Lucifer to Carpentier's Archangel Gabriel. The fight, which grossed a then staggering $1,626,580, was the first of Rickard's million-dollar gates. By 1927 the perception of Dempsey as unpatriotic had dissipated, and he was the fallen warrior seeking to defy the Fates.

Of course, there was that other powerful undercurrent nourishing Dempsey's enormous popularity: Born in Manassa, Colorado, and raised there and in Utah, he was seen as a rugged individualist from the Wild West—the free-roaming hero that Hollywood was newly celebrating in film. The ninth of 11 children of a shiftless father who did not support his family, Jack left home mud-poor at 16, a loner who did everything from mining coal to hauling beets to picking fruit. Always scrounging for work, he lived in hobo jungles and "rode the rods" between towns, lying on the two narrow cables that ran along the bellies of railroad cars, and he fought countless fights in saloons and mining towns under the name Kid Blackie. Pushing his way into a bar full of lumberjacks with noses like door-knobs, he would announce, in the manner of John L. Sullivan, "I can lick any man in the house. For a buck." That's how his West was won.

Dempsey had a fighter's body, with long, supple arms, sloping shoulders and a perfect set of pins. He was a savage in the ring, a remorseless aggressor from bell to bell. He even whaled at sparring partners as though they were opponents. Box? Who said anything about boxing?

When Dempsey was young and lithe and fit, he would pace endlessly, moving back and forth across a room in his slightly pigeon-toed walk. "He was like something wild in a cage then," recalled his former trainer Jimmy DeForest a few days before the Long Count. "I said to him one night when he was walking around, 'You must have something serious in your life that makes you this way . . . something on your conscience.' He only laughed: 'I was always this way since ever I can remember.'" Dempsey was often likened, as Jimmy Jones expressed it, to a pouncing cat. In newspaper accounts of the Long Count, he would be described by turns as "an infuriated animal" and "a wounded lion" and "pantherlike."

Dempsey's professional career was a long and profitable extension of his mining camp brawls. He was a darkly tanned man of 6' 1" and 187 pounds when he showed up in Toledo to meet Willard for the title in 1919. Willard was a veritable lumberjack at 6' 6½" and 245, but Dempsey had chopped down men that size before, and he attacked Willard from the first bell. Before the round was over, Willard had been on the deck seven times, and Dempsey had caved in the right side of his face, shattering the cheekbone in 13 places with a single left hook. Willard did not come out for Round 4. "He had the best left hook in boxing history," ring historian Bert Sugar says of Dempsey.

Never was Dempsey more the wounded cat than in his 1923 title defense against Luis Firpo of Argentina, a melee that has been called the wildest, most thrilling heavyweight bout of all time. It began when the 220-pound Firpo, sidestepping Dempsey's charge, dropped the champion within seconds of the opening bell. By the end of the first round Firpo had been down seven times, Dempsey twice. At one point Firpo shoved and belted Dempsey through the ropes and into the press row. It took a reporter and a Western Union operator to push the enraged, screaming champion back into the ring. The two fighters somehow survived the round, but Firpo never made it through the second. A left hook dropped him for the ninth and final time.

Dempsey came under attack in the press for barroom fouls—hitting on the break and striking Firpo as he climbed to his feet—but fight fans loved him. "He was uncontrolled and uncontrollable violence," says Randy Roberts, author of the 1979 biography *Jack Dempsey: The Manassa Mauler.* "He was the Mike Tyson of his day, always portrayed as an animal, with the outlaw image. But there was an authenticity about him. Dempsey was exactly who he was. He was comfortable being himself. The love for Dempsey was the love for a person who always wanted to be himself. No airs."

Tunney was his antithesis, real as well as perceived. He represented an altogether different set of values and aspirations. He was born in New York

City, the son of an Irish Catholic stevedore, and raised in a Bank Street row house not far from the Hudson River in Greenwich Village. Tunney first learned to fight as an amateur at local clubs, but not until he joined the Marine Corps and went to Europe with the American Expeditionary Force in World War I did he begin to box seriously. After winning the AEF's light heavyweight title, he decided to turn pro and, on returning to the States, to take aim at Dempsey's title. Unlike the onetime desperate hobo, Tunney seemed to spring straight out of a Horatio Alger novel. He suggested one of those young heroes who, in pursuit of self-improvement, studies hard, lives clean, sleeps tight, and practices self-discipline. He thought of himself as a pugilist, not a fighter, and he approached boxing as Capablanca approached chess.

"I thought of pugilism as a fencing bout of gloved fists rather than an act of assault and battery," Tunney wrote in *Arms for Living*, his 1941 autobiography. "More intricate than fencing because you wield two weapons, more of the chess play of blow and counterblow. . . . I became absorbed in the rational processes of the jab, the hook, side step and counter, the feint, the lead." He would do to Dempsey what Corbett, the defensive master, had done to the brawling Sullivan in 1892, boxing him silly and taking the title from him. "Defense was my natural technique," Tunney wrote, "the science of sparring, the strategy of it, thinking expressed with boxing gloves."

In fact, on his long and logical climb to Soldier Field, Tunney did just what he had planned all along. While working his way up, he defeated Battling Levinsky to win the light heavyweight title in 1922 and became one of the finest boxers that division has ever known: a crafty, clever mover and puncher who studied his opponents, developed strategies for beating them and always showed up trim, prepared, and in control. That was how Tunney climbed into the ring against Dempsey in Philadelphia in 1926.

For 10 rounds Dempsey hardly landed a solid blow, while Tunney sliced and pounded him bloody and nearly blind. When the fight was over, Dempsey's eyes were swollen into slits. He wanted to acknowledge the new champion but could not see his way across the ring. "Take me to him," he muttered to an aide. There, whipped and bowed, he hugged Tunney and turned and left—more popular in defeat than he had ever been in victory.

Just as Dempsey was a 19th-century man, a simple, straight-talking natural from the vanishing Old West, so Tunney was a 20th-century creation, a more complex hybrid from the city. "In the 1920s, American society was increasingly becoming the society of Sinclair Lewis's George Babbitt," says Richard Davies, a professor of sports history at the University of Nevada at Reno. "A society of business and industry, of technology and organization, increasingly bureaucratized, urbanized and regimented. Tunney represented this kind of life in which Americans were being captured. Dempsey represented those values and that way of life that Americans once had and lost, the rugged, self-made individualist. It is one of the reasons that he was so popular."

And Tunney was not. He made the mistake of reading books and often came across in public as an aloof, condescending snob who had what the *New York Times* called "an unconcealed dislike for the sport." Arriving in Chicago to begin training for the rematch, he told a large gathering that he was not in town for a fight. "I'm here to train for a boxing contest," he said. "I don't like fighting. Never did." In camp one day, bristling over Rickard's talk of a possible $3 million gate and Tunney's $1 million payday, the champion said, "I deprecate this insistent talk of money. . . . It is useless and disgusting."

While Dempsey trained at Lincoln Fields, a racetrack south of Chicago, Tunney did his sparring at the Cedar Crest Country Club in Lake Villa, Illinois, a resort town 50 miles northwest of the city. While Dempsey spent his leisure time playing pinochle and wrestling with bent-nosed pugs, Tunney passed his hours with Eddie Eagan, tediously identified in the prints as "a Yale Rhodes scholar and amateur boxing champion," or curled up in a library with W. Somerset Maugham's *Of Human Bondage*.

Tunney had been in training since late May, and he appeared even keener and more confident than he had been the year before. He had already won two major battles before the first bell. He had been granted his demands for a 20-foot ring—Dempsey had wanted a tighter 18-footer—and for strict enforcement of the knockdown rule. Tunney's handlers did not want Dempsey hovering near a stricken Tunney, as he had done against Willard and Firpo, waiting to pounce before Tunney even straightened up.

Those two victories aside, Tunney should have been an overwhelming favorite to win the rematch, but in the days leading up to the fight, as Chicago filled with gamblers, a surge of Dempsey money had turned him from a 7-to–5 underdog to an even money proposition. No doubt the enormous sentiment for Dempsey was at work here—the hope that he would win overpowered rational judgment—but rumors also had been intensifying that the fight was in the bag for the former champion. Davey Miller, who ran a pool hall with a gambling room upstairs, was the leading referee in Chicago in those days, and he was expected to be the third man in the ring. Word had gotten out that mob boss Al Capone had bet $45,000 on Dempsey. When Dempsey's former manager, Doc Kearns, arrived in town, he visited Capone and asked him how he thought Dempsey would do.

"'I got a big bet on him that says he wins,'" Kearns would recall Capone saying. "'Not only that, I've let the word get out that he'd better get a fair shake. Nothing preferential, understand. But a fair shake.'"

This did not bode well for Miller. In his 1938 book *Farewell to Sport*, Paul Gallico wrote that "Davey Miller was Capone's man, and blatantly so." The Chicago boxing officials responsible for picking the referee had heard not only about Capone's bet but also about a brother of Miller's putting $50,000 on Dempsey. Seeking to minimize the risk of scandal, the officials sat Miller and put Barry in the ring, where now he is standing about five feet from Tunney and still counting.

Two!

Tunney, sitting in a slouch with his left hand clutching the middle rope, is looking at the canvas and trying to sit up. . . .

Three! . . . Four!

Until now in a daze, his face vacant, Tunney suddenly raises his eyes from the deck and looks up at Barry as he continues the count. . . .

Five!

Tunney shifts his gaze away from Barry to his corner, directly across the ring. . . .

Six!

"Stay down!" his corner is yelling above the din, urging him to use the full count. "Stay down!" Barry moves closer to Tunney and is now standing almost over him as Barry raises his arm higher and drops it farther in a more distinct toll. . . .

Seven!

Directly behind Barry, outside the ring in Dempsey's corner, Dempsey's trainer, Leo Flynn, stands and holds up his right hand, palm facing out toward the fighter, to warn him not to leave the neutral corner early. . . .

Eight!

Barry tolls his right arm deeper. . . .

Nine!

Still holding the rope, Tunney pulls himself to his feet.

He had been down about 14 seconds in all, the first time he'd ever been on the floor in his career, and he did the only thing he knew how to do to survive. He had trained running backward for miles, planning for all contingencies, and he was running backward and sideways now as Dempsey chased him from post to post and from rope to rope. This was Dempsey's golden chance. Tunney ran and danced away. Dempsey lunged and missed with a hook. Tunney skipped left and darted right. He was trying to clear his head. He was in superb physical shape, which saved him, and as the seconds wore on, Dempsey began to slow. He was tiring of the chase. At one point he waved his left arm in a beckoning gesture. "Come on and fight!" Dempsey said.

Tunney wanted no more of him in the seventh. "Now, wasn't that a silly thing to say to me?" Tunney said later. "Do you really think he believed I was going in to make that same mistake all over again?"

Tunney survived the round, of course, but Dempsey really did not. It had exposed him for the aging, shot fighter that he was. "He had punched himself out," Povich says. Dempsey had no legs either, and after Tunney caught him with a straight right in the eighth, dropping him to his knees, he had nothing left.

Dempsey was in desperate trouble, but he hung on through the 10th. "In the last round Tunney was pecking away at Dempsey's face, and it looked like a piece of beefsteak," recalls Jones. "If that fight had gone any longer, Tunney would have won by a knockout. Whupped him outright!"

"We were devastated when Tunney won," says Studs Terkel, then a 14-year-old Chicago boy and later a prize-winning author. "Devastated! Who was this guy Tunney? This guy who recited Shakespeare? Dempsey *was* boxing in the '20s. Caruso was the opera, Chaplin was films, Ruth was baseball and Dempsey was boxing. We couldn't believe he had lost."

Of course, the Long Debate began swirling before the fighters reached the showers, raising two central questions that will forever go unanswered. Had Barry picked up the count in unison with the timekeeper at five, instead of starting again from one, would Tunney have been able to get up before the count of 10? Tunney says he could have arisen at Barry's count of three, when he first looked up at the referee. Had Barry started his count at five, leaving Tunney four fewer seconds to recover on the deck, would Tunney *then* have been able to escape Dempsey's initial charge across the ring?

Barry did not follow the rule as written, but the Illinois commission denied Dempsey's subsequent appeal. The Long Count was Dempsey's last fight, and no other ending to it could have served him half as well. Says Povich, "The loser, Dempsey, emerged from the fight as the hero—gypped out of a legitimate comeback for the title. This was, in a sense, the best and luckiest thing that ever happened to him. The general impression was that the fight was stolen from him. It served Dempsey like nothing else could have as far as his popular image was concerned."

Dempsey and Rickard remained close friends after the Long Count. In late 1928, in a deal sealed by a handshake, they agreed to become partners in the fight-promoting business. In January 1929 an ailing Rickard summoned Dempsey to his hospital bed in Miami. He had just undergone an emergency appendectomy. "I got it licked," Rickard said. "When I want you, I'll call you." He called a few hours later. Rickard died in Dempsey's arms.

To those in the fight game Tunney remained a remote figure the rest of his life. He had one title defense after the Long Count, earning $625,000 for knocking out a plodder named Tom Heeney in July 1928, and then quit, vacating the title. Along the way he had truly reinvented himself, like Fitzgerald's Gatsby, and his marriage to Polly Lauder, a wealthy socialite, lifted him further, from the streets of Greenwich Village to the blue lawns of Greenwich, Connecticut. He once lectured on Shakespeare at Yale, and he took walks in Europe with George Bernard Shaw. He became a business executive and virtually disappeared from the fight game.

In 1965, a year after Cassius Clay took the heavyweight title from Sonny Liston, Tunney went to Washington, D.C., to see his son John sworn into Congress. "I don't know anything about the heavyweights except Liston and Clay and [Floyd] Patterson," the former champion said. "And they are so bad, I have lost interest."

A heavy drinker, Tunney died of blood poisoning on Nov. 7, 1978. His funeral was private. He and Dempsey had stayed in touch over the years, and Dempsey was shaken by his passing. "I feel like a part of me is gone," he said. "As long as Gene was alive, I felt we shared a link with that wonderful period of the past. Now I feel alone."

The thing about Dempsey, though, is that he rarely *was* alone. By the time he died of heart failure on May 31, 1983, his life had been long and full of wonders, from his time as a saloon tough through the championship years and even beyond. Nine months after Rickard died, Dempsey lost his fortune in the stock-market crash. "Four million dollars in one day," says his daughter Barbara. But he had been broke before, and he picked himself up and fought more than 100 exhibitions, did some refereeing and acting and, still smarting from the old slacker label, enlisted in the U.S. Coast Guard at the outbreak of World War II. He served in the Pacific.

Of all the things Dempsey did over those postfighting years, though, nothing did more to establish him as an enduring landmark of his times than his life as a Manhattan restaurateur. He was the warmest of handshakers and the softest of touches. First at 50th Street and Eighth Avenue and later on Broadway, Jack Dempsey's Restaurant was a shrine for out-of-town visitors—whom he inevitably greeted with "Hiya, pally"—and a hangout for old boxers and a medley of sporting figures. Dempsey sat by the window waving at passersby.

"He never forgot where he came from," says his widow, Deanna. "He never forgot who he was." He greeted and schmoozed and told stories. About riding the rods. About the mining towns. About the day he beat Willard in the roaring Ohio heat. And always the one about the Long Count, under the lights at Soldier Field, and the night he lost but won.

September 1997

"THE FIGHT'S OVER, JOE"

*More than two decades after they last met in the ring,
Joe Frazier is still taking shots at Muhammad Ali,
but this time it's a war of words*

I t is always the punch a fighter does not see that hurts the most, and the little girl was so sweet and innocent-looking, standing shyly at her mother's side, that there was no way Joe Frazier could have seen it coming.

The former heavyweight champion of the world was sitting under a tent on the banks of the Delaware River in Philadelphia, at a place called Penn's Landing, where his touring autograph show had set up shop at an outdoor festival. With his son Marvis, Joe trains and manages fighters out of his Broad Street gym in Philly, but he also spends an inordinate amount of time signing his name in that long, sweeping script on photographs of himself and on merchandise from his portable store. On this languid September afternoon, under a sign that announced MEET YOUR PHILLY SPORTS HEROES, flanked by stacks of SMOKIN' JOE hats ($10) and T-shirts ($23), Frazier was signing everything put in front of him, gratis, schmoozing with parents as he posed for pictures with their children and hamming it up for the cameras. He was all grins and merriment for the scores of people who had waited in the sun for an audience.

At about 2:30 p.m., Frazier looked up and saw a petite and demure 10-year-old, Ginnysue Kowalick, her head slightly bowed, standing across the table. "My daughter doesn't know you too well, Joe," said the girl's mother, Marilyn Kowalick. "She has a question, but she's too shy to ask."

Frazier nodded. "O.K." he said.

"She wants to know if you ever beat Muhammad Ali," Marilyn said.

A scowl passed like a shadow down Frazier's face, and for a long moment he sat reeling in his chair, leaning back as his eyes rolled wildly from side to side, and he groaned, groping for words: "Agghh. . . . Ohhh. . . . Agghh. . . ."

Alarmed at Frazier's reaction, Marilyn leaned forward and said, "I'm sorry."

At last reassembling his scattered faculties, Frazier looked at Ginnysue and said, "We locked up three times. He won two, and I won one. *But look at him now*. I think I won all three."

Two days earlier, at the Essex House in New York City, the object of Frazier's turbulent emotions sat folded on a couch in a suite of rooms overlooking Manhattan's Central Park. He lay back and fumbled with his third package of shortbread cookies. White crumbs speckled his black shirt—the remains of his day, the emblematic story of his life. Ali had just spent most of an afternoon signing a limited edition of large photographs that showed him, dressed in luminous white, holding the Olympic torch during the opening ceremonies of the 1996 Games in Atlanta. He was in New York for the screening of yet another documentary celebrating his life, this one a TNT production with the unlikely title, *Muhammad Ali: The Whole Story.*

Ali speaks in barely a whisper now, unless he has an audience, and then his voice rises raspingly, just enough to carry a room. Surrounded by a small group of fans and followers at the Essex House earlier that day, he could not resist the chance to perform. He raised his right fist in the air and said, "This is the piston that got to Liston!" He also asked the gathering, "Know what Lincoln said when he woke up from a two-day drunk?"

A dozen heads craned forward. Ali's eyes widened in shock. "I freed the *whooo?*" he blurted to the nearly all-white audience. High, nervous laughter filled the room.

"I saw Joe Frazier in Philly last week," a voice nearby said quietly.

Ali's eyes grew wide again. "Joe Fraysha?" he whispered.

He has known for years of Frazier's anger and bitterness toward him, but he knows nothing of the venom that coursed through Frazier's recent autobiography, *Smokin' Joe.* Of Ali, Frazier wrote, "Truth is, I'd like to rumble with that sucker again—beat him up piece by piece and mail him back to Jesus. . . . Now people ask me if I feel bad for him, now that things aren't going so well for him. Nope. I don't. Fact is, I don't give a damn. They want me to love him, but I'll open up the graveyard and bury his ass when the Lord chooses to take him."

Nor does Ali know what Frazier said after watching him, with his trembling arm, light the Olympic flame: "It would have been a good thing if he would have lit the torch and fallen in. If I had the chance, I would have pushed him in."

Nor does Ali know of Frazier's rambling diatribe against him at a July 30 press conference in Atlanta, where Frazier attacked the choice of Ali, the Olympic light heavyweight gold medalist in 1960 and a three-time heavyweight champion of the world, as the final bearer of the torch. He called Ali a "dodge drafter," implied that Ali was a racist ("He didn't like his white brothers," said Frazier) and suggested that he himself—also an Olympic champion, as a heavyweight, in 1964—would have made a better choice to light the flame: "Why not? I'm a good American. . . . A champion is more than making noise. I could have run up there. I'm in shape."

And while Frazier asserts at one turn that he sees "the hand of the Lord" in Ali's Parkinson's syndrome (a set of symptoms that include tremors and a masklike face), he also takes an eerily mean-spirited pride in the role he believes he played in causing Ali's condition. Indeed, the Parkinson's most likely traces to the repeated blows Ali took to the head as a boxer—traumas that ravaged the colony of dopamine-producing cells in his brain—and no man struck Ali's head harder and more repeatedly than Frazier.

"He's got Joe Frazier-itis," Frazier said of Ali one day recently, flexing his left arm. "He's got left-hook-itis."

Ali's wife, Lonnie, shields him from such loutish and hateful pronouncements. "I don't want him hearing negative things," Lonnie says. "It's trash."

Ali has been living rent free in Frazier's head for more than 25 years, ever since Ali—after being stripped of his heavy-weight championship in 1967 for refusing induction into the U.S. Army, and then serving a $3^1/2$-year suspension from boxing—emerged from his banishment and immediately set about regaining his title, which by then was held by Smokin' Joe. At Ali's urgent pleading, Frazier backed him in his fight to regain his boxing license, but no sooner had that been accomplished than Ali began cruelly berating his benefactor, a man who had grown up mule-poor in Beaufort, South Carolina, the son of a struggling farmer and bootlegger. The young Frazier had migrated to Philly, taken up boxing and become the precursor of Rocky Balboa, training by tenderizing sides of beef in a kosher slaughterhouse with his sibilant left hook.

Over the next five years, from their first fight in New York City, on March 8, 1971, until their third and last in Manila on Oct. 1, 1975, Ali humiliated and enraged and ultimately isolated Frazier, casting him as a shuffling and mumbling Uncle Tom, an ugly and ignorant errand boy for white America. But the most lasting characterization of all was the one Ali coined on their way to the Philippines in '75, the one that came near the end of the singsong rhyme he would deliver with that mischievous smirk on his moon-bright face: "It will be a killa and a chilla and a thrilla when I get the gorilla in Manila!"

Of all the names joined forever in the annals of boxing—from Dempsey-Tunney to Louis-Schmeling, from Zale-Graziano to Leonard-Hearns—none are more fiercely bound by a hyphen than Ali-Frazier. Not Palmer-Nicklaus in golf nor Borg-McEnroe in tennis, as ardently competitive as these rivalries were, conjure up anything remotely close to the epic theater of Ali-Frazier. Their first fight, snagged in the most turbulent political currents of our time, is widely viewed as the greatest single sporting event of this half century. And the third fight—for its savagery, its shifting momentum and its climactic moment, in which the two men sat battered on their stools—is regarded, by consensus, as the most surpassing prizefight in history.

So here it is, 25 years after Ali-Frazier I, and Frazier is burning like the flame that Ali set off with his Olympic torch. Feeling that history has treated him unfairly, Frazier is haunted and overshadowed by his old tormentor, the very figure he did most to help create. Frazier was one of the greatest of all gladiators, but today he finds himself cast as just another player in the far larger drama of Ali's life. He is trapped and frozen in the Ali mystique, a dragonfly embedded in the amber of Ali's life and times.

For Ali is as near to a cultural saint as any man of our era. His appearance on the Atlanta stage was a window, thrown suddenly open, on the long journey he has taken through the lights and shadows of our unresolved past—America's past. As his left arm shook, he lit the flame and choked the breath of a nation. His life has become an extended public appearance: He swims among crowds wherever he goes, leading with the most recognizable chin on the planet. He tells old knock-knock jokes, receives visitors like a Middle East potentate and signs off on the next book about his life. And now and again, just for old times' sake, he leans over to whisper in Joe Frazier's ear.

As he did when his eyes widened in that suite at the Essex House. And then he gave the impish grin. "Joe Fraysha?" Ali said. "You seen the gorilla? From Manila?"

The geometry of the lives of Ali and Frazier is forever fixed in history. The line between them, once as curved and sweeping as a left hook and as long as a flicking jab, is today as irreducibly short as the one that joins their names. The two men left each other scarred in different ways. Ali's wounds are visible on the surface; you can see them on his face. Frazier's wounds lie deeper within; you can hear them in the pain in his voice.

There had never been a night like this one in New York City. By 10:30 P.M. on the evening of March 8, 1971, when the two fighters climbed into the ring at Madison Square Garden, Ali in red trunks and Frazier in green-and-gold brocade, there was a feral scent and crackle to the place. The Garden was a giant bell jar into which more than 20,000 people had drifted, having passed through police barricades that rimmed the surrounding streets. They came in orange and mint-green and purple velvet hot pants, in black leather knickers and mink and leopard capes, in cartridge belts and feathered chapeaux and pearl-gray fedoras. Some sported hats with nine-inch brims and leaned jauntily on diamond-studded walking sticks. Manhattan listed toward Babylon.

"I looked down from the ring, and it was a sea of glitter," recalls Eddie Futch, who was then Frazier's assistant trainer. "I have never seen any boxing event that had so many celebrities."

Angelo Dundee, Ali's trainer, was making his way through the tumult to the ring when he heard someone call his name: "Hey, Ange!" Dundee looked up. Frank Sinatra snapped his picture; the singer was working for LIFE magazine. Burt Lancaster was doing radio commentary. Ringside seats had sold for $150, but scalpers were getting $1,000. "Plumage, pimps and hustlers," says Bobby Goodman, the fight publicist. The fighters were each getting a record $2.5 million, an astronomical sum in those days, and the worldwide television audience was 300 million. The Garden ring was the wrist on which America was checking its pulse.

The boxer-dancer with the beautiful legs had arrived to do battle against the puncher-plodder with the thick thighs. Of course, the fans had come to see more than a classic clash of styles. The match was billed as the Fight of the Century, and the sporting world had been waiting for it for more than three years, ever since Frazier knocked out Buster Mathis in 11 rounds on March 4, 1968, to win the vacant New York heavyweight title and begin laying claim to being the toughest man on earth—the toughest, at least, with a passport. The previous year Ali had been stripped of his world championship and his freedom to travel abroad, and during his ensuing 43-month absence from the ring, Frazier buried his implacable hook into every heavyweight who stood in his way, finally winning the vacant world title on Feb. 16, 1970, by knocking out Jimmy Ellis in the fifth round.

During his exile Ali, who had to earn his money on the college lecture circuit, began to knock at Frazier's door, seeking help to get back his license to fight, saying that an Ali-Frazier match would make them both rich. "He'd come to the gym and call me on the telephone," says Frazier. "He just wanted to work with me for the publicity so he could get his license back. One time, after the Ellis fight, I drove him from Philadelphia to New York City in my car. Me and him. We talked about how much we were going to make out of our fight. We were laughin' and havin' fun. We were friends, we were great friends. I said, 'Why not? Come on, man, let's do it!' He was a brother. He called me Joe: 'Hey, Smokin' Joe!' In New York we were gonna put on this commotion."

For Ali, the most gifted carnival barker in the history of sports, the commotion was father to the promotion. So when Frazier stopped his car in midtown Manhattan and walked into a store to buy a pair of shoes, Ali leaped out, his eyes bulging, and cried, "It's Joe Frazier, ladies and gentlemen! Smokin' Joe! There he is! He's got my title! I want my title! He ain't the champ, he's the chump. I'm the people's champ!"

Frazier, a proud and soft-spoken rural Southerner, had never witnessed anything like this. It rattled him at first. Butch Lewis, a companion of Frazier's and later a promoter himself, explained to him what Ali was doing: "He's not disrespecting you. This is Ali! This is what will make the payday. *This is not personal.*"

Lewis says the men shared more than anyone knows. Frazier knew that Ali was in need of money. On at least two occasions, Lewis says, Frazier slipped Ali cash when he needed it, once giving him $2,000 to pay an overdue bill at the City Squire Motor Inn in New York City. But now Ali was dabbing curare on the tip of his rhetoric.

All through Ali's youth in Louisville and his early years as a champion, he had been a blend of his chesty, arrogant, yakety-yak father, Cassius Clay Sr., and his gentle, uncommonly sweet mother, Odessa. "Ali is softhearted and generous to a fault," says his former fight doctor, Ferdie Pacheco. "Essentially a sweet guy whose whole demeanor aims to amuse, to entertain and be liked." Yet there was a period in Ali's life, after he revealed that he had joined the separatist Black Muslims in 1964, when that side of his personality disappeared—"when he was not particularly pleasant to anyone," says Pacheco, recalling the two years before Ali's exile, when he fought Floyd Patterson and Ernie Terrell. "He was a hateful guy."

Neither Patterson nor Terrell would call him Ali—they used what he called his "slave name," Cassius Clay—and so in the ring he played with each of them as a cat would with a wounded mouse, keeping them alive to torture them. "What's my name?" he demanded of them as he landed his punches at will. Goodman, who was Terrell's publicist then, says, "He gave Ernie a merciless beating around the eyes. Ernie had double vision for a long time."

If Ali emerged from his exile years a softer man, as many contend, he had not forgotten how to sting and wound an opponent. "There was an awful mean streak in Ali," says Dave Wolf, then one of Frazier's confidants. "He did to Joe verbally what he did to Terrell physically."

The Ali who had laughed and bantered with Frazier, who had raised all that good-natured commotion in Manhattan, now appeared to be a man transformed—stripped of his disguise. "Joe Frazier is too ugly to be champ," Ali said. "Joe Frazier is too dumb to be champ. The heavyweight champion should be smart and pretty, like me. Ask Joe Frazier, 'How do you feel, champ?' He'll say, 'Duh, duh. duh.'" That played to the most insidious racial stereotype, the dumb and ugly black man, but Ali reached further: "Joe Frazier is an Uncle Tom." And further: "Ninety-eight percent of my people are for me. They identify with my struggle. . . . If I win, they win. I lose, they lose. Anybody black who thinks Frazier can whup me is an Uncle Tom."

In fact, because of Ali's work for racial justice and because of the sacrifices he made in his stand against the Vietnam War, the vast majority of blacks—as well as an increasing number of whites—saw his battles as theirs and were drawn to him as a force for social change. The most prominent voices of the 1960s, a decade torn by conflict and rebellion, had been silenced. Dr. Martin Luther King Jr. was dead. Bobby Kennedy was dead. Senator Eugene McCarthy had drifted like a blip off the screen. Ali alone remained alive in the ruins—the most commanding voice for and symbol of the decade's causes.

In the months leading up to the fight, he brought to bear all the horsepower of his eloquence. His demeaning of Frazier, Ali now says, had but one purpose: "To sell tickets." Of course, Frazier says there was no need to sell anything, because their purses were guaranteed, but this argument ignores the fact that Ali was always selling more than tickets. The consummate performer, he was selling himself. And there are those who say that Ali's rhetoric was merely a part of his act, the tappety-tap-tap of his every-day walking shtick. But whatever compelled him to violate all canons of fairness and decency in his portrayal of Frazier—whether it was meanness, bravado or a calculated plan to enrage and rattle his opponent— he succeeded in isolating Frazier from the black community.

And Frazier? He felt manipulated, humiliated, and betrayed. "He had me stunned," Frazier says. "This guy was a buddy. I remember looking at him and thinkin', What's wrong with this guy? Has he gone crazy? He called me an Uncle Tom. For a guy who did as much for him as I did, that was cruel. I grew up like the black man—he didn't. I cooked the liquor. I cut the wood. I worked the farm. I lived in the ghetto. Yes, I tommed; when he asked me to help him get a license, I tommed for him. For him! He betrayed my friendship. He called me stupid. He said I was so ugly that my mother ran and hid when she gave birth to me. I was shocked. I sat down and said to myself, I'm gonna kill him. O.K.? Simple as that. I'm gonna kill him!"

So by the time they climbed through the ropes that night in the Garden, the lure of the fight went far beyond the exquisitely contrasting ring styles of the two men. For many viewers Ali was still the mouth that poured, the renegade traitor and rabble-rouser whose uppity black ass needed dusting. For many others, of course, he symbolized all successful men of color who did not conform in a white man's world—and the hope that one, at least *one*, would overcome. Frazier had done nothing to earn the caricature of Uncle Tom, but Ali had lashed him to that stake as if to define their war in black and white. Frazier knew the scope of Ali's appeal. A Bible-raised man, he saw himself as David to Ali's Goliath.

"David had a slingshot," Frazier says. "I had a left hook."

For 14 rounds, almost a full hour in which the Garden never stopped rocking, Frazier pursued and pounded the former champion like a man simultaneously pushing a plow and chopping wood. Ali won the first two rounds, dancing and landing jabs and stinging rights, but by the third, under a remorseless body attack climaxed by a searing hook to the ribs, his feet had begun to flatten, and soon he was fighting toe-to-toe, his back pushed against the ropes.

It was a fight with two paces, fast and faster, and among its abiding images is that of Frazier, head down and body low, bobbing and weaving incessantly, taking lashing lefts and rights from Ali, then unloading that sweeping hook to the jaw, and Ali waving his head defiantly—*No, no, that didn't hurt*—and coming back, firing jabs and hooks and straight rights to Frazier's head. It was soon clear that this was not the Ali of old, the butterfly who had floated through his championship years, and that the long absence from the ring had stolen his legs and left him vulnerable. He had always been a technically unsound fighter: He threw punches going backward, fought with his arms too low and avoided sweeping punches by leaning back instead of ducking. He could get away with that when he had the speed and reflexes of his youth, but he no longer had them, and now Frazier was punishing him.

Frazier quickened the tempo in the third and fourth, whaling Ali with lefts and rights. Ali moved as he fired jabs and landed rights and shouted at Frazier, "Do you know I'm God?"

"God, you're in the wrong place tonight," Frazier shot back. "I'm takin' names and kickin' ass!"

The Garden crowd was on its feet. Frazier mimicked Ali in the fifth, dropping his hands and laughing as Ali struck him with a left and a right. Frazier's ferocious head and body attacks began to slow Ali down, but the former champion scored repeatedly as Frazier moved in, and by the start of the eighth the crowd was chanting, "Ali! Ali! Ali!" Looking inspired, Frazier bore in, crashing a hook on Ali's head and following it up with two rights. After Ali mockingly tapped him on the head, Frazier drove a fiery hook into the ex-champ's jaw, and after the bell that ended the round members of the crowd were chanting, "Joe! Joe! Joe!"

Starting the 11th Frazier was winning on two of the three cards, and it was here that he took possession of the fight. As Ali stood in a neutral corner, Frazier stepped inside and let fly a thunderous hook to the jaw that snapped Ali's neck and buckled his legs. Ali looked gone. A hard right sent him sagging on the ropes. Another wobbled him again. At the bell he was still on his feet, but he moved shakily back to his corner.

If Ali-Frazier I was the most memorable athletic event of our time, surely it was the 15th round that made it so. About twenty seconds after the opening bell, Frazier threw the most famous left hook in boxing history and raised the evening to the realm of myth. The punch began south of his brocade trunks, somewhere down in Beaufort, and rose in a whistling arc that ended on the right side of Ali's jaw, just above the point of the chin. Ali sprawled on his back, the tassels on his shoes flying in the air. "I looked up." Ali says today, "and I was on the floor."

Frazier turned and walked away. Earlier in the fight, after pounding Ali with hooks to the head, he had asked his cornermen, "What is keeping this guy up?" Now he asked it again as he turned and saw Ali climb slowly to his feet at the count of four. Frazier won a unanimous decision—"I kicked your ass!" he would yell at Ali as the final bell sounded—but among the enduring moments of that night was the one in which a battered Ali rose off that deck.

The two fighters sent each other to the hospital. Ali went briefly for a swollen right jaw, which made him appear to need a tooth extraction, and a lumpy-faced Frazier was in and out for two weeks for treatment of exhaustion, high blood pressure and kidney problems. The two men also left each other irreversibly diminished. They would never be the same fighters again.

Thirty-five months would pass before they would meet for Ali-Frazier II, on Jan. 28, 1974, at the Garden. But by then the context in which they fought had changed so dramatically that there is no comparing the two bouts. On Jan. 22, 1973, Frazier had lost his title when George Foreman hit him a few times with his wrecking-ball right and knocked him senseless in the second round in Kingston, Jamaica. So there was no championship at stake in Ali-Frazier II. By then, too, the social causes of the '60s were no longer issues of great ardency. But the Vietnam War had become such a national plague that Ali's popularity had climbed at roughly the same rate that the war's had declined.

The only thing that remained the same was Frazier's incandescent animus toward Ali, unappeased by his victory in '71. Five days before the second fight, sitting together before a national TV audience on ABC, they were discussing the first bout when Frazier referred to Ali's visit to the hospital. "I went to the hospital for 10 minutes," Ali shot back. "You went for a month."

"I was resting," Frazier said.

"That shows how dumb you are," Ali said. "People don't go to a hospital to rest. See how ignorant you are?"

Frazier had not had much formal schooling, and Ali had touched his hottest button. "I'm tired of you calling me ignorant all the time," snapped Frazier. "I'm not ignorant!" With that, he rose and towered over Ali, tightening his fists, his eyes afire. When Ali's brother, Rahaman, rushed to the stage, Frazier turned to him and said, "You in this too?" Here Ali jumped to his feet and grabbed Frazier in a bear hug. They rolled off the stage and onto the studio floor, and Goodman remembers Frazier holding one of Ali's feet and twisting it, like the head of a chicken, while Futch screamed, "Joe! Joe! Don't twist off his foot! There won't be a fight."

Ali was bug-eyed as Frazier left in a fury. "Did you see how wide Clay's eyes opened up?" Frazier said. "Now I really got him scared!"

Frazier got nothing. Ali won an easy 12-round decision, nearly knocking Frazier out in the second round and then clinching and smothering whatever attack Frazier tried to mount inside. Indeed, Ali put on a boxing clinic, fighting at his range instead of Frazier's, and many of Frazier's sweeping hooks appeared to lack the snap they'd had three years before. The Ali-Frazier rivalry might have ended right there, in fact, if Ali had not taken events into his hands so magnificently nine months later, on Oct. 30 in

Kinshasa, Zaire, knocking out Foreman—the baddest man on the planet—in an upset that staggered the memory and fired the imagination.

Ali's victory in Africa eventually led to Ali-Frazier III, the final combat, in the Philippines. Here the two fighters got guaranteed purses, $4.5 million for Ali and $2 million for Frazier, plus a percentage of the gross. Once again Ali had become the largest draw in sports, and once again he went at Frazier with a vengeance, correcting his diction and carrying around, in his shirt pocket, a small rubber gorilla. At a press conference before the fight, Ali pulled out the doll in front of Frazier and began beating it, saying, "All night long, this is what you'll see. Come on, gorilla! We're in Manila! Come on, gorilla, this is a thrilla!" Black people cringed, but not a few whites laughed, and Frazier felt again the heat of his simmering anger.

No one knew what to expect when these two aging fighters came together that morning in Manila. Several major U.S. newspapers didn't bother sending a writer to cover the fight. But those who were there witnessed prizefighting in its grandest manner, the final epic in a running blood feud between two men, each fighting to own the heart of the other. The fight called upon all of their will and courage as they pitched from one ring post to another emitting fearful grunts and squeals.

By the end of the 10th round Ali looked like a half-drowned man who had just been pulled from Manila Bay. His aching body slumped, glistening with sweat. He had won the early rounds, snapping his whiplike jab on Frazier's face, but as in '71 Frazier had found his rolling rhythm after a few rounds, and by the fifth he had driven Ali into his corner and was thumping his body like a blacksmith. Ali's trainer was frantic. "Get outta the goddam corner!" screamed Dundee. It was too late. The fight had shifted from Ali to Frazier.

For the next five rounds it was as if Frazier had reached into the darkest bat cave of his psyche and freed all his pent-up rage. In the sixth he pressed and attacked, winging three savage hooks to Ali's head, the last of which sent his mouthpiece flying. For the first time in the fight, Ali sat down between rounds. Frazier resumed the attack in the seventh, at one point landing four straight shots to the body, at another point landing five. In the ninth, as Ali wilted, the fighting went deeper into the trenches, down where Frazier whistles while he works, and as he landed blow upon blow he could hear Ali howling in pain. In his corner after the 10th, Ali said to Pacheco, "This must be what dyin' is like."

Frazier owned the fight. He was sure to regain his title. And then came the 11th. Drew (Bundini) Brown, Ali's witch doctor, pleaded with him, "Go down to the well once more!" From wherever it is that such men draw the best and noblest of themselves, Ali emerged reborn. During the next four rounds he fought with a precision and fury that made a bloody Frazier weave and wobble. In the 12th Ali landed six consecutive punches to Frazier's head, and moments later he slammed home eight more. By the end of the round an archipelago of lumps had surfaced around the challenger's eyes and brow.

Futch could see Frazier's left eye closing. Before the 13th he told his boxer, "Move back and stand up a little, so you can see the target better." That was just what Ali needed, more room and a taller man to fire at. "Boy, did he take advantage of that," says Futch. Ali threw punches in flurries, so many blows that Frazier reeled helplessly. A right cross sent Frazier's white mouthpiece twirling four rows into the seats. Futch kept thinking, *Ali has to slow down. He cannot keep this pace. Not into the 14th round!* By then Frazier's face was a misshapen moonscape, both eyes closing, and in the 14th Ali fired barrages and raked a nearly blind Frazier with rights and lefts. Futch stared at Ali and thought, *Incredible!* When the bell tolled, it tolled for Joe.

"The fight's over, Joe," Futch told him before the beginning of the 15th.

Frazier jumped from his stool. He said, "Eddie—"

"Just sit down, Joe."

A benumbed and exhausted Ali, his lips scraped raw, lay on a cot in his locker room in Manila and summoned Marvis Frazier, Joe's 15-year-old son, to his side. "Tell your dad the things I said I really didn't mean," Ali said.

Marvis reported back to his father. "He should come to me, son," Joe told him. "He should say it to my face."

Back in the States, Ali called Lewis and asked him for Frazier's private number. Ali told Lewis that he wanted to apologize to Frazier for some of the things he had said. Lewis called Frazier, but, he says, Frazier told him, "Don't give it to him."

In the 21 years since then, Ali and Frazier have seen each other at numerous affairs, and Frazier has barely disguised the loathing he feels toward his old antagonist. In 1988, for the taping of a film called *Champions Forever*, five former heavyweight title holders—Ali, Frazier, Foreman, Larry Holmes and Ken Norton—gathered in Las Vegas. A crowd of people were at Johnny Tocco's Gym for a morning shoot when Frazier started in on Ali, who was already debilitated by Parkinson's. "Look at Ali," Frazier said. "Look what's happened to him. All your talkin', man. I'm faster than you are now. You're damaged goods."

"I'm faster than you are, Joe," Ali slurred. Pointing to a heavy bag, Ali suggested a contest: "Let's see who hits the bag the fastest."

Frazier grinned, not knowing he was back in the slaughterhouse. He stripped off his coat, strode to the bag and buried a dozen rapid-fire hooks in it, punctuating each rip with a loud grunt: "Huh! Huh! Huh!" Without removing his coat, Ali went to the bag, assumed the ready stance and mimicked one Frazier grunt: "Huh!" He had not thrown a punch. He turned slowly to Frazier and said, "Wanna see it again, Joe?" In the uproar of hilarity that ensued, only Frazier did not laugh. Ali had humiliated him again.

After the shoot, at a luncheon for the fighters, Frazier had too much to drink, and afterward, as people milled around the room and talked, he started walking toward Ali. Thomas Hauser, Ali's chronicler, watched the scene that unfolded over the next 20 minutes. Holmes quietly positioned himself between Ali and Frazier. "Joe was trying to get to Ali," Hauser says, "but wherever Joe went, left or right, Holmes would step between him and Ali. Physically shielding him. Joe was frustrated. After about 10 minutes of this, Foreman walked up to Larry and said, 'I'll take over.'" So for the next 10 minutes Frazier quietly tried to get around 290 pounds of assimilated Big Macs. At one point Frazier leaned into Foreman, but Foreman only leaned back. "Keep it cool, Joe," Foreman whispered. "Be calm."

Ali had no idea this was going on. "He was walking around like Mr. Magoo," says Hauser. "He was oblivious."

While Frazier's hostility toward Ali was well known to the fight crowd, it was not until his book came out last spring that he took his venom public. When Phil Berger, who wrote the book, began interviewing Frazier last fall and heard what he wanted to say about Ali, he warned Frazier of the damning impact it would have. "Ali's become like a saintly figure," Berger said.

Too bad, the fighter replied. "That's the way I feel."

With his book and his unseemly harangue against Ali at the Olympics, which had the strong whiff of envy, Frazier may have done himself irreparable damage among the legions who have admired him so steadfastly. What he wants from Ali is an apology for those long years of vilification—the apology he did not want to hear when Lewis called him on Ali's behalf after Manila.

Ali has expressed contrition more than once for the things he said. In Hauser's 1991 oral history *Muhammad Ali: His Life and Times*, Ali says, "I'm sorry Joe Frazier is mad at me. I'm sorry I hurt him. Joe Frazier is a good man. I couldn't have done what I did without him, and he couldn't have done what he did without me."

Wolf understands Frazier's rage, but he sees Ali today and does not see the man behind the cruel jibes of the past. "I'm not sure that part exists anymore," Wolf says. "Whether it is the Parkinson's or just maturing, that part of him is gone." So that leaves Frazier, imprisoned in the past, raging against a ghost.

Lewis, still a close friend of Frazier's, has pleaded with him to cut Ali loose. At the real root of Frazier's discontent, says Lewis, is his sense that history has not dealt with him fairly—that his Olympic triumph and his heavyweight championship years have been forgotten, and that time has turned him into just another stitch in the embroidery of Ali's legend. "You have your place in history, and Ali has his," Lewis tells Frazier. "You can't reflect back in bitterness. Let it go."

Futch's gentle voice still rings the clearest. His words in Manila, after 14 savage rounds that left Frazier's eyes nearly as blind as his heart is now, still echo faint but true. "The fight's over, Joe. . . . The fight's over, Joe. . . . The fight's over, Joe."

September 1996

Joe Frazier, now 58, still lives above the South Philly gym that carries his name, making his appearances, signing those autographs. Seven years after Ali lit the flame in Atlanta, at the 2002 NBA All-Star game in Philadelphia, the two men were seen together at courtside during the playing of "Lift Every Voice" and "America the Beautiful." Ali was having trouble standing, and Joe kept a supporting hand under Ali's left arm to keep him steady, helping his old nemesis in a way he never had. "We sat down and made up," Frazier told Rich Hofmann of the Philadelphia Daily News. *"Life's too short. He said his apology and I accepted it . . . 'Let's bury the hatchet, please.'"*

YOUNG CASSIUS

At 50, Muhammad Ali is a much-admired figure, just as he was in his formative years as a fun-loving but purposeful youth in Louisville

"AS A KID IN LOUISVILLE, THE CITY SEEMED SO BIG TO ME. NEW YORK SEEMED SO BIG. CHICAGO SEEMED BIG. AND LONDON, ENGLAND, SEEMED FAR AWAY. AFRICA WAS FAR AWAY. I WAS CASSIUS CLAY THEN. I WAS A NEGRO. I ATE PORK. I HAD NO CONFIDENCE. I THOUGHT WHITE PEOPLE WERE SUPERIOR. I WAS A CHRISTIAN BAPTIST NAMED CASSIUS CLAY."

—*Muhammad Ali, Nov. 22, 1991*

Cassius Clay was cruising west on Walnut Street, through the black part of Louisville known as the West End, consorting with the world from behind the wheel of a Cadillac convertible. It was the autumn of 1960. Clay was only 18, a few days away from his first professional fight and just beginning to yank the clapper in the national bell tower, the one he would use forever after to announce his arrival. Almost standing in the car, the youngster yelled over and over, to everyone he passed, "I'm Cassius Clay! I am the greatest!"

The girl sitting next to him, the one sinking demurely in her seat, trying to look as inconspicuous as possible in a pink Cadillac in the middle of black Louisville, was Wilma Rudolph, a 20-year-old college student who was visiting Clay from Tennessee State. They were a matched pair, two links on the fresh cuffs of history, as they drove that October afternoon. Clay was, by consensus, the finest amateur boxer in the world. Only two months before, at the Olympic Games in Rome, the 178-pound youth had won the gold medal in the light heavyweight division by whipping Zbigniew Pietrzykowski, a portly coffeehouse keeper from Poland. The white trunks Clay showed off to West End neighbors on his return were stained a candy pink by the Polish fighter's blood. Rudolph was the fastest woman on earth. Her victories in three sprints—the 100 and 200 meters and the 4 × 100-meter relay—had made her the first American woman to win three gold medals in a single Olympics.

The two athletes had become friends in the days they spent together in Rome. Clay was sweet on Rudolph, but he was too shy to tell her how he felt. His diffidence with girls was painful. He had fainted dead away the first time he kissed one, two years earlier, and it took a cold washcloth to bring him to. So he concealed his shyness in bravura.

"I can still see him strutting around the village with his gold medal on," recalls Rudolph. "He slept with it. He went to the cafeteria with it. He never took it off. No one else cherished it the way he did. His peers loved him. Everybody wanted to see him. Everybody wanted to be near him. Everybody wanted to talk to him. And he talked all the time. I always hung in the background, not knowing what he was going to say."

His six-year amateur career had taken him to many American cities, from San Francisco to New York, but the journey to Italy had been his first outside his native land, and gold medal and all, it had been a turning experience in his life. Clay's triumphant return to River City, with police sirens leading the 25-car motorcade through the streets, raised a clamor usually reserved in those latitudes for the Kentucky Derby winner. Not since 1905, when cumbersome Marvin Hart whipped Jack Root to win the heavyweight championship of the world, had Louisville produced a fighter of such celebrity.

Now there he was, driving up Walnut Street, waving at the crowds and stopping at an intersection and rising to announce himself. "And this," he yelled, "this is Wilma Rudolph. *She* is the greatest!"

"Sit down," she said.

"Come on, Wilma. Stand up!"

Crowds were stopping on the street and craning to look inside the car. "No, I can't do that," she said.

"Yes, you can," said Clay. "Stand up, Wilma! Come on."

Wary of crowds, she began sinking lower, covering her face with her hands, trying to crawl inside the glove compartment, slowly disappearing in the cracks of the seat. It was no use. "Look!" Clay said, pointing down to her. "Here she is, down here! It's Wilma Rudolph. She is the greatest! And I'm Cassius Clay. I am the greatest! Come on, Wilma, stand up!"

There was no place to hide with Cassius Clay on Walnut Street. So she rose, reluctantly, for the gaping crowds. What would be the longest running circus in American sport was pushing off. "I saw him at the very beginning," says Rudolph. "It was bedlam. I always told him, 'You should be on stage.'"

On Walnut Street, of course, he already was. This was more than 31 years ago—in a different incarnation, as Muhammad Ali, he turns 50 on Jan. 17—and that rarest of all careers, spanning two decades and part of a third, was only beginning. On Oct. 29, 1960, in his first pro fight, he won a six-round decision from heavyweight Tunney Hunsaker, the police chief of Fayetteville, West Virginia. Clay emerged unscathed and promptly crowned himself king. One of his cornermen for that fight was George King, a former amateur bantamweight from Louisville who first met the 12-year-old Clay when the youngster began hanging around trainer Fred Stoner's all-black boxing team at the Grace Community Center. With Rome and Hunsaker behind him, Clay was not a boy anymore.

"Where'd you get that name?" he asked King one day. "You ain't big enough to be a king. They ought to call you Johnson or somethin'. There's only one king."

"Who's that?" asked George.

"You're lookin' at him," Clay said.

Clay's days in Louisville were numbered. By the end of the year he had moved to Florida and was fighting out of Angelo Dundee's Fifth Street Gym in Miami Beach. Increasingly the town of his birth and boyhood became a place more of memory than of moment. Gone were the days when he skipped down the halls of Central High between classes, shadow-boxing as he danced past knots of tittering students, stopping to throw a flurry that would fall just short of an incoming freshman's outgoing nose, then ducking into a washroom to box himself silly in front of a mirror. Gone was the laughter in the classrooms when Central's tall, scholarly principal, Atwood Wilson, would flip on the school intercom and, tugging on his suspenders, gravely intone his warning: "You act up, and I'm going to turn Cassius Clay on you." Gone were all those early mornings when young Clay raced the school bus for 20 blocks east down Chestnut Street, waving and grinning at the faces in the windows as he bounded past pedestrians scurrying to work.

"Why doesn't he ride to school like everybody else?" a sleepy-eyed young Socrates asked on the bus one day.

"He's crazy," replied one of Clay's classmates, Shirlee Lewis Smith. "He's as nutty as he can be."

Young Clay was an original, sui generis, a salad of improvisations—unpredictable, witty, mischievous, comical. An indifferent student, he lived within his own world during class, day-dreaming by the hour. "Most of the time, when he wasn't paying attention, which was often, he'd be drawing," recalls his senior English teacher, Thelma Lauderdale. "But he never gave me any trouble. Shy and quiet in my class. Meditative."

She never met the other Clay. Beyond her doors, flitting here and over there, he was forever a cutup. "He was a jolly-go-happy guy," says Jimmy Ellis, a boyhood friend who also went on to become heavyweight champion of the world.

"He was just a playful person," says Indra Leavell Brown, a friend of Clay's since childhood. "He had a lot of friends. We'd eat in the cafeteria, and he'd come in and crack his jokes and say little silly things and have all the table laughing."

"He always used to tell me he was in love with me," says Dorothy McIntyre Kennedy, who knew Clay from the time he was 12. "But he always made a joke out of everything. I *never* took him seriously. It was like he never wanted to grow up. He always wanted to be this *person*—the class clown."

Clay was different, all right, as elusive as the butterfly he would soon proclaim himself to be, inventing and reinventing himself as he went along. He dated Mildred Davis for a spell his senior year, and she remembers the Monday after he won the Golden Gloves championship in Chicago, when he showed up at school bearing in his hands, like an offering, a golden pendant. "A little gold glove, with a diamond embedded in it, on a gold chain," says Davis. "And he put it around my neck and said, 'I don't ever want you to take this off. I want you to wear this all the time.' And I said, 'Fine.' That was about 8:30 in the morning. At about 11, he came back and said, 'Someone else wants to wear it.' So he took it off and let someone else have it the rest of the day. And the next day, some other girl wore it. I never questioned him about it because he was always so silly. So silly. He wanted me to wear it forever, and I had it for about two-and-a-half hours."

Every day with Clay was an adventure, and Davis never quite knew what to expect from him. She hardly knew what to make of the bottle he was sipping from all the time. "He carried a bottle of water with fresh garlic in it," says Davis. "He would drink it, and he reeked of garlic. I remember asking him why he put the garlic in the water, and he said, 'I do that to keep my blood pressure down.' And he would do some of the craziest things with his eyes. He would come up to guys, make his eyes big, press his lips together and say, 'I'm gonna knock you out!' He always carried his money all folded up in a small change purse, like a little old lady. If you met him, there were things about him that you could never forget. Even in high school, he would always say, 'I'm not gonna let anyone hit me, as pretty as my face is. I'm almost as pretty as you.' He did have beautiful skin. And I'll never forget the night he said to me, 'Come on, I'll run you home.'"

That was the night of the variety show at Central High, a takeoff on *The Jackie Gleason Show* on television. "The girls would come out to announce the acts, and I was the last one, and I'd say, 'And away we go!'" says Davis. "Cassius was on the show that night. He was shadowboxing, as usual. That was his act. After the show he said, 'Come on, I'll run you home.' And I was thinking, He doesn't drive. How is he going to run me home?"

They left the school and started walking west on Chestnut. Pretty soon Clay began to jog in place next to her as she felt her way along the sidewalk in her high heels. "It was dark," says Davis. "He would run up ahead a block or two and jog back. He trotted beside me most of the way. That's what he meant by running me home. So I walked 13 blocks in my high heels. How *crazy* he was."

Davis and Clay took long walks together around Chickasaw Park that spring, watched television at the Clay house on Grand Avenue, sat together at her mother's dinner table over meat loaf and corn bread and cabbage. He was, at all times, unfailingly polite. "Would you like something to eat?" Mildred's mother, Mary, would ask. "Yes, ma'am," Cassius would say. Indeed, there was something old-fashioned about the way he viewed things.

"You know," he once told Mildred, "when we get married, you'll have to wear longer skirts."

"Why would I have to do that?" she asked.

"To look like a lady," he said.

That was not the only time he spoke of marriage to Davis. Clay always built models in his mind, including a make-believe world with a large, happy family of which he was the benevolent father. "We watched a lot of TV at his mother's house," recalls Davis, "and little kids would come over. He loved kids—he always liked to have five or six around him—and I remember one time, it was around Easter, and my mother wouldn't let me go to one of his fights. He came by after the fight, and we sat together on the front porch. At one point he said, 'Pretty soon we're gonna get married, and we're gonna get a real big house with a swimming pool. All the kids in the neighborhood are gonna come over—we're gonna have a lot of kids—and they'll all swim in the pool.'"

Clay was his mother's son. Odessa Grady Clay was a sweet, pillowy, light-skinned black woman with a freckled face, a gentle demeanor and an easy laugh. Everyone who knew the family in those days saw the kindness of the mother in the boy. In his sophomore year, when he was still 15, Cassius began working after school in the Nazareth College library, across town, for 60 cents an hour. He carried books from floor to floor, dusted the volumes and the shelves, waxed the tables and dry-mopped the brown linoleum floors. The first day he walked into the library, Sister James Ellen Huff, the librarian, was struck by his shy, gentle manner.

"Do they call you Cash?" Sister Huff asked.

"No, ma'am," he said. "I'm Cassius Marcellus Clay."

"He had his mother's sweetness," says Sister Huff.

In fact, when Clay talked about his parents at all, it was of his mother. "Everything related to his mom," says Indra Brown. "He would say, 'My mother comes first, before anybody. My mom will be treated right.'"

Of course, all the diversionary commotion he created in his life—the incessant shadowboxing and grandstanding, the flights of fantasy into becalmed worlds of aqua pools and frolicking children—mirrored and masked the chaos of his life at home, where violence and turmoil often came and went with his father, Cassius Sr., a gifted religious muralist and commercial sign painter. The old man, chesty and fast-talking, had always cut a popular figure around town. "Everybody around Louisville knew Mr. Clay," says Yates Thomas, a boyhood pal of young Cassius's. "Up on his ladder painting signs."

And down along the streets, he moved from saloon to saloon, his rich singing voice belting out his favorite songs for the audiences bellying up to the bar. The elder Clay was a wild, free-roaming drunk and womanizer whose peregrinations around town made him a legend along the river's shore. "I just loved him," says West End liquor store owner John (Junior Pal) Powell, a longtime friend of Cassius Jr. "A fun-loving type of guy. But he did drink a lot. One time some lady stabbed him in the chest, and he came up to my apartment. I tried to get him to let me take him to the hospital, but he said, and he always talked real fast, 'Hey, Junior Pal, best thing you can do for me is do what the cowboys do. You know, give me a little drink and pour a little bit on the chest, and I'll be all right.'"

By the time he died, in 1990—of a heart attack, in his car, in a Louisville parking lot—Cassius Sr. had embroidered a long police rap sheet with his troubled history, most of it fueled by alcohol. Thomas Hauser, the author of *Muhammad Ali: His Life and Times,* an oral history of the fighter, says that an FBI investigation into Ali—initiated in 1966, the year before he refused induction into the armed forces—revealed that the elder Clay had been arrested nine times on charges that included reckless driving, disorderly conduct, and assault and battery. According to the file, Odessa thrice summoned the police seeking protection from her husband. The last file on him, obtained from the Louisville police department, showed he was arrested five times for drunken driving since 1975. Ali declines to talk about violence in the Clay household, but Hauser says he could imagine, in something that Ali once told him, a young Clay fleeing the early-morning chaos at home.

"I don't know what it was," Hauser recalls Ali saying, "but I always felt I was born to do something for my people. Eight years old, 10 years old; I'd walk out of my house at two in the morning, and look at the sky for an angel or a revelation or God telling me what to do. I never got an answer. I'd look at the stars and wait for a voice, but I never heard nothing."

The bars in Louisville closed at 2 A.M. Regardless of what things that go bump in the night drove the boy from his home at two in the morning, he would soon find his calling outside the thin walls of the bungalow on Grand Avenue. And when he did, predictably, he created another world for himself, floated through it, escaped into it until, at last, he used it to express himself like no other man of his time.

Clay was six pounds, seven ounces at birth, but by age three he had grown as big as a calf. One day, when he was still an infant, he jarred loose one of Odessa's front teeth. "We were lying in bed," she says, "and he stretched his arm out and hit me in the mouth. He just loosened the tooth. They couldn't straighten it. Finally it had to come out."

Cassius and his brother, Rudy, 18 months younger, would visit their uncle William Clay, and neighbors would bolt the doors. "One day they broke the birdbath in Mrs. Wheatley's yard," says William. "We called them the Wrecking Crew."

The sea change in his life occurred when, at age 12, he was attending a fair downtown and a rascal stole his new bike. Told a cop was downstairs in the Columbia Gym, Cassius went there to complain. In tears, he told his tale to the policeman, Joe Martin, who was training an amateur boxing team. "I'm gonna whip him if I can find him," said Cassius of the thief.

Martin remembers asking the boy if he could fight. "You better learn to fight before you start fightin'," Martin said.

Cassius looked around the gym at all the wondrous activity—the snap of the punching bags and the skipping of rope and the sparring in the ring. Finally, he said, "I didn't know this was here. Can I come?"

He was back the next day. "He didn't know a left hook from a kick in the ass," says Martin. "But he developed quite rapidly. I'd tell him what to do—how to stand, how to keep his arms and hands, how to punch. He'd be hitting the heavy bag, and I'd tell him, 'Cassius, there's a fly on that bag. I want you to hit him, but I don't want you to kill him. You got to turn the hand over. Snap punches. *Phew! Phew!*'"

Cassius loved to fire and turn the jab. Even at 12, when he was an 89-pound novice, he had a beguiling cocksureness that played well with the older amateurs in Louisville. George King first met Cassius during an intracity tournament at the Columbia Gym. Cassius was boxing for Martin's team, but he drifted over to Fred Stoner's team in the locker room and stood next to King, who was 21 years old and already married with a child. "I'm taller than you," Cassius said. "Do you think you could beat me?"

Soft laughter lifted among the older Stoner fighters. King smiled.

"Think you could stop this jab?" Cassius asked, throwing out two quickies. King pushed a jab toward Clay.

"My jab's quicker than yours," the boy said.

Rudell Stitch, then age 21, turned a thumb down. Fixing Stitch with a smirk, Cassius said, "Come on, I'll give you some of it, too."

All these years later, King's voice lilts at the memory. "We were down there, grown men, and he didn't give a damn," says King. "That's just the way he was. He'd pick at you, mess with your head, tease you to death. I kind of liked him. He was a neat lookin' kid, and he had all that personality. Everybody just took to him."

Over the next six years Cassius grew into a surpassing amateur boxer: 100 victories in 108 bouts; two consecutive national AAU championships, in 1959 and '60, both times as a light heavyweight; two straight national Golden Gloves titles, in '59 as a light heavy and the next year as a heavyweight; and, of course, an Olympic gold medal. "His secret was his unusual eye speed," says Martin. "It was blinding. The only other athlete I ever saw who had that kind of eye speed was Ted Williams. When he started fighting, Cassius was so fast with his eyes that you could give a guy a screen door and he wouldn't hit Cassius 15 times with it in 15 rounds. He was *different*. Quick as lightning for a big man, the quickest I ever saw."

He was born with phenomenal physical gifts, but unlike so many others, he nurtured them and squandered nothing. Indeed it was as if, in Martin's gym, Cassius had found the message in the silence of the stars. In high school he lived as ascetic an existence as possible for a teenager. Yates Thomas remembers Cassius showing up at school in the morning after buying two raw eggs and a quart of milk.

"He would break the eggs into the milk, shake it up and drink it," says Thomas. "He'd say, 'Now I'm ready to go to school. I'm the baaaaddest man in Looville!' All he thought of was fight-fight-fight. We used to go to a teenage place at night, and he'd stay till 10 o'clock, even on a Saturday night, and then he'd say, 'I'll see ya. I'm goin' home to bed.' He didn't smoke. He'd say, 'Ain't gonna put that stuff in my lungs.'"

At some point in his senior year Clay began to eschew pork, and for the same reason that he reeked of garlic. "Pork's not good for you," he warned Davis. "It raises your blood pressure." When Junior Pal offered him a grape soda early one morning as Clay was working out, Cassius waved him away. "The sugar and acid ain't good for you," he said.

Despite what was happening at home—or, more likely, because of it— he shunned alcohol. It was as if he were studying, high on his own Himalayan peak, the evanescent secrets of the butterfly. "He didn't chase women," Martin says. "And I never heard him say a curse word in my life. We used to go to a lot of towns, and he used to sit down and read a few pages of the Bible before he went to bed."

Clay's dalliances with women had far less to do with romance than with fantasy—his flirtations had the fizz life of a soft drink—and, according to Indra Brown, he was a virgin when he graduated from high school. "I know that for a fact, because he confided in me on things like that," she says. "He used to say to me, 'I will always have money. I'm not going to be a Joe Louis. Women are not going to drag me down. They are not going to be my downfall!'"

Late in his junior year he began doing experiments in the technique of kissing, and on his first try he nearly blew up the lab. Areatha Swint had first met Clay after a high school variety show, when she needed someone to walk her home. They dated for three weeks before he got around to asking her for a kiss goodnight. "On the night he did, it was late," Swint would recall in a newspaper memoir. "It must have been around 12:30 or one. We were being quiet because my mother had said there was no company after 12, and he didn't have any business being up that late because he was in training.

"I was the first girl he had ever kissed, and he didn't know how. So, I had to teach him. . . . When I did, he fainted. Really, he just did. He was always joking, so I thought he was playing, but he fell so hard. I ran upstairs to get a cold cloth. Well, when you live in the projects, a lot of times mother would wash and lay the towels on the radiator to dry. So I looked for one and got some cold water on it and ran back down the stairs."

She doused him with it. When he finally came to, Swint asked, "Are you O.K.?"

"I'm fine, but nobody will ever believe this," he said.

His shyness was such that at times the mere presence of girls struck him dumb. In 1959, recalls Wilbert (Skeeter) McClure, who was another young boxer, he and Clay were in Chicago for the Golden Gloves when Cassius began pestering him and a few other fighters to don their Golden Gloves jackets and head over to Marshall High, a largely black school, to meet some girls. McClure was in college and had no interest in high school girls, but Clay kept bugging him to go. McClure finally agreed, and so they visited the school for lunch. Girls were all over the place, eyeing this team of young gladiators with the new jackets. After Clay got his tray of food, he sat down, said nothing and never looked up.

McClure turned the needle. "You wanted to get us here," he said to Clay. "Come on. Do your thing."

Cassius sat frozen. Recalls McClure: "He was silent, staring at his plate and eating his food."

By this time, Clay was a minor celebrity back home. He had often been featured on *Tomorrow's Champions*, a local Saturday afternoon television program featuring young boxers, and his name had begun appearing in the Louisville *Courier-Journal* as far back as 1957, when he was 15 and he stopped a tough named Donnie Hall. The headline read: CLAY SCORES T.K.O. OVER HALL IN 4TH.

When Jimmy Ellis, a 17-year-old untutored roughneck from Louisville, saw that bout on *Tomorrow's Champions*, he went to the Columbia Gym to learn how to box. Says Ellis, "Hall was a friend of mine, and I figured, I can beat that other guy." So Ellis started fighting. History would soon be up to its old tricks, for it was Ellis, 11 years later, who would win the vacant heavy-weight championship after Ali was stripped of it for having refused to serve in the military during the Vietnam War. Ellis traveled frequently with Clay in their amateur years, and what he remembers most vividly about him was his almost boundless capacity for work in the gym.

"I don't know where he got the energy," says Ellis, who now works for the Louisville parks system. "He'd box and box. He'd box three or four rounds with one guy. Then he'd sit down. Then another guy would come into the gym, and he'd go three or four rounds with him. Then he'd come out and hit the heavy bag. And then he'd go three or four rounds with another guy."

And any time a professional fighter came to town, says Ellis, Clay would train where the pro trained. Dundee brought light heavyweight Willie Pastrano to Louisville in 1957, and they were sitting in their hotel room one day when the phone rang. Dundee took the receiver and heard this: "My name's Cassius Marcellus Clay. I'm the Golden Gloves champion of Louisville, Kentucky. I'm gonna win the Golden Gloves, and I'm gonna win the Olympics in 1960, and I want to talk to you."

Dundee invited him up. For the next three hours, recalls Dundee, Clay picked and probed and plundered his brain, asking him how his fighters trained, what they ate, how far they ran, how much they hit the bags. "He was a student of boxing," Dundee says. "He was so inquisitive. A very interesting young man."

Two years later Dundee and Pastrano were back again—Pastrano was only four years away from winning the light heavyweight crown—training for a fight in Louisville against Alonzo Johnson. There was young Clay again, this time hustling Dundee for a chance to spar with Pastrano. Dundee turned him down—he did not believe in matching amateurs against pros—but the kid persisted: "Come on, come on. Let me work with him."

So Dundee finally yielded. Pastrano sparred one round with Clay, and the boy danced around him. "In and out, side-side, in and out," says Dundee. "Stick-stick-stick. Move-move-move. He was so quick, so agile, Willie couldn't do nothing with him."

Dundee called it off, saying, "Willie, baby, you ain't gonna spar no more. You're too fine, baby."

Pastrano wasn't buying. "Bullshit!" he said. "The kid kicked the hell out of me."

So much of what came to characterize Ali as a fighter—his tactics in and out of the ring—he began cultivating as an amateur. Ellis recalls Clay working on opponents' minds as deftly as he would soon work on their chins. Says Ellis, "We'd be fighting in the wintertime, in Chicago, and there'd be his opponent sitting there sniffling or blowing his nose. Cassius would say, 'Man, you got a cold? I'm gonna knock you out—cold! You can't beat me if you got a cold. I'm gonna knock you out!'"

Martin says that long before Clay went berserk at the weigh-in before his first bout with Sonny Liston, in 1964, he had become a performer—even an artist—at the scales. He was being weighed on March 9, 1960, only hours before facing Jimmy Jones, the defending heavyweight titleholder in

Chicago's Tournament of Champions, when he turned to his trainer. "Mr. Martin," Clay said, "are you in a hurry to get away from here tonight?"

"Not really," said Martin. "Why?"

Clay pointed to Jones and said, "This guy over here, I can get rid of him in one round *if* you're in a hurry. Or, if you're in no hurry, if you want me to box, I can carry him for three rounds."

"I'm in no hurry," said Martin.

"I'll let him go three," Clay said.

The kid spun Jones like a top. Clay slipped the champion's heavy artillery in the first round, and then, according to the *Louisville Times*, he "deftly outboxed him the final two rounds."

Clay was on a path to glory, only six months away from the Rome Olympics, and by then he was rising at four in the morning, before first light, to climb into his sweats and strap on his work boots with the steel toes. At that hour John Powell was usually done sweeping out the liquor dispensary where he worked, and he would sit and listen to the wind blow outside. Recalls Powell: "I'd be sitting on the counter, and I could see his shadow coming around the corner from Grand Avenue. Clay was on his way to Chickasaw Park. Cold, dark winter mornings. You could see that shadow coming. Then here he comes, running by, with those big old Army brogans. He'd be the onliest person in the early morning. And I'd walk outside, and he'd stop and shadowbox. He once said to me, 'Someday you'll own this liquor store, and I'll be the heavyweight champion of the world.' Both of those came true, too."

Clay ran all over Louisville in those steel-toed boots—west to Chickasaw Park in the early morning, east down Chestnut racing the school bus, up and down Walnut Street, downtown and back again, the brogans clomping on the pavement, the fists flying, the litany always the same: "I'm gonna be the next world champion. You're gonna read about me. I'm the greatest!" At 10th and Walnut crowds of men used to gather around a peanut vendor, crack nuts and talk sports.

"Cassius Clay used to come up the street acting like he was hitting people," says Lawrence McKinley. "Shadowboxing and throwing punches in his heavy shoes. Nobody ever dreamed he'd be world champ."

One day one of the street-corner habitués, Gene Pearson, got tired of hearing the litany and vowed to put Clay in his place. "He ain't gonna be no champion," Pearson said. The next time Clay passed the corner, Pearson stepped out from behind a post and hit him with a straight right.

"Pow!" says McKinley. "As hard as he could. Clay like to go all the way down. He went to his knees, just like he was gonna fall, and he stopped himself and looked up at Gene, and he stretched his eyes real wide and he came up and—whew!—he must have hit Gene 15 or 20 times, so fast you could hardly see the punches, and Gene started saying, 'Get him off me! Get him off me! Yeah, you're gonna be the champ.' And Cassius went right on running up the street. Never said nothin'. The next time Cassius came by, one of the guys said, 'Are you gonna hit him again?' And Gene said, 'Hey, champ!'"

Clay was never a street fighter, and classmates can recall only one occasion when he was goaded into fighting. According to Indra Brown, the episode nearly brought Clay to tears. They were at a delicatessen across from the school when two kids began baiting Cassius, pushing him around and saying, "Come on, let's fight. You can fight." Clay kept backing off. "Leave me alone," he kept saying. "I don't want to do this. Leave me alone."

The boys pushed too far. "Cassius finally went after one of them," Brown says. "He floored him. A right hand. To the jaw. Cassius almost cried. I could tell by his voice. But that was the end of that. They never bothered him again."

He avoided all confrontations, including the civil rights demonstrations downtown in which blacks were involved during the late 1950s. Clay was born in a town where most of the public facilities were segregated. Until the barriers started coming down in the '50s, Chickasaw was the only park that blacks could use, and most of the libraries, restaurants and movie theaters were for whites only. Central was the all-black high school. When Clay was at Central, one of the teachers, Lyman Johnson, regularly led students on picket lines and lunch-counter sit-ins. Clay never participated, says Yates Thomas, except the one time that Thomas talked him into joining him on a picket line at a downtown restaurant.

Clay was standing on the sidewalk, says Thomas, when an eighth-floor window opened and a white woman emptied a bucket of water on the marchers below. "She emptied it right on his head," says Thomas. "She got him exactly. Water spilled all over him. He was just standing there."

That ended his career as an activist in Louisville. "He said he would never demonstrate again," says Thomas. "He never did." For years it was believed that Clay's activism began for real upon his return from the Olympics, when a Louisville restaurant refused to serve him and a white motorcycle gang threatened him. According to long-accepted Ali lore, Clay threw his gold medal into the Ohio River. In fact, says Hauser, "he lost it." And while Clay was turned away from restaurants on many occasions, the biker incident never happened.

His life had become so consumed by the rigors of boxing—aside from all the roadwork, he trained in two gyms, with both Martin and Stoner—it was something of a wonder that he made it through Central at all. But in his junior and senior years, Clay had as his ally the most powerful man at Central, the principal. Atwood Wilson adored the young man. At assemblies Wilson would embrace him onstage and announce, "Here he is, ladies and gentlemen: Cassius Clay! The next heavyweight champion of the world. This guy is going to make a million dollars!"

Academically Clay paddled in the doldrums—he ended up ranked 376th in a class of 391 students—but his failure at scholarship did not trouble the principal with the master's degree in education from the University of Chicago. What Wilson admired most of all was excellence, says Bettie Johnson, a counselor at Central, and no one at the school excelled at his job in life more than young Clay did. So the grades be damned. Clint Lovely, a Central student at the time, recalls Wilson saying, "Cassius doesn't need to know anything but how to fill out his income tax. And *I'm* gonna teach him that."

With graduation drawing near, there was a powerful sentiment among some teachers not to permit Clay to graduate because, says Johnson, he wasn't going to pass English. Thelma Lauderdale required a term paper from her English students, and Clay had not done his. "He wanted to do it on the Black Muslims," recalls Johnson, "and the teacher did not feel that was acceptable. The subject was controversial at the time. You have to understand what was going on in black thinking prior to the militancy of the sixties. Black Muslims were considered by blacks as very, very questionable people. Cassius was not a militant, outspoken guy. He always had this mischievous twinkle in his eye, like he had a private joke he was telling himself. He just had this interest in the Muslims."

Before a faculty meeting in the music room, Wilson rose and delivered his Claim to Fame speech: "One day our greatest claim to fame is going to be that we knew Cassius Clay, or taught him." At this point, says the former school librarian, Minnie Alta Broaddus, "I thought, Maybe he knows something I don't know."

Wilson argued that Clay had a unique set of gifts, that he was going to be the heavyweight champion of the world and that he should not be held to the rules governing the average student. No one in the room was more of a scholar than the eloquent Wilson—he was ruthless with any teacher he perceived as mediocre—but here he argued that Clay was so exceptional that he should not be denied a diploma simply because he could not parse a sentence or quote from *Macbeth*. "The coaches all thought it was great because they were always trying to play guys who were ineligible scholastically," says Johnson. "The academic people were outraged because they thought we were letting our standards down."

Wilson was unmoved. "Do you think I'm going to be the principal of a school that Cassius Clay didn't finish?" he said. "Why, in one night, he'll make more money than the principal and all you teachers make in one year. If every teacher here fails him, he's still not going to fail. He's not going to fail in my school. I'm going to say, *I taught him!*"

The Claim to Fame speech carried the day. Clay fulfilled his term paper requirement when Lauderdale permitted him to give an oral presentation to her class, a travelogue on his adventures touring various American cities as an amateur boxer. He passed. At the graduation ceremonies on June 11, 1960, Clay received a standing ovation as he strode to get his diploma. It was, in a sense, a classic final performance for the clown who would be king.

"I remember when he graduated," says Davis. "All the guys had white shirts and ties under their caps and gowns. And dress shoes. He had on a T-shirt, and he walked down the aisle in his brogan work boots. With the steel toes."

It is more than three decades later, the autumn of 1991, and Muhammad Ali is sitting with his head back and his eyes closed in the high-backed leather chair in the office behind his house on a farm in Berrien Springs, Mich. His 50th birthday is two months away. Out back, a horse in a pasture is galloping along a fence. Dusk, in orange silks, approaches from the west. Ali rises slowly from his chair and begins moving sideways across the room, dancing, sliding in and out, shooting out the jab, shadowboxing, daydreaming.

"I'll win the heavyweight championship back when I'm 50 years old!" he says. "Isn't that somethin'? Is that powerful? They can pay $20 million or $50 million to whoever I fight. Holyfield or Tyson. This is gonna shake 'em up. It's like a miracle, a dream. Muhammad Ali is back! Can you picture this?"

Ali sweeps left and right across the rug, stops in front of the hall door and sets his feet. He throws a flurry, snaps a jab, crosses with an overhand right—*Phew! Phew! Phew!*—comes back to his toes, slips back into the chair. He is breathing heavily as he leans back and closes his eyes again. His left hand, resting on his chest, is trembling. The grin is childlike, mischievous.

"Can you believe it?" he says. "Dancin' at 50! . . . Ooooohhh. . . . Dancin' at 50. Maaannnn. It'll be bigger than the moon shot! I'm dedicatin' the fight to the baby boomers, the people who were six years old when I beat Sonny Liston. Now they're thirty-four. I'll do the Ali shuffle!"

Back on his feet, he rolls to the left, stops, stutter-steps a shuffle, dances left and pulls back his head, dodging punches here and sliding there. Ali is inventing himself again, dreaming again, picking and messing with all of the old ghosts in new fantasies.

"I get a hundred million," he says. "Did you hear me say that? A hundred million dollars! In the first 25 seats there'll be 25 presidents. President of Egypt. President of Syria. Gaddafi. Mobutu. Kings. Can you imagine the security? Maaaannnn. A hundred million dollars for architects and builders to build a big school. If you had a chance to build a school, wouldn't you? Imagine: the Muhammad Ali School of Technology or whatever. Seventy-five classrooms. Big kitchen. Auditorium. My dream is to make lectures in the school, to 300 kids! Take them off dope. In the school that I built. Can you imagine that?"

Yes, of course. Three hundred kids, a big, happy family at last. And they can all go swimming in the pool.

January 1992

PART 3

BASEBALL

COLLISION AT HOME

*A century ago the best catcher in baseball,
Boston's Martin Bergen, waged a losing battle
against mental illness—a violent struggle
in which he was not the only casualty*

Early on the morning of Friday, Jan. 19, 1900, in a little wooden farmhouse on a snow-swept spit of land in central Massachusetts, the finest catcher the game of baseball had yet known—a gentle, churchgoing man, an attentive husband, a doting father of two—rose from the couch on which he had been sleeping and made his way in darkness to the kitchen stove. Martin Bergen, age 28, was about to build a fire.

Out back, in the barn where his father was sleeping, the cows needed milking and the hens and the horse feeding, but Bergen's circuitry had been shorting out for months, and he was no longer of this world. On this graying wisp of a winter dawn, those scolding humpbacked witches that had ridden him for years were hanging on more grimly now than ever: the paranoid delusions that had made him duck knife blades as he played behind the plate; the inclement spells of nervousness and catatonia; the fear of his impulse to violence; the lapses in memory; the fits of melancholy; and the fantasies, oh, the fantasies on the train.

He had "suffered spells" and "acted queerly," as people put it in those days, long before he joined the Boston club of the National League in 1896, and the fact that he had stuck there over four full years revealed how much a team was willing to endure to have him behind the plate. Though Bergen was only an adequate hitter, .265 lifetime, the Boston scribblers had crowned him the King of Catchers. He was the Charles Johnson of his day, a nimble fielder with a bullwhip arm who could snap the ball to second base without so much as moving his feet.

"As a catcher, Martin Bergen was the best the world ever produced," future Hall of Famer Jesse Burkett, a St. Louis outfielder, told the *Worcester Spy* in 1900. "No man acted with more natural grace as a ballplayer. There was finish in every move he made. His eye was always true and his movements so quick and accurate in throwing that the speediest base runners . . . never took chances when Bergen was behind the bat."

The Bostons, popularly called the Beaneaters, forgave Bergen's eccentricities while they were winning pennants in '97 and '98, but by the summer of '99, when the team began to struggle, his increasingly erratic behavior made him a lightning rod for discontent. That April his four-year-old son, Willie, had died of diphtheria while the Bostons were on the road, and it had troubled Bergen that he could not get home before the end of the religious service—late to his favorite child's funeral. "It's pretty tough that my boy should be taken away," Bergen lamented to neighbors, "but it seems a great deal harder still to think that I should just get home in time to see him being taken out of the door in a box."

Phantoms were wheeling like crows in his head. Increasingly distracted and morose, he skipped out on the ball club in the middle of a pennant race, in late July, and stole home to his 60-acre farm in North Brookfield, Massachusetts, for a couple of weeks, believing that his teammates were plotting to kill him. In passenger trains, heading to road games, he had sat with his feet in the aisle so he could see his assassins approach from either way. He believed that the National League had hired his personal physician, Louis Dionne, to poison him. He had cried like a frightened boy after unburdening himself of his paranoid fantasies to a reporter for the *Cincinnati Enquirer* and had begged the man not to write what he had said. (The reporter complied.) The clamor and cheering at games had been driving Bergen to a state of heightened agitation.

After his return to the team in August, he caught fewer and fewer games. He smoked heavily and chewed a 10-cent plug of tobacco every game. Dionne listened to his woes and diagnosed the problem as "tobacco heart"—frayed nerves due to excessive use of nicotine.

As the season drew to a close, with Wee Willie Keeler and the Brooklyn Bridegrooms pulling away to beat the Bostons for the flag, Bergen's mental condition grew more acute. He sought remedies from doctors and importuned three Catholic priests—Bergen rarely missed a Sunday Mass—to still the demons that had nested in his soul. He brooded in the clubhouse, staring into the distance for hours. Though of average stature, at 5' 10" and 170 pounds, he appeared to grow larger and more fearsome to his teammates, evolving into a semblance of James Wait in Conrad's *Nigger of the Narcissus,* who inspired such fear among his mates that they shrank from even looking at him. Boston club president Arthur Soden told his boys to be careful around Bergen.

The catcher's wife, Hattie, had told Dionne that she had no fear of him. Nor did she fear for their two children, six-year-old Florence, a pretty brunette in curls, and flaxen-haired Joe, three years younger. Martin liked to hitch up his horse and buggy and take the kids to pick up the mail in town. By January 1900, though, he was not getting along with his father, Michael, whose drinking had been a source of tension between them, and on the night of Jan. 18—when Michael was supposed to start living with the family on the farm—Hattie met her father-in-law at the door and refused to let him into the house. A row ensued. At one point Hattie hid Martin's shotgun under the sheets of their bed, in the same room where the two kids slept, and when Martin got up around 5:30 A.M. to make that fire, he had a couple of shotgun shells in one of his pockets.

Standing before the kitchen stove, he lifted the oven lids and scooped out Thursday's ashes. Then he gathered old papers and laid them on the grate. Crossing the kitchen in his stocking feet, he opened the woodshed door and went inside. He may have meant to break up some wood for kindling. The heavy woodsman's ax was in one corner of the shed. Bergen picked it up. There's no telling where his last hallucination took him, but in that shed he Jekylled into Hyde. He swept back into the kitchen, the ax in his hands, and cut the corner into the bedroom. Hattie saw him coming toward her. She got to her feet and raised her hands to protect herself.

Martin Bergen was born in North Brookfield, 55 miles west of Boston, on Oct. 25, 1871. He was one of six children raised by Michael and Ann Delaney Bergen. When Martin was a teenager, baseball was just coming to flower as the national game, with Cap Anson of the Chicago White Stockings and King Kelly of the Chicagos and then the Bostons running and scratching in their wools. Martin and his younger brother William practiced endlessly, both as catchers.

William, a smooth fielder, would play 11 years in the majors, most of them for the Brooklyns. His most enduring legacy would be a lifetime batting average of .170, still the lowest for any player with more than 3,000 at bats. Martin was cut from a better but softer grain of wood. Even as a kid, on Father James Tuite's team of altar boys, he had periodic tantrums, throwing down his gear and stalking off the field if another player earned more applause. He had a feel for the game, however, and he shaped his considerable athleticism to fit its languorous rhythms.

Everywhere Bergen went trouble followed. He began his run in minor league ball in Salem, Massachusetts, in 1892, where he hit .247, but the year was not over before he got into a beef with a teammate over what the *Sporting News* described as an "imaginary grievance" of Bergen's. He gave the other player "a bad beating." Bergen fought with other teammates that year over what they too maintained were imagined offenses.

At Northampton, Massachusetts, in '93, Bergen's prowess as a catcher began to draw attention, and he got offers from several other teams around New England. In '94 he landed in Lewiston, Maine, where he batted .321 in 97 games and caught brilliantly. "A phenomenal ballplayer," his teammate Jack Sharrott recalled years later in the *Worcester Evening Gazette*, but "so cranky that hardly anyone could get along with him and it was only by the greatest diplomacy that he was gotten along with at all."

Bergen performed so well in Maine that manager Jimmy Manning signed him to his Kansas City (Missouri) Blues in the talent-rich and hotly competitive Western League. There Bergen played to generally effusive reviews. After a 9–7 victory over Indianapolis in late July 1895, the *Kansas City Star* noted, "Bergen caught an excellent game yesterday and kept the visitors anchored to the bases all through the contest." What's more, it was not only his artful catching that was drawing notices. By July 1, Bergen was leading the Blues with a .407 average. "He is one of the cleanest hitters that ever played in Kansas City," the *Star* reported on June 23. His play suggested that he belonged at another level—in the only major league then in existence, the National League.

Mood swings aside—Bergen flipped from bright, expansive highs to dark, despondent lows—he was beginning to show a disturbing inclination to flee from his travails. He had met the pretty, fair-haired Hattie Gaines, who worked as a stitcher in the Batcheller shoe factory in North Brookfield, and they had been married in July 1893. He had urged her to join him in Kansas City, but she had chosen instead to stay with her family in upstate New York during the season. Living in a distant town without his wife left Bergen more unsettled than ever, and his erratic behavior incensed the tough Manning. Near the end of the '95 season, in one of his "spells," Bergen left the Blues over a perceived slight and went home to Massachusetts, never to return.

He would not be out of the game long. Bergen had ended up batting .372 for the Blues that season, with 188 hits and 118 runs scored in 113 games, so it was not any wonder that, at season's end, the desperately needy Bostons came after him. They had lost their formidable catcher, Charlie Bennett, in January 1894. (Leaving Wellsville, Kansas, on a hunting trip, Bennett was running to catch a moving train when he lost his grip, slipped and fell under the wheels. He lived but lost both legs.) Boston manager Frank Selee dispatched his best pitcher, future Hall of Famer Kid Nichols, to scout Bergen in Kansas City. "I saw at once that he was a good man," the Kid recalled in the Boston Morning Journal years later. The Bostons gave the Blues $1,000 and shortstop Frank Connaughton for Bergen, but the catcher sniffed a conspiracy against him, and Selee had to travel to North Brookfield to assure Bergen that he would be used properly and to mollify him over his salary complaints. In those days the National League had a salary cap of $2,400 per player, and Bergen wanted top dollar.

Two seasons would pass before Bergen made the maximum—a good part of '96 was lost to injury—but he began to bloom as a defensive catcher in '97. Some of his feats became legendary. In one game in Washington that year, he threw out seven runners trying to steal second base. "Bergen did throwing the like of which had never been seen in that city," said former New England League umpire William Fitzpatrick, a cousin of Bergen's.

The Bostons were charging toward their fourth pennant in seven years, and the catcher asserted himself as a respected and even crucial member of one of the greatest teams of the 19th century. Four of those Bostons would make it to Cooperstown: Nichols, who won 361 games in a 15-year career, had at least 30 wins per season seven out of eight years, from 1891 through '98, and pitched a staggering 532 complete games; outfielder Hugh Duffy, who holds the highest batting average for a season, .438 in 1894 (236 hits, including 18 home runs, in 539 at bats); outfielder Sliding Billy Hamilton, whose career record of 937 stolen bases stood until Lou Brock broke it in 1979; and third baseman Jimmy Collins, who hit .346 and .328 in the Bostons' last two pennant seasons of the 19th century.

They were solid, even brilliant, and Bergen was embraced as a mate. Between the lines he played the unruffled pro. John Gaffney, one of the premier umpires of those times, never knew Bergen as a complainer, this in an era noted for its theatrics. "I have been behind him umpiring for four years, and in that time he never raised a kick at any of my decisions," Gaffney told the Worcester Telegram in 1900. "The worst I ever heard him say was, 'Gaff, look out for the corners a little sharper.'. . . No man could catch more gracefully or do more with less apparent exertion than Bergen. Every move he made counted. He and [Dick] Buckley were the only two players I've ever seen who could throw to the bases without moving their feet. . . . That was one of Martin's strongest points. It . . . worked [sic] havoc with base runners."

If Bergen seemed odd off the field, he more than made up for it in the Bostons' run to beat the Baltimores for the '98 National League title. That year, Bergen bought his farm two miles outside North Brookfield for $1,650, putting $300 down, and for Christmas the club sent him a present fit for a young gentleman farmer with a family: "Two handsome horses, a carriage, sleigh, harness and a piano," reported the *Springfield Union*.

He was a favorite of the fans, so the money changers in the front office loved him. Bergen had hit only .248 in his second year in the majors, playing 87 games, but he came back in '98 to have his best season, hitting .289 over 120 games and earning his reputation as the best fielding catcher in the game. Yet that year he also grew increasingly hostile and unbalanced and, according to the *Boston Morning Journal*, "assaulted several of the most inoffensive members of the team while in the west."

All this came to a boil on July 28 in what the *Sporting News* would describe as a "sensational scene" instigated by Bergen over breakfast in the fancy dining room of the Southern Hotel in St. Louis. The night before, on the train bearing the team from Brooklyn, pitcher Vic Willis and other players had begun kidding one another. "Bergen took a hand in the fun-making," the *News* reported, "and good fellowship was the rule. Suddenly Bergen grew morose and refused to join in the horseplay. He growled at Willis, but no one paid any attention to it, as it was nothing unusual for him to relapse into one of his spells when he would not talk with or be talked to by anyone."

The next morning, Willis came down to breakfast and was escorted by the headwaiter to a seat next to Bergen. The 22-year-old Willis, a 6' 2" rookie on his way to winning 25 games that season, greeted his catcher as he sat down. "If you don't get away from me," snarled Bergen, "I'll smash you, sure!" Willis refused to move, and Bergen reached over and slapped him on the face. Smarting from the blow, Willis appeared ready to fight, but he checked himself. Several players urged him to another table, then out of the room.

Selee warned him not to retaliate. "I'll make a sacrifice of my personal feelings and swallow the insult in the interests of the club," vowed Willis, "but if Bergen makes another break at me, we'll settle the question of which is the better man." Bergen refused to apologize, claiming he was made the butt of jokes on that train, and Selee warned him against any further trouble, telling Bergen, "If you say the word, I'll begin negotiations at once to trade you." Bergen said that he wanted to stay but that nobody would make a fool of him. The other players, trying for a fifth pennant in eight years, admired Bergen as a hustling, hardworking player but were livid over the slapping incident.

"It's his disposition to be gloomy and morose and we give him all the latitude we can in order to keep peace with him," one unnamed player told the *News*. "That scrap with Vic Willis was an outrage. Bergen made an ass of himself and brought discredit on us all by his inexcusable conduct. . . . It is a surprise to me we were not all thrown out bag and baggage. . . . There is no boycott on Bergen, but there is nothing cordial in our relations with him and he so understands. He has made trouble with a good many of the boys and we just give him a wide berth. But he's a ballplayer, and once we get into a game, personal feelings are set aside in admiration of the artist, for such he is."

The Southern Hotel incident, suppressed by the writers at Selee's request during the season, finally broke in the *Sporting News* in mid-October—after Boston had won the pennant—but the story did not force the team to trade its star catcher. The club had come to perceive him as too valuable. Since the middle of the '98 season, however, the Bostons had been a house unevenly divided, an entire team set against one man. Matters could only grow worse.

In addition to paranoia, Martin Bergen most likely suffered from schizophrenia with a touch of manic depression. "If I had to make a diagnosis, that would be it," says Dr. Carl Salzman, professor of psychiatry at Harvard Medical School, who examined various contemporary accounts of Bergen's behavior. Schizophrenia, Salzman says, can be marked by delusions such as Bergen experienced: "a belief that something is happening that isn't, and it's usually threatening. Other symptoms are withdrawal, inability to socialize, or fear of socializing; flat or dull feelings, not the usual range of expression of emotion; and difficulty thinking and controlling one's thoughts. It's a brain disease that causes the person to be more vulnerable to the usual stresses of life."

Today someone like Bergen would be treated with drugs and psychotherapy, but at the turn of the last century "there weren't any medications to treat this illness," says Salzman. "There was no psychotherapy. Many people [with Bergen's symptoms] were put in hospitals and locked up." The only medicine Bergen seems to have been prescribed were bromides, mild sedatives that, according to Salzman, were "commonly used at that time to quiet people down, especially if they were very anxious or had trouble sleeping." Against Bergen's afflictions, though, bromides were worthless.

Meanwhile, the stresses on the field and off mounted through 1899. The crowds seemed to grow louder and closer around Bergen. His wife became ill with tuberculosis. His paranoid fantasies had become self-fulfilling. Following the St. Louis incident, his teammates indeed "gave him a wide berth" and were no longer cordial. After his son Willie died in April, Bergen began to imagine that players were making light of the boy's death and joking about it behind his back.

Later that spring, in front of the Burnet House Hotel in Cincinnati, sportswriter Harry Weldon of the *Enquirer* came upon Bergen in a "jolly good humor" and asked him what he thought of the pennant race. "Why, we will win the pennant in a gallop," boasted Bergen. "It's a cinch for us!" Then, Weldon would recall in the *Sporting News* the following January, a scowl came over Bergen's face. "But it won't make a damned bit of difference to me whether they win or not," he said.

"Why not?" asked Weldon.

"Because I won't be with this bunch much longer," Bergen said. "I am going to quit them. I am tired of traveling with a lot of knockers and backbiters. They are all giving me the worst of it. I'll shake the gang just as soon as we get to Boston."

Frank Killen, the Boston pitcher, was listening as Bergen spoke. Other teammates soon gathered around, and Bergen stopped talking. Ten minutes later, Weldon was talking to the manager, Selee, when Killen came over, took Weldon aside and said, "Marty is out there crying like his heart would break. He sent me here to ask you not to put anything in the paper about what he told you." Weldon promised. Then Killen turned to Selee and asked what the trouble was with Bergen.

"He is insane," Selee said. "I've done everything in my power to get along with him. He is possessed of the insane idea that none of us like him. I will have to get rid of him. He is the greatest catcher in the business, but . . . there is no use trying to keep him on the team."

Soden, the Beaneaters' president, had warned Selee that Bergen was dangerous and, he feared, might shoot someone. Players thought that Bergen was growing more and more detached from reality. Some attributed his eccentricities to drink, but he was known to be a temperate man and never hung out in saloons on the road, reading in his room after dinner rather than carousing with the boys. When the team played at home, Bergen, rather than stay at a hotel in Boston, commuted by train from North Brookfield.

In July, on their way to Cincinnati at the beginning of a long western road trip, the Boston players were gathered in groups in their special car, laughing and playing cards as Bergen brooded alone in a corner. The train stopped briefly in Washington, D.C. Suddenly, a New York player, whose team also had a special car hitched to the train, dashed into the Boston car and asked what was going on with Bergen. "We looked about the car, but could see nothing of him," Kid Nichols later recalled. "Then someone told us to look out on the platform. There was Bergen, with his grip in his hand, walking away from the train as fast as possible. Our train had started so we could not stop."

It would be the longest and most spectacular walkout of Bergen's career, and it infuriated the Bostons because it left them, as they contended for their third pennant in a row, with only their backup to catch game after game in the midsummer heat. The *Boston Globe's* T.H. Murnane, a former player who had become the most respected of the nation's baseball writers, journeyed to Bergen's farm in late July to get the story and found the shed full of hay, the corn crop healthy and Bergen standing in the barn doorway with little Florence and Joe. He complained to Murnane of all the catching he had done, of his shattered nerves, of his need for rest.

Two years before, following the '97 season, Bergen had told Murnane, "Many a time I have asked for a leave of absence simply because I thought I would go mad if I worked another day without rest." Now Bergen told the reporter, "Manager Selee would never listen to my reasons for coming home, always turning me off with the remark, 'That will cost you fifty dollars; you can't give me any stories.' At Chicago, on the last trip, at least four members of the Boston team went out of their way to abuse me every time I went to bat. They would call out, 'Strike him out!' . . . I left the club when it reached Washington. . . . I found manager Selee and the rest of the players were trying to avoid me."

Bergen's return to Boston, on Aug. 4, a little more than two weeks after he had left, turned out to be the crowning moment of his career. Against the Washingtons, Bergen nailed all three runners who tried to steal on him. The fans gave him an ovation every time he came to bat. In the ninth inning, with two out, the Bostons down 3–2 and men on second and third, Bergen drove a single to left that scored both runners and won the game. Fans vaulted the barricades at South End Grounds to shake Bergen's hand and pound him on the back. Wrote Murnane, "After the game Bergen was a mark for the crowd, who cheered him until he went out of sight."

His teammates were still riled over what Bergen had said about them in the interview with Murnane at the farm, and they were even more rankled by the ovations for Bergen, which suggested to them that the crowd had taken Bergen's side. The next day, before the game, the players demanded that Bergen retract what he'd told Murnane, but he refused. Claiming to the press that they had nothing but "the best of feeling for their comrade" and that they were not guilty of "the charges of keeping aloof from him," the players threatened to strike. They were 15 minutes late for the game, and they took the field only after Bergen resorted to the oldest dodge of all, saying that Murnane had "incorrectly quoted" him.

That September, Bergen went AWOL again. He returned unannounced a few days later, showing up at the ballyard in Brooklyn a few minutes before a game and donning his gear without speaking to anyone, not even Selee. Two days later Bergen was lounging with some Boston players outside Brooklyn's Hotel St. George, appearing to be in the best of moods, when two children began needling them. "Boston couldn't beat nuthin'," they said. According to the *Boston Evening Record*, "Bergen laughingly chased them, and when he caught them sat down on a curbstone, with one child on each knee, making them say, 'Hooray for Boston!' before he would let them go."

Late in the '99 season, with the Bostons trailing the Brooklyns, Bergen read some stinging rebukes of him in the press. The *Boston Post*, which blamed him for the club's woes, wrote that "Bergen has not a good friend on the team" and patronizingly referred to him as "the boy who will not mind." He had vowed to Murnane that he would never play for another team, but Selee and Soden talked openly of trading him.

Under increasing stress, Bergen felt he was going to pieces. Near the end of the season, while catching against Philadelphia, he experienced a psychotic episode that caused him to give up so many passed balls that Selee removed him from the game. As a pitch reached the plate, the *Springfield Republican* reported months later, Bergen would leap out of the way, letting the ball go by, because he imagined someone was standing next to him and making a "fierce stab at him with a knife." The next day, Oct. 10, a headline in the *Boston Globe* read BERGEN MAKES A FARCE OF HIS POSITION.

Bergen began acting wildly, complaining of the circus going on in his head and telling of an urge to run off into the woods. The day after the season ended, his brother William summoned Dionne. The doctor rode out to the farm Martin called Snowball and, according to accounts that appeared months later in the *Boston Herald* and other publications, found him pacing frantically in front of the house. "What's the matter?" Dionne asked.

"Doctor, my head is spinning," Bergen said. "I have lots of strange ideas."

"What sort of ideas?" Dionne asked.

"I have an idea that someone is trying to injure me," Bergen confided. "I don't know what I'm doing. I played ball all last summer, and people tell me I played fine, but I can't remember hardly any of it. In fact, I don't remember hardly anything about the last game—I played it in a trance—except that when it was all over, a man came up to me and said, 'Martin, you played great,' and he gave me a cigar, but I was afraid to smoke it. It was a big cigar, and it looked to me like poison. I thought this man had been told to . . . kill me."

Dionne mixed a bromide for him, but Bergen was reluctant to take it when Hattie poured it. The next day, during a second encounter with Dionne, Bergen confessed, "I thought someone in the National League had found out that you were my family physician and had arranged to give me some poison. I did not take it from my wife because I didn't wish hers to be the hand that poisoned me." Bergen had told Murnane that he walked out on teams when he was seized by an "uncontrollable" urge to cut for home. He told Dionne he had left the Bostons in July because he feared that players were trying to kill him, and that on his journey home he walked sideways through the cars so he could see his pursuers coming at him from either direction.

In November the doctor visited Snowball Farm to attend to the tubercular Hattie. He found her lying on the couch and coughing up blood. Martin was wringing his hands in anguish. "The sight of that blood drives me crazy!" he said.

On Sunday, Jan. 14, Bergen visited Dionne's office to pick up medicine for Hattie. Dionne inquired about his health. Bergen said he had visited a doctor in Kansas City during the summer. Curious about Bergen's memory, Dionne asked him what route he had traveled west. Bergen did not recall. He did remember playing baseball in St. Joseph, Missouri, he said, but that was all. As he left, he said, "This has been a very pleasant talk, and yet it's strange how it has rattled me. I'm almost crazy."

Four days later, on Thursday, Jan. 18, Bergen rose early on the farm, helped his father with the chores and cooked breakfast for his family. He had ordered $25 worth of groceries from Boston the day before, but he had no sleigh with which to fetch the goods from town, so he stopped at Mrs. Daniel Collins's farm and asked to borrow hers. She saw him walking his horse in harness onto her place, his two kids in tow. "Hello, here comes farmer Bergen!" she said. Like the fans in the stands, the gentlefolk around North Brookfield had never seen the dark side of Bergen. He laughed and said, "What kind of farmer do you think I make, Mrs. Collins?"

"I think you will make a very good farmer, Mr. Bergen."

Bergen shook his head and laughed again. "I don't think I will ever make a good farmer," he said.

He hitched the horse to the sleigh and set out with his father for town, leaving the kids behind with Mrs. Collins. In E.W. Reed's drugstore Martin ran into Dionne, to whom he apologized for not having filled the prescription the doctor had given him on Sunday. "I've only just got around to it," Bergen said.

The papers had been abuzz with trade talk involving Bergen, and one man in Reed's asked him, "Are you going to be playing ball, Martin?"

"No, I'll never play another game of ball," he said sadly. Michael Bergen stayed in town while Martin drove back to Mrs. Collins's place, where he picked up Florence and Joe and returned to the farm without his groceries, which had not yet arrived.

Martin was an early riser, as most farmers are, and the soundest guess is that the following morning he came off the couch where he'd slept at around half past five. Not long after, he rushed out of the shed, ax in hand, hallucinating in a psychotic fury, and raised the blade above Hattie as she stood by the bed.

Wielding the weapon with a batter's practiced force, Bergen brought it down on the left side of her head, crushing her forehead and killing her instantly. She fell on the bed with her arms still raised above her head, as if in supplication. Florence and Joe, in their nightclothes, ran screaming out of the room. Martin swept after them and caught the boy with the blade along the top of the head, severing the crown of his skull, then picked up the body outside the bedroom door and threw it to the bedroom floor. Florence had hidden behind a kitchen chair, but Bergen saw her and went after her. He missed her once with the ax, breaking a piece off the wooden chair, but killed her with a blow to the head in front of the stove.

Surrounded by his dead family, Bergen took his straight razor off the kitchen shelf, stood before the looking-glass above the sink and cut his throat with such force that he nearly decapitated himself. The razor fell on a table by the sink. Martin died next to Florence on the kitchen floor.

Later that morning Michael got up in the barn and went to the house. He tried the front door, but it was locked. He heard no movement inside. He went to Mrs. Collins's place and told her that the house, usually bustling in the morning, was silent, and that the curtains were drawn. "Go back and milk the cows," Mrs. Collins said, "and try to get into the house."

Near noon, Michael let himself in through the shed. He saw the carnage by the stove.

Less than eight years had passed since the most infamous ax murders in U.S. history: the hacking to death of Lizzie Borden's parents in Fall River,

Massachusetts, 63 miles southeast of North Brookfield. The Bergen mur-
der-suicide would not achieve such long-lasting notoriety, but the story,
involving one of the most famous ballplayers of the day, was strung in black
in the headlines of newspapers nationwide among the latest dispatches
from the Boer War.

The horror of what took place on Snowball Farm not only plunged the
little town of North Brookfield into mourning but also fetched sleighs with
bells ringing from miles around the countryside. Hundreds of people, some
of them riding in a horse-drawn taxi from town, gathered around the
Bergen house and peered ghoulishly through the windows as doctors,
policemen, the coroner and the undertaker moved around the bodies, trying to piece together what had happened.

The next day, in a steady rain, the bodies were taken in three hearses to
St. Joseph's Church in North Brookfield, where 800 mourners gathered
inside to hear the service. At least that many stood outside. Only two baseball men—an East Brookfield neighbor, 37-year-old Connie Mack of the
Milwaukee team, and Sliding Billy Hamilton, Bergen's roommate on the
road—attended the funeral.

"What a state his mind must have been in!" cried Jesse Burkett when he
heard the news. Horrified members of the Boston team were quoted endlessly in the papers—including all those who, taking Soden's advice, had
shunned Bergen. They had avoided him in life and had not attended the
funeral after his death. A number of them pleaded that they had mistakenly thought the service was on Sunday. Selee did send flowers.

The burial was in a single broad grave in St. Joseph's Cemetery. Bergen's
good friend T.H. Murnane, the writer and former ballplayer who had visited him at the farm six months earlier and found him standing and smiling with his two children in the barn doorway, sent 28 white flowers with
a background of ferns and a note that said, "May these flowers speak a word
of charity for Martin Bergen, who has done this insane deed."

The flowers were lying on Bergen's casket as the funeral train wound up
the hill to the cemetery.

June 2001

YANKEE STADIUM

It was a balmy morning in the Harlem River Valley that separates the Bronx from the island of Manhattan, and in the distance you could hear the clack and rumble of the elevated trains as they passed just outside the centerfield wall of Yankee Stadium. Inside the Stadium—as workers in yellow hard hats scurried about the scaffolding and pigeons pecked at the freshly planted sod—there was a sense of renewal in the air. It was Feb. 17, and George Steinbrenner's ballpark was undergoing its makeover for the 1999 baseball season, its final facial of the millennium. Only Monument Park, that brick-lined haven tucked behind the wall in left center, was untouched by the pneumatic drills and hammers.

For decades the Stadium has been one of New York's most popular tourist attractions, the Bronx's answer to the Empire State Building and the Statue of Liberty; on this sparkling Tuesday morning, tour guide Tony Morante was leading 20 visitors up the walkway into Monument Park when they all seemed to stop at once. There before them, rising like tombstones in the corner of a churchyard, were four marble slabs bearing bronze plaques depicting in bas-relief the merry visages of Yankees legends Babe Ruth, Lou Gehrig, Miller Huggins and Mickey Mantle. Deirdre Weldon had brought nine boys from Yorktown, New York, to celebrate the birthday of her son, Terry; as they all gathered reverently around, staring at the faces on the monuments staring back at them, 10-year-old Chris Raiano said aloud what all his friends were wondering.

"Are they all buried here?" he asked.

"No, they are not," Weldon replied. "Only the memories are. . . ."

Back in 1921, not long after the New York Giants' baseball team moved to evict the Yankees from the Polo Grounds in Manhattan—the Giants were sore that Babe Ruth's Yankees were outdrawing them—the Yankees' owners, beer baron Jake Ruppert and Til Huston, announced that they had

205

purchased a 10-acre lot across the river, in the Bronx, and that they planned to build a ballyard of their own. The Giants' manager, John McGraw, scoffed at the scheme. "This is a big mistake," said Little Napoleon. "They are going up to Goatville, and before long they will be lost sight of."

Today, nearly 80 years later, old Goatville is the richest repository of memories in American sports. It was way up there, in the wilds of the Bronx, that the New York Yankees won 33 American League pennants and 24 world championships. Close your eyes, and you can see, on the grainy film of memory, Lou Gehrig listening to the echoes of his farewell speech in 1939 . . . Al Gionfriddo twice looking over his shoulder and then reaching out for Joe DiMaggio's 415-foot drive in the '47 Series . . . Mickey Mantle's thunderous shot denting the copper frieze lining the upper deck in right . . . Reggie Jackson driving a knuckleball into the black tarp covering the seats in center for his third home run in the final game of the '77 Series . . . Yogi Berra leaping into Don Larsen's arms at the end of the Perfect Game . . . the dying Ruth, bracing himself on a bat, waving that last, long goodbye.

It was there, in 1928, in the very bowels of the place, that Notre Dame's Knute Rockne, at halftime of a scoreless tie against Army, exhorted his players to "win just one for the Gipper." It was there that Doc Blanchard ran with Glenn Davis in '44, when Army whipped the Irish 59–0, and it was there that Jack Dempsey flattened Jack Sharkey in '27, first scrambling his eggs with a low blow and then shaving his stubble with a short, sharp hook to the chin. Joe Louis fought in Yankee Stadium 11 times, and it was there in '38, in the most politically charged prizefight in history, that he knocked out Hitler's model of Aryan supremacy, Max Schmeling, at 2:04 of the first round. And it was there, too, that the New York football Giants waged all those wintery wars against the Bears, the Browns and the Baltimore Colts.

Of course, neither Ruppert nor Huston foresaw any of this when they bought the land from the estate of William Waldorf Astor for $675,000 and then shelled out $2.5 million for construction of the park. All they really had in mind, by way of mooning the Giants just across the river, was to build the largest, grandest ballpark in America. In the remarkably brief course of 284 working days, beginning on May 5, 1922, some 500 men turned 45,000 barrels of cement into 35,000 cubic yards of concrete. They made bleachers out of 950,000 board feet of Pacific Coast fir that came to New York by boat through the Panama Canal. They secured the grandstand seats with 135,000 steel castings and a million brass screws. They rolled out 16,000 square feet of sod.

When it was finished, the park had 36 ticket booths and 40 turnstiles that ticked like clocks as they counted the house. And what a house it was—a colossus, in fact, a three-tiered horseshoe that seated 70,000. F.C. Lane, in a 1923 issue of the *Literary Digest*, called it "the last word in ball parks. But not the least of its merits is its advantage of position. From the plain of the Harlem River it looms up like the great Pyramid of Cheops from the sands of Egypt."

It was the first ballpark in America to be called a stadium, which traces back to the ancient Greek and Roman word for a track for footraces, and the place had nothing if not room to run. When Ruth stepped out of the Yankees' dugout and onto the field for the first time, he looked around and declared, "Some ballyard!" It was short down the lines, 281 feet to left and 295 to right, but the fence flared out sharply in left and seemed to disappear at the 490-foot mark in dead center, creating an alley in left center that righthanded power hitters dubbed Death Valley. Wrote one bug-eyed scribbler in the *New York Sun*, "The flag pole seems almost beyond the range of a siege gun as it rears its height in distant center field."

The Yankee Stadium, as it was called then, had its grand opening on April 18, 1923, and more than 70,000 people—at the time the largest crowd ever to watch a baseball game—made their pilgrimage to see the Yankees play the Boston Red Sox. The roads around the Stadium were unpaved, and flivver dust choked the patrons massed at the turnstiles. The impatient crowd pressed forward, and it took a cordon of 200 policemen to keep it back. Baseball commissioner Kenesaw Mountain Landis arrived via the Interborough subway, promptly got caught in the crush of bodies outside the gates and had to be rescued by the cops. Inside, as John Phillip Sousa struck up the Seventh Regiment Band for *The Star-Spangled Banner*, the two rival managers, Huggins and Boston's Frank Chance, pulled the rope that raised the flag just inside the centerfield wall. The Yanks won the opener 4–1, on a homer by Ruth.

Grantland Rice, in the next day's *New York Tribune*, rolled up his sleeves and let fly with this lead: "A white streak left Babe Ruth's 52-ounce bludgeon in the third inning of yesterday's opening game at the Yankee Stadium. On a low line it sailed, like a silver flame, through the gray, bleak April shadows, and into the right field bleachers. And as the crash sounded, and the white flash followed, fans arose en masse . . . in the greatest vocal cataclysm baseball has ever known."

The saga of Yankee Stadium had begun, and it wasn't three innings old when Ruth claimed the place as his own. Because of its short porch in right, the House That Ruth Built was also known as the House Built for

Ruth. While placing the centerfield fence at the outer limits—or beyond—of most righthanded hitters, the mischievous Ruppert then took an even greater edge. He made the cracking of home runs a relatively facile exercise for lefthanded pull-hitting sluggers, of whom he had the greatest ever. Ruth's 54 homers in 1920 and his 59 in 1921—many of them over the Polo Grounds' short porch in right—had established the fan appeal of the home run and had launched the Babe as America's most charismatic athlete. Ruppert designed for Ruth a porch of his own.

Over the next 20 years, first through the power of Murderers' Row and then through the teams of DiMaggio, the Stadium became a kind of secular church in the Bronx. The Grand Concourse, two blocks north of the Stadium, was the main thoroughfare for an upscale neighborhood of handsome apartment buildings that had elevators and doormen. Many of the players lived up the hill in the Concourse Plaza, and kids used to meet them coming out the door and trail them to the Stadium.

John McNamara grew up there in the 1920s, and he recalls the day the bronze door of the players' exit burst open and out swept the Babe himself, wearing his signature raccoon coat. "He looked like a bear," says McNamara. "He was trying to get into this little roadster, but he was so big he couldn't. He took off his coat, handed it to me and said, 'Here, kid, hold the coat.' I took it like the Pope was handing me his cloak. When he got in, I handed it back to him. 'Thanks, kid,' he said, and drove off. What a thrill!"

In those days visiting teams often stayed at the New Yorker Hotel at 34th Street and Eighth Avenue in Manhattan and came to the ballpark on the C-line subway. "When I was a kid, I used to wait by the subway station at the Stadium and meet the players when they got off," says Arthur Richman, a senior adviser for the Yankees, who grew up in the Bronx. "I met the old St. Louis Browns there. They used to get me in."

As those championship pennants multiplied along the Stadium's facade—10 were fluttering there by the end of World War II—old Goatville became a national shrine. "If you'd never been to Yankee Stadium, you'd never been to the big leagues," says former big league pitcher Bill Fischer, who first played there with the White Sox in 1957. "It was like you had never *lived* until you played ball in that town."

Fischer's first trip there came near the end of the longest orgy of winning in Yankees history and in the history of baseball—the dozen years from 1947 through 1958—and at a time when major events in three sports had lifted the place to the zenith of athletic venues. There have been 30 world championship fights contested as main events at the Stadium. It was there that Rocky Marciano twice whipped Ezzard Charles in '54—the second time after Charles had butterflied Marciano's nose like it was a shrimp and opened a cut over his left eye; Marciano was bleeding so much by the eighth round that his corner feared the fight would be stopped. Bulling forward, increasingly desperate as the seconds ticked away, Marciano caught Charles in the eighth, dropping him with a long right hand for a count of four, and then chasing him across the ring and knocking him out with a left hook and a right cross.

Sugar Ray Robinson, pounding for pounding the greatest of all fighters, lost only 19 times in his 25-year career, but two of his most memorable losses came in that little ring set up over second base. On June 25, 1952, giving away almost 16 pounds to light heavyweight champion Joey Maxim, Robinson was hitting Maxim at will for 11 rounds, winning easily on all cards and about to take his third world title before deliquescing in the 104° heat. It was so hot that night that the referee, Ruby Goldstein, nearly keeled over and had to be replaced following the 10th round. Robinson's collapse began in the 12th, when he staggered around as Maxim pursued him and pounded his body. Robinson fell to the canvas in the 13th after missing Maxim with a wild right, and the crowd of 47,983 gasped as Robinson, slumped on his stool, was unable to answer the bell for the 14th. Thus he suffered the only knockout of his career, but it was the heat, not Maxim, that did him in.

And it was in Yankee Stadium in '57 that middleweight champion Robinson and welterweight titleholder Carmen Basilio, an onion farmer from upstate New York, skinned and peeled each other for 45 long minutes in what the New York Times called, "fifteen rounds of the most savage fighting ever seen at the Yankee Stadium." In a dramatic climax, ring announcer Johnny Addie called out a split decision and declared Basilio the new middleweight champ.

Bob Sheppard has been at the Stadium's public address microphone since 1951, announcing all regular- and postseason baseball games in his precise, resonant voice, but among his most cherished memories are those from the Giants' football games he worked. Sheppard was at the Stadium on Dec. 28, 1958, for the Greatest Game Ever Played, the overtime NFL championship game between the Giants and the Colts. What he remembers now is the Colts' final drive in regulation; losing 17–14, they had the ball on their own 14 with two minutes left. He can still see quarterback Johnny Unitas finding flanker Raymond Berry again and again. "It drove me crazy," Sheppard says. "We almost had it in the bag. The Colts only had two minutes and all those yards to go, and I thought, It's safe. We have a good defense. But what a magician that Unitas was! He had me saying, over and over and over on the P.A., *Unitas to Berry, first down. . . . Unitas to Berry, first down. . . . Unitas to Berry, first down!*" Steve Myhra kicked a field goal to tie the score 17–17, and the Colts won it in sudden death when fullback Alan Ameche plunged through a hole at the one to score. "A huge hole," moans Sheppard.

That game was played less than three months after the Yankees beat the Milwaukee Braves in the seventh game to win the 1958 World Series. That victory crowned a 12-year stretch in which the Yankees won 10 pennants and eight World Series—a record five titles in a row from 1949 to '53. The Stadium itself had changed very little since '23. By then the Yankees had installed those monuments close to the wall in center, the first, in 1932, honoring Huggins, who had died three years before, and then stones commemorating Gehrig ('41) and Ruth ('49). The monuments were in the field of play, and nothing tested a centerfielder more than having to run down a ball that was rattling around between the monuments and the wall. The Yankees shortened the Stadium's deepest fences in 1937—centerfield went from 490 feet to 461, left center went from 460 to 457 and right center from 429 feet to 407—but it still took a Thorlike blast to reach the bleachers. It is no wonder so many memories of those years involve outfielders dashing madly after long fly balls.

In the sixth game of the '47 Series, with the Yankees leading the Dodgers three games to two, DiMaggio came to bat with two men on in the sixth and the Dodgers leading 8–5. Leftfielder Al Gionfriddo was playing near the line when DiMaggio ripped a 415-foot drive toward the bullpen in leftfield. Gionfriddo, thinking he had no chance, took off after it anyway, head down. Twice he looked back over his left shoulder. On the rooftops of the nearby Gerard Avenue apartment buildings, men with binoculars watched him run and listened as Dodgers play-by-play man Red Barber shouted over the radio, "Gionfriddo's going *backbackbackbackback!*" DiMaggio was rounding first as Gionfriddo neared the wall: "I saw it coming over my head," Gionfriddo recalls, "and I knew I had to jump, and so I jumped, with my back toward the plate, and I reached out and caught the ball in midair, as I am turning, and I came down and hit the bullpen gate with my butt."

Barber cried out, "Oh, doctor!"

DiMaggio, that most taciturn of men, kicked the dirt as he pulled up near second base. "In all the years I played with him, that's the only time Joe showed any emotion," Yankees shortstop Phil Rizzuto says. "Ever." The Dodgers won the game 8–6 but lost the Series.

Rizzuto remembers Ruth's coming to the park long after he'd retired in '34, even when he was sick and dying of throat cancer, and sitting in the dugout cheerily spinning tales. "He used to sit on the bench in that camel hair coat and camel hair hat with that big cigar. His voice was just about gone with cancer, but he'd tell us stories about the old days, like how he'd eat hot dogs during games. Some innings, when he wasn't going to bat, he'd just stay out in rightfield and walk to the hot dog vendor under the stands and eat hot dogs among the people. . . ."

Two months before Ruth died, in '48, he returned a final time to celebrate the Stadium's 25th anniversary, and *Herald Tribune* photographer Nat Fein got a picture of him on a stool in the clubhouse. "He was so sick, it took two men to dress him," Fein recalls. "The Yankees were playing Cleveland that day, and Ruth took Bob Feller's bat and leaned on it, like a cane, as he's coming out of the dugout." Fein took a picture of Ruth from behind, with the number 3 on his back for the last time. That picture won the Pulitzer Prize in '49.

The Stadium touched everyone who played in it. Former Brooklyn pitcher Carl Erskine grew up in Anderson, Indiana (pop. 55,000), hearing about Ruth and Gehrig and DiMaggio and dreaming about playing in the Stadium one day. And there he was, in the '49 World Series, walking into the visitors' clubhouse recently vacated by the Yankees, who had switched dressing rooms. "We walked in, awestruck, a bunch of kids," says Erskine, "and here were two lockers with two uniforms in them: Ruth's and Gehrig's. All cleaned and pressed and hanging there. I think they did it on purpose: We'll shake these kids up *real* good.

"The Stadium had an aura. There was a feeling of privilege and almost a disbelief that you're walking on the same field as those greats of the past. I stood on the mound there one day, and I'm looking around at 70,000 people, and I had this thought: *That's more people than live in Anderson!*"

In the sixth game of the '51 Series, the Yankees were leading the Giants three games to two when rightfielder Hank Bauer struck a bases-loaded triple in the sixth, giving the Yanks a 4–1 lead that they carried into the ninth. The finish was a circus. The Giants loaded the bases with nobody out and Irvin coming to bat. Stengel called on lefty Bob Kuzava. Irvin hit a bolt to left center that Bobby Brown, the Yankees' third baseman, says traveled about 450 feet before left-fielder Gene Woodling chased it down. That scored the runner from third and advanced the other two. Bobby Thomson then struck a nearly identical shot to left center that Woodling grabbed on the run. The runner scored from third, making it 4–3. With the tying run on third, pinch hitter Sal Yvars came to bat. "I can still see it," Sheppard says. "Yvars hit a screaming line drive to right."

"I was holding my breath," says Rizzuto.

Bauer, playing deep, charged. "I saw it, and then I didn't see it," he recalls. He slid forward feet-first and snatched it off the top of the grass, ending the game and winning the Series. Brown laughs at the unlikely climax: "Monte Irvin and Bobby Thomson hit two balls 900 feet and Yvars hit a screaming line drive, and the next day one headline said, KUZAVA SHUTS DOWN GIANTS IN THE NINTH."

DiMaggio played in his last World Series that year; Mantle was playing in his first. One of the most important plays in Mantle's career took place in the second game of that Series. On a Willie Mays fly ball, Mantle, trying to get out of DiMaggio's way, stepped on a drain cover, tore ligaments in his right knee and collapsed. He lay motionless. "I thought he'd been shot, the way he went down," Yankees second baseman Jerry Coleman says. "That was the beginning of Mickey's long, agonizing problems with his leg."

Mantle was DiMaggio's heir apparent to the most venerated role in the Stadium's lore: the Yankee slugger. It was a legacy founded by Ruth from Opening Day in '23, and a parade soon trooped in his wake: Gehrig, DiMaggio, Berra, Mize, Mantle, Roger Maris. But none of them, not even Ruth, hit the ball as far as Mantle did. Twice in his career, batting from the left side, the Mick was a foot or two short of becoming the first man to drive a fair ball out of the Yard. Over the years, the fact that no one has ever done so became a central element of the Stadium's mystique.

On May 30, 1956, facing Washington Senators pitcher Pedro Ramos, Mantle drove a 2-and-2 fastball into the copper frieze along the rightfield roof. "I first thought it was just a pop fly," Ramos recalls, "but it carried like that new airplane that's gonna take a half hour from San Francisco to New York. If it had not hit the roof, it would have been in Brooklyn."

Seven years later Mantle busted a fastball from Bill Fischer, now pitching for the Kansas City Athletics, that hammered the same filigree. "You could hear everybody suck in their breath when it was hit," says Rizzuto. "It was on its upward arc when it hit that facade, and then it seemed to hesitate a moment before it dropped." Mantle proclaimed it the hardest ball he ever hit. Says Fischer, "Six feet over and it would have gone right through the gap by the bullpen and killed somebody waiting at the train station."

Perhaps the mother of all blasts in the Stadium came two years later when 6' 7", 255-pound Frank Howard of Washington smote a Steve Hamilton fastball down the foul line and over the upper deck in left, over the exits and over the roof and out of the park. It was foul by about four feet. "Nobody's ever hit a ball that far," says Yankees third baseman Clete Boyer. "It was like a shot out of a bazooka. I wish it had been fair. You had to see it to believe it."

Which is precisely what they were saying on that afternoon of Oct. 4, 1955, as the 2,838,000 citizens of Brooklyn danced out their doors and into the streets. For Brooklyn fans, the Stadium had come to be the embodiment of a wicked curse—a mammoth white oracle orchestrating their fate. Coming into their '55 Series with the Yankees, the Dodgers had been in seven World Series since 1916, and they had never won a championship. The Yankees had beat them four times (two of those in seven games) in the past eight years. Going into the seventh game of the '55 Series, each team had won on its home field, setting up what Harold Rosenthal of the *New York Herald Tribune* described at the time as possibly "the most dramatic Series game ever played."

Dodgers manager Walter Alston made two fateful moves that day. First, since the Yard was friendly to lefthanded pitchers, he sent Johnny Podres to the mound. Second, in the sixth inning Alston moved Jim Gilliam, an infielder playing leftfield that day, to second base—where he belonged—and replaced him with Sandy Amoros, a light-hitting outfielder with the range of an antelope.

The Dodgers were leading 2–0 in the sixth when Berra came to the plate with no outs, Billy Martin on second and Gil McDougald on first. Amoros was playing the lefthanded pull hitter toward center. "I threw a fastball that was high and about a foot outside," recalls Podres. "He shouldn't have even swung at it! But Yogi did." Berra sliced the ball down the leftfield line. Amoros got a good jump and began sprinting wildly toward the foul pole. Martin took off for third, and McDougald raced to second. As he rounded second, he saw Amoros closing on the ball. "When Amoros got near the fence, he put on the brakes, and it looked like he was leaning backward," McDougald recalls. "When I saw that, I took off for third. I was going to score! And then Sandy stuck out his hand. . . ."

All of Flatbush inhaled at once. Brooklyn fans had seen this all before, year after year—the killing Yankees rally, the final turn of the screw. Frozen now in time, that moment, that scene, is a museum piece, an autumn diorama worthy of its own corner at Cooperstown—the October light playing tricks in leftfield, McDougald racing toward third, the players in the dugouts on their feet, heads craning toward that corner, the ball slicing and Amoros reaching out. . . .

"The sun was devastating that day," says Coleman, "and there were dark shadows in front of Amoros. He never saw that ball. . . ."

"And then Sandy stuck out his hand," says McDougald, "and found that Easter egg."

Both runners skidded to a stop as Amoros turned and fired to shortstop PeeWee Reese, who fired to first baseman Gil Hodges and caught McDougald between second and third. "I felt like cutting across the diamond, but I think the coaches would have got mad at me," McDougald says.

It all seems so simple to Podres now: "Yogi hit that ball off me, and Amoros made the greatest catch in America."

The Dodgers won, their first and only World Series in Brooklyn, and Erskine remembers walking into the clubhouse when it was all over—the same clubhouse where Ruth's and Gehrig's uniforms had been left hanging clean and neatly pressed in '49—and feeling a tranquillity that he'd never felt before. "To go to their park and beat them, after all those frustrating years, just added a dimension to it," he says. "There was a quietness when we first walked in that clubhouse, almost a spiritual feeling, gratitude for this accomplishment. Then someone popped a bottle of champagne, and the lid blew off."

Just as it was about to do again on the afternoon of Oct. 8, 1956, when Dodgers pinch hitter Dale Mitchell came to the plate in the top of the ninth, the only man standing between Don Larsen and his perfect game. Larsen had pitched brilliantly, to be sure, but the elements had favored him that day. In the fall the Stadium is hard on hitters late in the day. As the sun sets behind the upper deck, a shadow gradually moves across the infield; there is a time when the ball is pitched out of the sunlight and into the shade—the ball seems to flicker on and off like a light. The glare also makes leftfield the hardest position to play in baseball at that time of year. "It gets late early out there," as Yogi once famously said.

In the second inning Jackie Robinson smacked a liner off third baseman Andy Carey's glove. The ball caromed to McDougald at short. "Luck, blind luck," McDougald recalls. Robinson's foot was six inches above the bag when Collins took the peg at first. "Out!"

In the fifth Hodges drove a ball into left center, a homer almost anywhere else, but Mantle, the fastest Yankee of them all, was in full flight, à la Gionfriddo, and made a sensational backhanded catch. And then Amoros hit a long drive down the right-field line that looked like a homer, but it hooked foul by inches.

By the sixth inning, Coleman recalls, excited Yankees on the bench began playing manager and moving players around on the field: Move here! Move there! Play up! Play back! Finally Stengel had had enough: "Shut up!" he hollered. "I'm managing this here ball club!"

By the time Mitchell, the 27th Dodgers hitter of the day, came to bat, a cathedral-like stillness had descended on the Stadium. "He was a tough contact hitter," recalls Sheppard. "I thought, Oh, no. The last out. The last player. Top of the ninth. My stomach was churning. It was silent. You don't shout, you just pray." Larsen's first pitch was outside, ball one. The second was a slider for a called strike. Mitchell then swung at and missed a fastball, strike two, then fouled off another fastball. Larsen's third fastball caught the outside corner of the plate. "I can see Babe Pinelli turning and calling, 'Steee-rike three!'" says Sheppard. "The exhalation! It filled the Bronx!"

And it still does, even though the Stadium is no longer what it was in the days when the Yankees shared the place with the football Giants and Louis and Marciano and Robinson. The Giants are long gone to Swampsville in New Jersey, and the last fight to be staged there was on Sept. 28, 1976, when Muhammad Ali feebly outpointed Ken Norton to keep his heavyweight title. In 1973, on the occasion of its 50th anniversary, the Stadium underwent major surgery. When all of King George's men put Yankee Stadium back together again, all those girders that blocked sight lines were gone, but so was Death Valley and the monuments, which were moved to the other side of the fence in left center. And with the infusion of righthanded power in the Yankees' lineup, most notably Dave Winfield in 1981, the fences kept coming in. "People want to see home runs," Steinbrenner said in 1984, as he prepared to bring the walls in again. "It hasn't been fair to our righthand hitters." Today, that original 460-foot power alley in left center is now 399 feet, and the centerfield wall, once 490 feet away, is now 408.

From the fall of '73 to the spring of '74, the men of the Invirex Demolition Co. busted up the Stadium with jackhammers and wrecking balls, turning Goatville into the greatest archaeological dig west of Cheops. Jay Schwall, the owner of Invirex, ordered the 30-ton copper frieze dismantled and melted down—including that section over rightfield that, he says, bore a dent from Mantle's bazooka shot in '63.

Bert Sugar, boxing historian and baseball aficionado, sifted through the artifacts and unearthed everything but Rockne's halftime speech. He walked away with Babe Ruth's ashtray and bat bag—"which looks like a cow's udder," he says—sheets of undistributed World Series tickets from

'48, the year the Yankees finished a close third, 2 1/2 games behind Cleveland; a set of first-down chains (*Unitas to Berry, first down*); Casey Stengel's shower door; and a full uniform worn by DiMaggio, a pair of Gehrig's pinstriped pants and Ron Swoboda's jockstrap.

Some things are immutable. The Bronx is up, and the Battery's down. And some things should never change. The old Grand Concourse neighborhood is not what it used to be. The doormen are gone, the elevators are going. The Concourse Plaza, where so many Yankees used to live, is now a home for senior citizens. There has been much talk lately of building a new Yankee Stadium on Manhattan's West Side. Or in New Jersey. For those whose lives have been touched by the spirit of Yankee Stadium, such a thought is tantamount to a sacrilege.

"Can you imagine moving the Statue of Liberty to Montauk Point?" says Sheppard.

"How about moving Carnegie Hall to Hoboken?" says Sugar.

Yankee Stadium may not be the house it was when Ruth built it, but it remains on the same plot of land Ruppert and Huston picked out when they decided to stick it to McGraw's Giants, and it has been hallowed by the triumphs and failures of the great athletes who played there and were, in turn, shaped by the experience.

Mickey Mantle used to have this recurring nightmare about the Stadium: He is dressed in his Yankees uniform, wearing spikes. He can hear Sheppard announcing the lineup one player at a time, his voice echoing like Gehrig's farewell. "Catching *catching*, number 8 *number 8*, Yogi *Yogi* Berra *Berra*. . . ." Mantle is outside, on the street, and he is trying, frantically, to get in. All the gates are locked, but he can see inside. The Stadium is full. He hears Sheppard call his name: "In centerfield *centerfield*, number 7 *number 7*, Mickey *Mickey* Mantle *Mantle*. . . ." He rattles the gates, a prisoner locked outside, but no one is there to help him, and he cannot get in.

Maybe this was Mantle's final legacy, this nightmare he bequeathed to us. That we would one day go to Yankee Stadium and the gates would be locked, the monuments moved, and we could not get in. And then not even the memories would be buried there.

June 1999

HE'S STILL NOT HOME FREE

The Mets' brilliant first baseman and team leader, Keith Hernandez, an indispensable man in the playoffs, must, as always, deal with doubts and demons and a love-hate relationship with his father

"EVERYBODY THINKS, BECAUSE YOU MAKE A LOT OF MONEY, THAT YOU HAVE A LOCK ON HAPPINESS. IT'S NOT TRUE. . . . I MOST FEAR BOREDOM AND LONELINESS, LIFE AFTER BASEBALL. LIFE AFTER BASEBALL EQUALS BOREDOM AND LONELINESS. I DON'T WANT TO BE A 50-YEAR-OLD GUY SITTING AND DRINKING BEER IN SOME PICKUP BAR WITH YOUNGER PEOPLE. I'VE SEEN IT. I DON'T WANT TO BE THAT."

Keith Hernandez

There is only one place where Keith Hernandez feels truly safe, only one place on God's green earth where he is at home. To be Keith Hernandez—arguably the finest fielding first baseman of all time, a lifetime .301 hitter, the indisputable leader of the New York Mets—requires just such a place, complete with a moat, wherein he can make a separate peace.

Oh, to be sure, he has that two-bedroom condo in that high rise in Manhattan, where he lives alone with his paintings and his books on the Civil War and his racks of wine and his new suits of clothes. Way up there, he can stand on the balcony on a summer night and look up at the lights on the Chrysler Building and down at the masses flowing along Second Avenue and say, as he did recently, "They can't get at me here."

But other things can, and they do. There is the telephone ringing, often incessantly. There are those long, empty spaces in his life in which self-doubt mounts and rides him like a witch. There are the periods of loneliness between girlfriends, which compel him to call his older brother, his closest friend, in a state of panic and say, "God, Gary, I don't like being by myself! There are 10 million people in New York and it's so lonely. I don't think I'll ever meet anybody again."

There is only one place of retreat away from all that turmoil, and that's where the earth is really green and the bases are white, where those wonderfully straight chalk lines embrace him in the orderly universe of baseball. Nothing intrudes upon him there. In fact, such is the intensity of his focus on the field that fellow players still marvel at Hernandez's performance in that fateful month of September 1985.

He had separated from his wife and three children and was in the first throes of a hostile estrangement. On Sept. 6 he appeared before a widely publicized Pittsburgh grand jury investigating drug dealer Curtis Strong, and for four hours testified about his use of cocaine between 1980 and early 1983, when he was playing for the St. Louis Cardinals. On the field, he was literally leading the Mets through a tight divisional title race with the Cardinals. In fact, just four days before he testified in Pittsburgh—an ordeal so physically draining that his suit was soaked through with sweat—he went 5 for 5 in San Diego.

Gary, a former minor leaguer who now sells insurance in northern California, says, "If I was about to go before a grand jury, I'd have been so distracted that I probably would have put my uniform on backwards. Keith seems to do better when he is under duress."

"I've never seen a guy, no matter what he has gone through, play like that under pressure," says Expo shortstop and former Met teammate Hubie Brooks.

Hernandez played with passionate clarity and grace that September. Despite what he was going through, he hit .373: 38 hits in 102 at bats. And he worked his usual wonders at first base on his way to winning his eighth straight Gold Glove.

So it's in that haven of the ball field where he finds his safety. "Baseball totally consumes me while I'm at the ballpark," Hernandez says. "If it hadn't been for baseball, I might have cracked. I've always been able to separate everything from baseball for three hours. Out in the field, no one can touch me. In a sense it's my sanctuary, a glass-house sanctuary. They can look in and see, but they can't touch."

There is one man, though, who can break through. John Hernandez, Keith's 63-year-old father, has been the most influential and dominant presence in his son's life. He is the man who taught him to play the game. He is the man who has so pushed and ridden him that at times they are barely on speaking terms. Only John ever broke into the sanctuary.

Just this summer—after a bitter falling-out over a dispute that had nothing to do with his father's being on his back, the usual source of their conflicts—Hernandez became so distracted that he sank into a batting slump that lasted two months. Keith had bought his father a satellite dish so that he could watch him play all over the country, yet the very thought that his father was watching infuriated him.

"I knew he was watching and I couldn't stand him watching," Hernandez says. "I'd be in the on-deck circle and I'd be thinking about him. I'd get up to the plate and be thinking about him. I'd go oh for 4 and I'd say to myself, 'Sit there and squirm.' I called Gary and said, 'I can't stand him watching me play.' I didn't have the concentration. It's the one time something got in between me and my play, and he doesn't even know it. That's why my slump was so bad."

Their relationship is complex, as is often the case between a father and son, but theirs is one right out of *The Great Santini*, filled with the sounds of clashing egos and the fury of resentments. John Hernandez, Juan to his son, is an obsessive and overbearing man who taught Keith how to hit and field, and the simple truth is that no one, no manager or batting instructor, knows the nuances of his swing half as well as his father does.

For years, John's understanding of Keith's stroke has been the tether that has kept these two men together. Keith knows that no one can help him out of a slump as quickly as his father; and so, throughout his career, he has often turned to his father for help. At the same time, he has felt the compelling need to break away from his father and make it on his own, to be his own man.

"It's a paradox," brother Gary says. "Keith wanted to feel he could stand up and do it on his own. By the same token, my dad gave Keith a real big advantage—an ace in the hole. For Keith not to use it, to go through the miseries of a slump when he could get out of it much sooner, was really ridiculous."

Ridiculous or not, Hernandez has tried over the years to cut the cord. "I've tried to pull away but he won't let me," says Keith. "We've had major falling outs. I'd tell him, 'Dad, I'm a man. I don't want to be reliant on you for my career. Dad, I'm 28. . . . Dad, I'm 30. . . . Dad, I'm 31. . . . Dad, I'm 32; I'm a man." There would be no conflicts ever if he wouldn't force his help. If he had said, 'Anytime you need me, I'm here,' things would have been much better."

But no, says Keith. "It was, 'If you don't want to hear this advice, you'll hit .240 this year.' He wants to take credit. He's told me, 'You wouldn't have made it without me pushing you.' You mean to tell me that of all the professional athletes in the world, all of them had a father that pushed and pushed and pushed on them? I find that hard to believe."

This relationship with his father has been the central conflict in Keith Hernandez's life. "He's got a love-hate thing for me," John says. "He loves me, but he hates me for some of the things I've made him do. He wants to love me, but he wants to fight me. He has so much natural ability that he takes the easy way out. I would step on him for getting bored. I forced him. 'Put out!' I told him. People have said, 'Hey, you made Keith.' No, I didn't make him. You could take another kid and do the same thing with him and he wouldn't do a damn thing. He had the talent, so he could do it. . . . So many people have told him that I've made him, and that is just burning inside of him."

The love-hate thing, if that is what it is, developed long after the care-free days when John first put bats and gloves in his sons' hands. That was in the blue-collar town of Pacifica, a coastal community embraced by the San Bruno mountains some 20 miles south of San Francisco.

John's parents emigrated to America from Spain in 1907 and settled in San Francisco. John was a Depression child, and he grew up in the city channeling most of his energies toward baseball. He was a high school phenom as a first baseman. He hit .650 his senior year. The Brooklyn Dodgers signed him in 1940, for a $ 1,000 bonus, and he began his minor league career in Georgia. "An outstanding hitter," said Al Rosen, who played against him.

Whatever, the end came too quickly. He was at bat. The lights were bad in centerfield, and he lost sight of a pitch; he was beaned so badly that his eyesight was never the same. He played some baseball for the Navy in World War II—alongside Stan Musial, in fact—but he gave it up shortly after the war. "It was a blow not being able to play again," John says.

He eventually joined the San Francisco fire department and moved with his wife, Jackie, to Pacifica. "It was a great place to grow up," Keith says.

"Got home from school, cut through the fence and ran through the arti-choke fields. There was love in my home. I have fond memories. Summers. Good weather and no school and a neighborhood of around 15 kids. We'd follow the creek back up to the mountains. Almost Huck Finn kind of stuff. And we played ball."

And played and played. Of course, John was the pusher and the shaker behind all this, determined to make his sons into ballplayers. "Baseball was like Dad's vocation," Gary says. "The fire department was something that put food on the table and paid the bills. His passion was baseball and teach-ing us to play it."

John Hernandez threw himself into it. In their garage he attached a rope to a ceiling beam and at the end of it tied a sock containing a tennis ball. He watched for hours as the two boys swung at it. John can still hear them whacking at that ball. "They'd swing, swing, swing," he says. "Bang, bang, bang. You can hear them all day long. When the sock wore out, I'd replace it. A jillion of them."

And there were all those days of batting practice. John threw the BP, teaching them the strike zone and how to hit to all fields. Now and then, he would pile the bats and gloves and balls in the car and announce, "We're gonna go hit!"

"Nah," Keith would say, "we don't wanna hit today."

And Dad would say, "Get your butts in the car. We're gonna hit!" Into the car they would go. John would spend hours hitting them ground balls and pop-ups at first base. They were going to be first basemen, just as he had been, by God! And then there were the baseball quizzes. "He gave us written tests," says Keith. "On situations. Thirty or forty questions. I was eight years old when these started. He would write out situations and read them to us, and we had to answer where we'd be on the field, where the first baseman was supposed to be on the field at all times. On cutoffs. Dou-ble plays. I knew fundamentals when I was eight year old."

John made his wife a part of his private baseball school, too. At Little League games, Jackie was in charge of taking the home movies. These were not home movies to be enjoyed on a Sunday afternoon. No. "We'd get the film back and he would go over the swings," says Keith. "Fundamentally. Every at bat."

John immersed himself in his boys' athletic lives, particularly Keith's. In Keith he saw early a potential major leaguer—the player that a high inside pitch out of those bad lights had kept him from becoming. Gary didn't have Keith's natural gifts, but he could play, too.

"If I hadn't had Dad's help, I wouldn't have become the baseball player I was," says Gary, who won an athletic scholarship at the University of California at Berkeley, where he became an All-American first baseman. "I don't think I could have gotten an education at Berkeley without that help. I was never one to turn my back on any advice my father gave me. I handled that differently than Keith did. He went through growing pains, and I think Dad was a little tougher on my brother. He was too hard on Keith.

"Don't get me wrong, though. Dad was always family-oriented. You could hug and kiss him, and you knew he was always going to be there for you. He'd stick up for you, not let you down."

But whereas Gary was outgoing, sociable and, in his father's words, "happy-go-lucky," Keith was intense, hyper, introverted and driven to succeed, even as a youngster. "He wanted it," John says. "He wanted it bad. I told him, 'If you want it that bad, I'm gonna teach you.'"

The thing about Keith, too, was that he was so sensitive and easy to hurt, prone to nightmares. "He'd wake up screaming," John says. "We'd try to calm him and he'd go 'No! No! No!' He told us later on that everything was moving fast and we were bigger than what we were and everything around the room was big. You could hardly wake him up. He had the fear of God in his eyes."

In contrast, his dad was tough and intimidating—from the old school of very hard knocks. John recalls the day when Keith came running up to the front door screaming that a neighborhood bully was after him. "Let me in!" Keith said. "Wayne's beating up on me!" His father opened the door and scolded him: "If you don't go out there and fight back, you can't come in the house anymore!"

John then slammed the door in Keith's face.

Like any son, Keith sought approval from his father, and it wounded him when he did not get it. Sitting in his den one evening last month, a reflective John Hernandez said, "Keith had that little inferiority complex, and I think he feared he would disappoint me. He thought I would never be satisfied with him."

And no wonder. When Keith was 13, his father thought he saw his son quit on the field, and when the ball game was over, he screamed at him: "Listen, don't you ever quit like that again! I don't care if you strike out 5,000 times! I don't want you to quit!" Keith was so shaken by the tirade that he went home, in tears, in the car of someone else's father. In another game, he went 2 for 3 at the plate, but his father chewed him out in front of several people: "You can't be a ballplayer the way you're hitting! You've got to come back on the ball and rock into it! All you were doing is hitting the damn ball!"

He drove his son. "Sure, I drove him," said John. "You can put that in the magazine. Put it down. That wouldn't bother me."

The Hernandezes moved from Pacifica to the nearby town of Millbrae when Keith was a sophomore. At Capuchino High, a school steeped in athletic tradition, Hernandez starred as a quarterback in football, a ball-hawking guard in basketball and, of course, a first baseman in baseball. Thinking that Keith the basketball player was passing off too much, John once got so furious that he told him, "If you don't take 18 shots a game, you come in here and I'll kick you right in the butt! They're making an ass out of you out there." Keith didn't see it that way and kept dishing off to the open man. So, there was John, screaming in the gym at his son, "Keith, don't be a fool! Shoot!" John regrets this now. "I agree it's wrong. I could not control myself. Jackie was embarrassed. I embarrassed Keith."

All of this hyperventilating came to a head in Keith's last game as a senior. He was just a few points shy of breaking a scoring record, but in the second half, the opposing team went into a full-court press. Keith wisely passed the ball off to the open men breaking for the basket. Capuchino won because Keith broke the press, though he fell just short of the record. He returned home smiling, until John, furious and upset, began berating his son, calling him "stupid" for not shooting and not breaking the record. Keith fled the room in tears.

That spring, the star first baseman for the Capuchino Mustangs quit the baseball team, with his father's support, after a dispute with the coach. That obviously spooked big league teams about his attitude, so the Cards were able to pick him up in the 40th round of the 1971 free-agent draft. When they showed little interest in signing him, Keith was ready to go to college. But that summer he tore up the Joe DiMaggio League, and the Cards went after him and signed him for $30,000. "Great coordination, a great stroke," says Bob Kennedy, then head of player development for St. Louis. "And he could really play defense. Very knowledgeable." At times the old man may have ridden Keith too hard, but he taught his son how to play the game.

Kennedy sped him through the farm system, and in 1974, his third season, when Keith was hitting .351 in Tulsa, he got the call to join the Cardinals. He batted .294 in 34 at bats and made the club to start the 1975 season. He was being hyped as the next Musial, a lefty with a sweet, fluid stroke. But he was suffering on and off the field.

Hernandez was filled with self-doubt about his playing, with all the inse-curities of a rookie in the bigs. Away from the park he was extremely shy, often lonely, uncomfortable in crowds and wary of women. He had done the bar scene with the players since he hit the minors, and that had fos-tered in him a negative attitude toward women. Even today he tends to pull back when he begins to feel emotional intimacy in his relationships.

"One of the negatives of the game is that you're 18 and impressionable, and you have the veterans drinking in bars, and you meet night people," he says. "Ballplayers are night people. You meet people who hang out in pickup bars. You meet more undesirables than desirables. At that age, I think it makes a lasting impression. You're guarded, really guarded. I pulled away, but I wanted a good relationship, I wanted to be happy with one woman."

He had no one, so he lived alone in an apartment outside St. Louis, at times in despair. "I didn't like myself," Hernandez says. "I didn't like that I was a grown man and didn't talk to people, that I was afraid and so shy. Invariably I called Gary. I was a grown man, an adult, and couldn't social-ize. Not just females. People in general. I would go to baseball functions, anywhere there were people, and I'd stand by myself and hope that nobody would talk to me. There were a lot of nights back in '75 when there was no one to go out with. I was the only single guy on the team. I was lonely, and I'd go home and cry because there was no one to go out with. At times it would just build up and build up: 'Why can't I meet somebody?' Brutal. I was miserable . . . a stranger in a strange land."

Just as bad, he was feeling no acceptance in the clubhouse. One day he was listening to a conversation between pitchers Bob Gibson and Al Hra-bosky two lockers away, and he chimed in with a thought of his own. Gib-son snapped at him: "Shut up, rookie! You're just a rookie. Speak when you're spoken to!"

Later that year, he was sitting at the end of the bench just before a game when Gibson, of all people, walked over and sat down right beside him. For seven straight innings, Gibson lectured Hernandez nonstop about baseball: "Now watch the pitcher. Pitchers have patterns and you can pick up pat-terns. Watch the lefthanded hitters and how a pitcher throws to them, how he works them. And know your catchers. They often call pitches that they can't hit themselves."

Gibson explained that if a catcher is a dead fastball hitter and he has trouble with the breaking ball, he may tend to call the breaking ball. If a catcher is a breaking ball hitter and has trouble with the fastball inside, he may tend to call the fastball in. And on and on it went, the great Gibson presiding.

"I was stunned," Keith says. "In the seventh inning I had to urinate, and he's in the middle of a sentence and I said, 'Bob, excuse me, let me go to the bathroom. Be right back." I couldn't pee fast enough. I couldn't get back fast enough." Dashing back, he sat down, and Gibson glared and said, "Don't you ever get up when I'm talking to you! Don't you ever do that again. I'm sitting here trying to help you, and you get up and leave!"

Hernandez is not being critical of Gibson. "He was the old school," says Keith. "It just blew my mind. I swore after that year I would never do that to a rookie, and I've never given a rookie any crap my whole career. I go out of my way to help them."

Hernandez was hitting .250 for the Cards when they sent him back to Tulsa in June 1975. The St. Louis batting instructor, Harry (the Hat) Walker, had been asking him to hit every pitch to the opposite field, no matter where it was in the strike zone. John Hernandez had taught him to go with the pitch, to all fields, and now Keith could no longer pull the ball. Slumping, he was benched and finally sent back to Tulsa. There, manager Ken Boyer tried to help him regain his old stroke. He ended up hitting .330 in Tulsa, and that was it for minor league ball.

From 1976 to '79 Hernandez evolved into the complete ballplayer. But his development was far from a smooth sail. There were those damnable slumps, those calls to his father to ask what he was doing wrong, those periodic collapses of confidence. But there always seemed to be someone willing to push him and nudge him in the right direction. "I always had people there for me as I was coming up, because I always doubted myself," he says. "I still have my doubts. I've always needed someone to push me."

The year 1976 was pivotal in his life, both in and out of uniform. The nightmarish sense of aloneness that had hounded him in 1975 vanished when he got himself a roommate, pitcher Pete Falcone. And that was the year, at last, that he found himself a girlfriend, Sue Broecker, whom he first spotted sitting behind the dugout at a home game. He had a batboy pass her a note—"Something I'd never done in my career"—and they began a courtship that led to their marriage two years later.

When he was in a slump that year, veteran outfielder Willie Crawford forced him to take extra batting practice. "He made me come out every day," says Hernandez. "Made me! He said, 'You're not playing, you've got to hit to stay sharp.'" And Preston Gomez, the third base coach, forced him to take 20 minutes of ground balls a day. "Preston knew how to hit ground balls hard, where you had to stretch out. He improved my range by five feet. He made you go that extra halfstep to get there."

And there was his father again, trying to help but pushing too hard and embarrassing his son. One day in Candlestick Park, Falcone looked from the dugout at Hernandez in the field and saw him waving his bare hand up and down by his face. "It was like he was waving at a bee hovering around his ear," Falcone says. Actually, Keith was signaling his father to be seated, please. John was in the stands, waving his arms to get Keith's attention so as to give him some advice. Keith later told him, "You look like you're waving planes in on an aircraft carrier. Sit down!"

With all the advice and help he was getting from all directions—everyone was always waiting for him to be the next Musial—he particularly cherished the counsel of Lou Brock. "My philosopher," Keith calls him. As a son of John Hernandez, Keith has long dwelled on the mechanics of his hitting stroke. When he would make an out, Hernandez would tell Brock something like, "Gee, my hands weren't right." To which Brock would reply, "Ah, shut up! I don't want to hear that. Keith, when you go to hit, there are only three factors involved: you, the pitcher and the ball. Once it's released, it's only you and the ball. It becomes the question of who's better, you or the ball."

Perhaps the most valuable message he heard from Brock was to take charge of the infield. "Be an agent of action," Brock would tell him. "Don't be an actor affected by events. When a pitcher looks over his shoulder at you, he's looking for a sign of strength. A nod. A fist. You're the first baseman. You're the last guy to hand the ball to the pitcher. Give him a sign of strength."

"I'm not comfortable doing that," Keith would tell him. "That's not me."

"You have to do it!" Brock would say. "Take charge!"

The teachings of Brock eventually sank in, but it took time. After hitting .291 with 91 RBIs in 1977, he got off to a fast start in '78—he was hitting .330 at the All-Star break. But he promptly went into a swoon that left him with a .255 average by season's end. "I don't know what happened," he says. "I fell apart."

At the beginning of 1979, his most important year in baseball, he was hitting .230 in April, and St. Louis sportswriters were calling for his benching. He seemed lost. The year before, his father had felt the growing resentment whenever he intruded with advice. Falcone's metaphor took on new meaning as John Hernandez's words buzzed around Keith's ear.

"I don't want to hear it," he told his father. "I'd rather 9-to-5 it than hear this." That is, leave baseball and get a 9-to-5 job. "Don't butt in anymore."

It used to be that they would talk by phone, before the days of the satellite dish, and John could tell him what to do without seeing him. "He would describe his feeling up at the plate, and I would tell him what he was doing wrong, and it worked," John says. "But now he shunned me."

Boyer, managing the Cardinals by then, finally pulled Hernandez out of that April shower. On a team flight one day, Hernandez's old Tulsa manager told him, "You're my firstbaseman. Don't worry about what's being written. I don't care if you hit .100. You'll be there every day." That's all Hernandez needed to hear. At year's end he was the NL batting champion with a .344 average, and he had 105 RBIs. Along with the Pirates' Willie Stargell, he was voted the co-MVP of the National League.

Suddenly, no longer was he the shy, insecure ballplayer he had been. He felt more comfortable in crowded rooms, mixing at banquets and parties. "I overcame it because of ego," he says. "The MVP! All of a sudden everybody was lauding me. All that public adulation. It helped me become more secure."

He put two exceptional years back to back, hitting .321 with 99 RBIs in 1980. He seemed to have finally found himself. But 1980 was the year, too, that he separated from his wife and found cocaine. In front of that Pittsburgh grand jury, he called it "the devil on this earth" and described how he went on a three-month binge during the 1980 season, suffering nosebleeds and the shakes. He says that he began using it when someone offered it to him and that he did not know much about the drug at the time.

"It was ignorance," he says. "Not much was known about cocaine then. It wasn't supposed to be addictive. You can do it once in a while and that's it. It will not have the lure to draw you back. That's false. It was the biggest mistake I ever made in my life. To this day I think about it and say, 'Oh, damn! How stupid can you be?'"

He says he used it only recreationally, mostly on the road and after games, and got off it on his own in early 1983 because he no longer liked the high. "You can't turn it off like a light switch," he says. "It has to run its course. You want to go to sleep and you can't. I didn't like the high anymore. I'm glad for that. It made it easier to get off. There is nothing good about it. I'm really proud I got off the stuff myself. I didn't go into rehab." In the meantime, Keith had led the Cardinals to the 1982 world championship.

There were rumors around baseball in 1983 that Hernandez had a drug problem, and Mets general manager Frank Cashen had heard them. When Cardinals G.M. Joe McDonald called Cashen and offered him Hernandez for pitchers Neil Allen and Rick Ownbey, Cashen made some inquiries about the rumors. "It did concern me, but I was told there was nothing to it," Cashen says. Cardinal manager Whitey Herzog says, "We needed pitching. Besides, Keith wasn't running out ground balls, and if there's one thing that gets to me, it's that. I would have traded Babe Ruth if he wasn't running out ground balls. The funny thing is, Keith never loafed on defense."

After the deal was made on June 15, 1983, Herzog called Hernandez into his office and broke the news. "We traded you to the Mets," said Herzog.

"Who?" said Hernandez, in shock.

"The Mets," said Herzog.

At the time, the Mets were in last place and appeared to be going nowhere.

One of the first things Hernandez did was call his agent, Jack Childers, and tell him he wanted to quit baseball. "Can I live off my deferred income?" Keith asked him.

"Wouldn't be enough," said Childers.

So off Hernandez went to join the lowly Mets. "I had probably the worst attitude in my career playing out that '83 season," he says. Soon after the trade, brother Gary watched Keith take batting practice one day in Candlestick Park. Mets coach Bobby Valentine, now the manager of the Texas Rangers, was throwing, and Hernandez was simply waving at the ball, sending dribblers back to him. "I wanted to throw up," Gary says. He followed Keith to the clubhouse and confronted him: "What was that out there? Who do you think you are? That man was out there throwing batting practice and you were wasting his time! Do you think you're better than the guys here? You're not! You've embarrassed yourself and you've embarrassed me."

Keith took the scolding and started playing ball. He finished the season at .297. At Gary's prodding, he signed a five-year, $8.4 million contract with the Mets. Gary told him that New York was a place where his skills would be showcased, where he would be at the top of the heap, where he could meet people and make connections for that life he feared after baseball. Gary told him, "The team is not that bad. They have young players coming up. You could be a vital cog to get the whole thing going. This is your chance to shine."

In spring training of 1984, Hernandez could see the promise, the many fine young players in the organization. What he brought to that '84 Mets team was everything he had learned from his father and all the helpmates who had followed. He emerged as what Brock had always told him to be: the agent of action. "That's the great bonus we got," says Cashen. "We knew he was a great fielder, a great hitter, but the thing that nobody knew here was that he was a leader. He took over the leadership of this ball club. Gave it something it just didn't have."

In 1984, with rookie Mike Fitzgerald catching, Hernandez not only took over the positioning of the infielders but also chattered constantly at the pitchers. "He knew every hitter in the league," say former Mets pitcher Ed Lynch. "He always reminded you: 'This guy is a high-ball hitter. Make him hit a breaking ball. . . .' 'Good fastball hitter.' If the count was 0–2, he'd say, 'Way ahead. Don't make a mistake.'" It got to the point, says Lynch, that he was always looking inquiringly to Hernandez when a hitter came to the plate. "If Einstein starts talking about the speed of light, you better listen to him," says Lynch.

While running the team, Hernandez also hit .311 for the year, with 94 RBIs. "That was the first time I was looked to for support," he says. "It was an emotionally draining year for me. When it was over, I was tired. I gave more of myself than at any time in my life." When the Mets got catcher Gary Carter the next year, the pressure to guide the pitchers was off, but everywhere else Hernandez's presence was still felt. "I can't remember an at bat I've had when he's not on the on-deck circle giving me information," says Lenny Dykstra. "He'll tell you, 'Make this pitcher get his curveball over. If you get on base, you can run on him.' What is so important is he knows the catchers. 'This guy's a pattern catcher: curveball, fastball outside, fastball inside.'"

He had become, to the Mets, simply the best and most valuable player in the franchise's history.

Now, three years later, Herzog says of the trade, "I think we did him a helluva favor. I think he knows we did."

He certainly does. "It was a rebirth for me," Hernandez says. "Something I needed. I was kind of dying on the vine in St. Louis. I had played there 8 1/2 years and everything was the same. I came here and got a new park, a new atmosphere, a new city. I got rejuvenated, like a complete blood transfusion. I've had more fun playing in New York the last three years than I ever had in my career."

It surprised him how much he came to enjoy New York. "There's so much here to fill your time—plays, parties, sporting events, great restaurants, museums. I love art." In fact, Hernandez owns a large impressionistic painting by the Spanish artist Beltran Bofill. He also has rows of books on the Civil War; he has been a buff for years. Hernandez, who has spoken at West Point on that war, will all of a sudden start chastising General George Meade for letting Lee get away after Gettysburg, as if it happened yesterday.

One of the first things Hernandez does when he gets up in the morning is begin the *New York Times* crossword puzzle. He'll take it with him to Rusty Staub's restaurant, where he often goes for lunch, and then he'll finish it in the clubhouse. "Lachrymose," he says as he lights up a cigarette. "That's probably 'teary.'"

His smoking habits are worthy of careful study. Hernandez usually smokes only at the ballpark, never at home. Two weeks after the season ends, he loses the urge and does not smoke again until he hits the clubhouse in spring training.

Despite his inner turmoil, Hernandez is a calming, reassuring influence on his teammates. He is looked upon with a reverence and affection rarely seen in a game played by men with large and often fragile egos. When Rafael Santana joined the club as a shortstop in 1984, it was Hernandez who took him aside. "He told me, 'Anything you need from me, any advice, just ask,'" recalls Santana. "He's my best friend on this ball club," says Darryl Strawberry. "I love him."

Ron Darling and Hernandez are especially close, and Darling sees a man of many natures: "He has a dichotomy of personalities—very personable, very caring, very loving, yet very tenacious and aggressive." Darling recalls the night this season in San Diego when he got yet another no-decision after manager Davey Johnson pulled him after seven fine innings. "The no-decisions had been piling up, and I was a little down. When I got back to my room, there was a bottle of Dom Perignon waiting, with a note from Keith." The note said, "Enjoy this. I hope it will help you forget. Your friend, Keith."

If only all of Hernandez's relationships were as smooth as the ones in the clubhouse. The divorce fight has grown more bitter, and Hernandez fears that it will end up in court and that his three children—Jessica, Melissa and Mary Elise—will suffer the most. His relationship with his father is more strained than ever, worsened now because Gary no longer mediates their disputes. The falling-out between Gary and John happened after baseball commissioner Peter Ueberroth ruled last February that Hernandez was one of seven players who had to either accept a one-year suspension from baseball or donate 10% of his base salary to a drug prevention program and 200 hours over two years to drug-related community service work. John wanted Keith to take the suspension, telling him, "You'll be subservient to this man the rest of your career!" Gary argued that Keith had gotten off easy and that he should pay the fine and serve the time. Gary and John haven't spoken since.

One day Keith asked his father, "Dad, I have a lifetime .300 batting average. What more do you want?"

His father replied, "But someday you're going to look back and say, 'I could have done more.'"

Hernandez's friends well know the conflict. Lynch says he once heard Keith say, "God, why doesn't he leave me alone?" Then, a half hour later, he heard Keith on the phone asking his dad for help with his stroke. After a game one night last year, Keith, whom everyone calls the Mex, turned to Staub, formerly Le Grand Orange, and said, "Orange, the Mex stinks. I talked to Juan last night."

"You look a little different swinging the bat," said Staub.

"Yeah, I talked to Juan and he said, 'I used to not see the word Mets on your shirt. Now I can. Bring your hands up.'"

Soon after Hernandez made the adjustment, he went on a tear. That is how well the father knows his son's batting stance. Lynch recalls answering the phone in Keith's condo and speaking to John, whom he had never met. "After I told him who I was, you know what he said? He said, 'You're pitching against the Cubs next week. Ryne Sandberg has been swinging at the first pitch lately.' I thought, this is Keith's dad."

Thanks, or no thanks, to John, Hernandez keeps performing at the highest levels. "I'm expected to hit .300 and drive in 90 runs," he says, "but there are times when I go out there and wish Darryl had this at bat, or Gary [Carter]. It doesn't happen often, but I'm human."

Gary Hernandez looks forward to the day when Keith retires. "There won't be the pressure that Keith puts on himself to be the top player that he is," says Gary. "He won't feel the pressure from Dad. And Dad will have to think about other things to do. They will be able to relate as human beings and not have everything keyed around Keith's performance. I won't be stuck in the middle. So things will be better all the way around."

Keith, too, thinks of retirement, of his life 10 years hence and the future he fears. He has this dream. "I want to be on the Pacific Coast. An accomplished sailor. A 30-foot boat. Sailing to Hawaii. Lying on the deck with a beer, with friends. Deep-sea fishing. Drop anchor and fish at night. Tranquil. The seas are calm. Nice breeze. The water is hitting the boat. Birds. The wind flapping a flag on the boat. The sound of water."

But of course. There he is, floating in middle age across the ocean. The boat, you see, is yet another sanctuary, surrounded by the biggest, most embracing moat of all.

October 1986

The New York Mets won the World Series in 1986, and they never would have gotten there without Hernandez. He not only hit .310, drove in 83 runs and led the National League in walks, with 94, but he picked up his young mates when they stumbled and carried them to the pennant. It was his finest hour as a player. He left the game in 1991, at age 37, following an injury-plagued season in Cleveland. Today he is earning solid reviews as a Mets' TV announcer, as a sharp, candid and often biting analyst of the players and the game.

PHILADELPHIA A'S

In his box festooned with bunting along the third base line, President Herbert Hoover had just quietly flashed the sign that the fifth game of the 1929 World Series was over. The president had buttoned up his overcoat. At his side, his wife, Lou, had taken the cue and pulled on her brown suede gloves. Around them Secret Service men were arranging a hasty presidential exit from Philadelphia's Shibe Park. Yogi Berra had not yet illuminated the world with his brilliant baseball epiphany—"It ain't over till it's over"—so how on earth were the Hoovers to know?

It was nearing 3:15 P.M. on Monday, Oct. 14, and the Chicago Cubs were beating the Philadelphia Athletics 2–0 behind the elegant two-hit pitching of starter Pat Malone. For eight innings, bunching a potpourri of off-speed pitches around a snapping fastball, Malone had benumbed one of the most feared batting orders in the history of baseball. At its heart were Al Simmons, who batted .334 and hit 307 home runs over his major league career; Jimmie Foxx, who once hit a home run with such force that it shattered a wooden seat three rows from the top of the upper deck at Yankee Stadium: and Mickey Cochrane, who batted .331 in the '29 regular season and is widely regarded as one of the finest hitting catchers ever to play the game.

Now it was the last of the ninth in a game Chicago had to win to stay alive in the Series. The Cubs were down three games to one, and all they needed to return the Series to Chicago was one more painless inning from Malone. Out at shortstop, scuffing the dirt, a 22-year-old Ohio country boy named Woody English had been watching Malone cut down the A's one by one. Only Simmons and Bing Miller, Philadelphia's rightfielder, had been able to rap out hits, a measly pair of singles.

Of the 50 players who suited up that day for the two teams, only English survives, and the 89-year-old former All-Star remembers savoring the prospect of returning to Wrigley Field for Game 6. "Malone could throw real hard, and he was throwing very well," English recalls. "All we needed was three more outs and we were back in Chicago for the last two games. It looked like we had it salted away."

As things would turn out, only the peanuts were salted. For this was the '29 Series, which had already proved to be one of the wildest, most twisting, most dramatic Fall Classics of all time. By the bottom of the ninth inning of Game 5, 24 Series records had been either broken or tied. The Cubs had struck out 50 times, and their surpassing second baseman, Rogers Hornsby, had fanned eight times.

This was the Series in which A's manager and part owner Connie Mack had stunned everyone in baseball by reaching around his pitching rotation—the strongest of its era, anchored by the sensational southpaw Robert (Lefty) Grove—and handing the ball in the opener to an aging, sore-armed righthander named Howard Ehmke. This was the Series in which Philadelphia, losing 8–0 in the seventh inning of Game 4, had come back swinging in what is still the most prolific inning of scoring in more than 90 years of Series history. Finally, this was the Classic that crowned a regular season in which the A's had won 104 American League games and finished a thumping 18 ahead of the second-place New York Yankees, the vaunted pinstripes of Babe Ruth, Lou Gehrig, Tony Lazzeri and Bill Dickey.

The 1927 Yankees, who won 110 games and finished 19 ahead of second-place Philadelphia, are traditionally venerated as the finest team ever assembled. In fact, according to most old-timers who played in that era, the 1927 and '28 Yankees and the 1929 and '30 Athletics matched up so closely that they were nearly equal, with the A's given the nod in fielding and pitching and the Yankees in hitting.

"I pitched against both of them, and you could flip a coin," recalls Willis Hudlin, 90, who won 157 games for the Cleveland Indians between 1926 and 1940. "They both had power and pitching. A game would be decided on who was pitching and what kind of a day he had. You could throw a dart between 'em."

In truth, the chief difference between the two teams had less to do with how they played in any given game than with where they played their home games. Many veteran baseball observers believe that the Yankees' far more exalted status in history is due largely to the fact that they played in New York, in media heaven, where the manufacture of myth and hype amounts to a light industry. Regardless, these observers agree that those old A's were the finest baseball team to play in Philadelphia and the greatest team that almost no one remembers.

"Those A's never got the credit they deserved," says Shirley Povich, 91, the retired sports editor of the *Washington Post,* who covered both teams. "The A's were victims of the Yankee mystique. Perhaps the 1927 Yankees were the greatest team of all time. But if there was a close second, perhaps an equal, it was those A's. They are the most overlooked team in baseball."

Indeed, from 1929 to '31 the A's were a juggernaut quite as formidable as the Yankees had been between '26 and '28. Both teams won three consecutive pennants and two of three World Series; both teams lost a seven-game Series to the St. Louis Cardinals (the Yanks in '26 and the A's in '31). Statistically the New York and Philadelphia mini-dynasties were remarkably even: The A's had a record of 313–143 (.686) between 1929 and '31: the Yanks, 302–160 (.654) between 1926 and '28. And while Philadelphia scored six fewer runs than the Yankees—2,710 to 2,716—the A's had five fewer runs scored against them: 1,992 to 1,997. That represents a difference between the two teams, in net scoring, of *only one run.*

The Yankees had the best single year at the plate, hitting .307 and scoring 975 runs in 1927. The Athletics' strongest offensive showings came in '29, when they batted .296, and '30, when they scored 951 runs. On defense the A's were clearly superior; over their three-year reign they committed only 432 errors, 167 fewer than the Yankees made during their era of supremacy.

Old-timers assert that if there was any position where those forgotten '29 A's had the edge over the '27 Yankees, it was behind the plate. The Yankees platooned two mediocre catchers, Pat Collins and Johnny Grabowski. In contrast, the A's started Cochrane, a lifetime .320 hitter who competed with the kind of fiery abandon that would one day characterize Pete Rose. On top of all that, Cochrane played his pitchers like violins.

The finest of them was the sullen, hard-assed Grove—"the greatest left-handed pitcher I ever saw," says Chief Hogsett, 92, who won 63 games for three American League teams between 1929 and '38. Grove was the premier stopper of his era. "He could shut you out any day," Hudlin says. "The Yankees didn't have any pitcher that overpowering."

The Athletics had no compromising weakness. "They had it all," says Ray Hayworth, 92, who caught for the Detroit Tigers from 1926 to '38. "Great pitching and great hitting and exceptional defense. And they first proved themselves to be a great baseball team in the '29 Series."

In the bottom of the ninth that Oct. 14 at Shibe, Malone quickly fanned Walter French, the pinch hitter who led off for the A's, and English again sensed that Game 5 belonged to the Cubs. He was not alone. Hundreds of people in the crowd of nearly 30,000 began watching the game over their shoulders as they made for the exits. Then, just as surely as Malone had the game in hand, it all began to unravel. The pitcher had two strikes on Max Bishop, the A's second baseman, when Bishop slashed a single past Chicago third baseman Norm McMillan and down the line in left. At once the departing crowds stopped in the aisles and at the exits and turned around. Even President Hoover decided not to forsake his seat.

Next up at the plate was Philadelphia centerfielder George Haas. His sad eyes and long, tapered face had inspired his nickname, Mule, but there was nothing plodding about his baseball. Haas was a fluid, quick-jump fielder and, when the screws were tightening, a ferociously intense all-fields hitter. He had batted .313 during the regular season. In fact, he was one of six A's—along with Simmons (.365), Foxx (.354), Miller (.335), Cochrane (.331) and Jimmy Dykes (.327)—who had hit over .310 with more than 400 at bats that year. Haas was heard muttering an oath as he went into the box. The curse, according to *Chicago Tribune* columnist Westbrook Pegler, was "a noise which the baseball players bandy back and forth from bench to bench during the season and the intent is strictly contumelious."

Malone studied the signs from catcher Zack Taylor and fired his first pitch right into Haas's wheelhouse, and the Mule struck the ball flush, lifting it in a high arc past rightfielder Kiki Cuyler and toward the row houses on North 20th Street, where hundreds of people sitting on makeshift rooftop bleachers and leaning out windows saw the ball bounce on the pavement. For eight innings, according to one writer, Shibe had been as solemn as "a convention of morticians." Suddenly it erupted. "The place went up in a roar," English recalls.

Bishop skipped over second base and then slowed down, waiting for Haas to catch up to him, and shook Mule's hand before trotting on toward home. From the presidential box the mayor of Philadelphia, Harry Mackey, sitting two seats to the left of Hoover, vaulted over the railing and embraced Haas as he swam into the arms of teammates gathered at the dugout.

Up in the press box the rhapsodies began. Cy Peterman, writing for the *Evening Bulletin* of Philadelphia, penned this ode to the homer by Haas: "They sing of joy when long lost sons come home. They prate of happiness when wars are done. But did you ever see a homer in the ninth that tied the score? There, ladies and gentlemen, is joy."

Standing at short, English could feel the game slipping away. In front of him Malone stepped off the mound toward home and stuck out his jaw at his catcher, yelling angrily, "You asked for that one!"

Taylor walked forward and tried to calm Malone. "How was I to know?" the catcher asked. "Bear down now and win it back in the 10th. You're the one to do it."

Just then, up to the plate went the menacing Cochrane, who was hitting .429 in the Series. Malone settled down at once and got the A's catcher to bounce a ground ball to Hornsby for the second out. The pitcher was now one out away from extra innings, but his woes were far from over. The Philadelphia leftfielder, Simmons, with his weak ankles and heavy thighs, went lumbering to the batter's box like Br'er Bear in the Uncle Remus tales, carrying on his shoulder his 38-inch-long club. At times like this nobody, except perhaps Foxx, could stir the crowds at Shibe in the manner of the former Aloysius Harry Szymanski, the son of a Polish immigrant from Milwaukee.

Simmons was known as Bucketfoot Al for his unorthodox hitting stroke: Instead of stepping toward the pitcher when he swung, he stepped toward third base, into the bucket. As awkward as the maneuver looked, however, Simmons unfailingly leaned into pitches, driving through them with his left shoulder. Most pitchers were terrified of him because he could drive the ball to all parts of the park. "He had the best power to the opposite field of any hitter I saw," says Hayworth. "He used to hit the ball over the right-field scoreboard like a lefthanded hitter."

Indeed, for years Simmons's line drives beat like distant drums off the right-centerfield fence at Shibe. On the eve of the '29 Series, in the *Evening Bulletin*, Ty Cobb had called Simmons "the gamest man in baseball with two strikes on him." Whenever the A's were compared to the Yankees, Simmons was Gehrig to Foxx's Ruth.

For kids who haunted the perimeters of Shibe, Simmons was the grist of legend. This was a time when players often lived in private homes near the ballparks where they played. Simmons lived at 2745 North 20th Street, across the street from Shibe's rightfield fence, in a second-floor bedroom in the home of Mr. and Mrs. A.C. Conwell. Simmons was a notoriously late sleeper, and the discreet Mrs. Conwell would ask neighborhood boys to awaken the star so he would not miss batting practice. One of the lads was Jerry Rooney, whose family lived three doors away, and at age four, he recalls, he entered Simmons's room and whispered to him, "It's time to wake up, Al. You're in a slump, and it's time to go to batting practice."

He was in no slump now. Simmons had an oft-expressed contempt for pitchers. "They're trying to take bread and butter out of my mouth," he used to say. Going to bat against Malone, Simmons treated the pitcher as if he were throwing batting practice. On the second pitch Simmons stepped in the bucket and lofted a drive to right center that looked like a home run. It fell just short, but by the time centerfielder Hack Wilson played the ricochet off the score-board, the crowd was on its feet, singing, and Simmons was pulling up at second.

Malone walked Foxx intentionally, setting up a force at three bases, and then Miller stepped into the box, looking for a curve that never came.

Shibe Park, which had opened in 1909, occupied a single city block of North Philly. The stadium, bounded by streets on all four sides, was at the center of a predominantly Irish neighborhood of row houses and small factories. Like a ballpark in a Norman Rockwell painting, Shibe had knotholes in the wooden fence in rightfield where dozens of smudge-nosed boys lined up daily to peer in, as if looking into a giant magic egg. To hear oldtimers in Philadelphia remember it, Shibe was a stunning shag rug of deepest green, its paths and boxes and pitcher's mound immaculately manicured, in the middle of a city blackened by factory chimneys and coal-burning locomotives. "Shibe was this perfect place," says Walt Garvin, a 76-year-old Philadelphia native. "Everything was green. No advertisements on the fences. Neat and clean and perfectly kept."

The Phillies played in the dilapidated Baker Bowl, six blocks east of Shibe on Lehigh Avenue, and attending one of their games in those days was tantamount to slumming. From the first year a Philadelphia team played in the World Series—back in 1905, when the New York Giants defeated the A's four games to one—until the Whiz Kids won the pennant for the Phillies in 1950, this was an American League city, a town whose heart belonged to the A's.

That first Athletics-Giants Series, not incidentally, had powerful social overtones. It set the tall, reserved, lace-curtain Irishman from Massachusetts, Cornelius McGillicuddy, against the scrappy shanty Irishman from New York, John McGraw. But the 1905 Series represented something broader than the class divisions among the immigrant Irish on the Eastern seaboard. It symbolized the historic struggle for primacy between the two largest and most prosperous cities in the U.S.: New York and Philadelphia.

In Colonial days Boston had been the first U.S. city in size and importance. But by the end of the 18th century Philadelphia had become ascendant, and so it remained until the mid–1800s, when New York took over as the economic and cultural mecca of the New World. In the early days of the 20th century Philadelphia was the nation's second city, and its teams' most memorable clashes on baseball diamonds—first against the Giants and later against the Yankees—expressed the city's aspiration to reclaim its place as the nation's center.

"The battle between New York and Philadelphia in baseball was symbolic of that battle for urban supremacy," says Bruce Kuklick, Nichols Professor of American History at Penn and author of *To Every Thing a Season: Shibe Park and Urban Philadelphia*. And at the center of the battle, always, was Mack.

It was he who pieced together the powerful A's team that whipped Chicago in the 1910 World Series, four games to one, and then twice crushed the Giants, 4–2 in 1911 and 4–1 in 1913. And it was Mack who, after selling the stars of those teams to avoid a bidding war with the emerging Federal League, ultimately retooled the A's into an even better team through a series of remarkably sage moves in 1923, the year he bought a curveball artist named Rube Walberg; in '24, the year he took rookies Simmons and Bishop to spring training; and in '25, the year he obtained Cochrane and Grove from minor league clubs and, at the urging of one of his retired sluggers, Frank (Home Run) Baker, picked up a grinning, moon-faced farm boy from the Eastern Shore of Maryland: Foxx.

Thus the A's acquired four future Hall of Famers—Simmons, Grove, Cochrane and Foxx—in two remarkable years. By 1928, still fishing, Mack had plucked Haas out of the minors and added a strapping 6' 4" graduate of Swarthmore College, George Earnshaw, who threw a blazing heater and a nasty snake. By then Mack was also recycling through Shibe some of the greatest has-beens in the annals of the game, including Cobb and fellow outfielder Tris Speaker. John Rooney, Jerry's brother, recalls the day in 1928, when he was five, that his father took him to the roof of their row house at 2739 North 20th Street. Pointing to the A's outfielders, the elder Rooney said, "See those three men? I want you to remember them. They are Ty Cobb, Tris Speaker and Al Simmons. Three of the greatest ballplayers of all time."

The Yankees won successive World Series in 1927 and '28, but the latter year it took all they had to keep the salty, emerging A's from stealing the pennant. New York finished 2½ games in front of Philadelphia, but what hurt Athletics fans was not so much losing but losing to the *Yankees*. "They were terribly disliked in Philadelphia," says Allen Lewis, who in 1928 was an 11-year-old A's fan and who later would become a baseball writer for the *Philadelphia Inquirer* and a member of the Veterans Committee of the Baseball Hall of Fame. "The papers used to write 'Noo Yawk Yankees.' It was ridiculous, but they did."

All of which made '29 the sweeter for the waiting. The A's clinched the pennant on Sept. 14. They had become the new irresistible force in baseball. And while Mack had a superb pitching rotation—Grove finished 20–6 and Earnshaw 24–8—it was he, the manager, who threw the most sweeping curve in World Series history. Two weeks before the season's end, Mack secretly decided to start the Series with Ehmke, a 35-year-old journeyman who had pitched fewer than 55 innings during the year. Mack confided his decision to Ehmke, sending him to scout the Cubs, but told no one else.

The press speculated that Earnshaw or Grove would pitch in the opening game, and not even Ehmke believed that Mack would stay true to his word, enabling him to fulfill his dream of starting in a World Series. As the players warmed up at Wrigley Field, Mack refused to name his starter. At one point Ehmke sat down on the bench next to his manager. "Is it still me, Mr. Mack?" he asked.

"It's still you," Mack said.

Fifteen minutes before game time, Ehmke took off his jacket and started to warm up. Jaws dropped in both dugouts. Grove and Earnshaw stared at each other in disbelief. Ehmke hadn't pitched in weeks. Simmons was sitting next to Mack, and he could not restrain himself. "Are you gonna pitch *him?*" Simmons asked.

"You have any objections to that?" Mack answered.

Simmons shook his head. "If you say so, it's all right with me," he replied.

Over the next three hours, in one of the most dazzling performances in World Series history, Ehmke struck out 13 batters, then a Series record, with a bewildering array of sneaky-quick fastballs and off-speed curves. Looking loose-jointed and nonchalant, Ehmke at times seemed half asleep. "He looked like he didn't give a damn what happened," English recalls. "He threw that big, slow curveball that came in and broke away from right-handers." All but one Cubs starter, first baseman Charlie Grimm, hit from the right side, and Ehmke twice struck out Chicago's toughest batters—Hornsby, Wilson and Cuyler—throwing junk. "Ehmke was a change from the guys we were used to, who threw hard," English says. "Not many pitchers used that stuff against us."

Ehmke went all nine innings and won the game 3–1. Mack would relish that victory the rest of his days. "It was beautiful to watch," he would recall years later.

"That was the surprise of the century," says Hudlin. "Nobody would have done that but Connie Mack. Howard just wasn't that kind of pitcher. I don't know how Connie figured it. A hunch, I guess. Then Howard went out and made monkeys out of the Cubs."

Ehmke's memorable pitching aside, the Series of '29 showed why that year's Athletics, if overshadowed by the '27 Yankees, have been admired by baseball insiders as one of the best teams in history. Foxx, the first baseman who was known as both Double X and the Beast, hit 33 home runs and batted in 117 runs during the season, and twice he hit prodigious homers in the World Series to put the A's in front to stay: a 400-foot solo shot in Game 1, in which Ehmke pitched so brilliantly, and a three-run line drive that helped propel Philadelphia to a 9–3 victory in Game 2, in which Grove and Earnshaw fanned 13 Cubs between them.

Foxx retired after the 1945 season with 534 home runs, 1,921 RBIs and a lifetime batting average of .325, but numbers hardly express the high and delicious drama he brought to the plate. He used to cut off the sleeves of his uniform to show off his picnic-roast arms, and he could drive balls 500 feet on a line with a whip of his powerful wrists. Stories of his most titanic clouts have all the ingredients of myth. "I think he had more power than Ruth or Gehrig," says Mel Harder, who won 223 games for the Indians between 1928 and '47.

It was Lefty Gomez, the Hall of Fame pitcher for the Yankees, who threw the ball that Foxx drove into the upper deck in Yankee Stadium, splintering the back of that seat. Many years later Gomez was sitting at home with his wife watching U.S. astronauts on television as they walked the surface of the moon collecting rocks in a sack. At one point an astronaut picked up what appeared to be a white object.

"I wonder what that is," said Gomez's wife.

"That's the ball Foxx hit off me in New York," Lefty replied.

After winning the first two games of the '29 Series at Wrigley, the A's went home to Shibe looking for a sweep. The Cubs won the third game 3–1 behind the pitching of Guy Bush, but that merely set up the most spectacular game of the Series—one that drew upon the resources of Philadelphia's most formidable pitcher and all the power of its batting order.

By the middle of the seventh inning of Game 4, the Cubs were winning 8–0, and they were riding the A's mercilessly. In the dugout Bush had been celebrating each run by donning a blanket as if it were a headdress and doing what one writer described as "a mock Indian war dance" along the Cubs' bench.

Mack was at the point of surrendering the game when a frustrated Simmons, who earlier had swung so hard on a third strike that he had fallen
down, took a cut at Charlie Root's third pitch in the bottom of the seventh and struck a thunderous home run that bounced on the roof of the
pavilion in left, making the score 8–1. Four successive A's batters then hit
singles: Foxx to right; Miller to center; Dykes to left, scoring Foxx; and
shortstop Joe Boley to right center, scoring Miller. With the score 8–3,
George Burns, hitting for pitcher Ed Rommel, popped up to English for
the first out.

After Bishop singled to center, scoring Dykes, Cubs manager Joe
McCarthy called on Art Nehf to relieve Root, who was booed as he walked
off the field. "They ought to have cheered him," English says.

On every afternoon of the '29 Series thousands of people jammed City
Hall Plaza in downtown Philly to hear the play-by-play piped through
speakers and to follow the movement of steel figures on a large magnetic
scoreboard. Hundreds watched from open windows at City Hall and nearby
office buildings. On other city corners thousands more gathered around
P.A. systems that blared the play-by-play. During Game 4 the crowd's
voices rose each time the A's scored in the seventh.

Haas went to the plate to face Nehf. The Mule stroked a low liner to
center. English turned and saw Mack Wilson lose the ball in the sun. "It
went over his head," English says, "and he turned and ran for it." Boley
scored. Bishop chased him home. The ball rolled to the wall. Haas rounded
third and raced to the plate for an inside-the-park home run. In the A's
dugout Dykes pounded on the man standing next to him. "We're back in
the game!" Dykes shouted. Reeling under Dykes's blows, the man fell
against the bats and knocked them over. It was the spindly Mack.

Never once had Dykes seen his manager leave the bench. Mack usually
just sat there, dressed in a dark suit, like an undertaker, and moved his
fielders around with a wave of his scorecard. But he left his seat that day.
"I'm sorry," said Dykes.

The 67-year-old skipper just smiled. "That's all right, Jimmy," he said.
"Wasn't it wonderful?"

At Mason's Dance Hall in Philly, in a crowd gathered around a radio set
on a table, 12-year-old Carmen Cangelosi leaped to his feet, screaming, as
the announcer described Haas galloping home: "They're gonna win now!
They're gonna win now!" City Hall Plaza erupted in howls.

The score was 8–7. Nehf walked Cochrane and was relieved by Sheriff
Blake. Simmons met Blake with a single to left. Foxx then singled through
the box, scoring Cochrane and tying the game up. At Philadelphia's

Franklin Field, where Allen Lewis was in a football crowd of 30,000 watching Penn play Virginia Poly, the makeshift baseball scoreboard in the west stands had shown the Cubs leading 8–0. "And then the crowd erupted," says Lewis. "In the bottom of the seventh, they put '8' up on the board. Play on the field stopped, and the players all turned around and looked up. I can still see that today."

Malone was brought into the game to face Miller. Trying to brush the batter back, Malone grazed him with the first pitch, loading the bases. All that English remembers of the waning moments of that historic seventh inning was the ball cracking off Dykes's bat and flying into deep left, and Riggs Stephenson going back and reaching up but fumbling the ball. "He should have made the catch," English says. The ball bounced off the wall. Simmons and Foxx scored.

The A's led 10–8. Malone then fanned Boley and Burns to end the inning.

When Mack called on Grove to pitch the last two innings, not a boy in all of Philly doubted the game's outcome. Grove was a lanky 6' 3", and in his windup he looked like an oil rig: His head and hands and torso rose and dipped rhythmically—once, twice, three times—until they rose a final time and he fired. "I can still hear Grove's fastball popping into Cochrane's glove," says former A's fan John McLaughlin, 77. No one in Grove's day threw a baseball harder, and there are those who believe he threw the hardest of all time.

The *Washington Post*'s Povich remembers a day in the mid–1930s when Bob Feller was the phenom of the hour and was to pitch at Washington's Griffith Stadium against the Senators. The retired Walter Johnson, an old friend of Povich's, was living in Maryland, and Povich invited him out to Griffith to see the kid with the heater, once clocked at 103 mph. "Walter was the most modest man you would ever know," Povich says. "And he's looking at Feller for a couple of innings and saying, 'Oh, he's fast!' Then a little while later he says, 'Oh, my! He's fast!' And then I popped the question: 'Does he throw as fast as you did?' And Walter said, 'No. And I don't think he's as fast as Lefty Grove.'"

Grove's best fastball came in at the letters and rose out of the strike zone. "If you took it, it would be a ball," English says. "But if you had two strikes on you, you couldn't take it. It was that close, and he had great control."

Tales of Grove's exploits abound. One afternoon while leading the Yankees 1–0 in the ninth inning, Grove gave up a triple to the leadoff hitter, shortstop Mark Koenig. Throwing nothing but darts, Grove then struck out Ruth, Gehrig and Bob Meusel. On nine pitches.

Grove had a Vesuvian temper that was quite as famous as his fastball, and he left behind him a trail of wrecked watercoolers and ruined lockers. There were many days when players, particularly skittish rookies, dared not speak to him as he observed the world from the long shadows of his bony scowl. One day in 1931, against the woeful St. Louis Browns, Grove was trying to win his 17th straight game without a loss—and thereby set an American League record—when a young outfielder named Jim Moore, substituting for the ailing Simmons, misjudged an easy fly ball and, ultimately, cost Grove the game, 1–0. Grove swept into the clubhouse like the Creature from the Black Lagoon. He picked up a wooden chair and smashed it into splinters. He then tried to rip off his locker door and settled for kicking it in. His rage unappeased, he tore off his uniform, sending buttons flipping like tiddlywinks, and shredded it like a rag. He bellowed, "Where is Simmons? He could have caught that ball in his back pocket!" Grove refused to speak to anyone for a week, and it was years before he forgave Simmons for staying out sick that day.

After his team stormed back to take the lead in Game 4 of the '29 Series, Grove took to the mound for the final two innings. He faced six batters and blew the ball past four of them. Hornsby, swinging late, flied to Miller to end the game.

There were celebrations in the streets of Philadelphia that night. The A's miraculous victory was the biggest story of the day. No wonder Hoover and his wife went north behind the locomotive *President Washington* to be on hand for Game 5.

Prohibition was still the law, and as Hoover walked across the field to Shibe's presidential box at 1 p.m., the crowd chanted, "Beer! Beer! We want beer!" What the crowd ended up with was something even headier: Simmons standing on second with the score tied in the bottom of the ninth, and Bing Miller, known as Old Reliable, at the plate. Miller was looking for his favorite pitch—"He was the best curveball hitter in the league," old-timer Hayworth says—so Malone whipped two fast-balls past him for strikes.

"I thought, It will be another fast one," Miller would later recall. So he shortened his grip and moved closer to the plate. Malone threw another fastball, and Miller swung. To this day English can see the ball flying over Hornsby's head, dropping in right center and rolling toward the fence. Simmons charged home to win the game 3–2. The Series was over.

Mack always said that the 1929 World Series was the greatest he ever saw, and that a diorama of that final moment should be built and set in a special corner at Cooperstown: Here is Wilson chasing Miller's double to the fence. Over there is Simmons plowing toward home, his spikes chopping up dirt on the path. In the middle is Malone, standing on the mound with his head down. And there is Hoover on his feet, applauding, and Mayor Mackey leaping from the box again, this time tossing his hat in the air, while all the A's charge out of the dugout onto a perfectly manicured patch of green.

It was the last World Series game that America would watch in innocence. Fifteen days later, on Black Tuesday—Oct. 29, 1929—the stock market would crash, and the country would begin to slide into the Great Depression. Nothing would ever be the same. While the A's would win the World Series again in 1930 and a third straight pennant in '31, their fate would mirror the desperate nature of the times. By the end of 1932, scrambling to stay afloat financially, Mack had sold Simmons, Dykes, and Haas to the Chicago White Sox for $100,000. In December '33 Mack sent Grove, Walberg, and Bishop to the Boston Red Sox for $125,000 and two nobodies, and Cochrane to the Tigers for $100,000 and one nobody. Foxx hit 58 home runs in 1932 and another 128 in the three years after that, but following the '35 season, Mack sold him to the Red Sox for $150,000 and two players. Through the 1930s and '40s the A's never got near another pennant and often had the worst team in baseball.

Of course, New York won the battle for urban supremacy. The A's were Philadelphia's last illusion of ascendancy. The poignant aftermath to all this was that the Yankees led the lobby that drove the A's out of Philadelphia and into Kansas City for the 1955 season. Like conquered slaves, the Kansas City A's became a sort of farm team for the Yankees, and over the years they helped feed New York players such as Roger Maris and Clete Boyer. The A's moved to Oakland in 1968 and won three straight World Series, from 1972 to '74. Then, when owner Charles Finley began feeling financial pressures, much as Mack had years before, the Yankees fed on Oakland's remains. Two of the A's best players, Jim (Catfish) Hunter and Reggie Jackson, figured prominently on the Yankees' 1977 and '78 championship teams.

The A's of '29 to '31 left a generation of Philadelphians with memories of what it was like to have a team that ate the great Yankees for dinner, with Cubs on the side. Today, most fans who recall the A's of that era well are in or nearing their 80's. What they all remember most vividly is that '29 World Series—the day Ehmke whipped the Cubs, the day the A's scored 10 in the seventh and the day Simmons scored from second to win the final game.

Carmen Cangelosi still remembers sitting in Mason's Dance Hall and listening to that seventh inning of Game 4 on the radio. "That inning made me a baseball fan for life," says Cangelosi, 78, a retired graphic artist. "I was an Athletics fan for life. I still know all the players. I know where they played. I know their nicknames: Bucketfoot Al. Double X. Old Reliable. Lefty. Mule. I know that 10-run inning and who scored and how they scored. Just like it was yesterday at Mason's. I remember when they won the World Series. There was a buzz in the air. An energy. You felt good about yourself, about your city, about everybody around you.

"It broke my heart when they moved. They're long gone, but I remember everything. I sometimes go to sleep thinking about them. What a team!"

August 1996

PART 4

FOOTBALL

BOB KALSU

"THE FEELING HAD GONE OUT OF EVERYTHING. IT WAS LIKE WE WERE
ZOMBIES. YOU DIDN'T CARE ANYMORE. JULY WAS TERRIBLE. THE
[NORTH VIETNAMESE] WHACKED RIPCORD, THAT HILL WE WERE ON,
WITH MORTARS AND ROCKET FIRE. DAY AFTER DAY, NIGHT AFTER
NIGHT. I WAS GETTING SHELL-SHOCKED. I DIDN'T CARE IF I GOT OUT. AT
NIGHT YOU COULD HEAR THE GOOKS YELLING FROM THE JUNGLES ALL
AROUND, 'GI DIE TONIGHT! GI DIE TONIGHT!' THIS WAS OUR
DEATHBED. WE THOUGHT WE WERE GOING TO BE OVERRUN."

—Spc. 4th Class Daniel Thompson,
wireman at Firebase Ripcord, Vietnam, July 1970

There were always lulls between the salvos of incoming mortars,
moments of perishable relief. The last salvo had just ended, and the dust
was still settling over Firebase Ripcord. In one command bunker, down
where the reek of combat hung like whorehouse curtains, Lieut. Bob Kalsu
and Pfc. Nick Fotias sat basting in the jungle heat. In that last salvo the
North Vietnamese Army (NVA), as usual, had thrown in a round of tear
gas, and the stinging gas and the smoke of burning cordite had curled into
the bunkers, making them all but unbearable to breathe in. It was so sweltering inside that many soldiers suffered the gas rather than gasp in their
hot, stinking rubber masks. So, seeking relief, Kalsu and Fotias swam for
the light, heading out the door of the bunker, the threat of mortars be
damned. "Call us foolish or brave, we'd come out to get a breath of fresh
air," Fotias recalls.

It was Tuesday afternoon, July 21, 1970, a day Kalsu had been eagerly
awaiting. Back home in Oklahoma City, his wife, Jan, was due to have their
second child that very day. (They already had a 20-month-old daughter, Jill

Anne.) The Oklahoma City gentry viewed the Kalsus as perfectly matched links on the cuff of the town. Jan was the pretty brunette with the quick laugh, the daughter of a successful surgeon. Bob was the handsome, gregarious athletic hero with the piano-keys grin, the grandson of Czech immigrants for whom American had been the promised land and Bob the promise fulfilled. As a college senior, in the fall of 1967, the 6' 3", 220-pound Kalsu had been an All-America tackle for Oklahoma, a team of overachievers that went 10–1, beating Tennessee in the Orange Bowl. The next season, after bulking up to 250 pounds, Kalsu had worked his way into the starting offensive line of the Buffalo Bills, and at season's end he had been named the Bills' rookie of the year.

While in Vietnam, Kalsu rarely talked about his gridiron adventures. Word had gotten around the firebase that he had played for the Bills, but he would shrug off any mention of it. "Yeah, I play football," he would say. What he talked about—incessantly—was his young family back home. Jan knew her husband was somewhere "on a mountaintop" in Vietnam, but she had no idea what he had been through. In his letters he let on very little. On July 19, the day after a U.S. Army Chinook helicopter, crippled by anti-aircraft fire, crashed on top of the ammunition dump for Ripcord's battery of 105-mm howitzers, setting off a series of explosions that literally sheared off one tier of the hill, the bunkered-down lieutenant wrote his wife. He began by using his pet name for her.

Dearest Janny Belle—

How're things with my beautiful, sexy, lovable wife. I love & miss you so very much and can't wait till I'm back home in your arms and we're back in our own apartment living a normal life. The time can't pass fast enough for me until I'm back home with all my loved ones and especially you Jan and Jilly and Baby K. I love and need you so very much.

The wind has quit blowing so hard up here. It calmed down so much it's hard to believe it. Enemy activity remains active in our area. Hopefully it will cease in the near future.

I'm just fine as can be. Feeling real good just waiting to hear the word again that I'm a papa. It shouldn't be much longer until I get word of our arrival. . . .

I love you, xxx–OOO.

Bob

Kalsu was, in fact, involved in the gnarliest battle going on at the time in Vietnam: an increasingly desperate drama being played out on the top of a steep, balding shank of rock and dirt that rose 3,041 feet above sea level and 656 above the jungle floor. From the crest of this two-tiered oblong promontory, on a space no bigger than two football fields, two artillery batteries—the doomed 105s and the six 155-mm howitzers of Battery A, Kalsu's battery—had been giving fire support to infantrymen of the 101st Airborne Division, two battalions of which were scouring the jungles for North Vietnamese while pounding the ganglia of paths and supply routes that branched from the Ho Chi Minh Trail in Laos, 12 miles to the west, spiderwebbing south and east around Ripcord through Thuathien Province and toward the coastal lowlands around Hue.

Atop that rock, Kalsu was caught in a maelstrom that grew stronger as July slouched toward August. On July 17, four days before his baby was due, Kalsu was made the acting commander of Battery A after the captain in charge was choppered out to have a piece of shrapnel removed from a bone in his neck. Kalsu and his men continued their firing missions as the NVA attacks intensified. With a range of 13 miles, Battery A's 155s were putting heavy metal on enemy supply lines as far off as the A Shau Valley, a key NVA logistical base 10 miles to the southwest, helping create such havoc that the enemy grew determined to drive the 300 or so Americans off Ripcord. As many as 5,000 NVA soldiers, 10 to 12 battalions, had massed in the jungles surrounding Ripcord, and by July 21 they were lobbing more than 600 rounds a day on the firebase, sending the deadliest salvos whenever U.S. helicopters whirled in with ammo and soldiers raced for the helipad to carry the shells on their shoulders up the hill.

Kalsu humped those 97-pound explosive rounds along with his men, an officer exposing himself to fire when he could have stayed in the bunker. "A fearless guy, smart, brave and respected by his troops," recalls retired colonel Philip Michaud, who at the time was a captain commanding the ill-fated battery of 105s. "Rounds were coming in, and he was out there. I told him a few times, 'It's good to run around and show what leadership is about, but when rounds are blowing up in your area, you ought to hunker down behind a gun wheel. Or a bunker.' The guy thought he was invincible."

The grunts loved him for it, and they would have followed him anywhere. David Johnson always did. Kalsu and Johnson, by most superficial measures, could not have been more different. Kalsu was white and the only child of middle-class parents—city-bred, college-educated, married, a father, devoutly Catholic. Johnson was black and the seventh of 11 children raised on a poor farm outside of Humnoke, Arkansas. He was single and childless, a supplicant at the Church of God and Christ. What the two men shared was a gentleness and childlike humanity that reached far beyond race. So James Robert Kalsu, 25, and Spc. 4th Class David Earl Johnson, 24, became inseparable. "They just clicked," recalls former sergeant Alfred Martin. "You saw one, you saw the other."

That lull in incoming fire on July 21 nearly brought the two friends together again. Johnson was standing outside Kalsu's bunker on the pockmarked hill. Cpl. Mike Renner, a gunner, was standing by his 155 with a sergeant who was dressing him down because the jack on the gun had broken, leaving the crew unable to raise it to a different azimuth. At that moment Kalsu and Fotias rose out of the bunker. They stood at the door for a moment, Fotias with his back to it, and Kalsu started reading to him from a piece of paper in his hand. "[It was] a letter he had received from his wife," Fotias says. "I remember the joy on his face as he read the letter to me. He said, 'My wife's having our baby today.'"

Some rounds you heard falling, some you didn't. Fotias did not hear this one. Jim Harris, the battalion surgeon, was across the firebase when he heard the splitting crack and turned his head toward it. The 82-mm mortar landed five feet from the bunker door. "I can still feel the heat of the blast coming past me and the concussion knocking me over," says Renner. "It flipped me backward, my helmet flew off, and the back of my head hit the ground."

Johnson fell sprawling on the ground. Fotias, at the mouth of the bunker, saw the sun go out. "I remember this tremendous noise," he says, "and darkness. And being blown off my feet and flying through the door of the bunker and landing at the bottom of the steps, six feet down, and this tremendous weight crushing me. I couldn't see. I couldn't hear. I had dirt in my eyes, and my eyes were tearing. I rubbed them, and then I could see again. I pushed off this weight that was on top of me, and I realized it was Bob."

Kalsu was really a boy trapped inside a large man's body—a player of pranks whose high-pitched cackle would fill a room. He laughed so heartily that he drooled, the spittle coursing from the corners of his mouth down around his dimpled chin and on down his chiseled neck. Once, on hearing the punch line of an off-color joke, he slammed a fist so hard on an adjoining barstool that the stool broke into pieces. He had the appetite of a Komodo dragon, but he loved kids even more than food. Some valve must have been missing in his psyche: His ego, unlike that of most jocks, was not inflatable. He always favored the underdog (he arranged the selection of one girl as high school homecoming queen because no one paid her much mind), and he turned down a high school sports award on grounds that he'd already received too many. "It'll mean more to somebody else," he told his mother, Leah.

Kalsu was born in Oklahoma City on April 13, 1945, and he came of age in the suburb of Del City at a time when coach Bud Wilkinson was leading Oklahoma through its gilded age. From 1953 into '57 the Sooners won 47 consecutive games, still a record for a Division I school, and finished three straight seasons ('54 to '56) undefeated. Twice during that run, in '55 and '56, they were national champions. Like every other 18-year-old gridiron star in the state, Kalsu aspired to play in Norman. Even as Wilkinson's program faltered in the early 1960s—the Sooners were 16–14–1 in the first three years of the decade—the coach's aura was so strong that there was only one place for a local kid to go. When Wilkinson recruited Kalsu out of Del City High in '63, Kalsu signed on.

He was not the first in his family to make the big time in Oklahoma college sports. Bob's uncle, Charles Kalsu, played basketball at Oklahoma State for Henry Iba, whose legend in college hoops was writ as large as Wilkinson's was in football. The 6' 6" Charles was a second-team All-America in 1939 and played pro ball with the old Philips 66 Oilers. Charles's brother Frank Kalsu, three inches shorter and two years younger, yearned to follow him to Oklahoma State. "Frank and Charles were extremely competitive," recalls their younger brother, Milt. "Frank went to Stillwater thinking he could play. He lasted half a semester and came home." Frank married Leah Aguillard, of French Canadian ancestry, became a sheet-metal worker at Tinker Air Force Base in Midwest City, Oklahoma, and settled in Del City.

Frank saw in his son, Bob, an open-field run at fulfilling the dreams that he had left behind in Stillwater. "That's what made him drive his son to be a college athlete," Milt says. "He'd wanted to play basketball for Iba." Frank put the teenage Bob on a rigorous conditioning program long before such regimens were common. Milt still remembers Bob chuffing through four-mile cross-country runs among the tumbleweed and jackrabbits while Frank trailed behind him in the family car.

Early on, the boy began to live for the playing of games, for competition, and he approached everything as if it were a last stand. "He played every kind of ball imaginable," says Leah. "He was even on a bowling team. He loved to play cards—canasta, hearts. We'd play Chinese checkers head-to-head. We played jacks when he was seven or eight. He played jacks until he was in *high school*. He'd never quit when he lost. He'd say, 'Mom, let's play another.'"

Bob liked football well enough—the butting of heads, the grinding contact, the fierceness of play in the trenches—but the game he loved most was golf. He was a four or five handicap. On Sundays, Bob would go to 7 A.M. Mass at St. Paul's Church so he and Uncle Milt could make an 8:30 tee time. They sometimes got in 54 holes in a day, and they spent hours behind Bob's house hitting balls, always competing. "We'd see who could get [the ball] closest to a telephone pole," Milt recalls.

Kalsu never played a down for Wilkinson, who resigned after his freshman season. However, over the next four years, including a redshirt season in 1964, Kalsu matured into one of the best offensive linemen ever to play for the Sooners. He also developed his talent for leading men, which was as natural as the stomping, pounding gait that would earn for him the nickname Buffalo Bob. Steve Campbell, three years behind him at Del City High, remembers summers when Kalsu, preparing for the next Oklahoma season, would call evening practices for high school players and run them as if he were a boot-camp sergeant. He simply put out the word that he would be working out at the high school and that all Del City players should be there.

Kalsu would appear in a jersey cut off at the sleeves, in shorts and baggy socks and cleats, and begin sending the young men through agility and running drills, racing up and down the field with the players and finally dividing them up for a game of touch football. "We were ready and willing followers," Campbell says. "He had a very commanding air about him."

Fact is, in his comportment on and off the field, Kalsu rarely put a cleat down wrong. "He did everything the way you're supposed to," says former Sooners defensive end Joe Riley, who was recruited with Kalsu. "He didn't cut classes. He never gave anybody a minute's trouble. He became the player he was because he believed everything the coaches told him. He didn't complain. We'd all be complaining through two-a-days, and he'd just walk around with a little smirk on his face. He was a little too goody-goody for some of us, but we respected him. And once you got to know him, you liked him."

By his third year of eligibility, 1966, Kalsu was starting on a squad that was showing signs of a pulse. The year before, in Gomer Jones's second season as coach, the Sooners had gone 3–7, and Gomer was a goner. In '66, under new coach Jim Mackenzie, Oklahoma went 6–4. When

Mackenzie died of a heart attack in the spring of '67, Chuck Fairbanks took over, and his rise to the practice-field tower presaged the sudden ascension of the team, which would have one of the wildest years in Sooners history.

Like their 2000 counterparts, the '67 Sooners had not been expected to win their conference, much less make a run at the national title. For guards Eddie Lancaster and Byron Bigby, the tone of the season was set on the first play of the first game, against Washington State in Norman on Sept. 23, when they double-teamed a defensive lineman and rolled him seven yards down the field, springing tailback Steve Owens for a 12-yard gain. Next thing Lancaster knew, Kalsu was standing over him and Bigby and yelling, "Good God, awright! Look at this! Look at what you did!"

Bigby turned to Lancaster and said, in some amazement, "You know, we can do this." The Sooners won 21–0. They kept on winning too and nearly pulled off the whole shebang, losing only to Texas, 9–7. Kalsu was smack in the middle of it all. Elected team captain, he took the job to be more than that of a figurehead. He took it to mean that he should lead, which he did in the best way, by example.

Steve Zabel, an Oklahoma tight end at the time, recalls the day Buck Nystrom, the offensive line coach, got peeved at the taxi squad players who were going against his linemen in the "board drill," in which two players lined up at opposite ends of an eight-foot-long plank and ran into each other like mountain goats, the winner being the one left standing on the board. Disgusted by what he saw as a lack of intensity, the 215-pound Nystrom—"the meanest coach I was ever around," says Zabel—got on the board and turned his cap backward. Without pads or a helmet, he took on all his linemen, one by one. Finally, Kalsu got on the board.

Kalsu, at 220 pounds, had become the biggest hammer on the Sooners' offensive line. He took off down the board. "He hit Buck so hard that he lifted him off the board and planted him on the ground with his helmet on Buck's chest," says Zabel. "Everybody was running around yelling, 'Kalsu killed him! Kalsu killed Buck!'"

That night Zabel and center Ken Mendenhall were walking into a Baskin-Robbins when Nystrom came out, holding an ice cream cone in one hand and his two-year-old son, Kyle, in the other. He was wearing the same T-shirt he'd worn at practice, and his arms were discolored. "Zabel! Mendenhall!" Nystrom blurted. "Wasn't that the greatest practice you ever saw?" He handed his cone to Zabel, the boy to Mendenhall, and raised the front of his shirt, revealing the black-and-blue imprint of a helmet. "Look at this!" he said gleefully. "Boy, ol' Bob Kalsu liked to kill me!"

On the field that year Kalsu was everywhere, urging the troops on, picking them up off piles. Every time Owens, the tailback, looked up from the ground, there was Kalsu. Owens would win the Heisman Trophy in 1969, but in '67 he was an unbridled galloper who often ran up the backs of Kalsu's legs. One day the exasperated captain took Owens aside. "Listen, Steve, I'm on *your* side," he said. "Find the hole!"

Owens was in ROTC, and he remembers Kalsu, a cadet colonel, marching his battalion around the parade grounds like so many toy soldiers. "He was all over us all the time," says Owens. "He took *that* job seriously too."

Before Kansas State played Oklahoma, Wildcats coach Vince Gibson, who had been studying film of the Sooners, approached Fairbanks on the field. "Kalsu is the best blocking lineman I've ever seen," Gibson said. In fact, after the Sooners' coaches studied all their game film of 1967, Fairbanks said that "our average gain on all plays going over Kalsu, including short yardage and goal line plays, is 6.2 net yards rushing. . . . This is what we coaches grade as . . . near perfection."

Kalsu "wasn't better than other players because of his ability," Fairbanks recalls. "He was better because he was smarter and technically better. He was a little more mature in his evaluation of what was happening on the field. There were no problems coaching him. You didn't have to try to motivate him. He came to practice every day with a smile on his face."

At season's end Kalsu appeared to have it all. An appearance in the Orange Bowl. All-America honors. A solid chance at a pro football career. And his marriage, after the Orange Bowl, to Jan Darrow. She and Bob had had their first date on Oct. 15, 1966, and she knew that very night she'd found her mate. "A really cute guy who made me laugh," she says. "I came home, threw myself on my sister Michelle's bed and said, 'I just met the man I'm going to marry.'"

Jan was the third of nine kids—five girls and four boys—and by the summer of 1967 Kalsu had been embraced as the 10th sibling in the Darrows' seven-bedroom house on Country Club Drive. "I always wanted brothers and sisters, and now I got 'em," he told Ione Darrow, the mother of the brood. Kalsu may have been a fearsome lineman, but what the Darrows discovered was a large, lovable kid who liked to scare trick-or-treaters by jumping from behind trees and who failed grandly in his experiments as a pastry chef. Diane Darrow, four years older than Jan, walked into the kitchen one day and saw Bob with his huge hands in a mixing bowl, squashing the batter. She asked him what on earth he was doing. He said he was making an angel food cake for Ione's birthday. Diane wondered why he wasn't using a wooden spoon. "The box says mix by hand," he said.

Around the Darrows' dinner table, everyone would stop to watch the spectacle of Kalsu's eating. Whole salads disappeared at two or three stabs of a fork. Glasses of orange juice vanished in a single swallow. Kalsu could devour a drumstick with a few spins of the bone, stripping it clean. He also played games endlessly with his new siblings, cheerfully cheating at all of them.

Bob and Jan were married on Jan. 27, 1968, and when they returned from their honeymoon in Galveston, Texas, during spring break, the Darrow family sang the news: "Buffalo Bob, won't you come out tonight?" He had been drafted in the eighth round by the Bills of the American Football League. The NFL's Dallas Cowboys and the AFL's Denver Broncos had also shown interest, but both had backed away, leery of Kalsu's military commitment. Having completed ROTC, he would be commissioned a second lieutenant after graduation in May. He was not immediately called to active duty, however. By the time he reported to the Bills that summer, Jan was six months pregnant.

Inside a few weeks with the Bills, Kalsu had worked his way into the lineup, taking the place of the injured Joe O'Donnell at right guard and starting nine games that season. No one watched Kalsu more closely than Billy Shaw, Buffalo's left guard and a future Hall of Famer. Shaw was 29 in '68, nearing the end of his career, and he saw Kalsu as a threat to his job.

"Bob had a lot of talent," says Shaw. "He had real good feet, and he was strong, good on sweeps. In those days we had only one backup, and he was Joe's and my backup. Our forte was foot speed, and Bob was right there with us. He really fit in with how we played, with a lot of running, a lot of sweeps, a lot of traps."

Shaw and O'Donnell were mirror images of each other—both 6' 2" and about 252 pounds—and when Kalsu joined them, the three looked like triplets. At the Bills' urging, the 6' 3" Kalsu had gained weight by lifting weights and devouring potatoes and chicken ("His neck got so big that even his ties didn't fit him anymore," says Jan), and he was listed at 250 pounds on the Bills' roster. "The thing I noticed is that he was so mature for a young player," says Shaw. "He wasn't your normal rookie. He wasn't in awe."

Bob Lustig, the Bills' general manager at the time, says Kalsu "had a good future in pro football." Lustig recalls something else: "He not only had the talent, but he also had the smarts. He didn't make the same mistake twice."

Kalsu also brought to Buffalo the same love of horseplay and mischief that had marked his days in Oklahoma. He and one of his rookie roommates, John Frantz, a center from Cal, filled a trash can with water and carried it into the head at training camp. They thought their other roommate, rookie tackle Mike McBath, was sitting on the toilet in one of the stalls. They lifted the can and dumped the water over the metal wall. They heard a thunderous bellow that sounded nothing like McBath. It was six-year veteran Jim Dunaway, Buffalo's 6' 4", 281-pound defensive tackle, who rose from the dumper like Godzilla and screamed, "Whoever did that is dead!"

Kalsu and Frantz bolted in a panic and hid in the closet of their room until Hurricane Dunaway had blown over, and they laughed every time they saw the big tackle after that. "Bob was always stirring the pot," says Frantz. "As good an athlete as he was, he was an even better person."

Frantz and McBath used to hit the night spots, chasing girls, but no amount of coaxing could get Kalsu to go along. "Some of the married guys chased around, but Bob, never," says Frantz. "He loved his wife and his kid. He was totally at ease with himself, confident in who he was. We'd go out, and he'd laugh at us: 'You guys can do what you want. I've got what I want.'"

Only seven active pro athletes would serve in Vietnam: six football players and a bowler. Most other draftable pro athletes elected to serve in the reserves. Kalsu's family and friends urged him to go that route. "I'm no better than anybody else," he told them all. "If I don't go, someone else will have to go in my place." It was early 1969. The Vietnam War was still raging a year after the Tet Offensive, and there was no hope of its ending soon. Frantz pleaded with Kalsu to seek the Bills' help in finding a slot in the reserves. "John, I gave 'em my word," Kalsu said, referring to his promise, on joining ROTC, to serve on active duty. "I'm gonna do it."

"Bob, it's hell over there," Frantz said. "You've got a wife, a child."

Kalsu shook his head. "I'm committed," he said.

That September, after nearly eight months at Fort Sill in Lawton, Okla, Kalsu came home one day looking shaken. His uniform was soaked with sweat. "I have orders to go to Vietnam," he told Jan.

They spent his last weeks in the country at her parents' house, with Jan in growing turmoil over the prospect of losing him. They were in the laundry room washing clothes when she spoke her worst fear. "What if you die over there?" she asked. "What am I to do?"

"I want you to go on with your life," he said. "I want you to marry again." She broke down. "I don't want to marry again," she said. "I couldn't."

"Jan, I promise you, it'll be all right."

They had been married in the St. James Catholic Church in Oklahoma City, and a few weeks before he left, they went there together. Jan knelt before the altar. "If You need him more than I do," she prayed silently, "please give me a son to carry on his name."

Bob was gone before Thanksgiving. In one of her first letters to him, Jan gave Bob the good news: She was pregnant again.

If his letters didn't reveal what he was facing in Vietnam, Jan got a sense of it in May 1970 when, seven months pregnant and with Jill in tow, she met him in Hawaii for a week of R and R. Bob slept much of the time, and he was napping one day in their room when fireworks were set off by the hotel pool. "He tore out of that bed frantic, looking for cover," Jan says, "terror and fear on his face. I got a glimpse of what he was living through."

At the end of the week they said goodbye at the airport. "Bob, please be careful," she said.

"You be careful," he said. "You're carrying our baby."

Jan returned to Oklahoma, Bob to Vietnam—and soon to Firebase Ripcord. For the last three weeks he was on that rock, it was under increasing siege, and his men saw him as one of them, a grunt with a silver bar working the trenches of Ripcord and never complaining. "He had a *presence* about him," says former corporal Renner. "He could have holed up in his bunker, giving orders on the radio. He was out there in the open with everybody else. He was always checking the men out, finding out how we were, seeing if we were doing what needed to be done. I got wounded on Ripcord, and he came down into the bunker. My hands were bandaged, and he asked me, 'You want to catch a chopper out of here?'" Renner saw that Kalsu had been hit in the shoulder. "I saw the bandage on him and saw he was staying. I said, 'No, I'm gonna stay.'"

The men of Battery A, trapped on that mountaintop, bonded like cave dwellers in some prehistoric war of the worlds. "Our language and behavior were pitiful," says Renner. "We behaved like junkyard dogs. If you wanted to fight or tear somebody else up, that's what you did. It was the tension. But I never heard Lieutenant Kalsu cuss. Not once. He was *such* a nice guy."

As was the other gentle soul of the outfit, David Earl Johnson. "A kind, lovable person," recalls his sister, Audrey Wrightsell. Growing up in their little Arkansas community, David played most sports. His junior high coach, Leo Collins, says that David was good at just about everything and best at basketball and track. "One of the best athletes you could ever wish for in a small school," says Collins. "He was so easy to manage, a coach's dream."

Like Kalsu, Johnson did not take the easy way out of the war. He was paying his way through Philander Smith College in Little Rock, majoring in business administration, when he decided not to apply for another student deferment. "I'm tired of this," he told Audrey. "I'm gonna serve my time."

So it was that Johnson landed on Ripcord with Kalsu, in the middle of the most unpopular war in U.S. history. In May 1970, during a protest against the war at Kent State in Ohio, National Guardsmen had fired on student protesters, killing four. Criticism of the war had become so strong that, as the NVA massed to attack Ripcord, the U.S. command in Vietnam decided not to meet force with more force, which would have put even more body bags on the evening news. So Ripcord was left twisting in the boonies.

The men made the most of their fate. Kalsu tried to make a game of the darkest moments. He and Big John, as Johnson was known, "were always laughing and joking," says former sergeant Martin. "For [them], everything was a challenge." When the sling-loads of ammunition would arrive by chopper, Kalsu would call out, "Let's get that ammo off the pads!" He and Johnson would take three of those 97-pound shells apiece and hump them up the hill together. The contest was to see who could carry the most. "Johnson was the biggest man we'd seen until Kalsu came along," says Martin.

They died together at five o'clock that summer afternoon. Fotias rolled Kalsu off him and saw the flowing wound behind the lieutenant's left ear. Kalsu was pulled out of the bunker, not far from where Johnson lay dead, and Doc Harris came running over. He looked down at Kalsu and knew that he was gone.

Renner, dazed from the concussion, saw that Kalsu was dead and picked up Beals, wounded in the blast, and started to carry him to the aid station. "Lieutenant Kalsu has been killed," Renner said. "I don't know what the hell we're gonna do now."

In a hospital where he had been flown after taking shrapnel, Martin got word that Kalsu and Big John were dead. "I sat there and cried," he says.

That evening, the battalion commander on Ripcord, Lieut. Col. Andre Lucas, learned of Kalsu's death. Lucas would die two days later, as the firebase was being evacuated, and for his part in defending it he would win the Congressional Medal of Honor. As battled-hardened as he was, he seemed stunned by the news about Kalsu. "The tone went out of the muscles on his face, and his jaw dropped," Harris says.

On July 21, 1970, James Robert Kalsu thus became the only American professional athlete to die in combat in Vietnam.

At 12:45 A.M. on July 23, at St. Anthony Hospital in Oklahoma City, Jan Kalsu gave birth to an eight-pound, 15½-ounce boy, Robert Todd Kalsu. When Leah Kalsu visited her that morning, Jan fairly shouted, "Bob is going to jump off that mountain when he finds he has a boy!"

That afternoon, as the clan gathered in the Darrow house to head for a celebration at the hospital, there was a knock at the front door. Sandy Szilagyi, one of Jan's sisters, opened it, thinking the visitor might be a florist. She saw a uniformed Army lieutenant. "Is Mrs. James Robert Kalsu home?" he asked.

Sandy knew right then. "She's at St. Anthony Hospital," she said. "She's just given birth to a baby."

The young lieutenant went pale. Turning, he walked away. Sandy called Philip Maguire, the doctor who had delivered the baby, and told him who was coming. At the hospital, the lieutenant stepped into Maguire's office and sat down. He was shaking. "Do you think she'll be able to handle this?" he asked. "I don't know what to do. I'm not sure I can do this."

Maguire led the officer to Jan's room, slipped into a chair and put his arm around her. "Jan, there's a man from the Army here to see you," he said.

"Bob's been killed, hasn't he?" she said.

The officer came in and stood at the foot of the bed. He could barely speak. "It is my duty . . ." he began. When he finished, he turned and left in tears.

Jan asked to leave the hospital immediately with her baby. She did one thing before she left. She asked for a new birth certificate. She renamed the boy James Robert Kalsu Jr.

The funeral, a week later at Czech National Cemetery, brought people from all around the country, and the gravesite service was more anguished than anything Byron Bigby, Kalsu's old Sooners teammate, had ever seen. "I looked around," he says, "and there was not a dry eye. We walked out of there biting our lips."

Barry Switzer, who had been a young assistant under Fairbanks during the '67 season, was walking to his car when he turned and looked back. What he saw haunts him still. "Bob's daddy got his wife and Jan back to the car," Switzer says. "After everyone was gone from the gravesite, he went back and lay down on the casket."

Three decades have passed since Kalsu died. Jan has sought ways to deal with the void, but times were often difficult. She struggled financially, frequently living from one government check to another, determined to remain at home while raising her kids.

She did not have a serious relationship with a man until the mid-'80s, when she began seeing Bob McLauchlin, an Oklahoma businessman. In 1986 they visited the Vietnam Veterans Memorial in Washington, D.C. They found Kalsu's name on the wall, and McLauchlin shared Jan's bereavement. They married in 1988. Last fall McLauchlin took Jill and Bob Jr. to a reunion of Ripcord survivors in Shreveport, Louisiana. Her children persuaded Jan not to go. They didn't want to see her cry as she had for so many years.

Jill and Bob Jr. have suffered a keen ambivalence for years. From all they have heard about their father from Jan and the Darrow clan, they have grown to love and admire him without having known him. They are proud of all he accomplished and of the honorable way he conducted his life, but they are angry at him too. They grew up fatherless, after all, having to comfort a lonely, grieving mother whose pain and struggles continually touched them.

The children turned out well. Jill, outgoing and warm, is a housewife in Oklahoma City, the mother of three with a fourth on the way. Bob, soft-spoken and reflective, is an aviation lawyer in Oklahoma City and the father of two. Asked what he would say to his father, Bob says, "I would embrace him and tell him I love him. It would not be derogatory, and it would not be mean, but I would ask him, 'Did you fully contemplate the consequences of your decision? I feel like I lost out, and I wish you had not made the decision to go.'" Bob Jr. considers what he's said for a moment, then goes on: "I'm equally proud he made the decision. That's the kind of man I want to be, to have the integrity that he had." That, of course, is the rub. Bob Kalsu made that decision precisely because he was the kind of man he was.

All who knew him remember him in different ways. The clan, as a family man. The football players, as a tough jock. Then there are those who knew Kalsu on that terrible hill. They have the most painful and poignant memories of him. Fotias has trouble talking about Kalsu, his voice soft and filled with sorrow. So does Renner. He walked over to Kalsu's body lying outside the bunker and peered into his motionless face. He would see that face for years. Now, however, "I can't see the face anymore," Renner says. "I can see his silhouette. I can't see a lot of their faces, only their silhouettes."

Renner is having trouble getting out the words. They come in a whisper. "I've thought of him every Memorial Day," he says. "In my heart, I pay homage to him. And Johnson. They are all very important." He closes his eyes and bows his head and quietly weeps.

July 2001

On August 9, 2002, in a ceremony at Ft. Campbell, Kentucky attended by more than 200 people—including Renner and Martin, from Firebase Ripcord; Kalsu's uncle Milt and mother Leah; and Jan and her husband and two children, with a host of grandchildren in tow—the 101ˢᵗ Airborne Division saluted the memory of the man by naming its Replacement Company after him—"one of the Division's most heroic Screaming Eagles."

THE BALLAD OF
BIG DADDY

*Big Daddy Lipscomb, whose size and speed
revolutionized the defensive lineman's position in the late
'50s, was a man of insatiable appetites: for women,
liquor and, apparently, drugs*

"I TELL YOU SOMETHING TRUE AS LIFE,
AND, BIG DADDY, YOU BETTER BE BELIEVIN';
YOU LAY THAT NEEDLE DOWN RIGHT NOW,
OR YOUR FRIENDS WILL ALL BE GRIEVIN';
YOU LAY THAT NEEDLE DOWN, BOY,
OR YOUR WOMEN WILL BE GRIEVIN'."

—*Edward Linn from
"The Sad End of Big Daddy Lipscomb,"
The Saturday Evening Post, July 27, 1963*

All day long, from 10 in the morning until 10 at night, the line of mourners stood four abreast along Madison Avenue in Baltimore. They had come from all over, thousands of them—black and white, young and old, men and women and children—and at times they reached such numbers that the line from the mean streets to the open steel-gray coffin extended more than two blocks. So many people, so many mournful faces. Cheek by jowl, for 12 hours, they filed into old Charlie Law's funeral home.

264 / My Turf

In one door and out another. In one mood and out another. In one era and out another.

In all his years Lenny Moore had never witnessed a spectacle quite like it. "It was overwhelming," recalls the Baltimore Colts' Hall of Fame running back. "You'd have thought it was a big movie star in there. Or a head of state. Biggest thing I ever saw like that in this town."

It was more than 35 years ago, on Sunday, May 12, 1963, and Eugene (Big Daddy) Lipscomb, dressed in a white silk tie and midnight-blue suit, was lying quite handsomely in state, in an outsize casket rimmed in pillowy white. He looked larger in death than he had in life, all 6' 6" and 306 pounds of him: larger than the legend he had spawned, with his size 56 suits and custom-made jockstraps; larger than the memories of his exploits on the football field, on which he nailed 225-pound fullbacks with one-arm tackles and chased down fleeting halfbacks; larger even than his ravenous appetites for women and whiskey.

Two days earlier, after a Thursday night of drinking and cavorting with two ladies of the night, Lipscomb had collapsed in the kitchen of a house on North Brice Street in southwestern Baltimore, the victim of an overdose of heroin. He was 31 years old, and the city's assistant medical examiner, Dr. Rudiger Breitenecker, found enough dope inside him to have killed five men. Lipscomb died in the ambulance bearing him to Lutheran Hospital.

He had lived his life in all the suburbs of chaos. He was survived by a 1963 yellow Cadillac convertible, at least one fiancée and three ex-wives, the second of whom he had married in Tijuana, Mexico, while he was still wed to the first. All over Pittsburgh, where he had played the previous two years, the Steelers and their followers cried out the same lament. "The best man I ever saw at knocking people down," Pittsburgh coach Buddy Parker said.

Lipscomb, a three-time All-Pro defensive tackle, played 10 years in the NFL, including five memorable seasons with the Colts, from 1956 through '60. In his final game, the Pro Bowl in January '63, he was voted lineman of the game. He was widely perceived as a natural wonder, like the Painted Desert or the Devil's Anvil. He was, in fact, the prototype of the modern lineman, the first 300-pound Bunyan endowed not only with enormous power but also with the two qualities usually denied men of his size: agility and speed. His belly did not roll out of his pants. He was hard and trim, and the fastest interior lineman in the league.

Gino Marchetti, the Colts' Hall of Fame defensive end, says he and his teammates used to call Lipscomb "our fourth line-backer. He was big, fast, strong, and agile. Really, *really* great." In fact, Baltimore's defensive coach in Lipscomb's day, Charley Winner, considered changing Lipscomb's position. "I remember one game against Green Bay," Winner says. "They had a fast back named Tom Moore, and Big Daddy dropped off the line to cover a pass. He chased Moore for 40 yards and then knocked down the pass in the end zone. I wanted to make him a linebacker, but we couldn't replace him on the line."

He had huge arms and hands—when he was first spotted by the track coach at Camp Pendleton, where Lipscomb served in the Marine Corps from 1949 to '53, he was lifting a 41-pound piece of a cannon with his fingertips—and the wingspan of a pterodactyl, seven feet, which made him a fearsome pass and field goal blocker and a constricting tackler from sideline to sideline. "One of the best tacklers there ever was," Weeb Ewbank, the Colts' coach in the late '50s and early '60s, recalled shortly before he died in November. "When Big Daddy wrapped a guy up with those long arms, he stayed wrapped."

Raymond Berry, Baltimore's All-Pro receiver in those days, cherishes one memory of Lipscomb on the field. The Colts were playing the Philadelphia Eagles, and Berry was standing on the sideline when the Eagles' fullback, 225-pound Clarence Peaks, took a handoff, started to his right, and cut back toward the middle. "Then I see Big Daddy Lipscomb. He was flowing down the line of scrimmage in pursuit, and he sticks out his arm," Berry says. "Peaks hit Big Daddy's arm, and it knocked him backwards. Backwards! He arm-tackled Clarence Peaks! That was the kind of play he brought to the game."

He also brought it to a working-class city in which Moore, Berry and quarterback Johnny Unitas—along with a defensive line that included Marchetti, Art Donovan and Don Joyce—were the patron saints of the common folk. The Colts won the NFL championship two years in a row, in 1958 and '59. Berry remembers the relationship between town and team as a unifying force that cut across racial, social, and economic lines: "It was a marriage, practically a honeymoon, between a team and a city."

Big Daddy, a man of the streets, was among the most beloved of all Colts. He was the quintessential "gentle giant" who picked up opposing players after knocking them down. "Are you all right, Sweet Pea?" he asked Los Angeles Rams quarterback Billy Wade, extending him a hand after crushing him in a pile-on. Big Daddy once gave his bed to a derelict man who had passed out drunk in a driving Baltimore snow, and he bore ghetto children on his mammoth shoulders through the city's streets. More than once he stopped his car when he saw a kid running barefoot in the winter. "Why don't you have shoes on?" he asked one boy.

"I don't have any shoes," the boy said. Lipscomb drove him home, and minutes later he was escorting the boy and his mother through a clothing store, buying shoes and jackets and pants for the kid.

"I saw him do that three or four times," says Johnny Sample, a Colts defensive back at the time. "A heart of gold."

No wonder, then, that a crowd upward of 20,000 came to see him off at Charlie Law's. At 10 P.M., the hour of closing, Law called Geraldine Young, the wife of former Baltimore running back Buddy Young, and asked what he should do. Geraldine had made all the funeral arrangements, picking out the coffin and suggesting how the body should be prepared for viewing. ("Don't put too much make-up on him, Charlie," she had said. "Don't make him look ashen.") His remains were to be shipped to Detroit that night for the funeral and burial, and Law was running out of time. "There's still a line two blocks long," he said. "What should I do?"

Geraldine thought for a moment. She had been at the funeral home earlier in the day and had stared in disbelief at the lines of people filing by to pay their last respects. "If the people are there, Charlie, let them see him," she finally told Law. "This is a great testimony to Big Daddy."

In another kind of testimony, women arrived from all points, at all hours. "He always had three or four ladies," Geraldine says. One of them, a singer who had flown in from Canada, where Lipscomb had wrestled professionally in the offseason, arrived not long after Law had closed his place at midnight, and she lighted like a lost starling on the Youngs' porch. Touched by her story, Buddy called Law at home, and a mortuary attendant working late let her in for a private viewing. "Thank you!" she cried after Buddy made the call. "I've just got to see him one more time!"

Big Daddy, who found football easy enough, life hard enough
To—after his last night cruising Baltimore
In his yellow Cadillac—to die of heroin;
Big Daddy, who was scared, he said: "I've been scared
Most of my life. You wouldn't think so to look at me.
It gets so bad I cry myself to sleep—"

—RANDALL JARRELL,
SAY GOOD-BYE TO BIG DADDY

At night before he went to sleep, when he was living in Baltimore with Colts tackle Sherman Plunkett, Lipscomb would slide his bed against the door so no one could get in. He kept a gun under his pillow. He would tie

Plunkett's giant dog to the end of the bed to keep at bay the flitting ghosts that went bump in his night. "I don't know what the hell he was scared of," says Donovan, "but he was scared to death of something."

Lipscomb was never sure himself. One day he might play the ebullient, knee-slapping comic and raconteur, the Colts' most irrepressible cutup; the next day an altogether different incarnation might appear in one of his tailored suits: a sullen, unapproachable ogre who wore a scowl for a mask, the phantom of his own dark opera. More than once, says Moore, Lipscomb inexplicably burst into tears. One night when Moore and Lipscomb were roistering through Baltimore in the back of a cab, Moore says, "he just broke down and started crying, and I said, 'What's wrong with you, man?' He said, 'Ah, the Daddy ain't right. The Daddy ain't right.'"

"He cried periodically," Luke Owens, a Colts teammate, says. "You'd walk up, and his mind would be somewhere else, and you'd look, and he was crying. 'Just a sad day,' he'd say."

Given to bouts of insomnia, Lipscomb paced the nights away. In the hot and airless dormitory at Western Maryland College, where the Colts set up training camp each summer, the players kept the doors and windows open in their rooms. Baltimore defensive end Ordell Braase recalls seeing Lipscomb, like a sentry on duty, walking the narrow hallways at night.

"He was a troubled guy," says Braase. "I remember waking up at four in the morning, and he'd be pacing those halls. I think the haunts of his childhood pursued him to the end of his life."

Lipscomb was born in Uniontown, Alabama, to a family of cotton pickers, on Aug. 9, 1931. He never knew his father, who fell ill and died in a federal Civilian Conservation Corps camp, and he was only three when his mother, Carrie, took him, her only child, north to Detroit. They lived in a rooming house in the Black Bottom ghetto on the East Side. "His mother was a fast lady, and she was tough," recalls Charles Bailey, one of Lipscomb's boyhood friends. When Gene, as his childhood pals knew him, was 11, Carrie's boyfriend stabbed her 47 times at a bus stop on Lafayette Street. Gene was fixing himself breakfast when a policeman came by to tell him what had happened, his hand on the boy's shoulder. She had died on the street.

Owens still wonders where Lipscomb got those gruesome photos he used to carry with him. Owens was visiting Lipscomb one day in Pittsburgh in the early '60s, and they were having lunch at a hot-dog place downtown when Lipscomb pulled out a sheaf of photos: black-and-white highlights from his early years as a Ram, from '53 to '55; photos from his glory days as a Colt. In this group was a gallery of pictures taken in a grainy winter dusk in Yankee Stadium on Dec. 28, 1958, showing scenes from the Greatest Football Game Ever Played, in which Baltimore beat the New York Giants 23–17 to win the NFL championship in the first sudden-death overtime in league history. Lipscomb also told Owens about his childhood, about growing up in Detroit, about the day his mother was killed. Owens didn't know if he had heard right. "Your mother was killed?" he asked. Here Lipscomb pulled out another passel of photos, taken by a homicide photographer.

"This is my mother," he said. "She was murdered."

Owens suspected this was Lipscomb's idea of macabre humor. He says, "I asked him, 'Are you serious?' I waited for him to tell me it was a joke, but he was very serious. They were pictures of his mother's murder scene . . . a horrible death. I looked at her, and I looked at him, and he had the strangest look on his face. I finally said, 'Let me see some more football pictures.'"

After he was orphaned, Gene moved in with his maternal grandfather, Charles Hoskins, in the old man's Detroit apartment building. The boy had already worked for years, setting pins in a bowling alley when Carrie was still alive, and he did even harder time after she died. "I had to buy my own clothes and pay room and board to my grandfather," he told the *Saturday Evening Post* in 1960. "I washed dishes in a café, loaded trucks for a construction gang and helped around a junkyard. One year I ran a lift in a steel mill from midnight until seven in the morning. Then I changed clothes and went to school."

At 6' 4" and 220 pounds, he was a sixth-grade Sasquatch, and schoolmates teased him about his clothes, which he was forever outgrowing, and about the special desk he needed in class. "I was a freak," he would tell his Colts teammate Joyce. When he struggled to spell simple words such as apple, the other kids giggled and called him Dumbo. All through his life, nothing could arouse the fury in him faster than the old taunts of dummy and big stupe that he had heard as a boy.

Life was no easier at home. Gene had a close if turbulent relationship with Hoskins, who once tied him to his bed, stripped him and beat him for stealing a bottle of his whiskey. "My grandfather loved me, all right, and did the best that he knew how," Lipscomb said. "But for some reason it was always hard for us to talk together. Instead of telling me what I was doing wrong and how to correct it, my grandfather would holler and whip me."

Gene's only triumphs were on the athletic fields of Miller High, where he learned to play football and basketball. But even those experiences ended badly when a rival coach caught him playing semipro basketball and softball, and he was declared ineligible for sports his senior year. On the advice of his football coach, Will Robinson, he dropped out of school and joined the Marines in 1949. He was awkward and blubbery and psychologically soft, but the rigors of Marine Corps life soon changed all that. At Camp Pendleton he won the shot put championship of the Second Marine Division. By the fall of 1952 *The Pendleton Scout*, the base newspaper, was feting him as the "stellar end" on the camp's football team and, at 6' 6" and 267 pounds, "one of the fastest men on the squad."

"The Marines turned his life around," Bailey says. "He shed all that fat and got in shape and became a real man." In 1953, when the Rams' young public relations director, Pete Rozelle, spotted Lipscomb at Pendleton and signed him up—the NFL commissioner-to-be scouted the Marines in those days—not a soul in Black Bottom could fathom the news. "All of us could have stood on our heads," Bailey says. "Pro ball. Damn! We couldn't believe it!"

Nor could all those offensive tackles when they found themselves facing the huge Lipscomb across the line. When Lou Creekmur, the Detroit Lions' future Hall of Famer, first beheld him in a game in 1954, he thought, I've got to block *this*? Still, Lipscomb fell easy prey to traps and tricks in those early years. Because he had never played football in college, where players are drilled endlessly on the fundamentals of the game, he entered the NFL with nothing to sustain him but his size and talent. He stood up straight at the line of scrimmage, making what Creekmur calls a "beautiful target" to hit low.

"He was as raw as liver with the Rams," Creekmur recalls. "In the service he could get away with standing up straight and muscling people around, but he couldn't do that in the pros. All you had to do was get under his arms and hands, and his body was so huge that once you got it moving in one direction, it was going over."

Lipscomb was most vulnerable, however, to the taunts hurled at him by opposing linemen. Creekmur, known as the Smiling Assassin, baited him all the time. The Rams called Lipscomb Big Daddy, and Creekmur would tell him, "So you're Big Daddy, huh? I'm comin' atcha! Let's see how big you are."

"I used to get him so pissed off that he wanted to kill me," Creekmur recalls. "You could see the steam coming out of his ears."

There was something almost comic about Lipscomb's early adventures on the field. Stan Jones, the Chicago Bears' Hall of Fame offensive guard, remembers a game in Los Angeles in which the Bears' placekicker, George Blanda, lined up to kick a field goal. Suddenly, behind the Rams' defensive line, loomed Lipscomb with safety Don Burroughs sitting on his shoulders like a boy astride his father. The 6' 4" Burroughs had his hands above his head to block the field goal.

"They must have been 10 feet in the air," says Jones. "Then Blanda hooked the kick short, and everybody started chasing it. Big Daddy was unaware that Burroughs was still on his shoulders, and *he* was running down the field after the ball." It resembled a circus act, with Lipscomb lumbering along and Burroughs riding him, until Chicago guard Herman Clark slanted by and cut them down.

The Bears' owner and coach, George Halas, stomped along the sideline screaming, "Next thing you know, they'll be throwin' helmets at the ball!" The Lipscomb-Burroughs field goal defense was soon declared illegal.

That improbable scene mirrored Lipscomb's life off the field and on. His two years with the Rams were the most chaotic of his life.

> Don't weep for me, Little Daddy,
> Don't bother with no prayer;
> I don't want to go to heaven
> Unless they swing up there.
> Don't take me up to heaven, Please, Lawd,
> 'Less there's kicks and chicks
> Up there.
> —THE SAD END OF BIG DADDY LIPSCOMB

For those who knew him well, Lipscomb was a house divided, a split-level in which two distinct personalities coexisted. In the home of Rams fullback Deacon Dan Towler and his wife, Roslyn, Lipscomb was warm and deferential, the same great fuzzy bear who called everyone Little Daddy and later addressed Geraldine Young as Sweetie Cakes and swung her children on his arms. "He had this gentle spirit," Towler says. "He was a prince." The other, darker Lipscomb drank to excess, partied and gambled to all hours, and tore up hotel rooms.

One day in California he leaped from lineman Harry Thompson's car and attacked a motorist who had cut them off. Lipscomb put his fist through the offending driver's window. Thompson stopped the bleeding with a tourniquet fashioned from a towel he kept in his car. "Damn, I wish I hadn't done that," Lipscomb sighed.

"He had no control over himself," Towler says. "He was a paradox. The way he acted *in* my house and *out* of my house, it was like Dr. Jekyll and Mr. Hyde. His animal nature often was unchecked."

Nowhere did that nature roam more freely than with women. Towler says Lipscomb regarded them not as human beings but as toys. He was utterly indiscriminate. "He loved the maids in the hotels," says Rams running back Tank Younger, his roommate on the road. "I remember him saying to me, 'Why don't you disappear? I want to take care of this maid.' Every time he heard a vacuum cleaner crank up, his dick got hard."

He also had an unsettling tendency to run with unsavory sycophants from the ghetto world in which he was raised. "These were the people he identified with," says Younger. "He had never finished high school, and they didn't have any education either. He understood them, and they understood him."

His marital life pitched along in a state of rolling turmoil. Lipscomb married his first wife, a Detroit woman named Ophelia, on Sept. 23, 1950, when she was 25, he 19. "A friend of mine who studies psychology tells me I was trying to find another mother," Lipscomb told the *Saturday Evening Post*. "I suppose I was." They separated on March 15, 1954, but were not granted a divorce, according to court papers, until Dec. 28, 1956. A year before that, on Dec. 17, 1955, Lipscomb had married a Houston nurse named Erma Jewel in Tijuana. Five months later, after learning that her marriage was bigamous, Erma filed for an annulment. In court papers she also accused Lipscomb of having physically abused her on three occasions and of having threatened "that she would not live to enjoy her 1956 Mercury automobile." The marriage was annulled on Aug. 17, 1956.

Four years later, in that *Saturday Evening Post* article, Lipscomb did not own up to the act of bigamy—"I divorced my first wife, married another girl and divorced her," he said—and he made light of what happened to Erma's car. Erma had not been harmed, but the same could not be said of the vehicle. "I didn't mind losing the second wife as much as losing the 1956 Mercury," Lipscomb said. "After she took possession I poured a box of sugar down the gas tank. When she told me she had to buy a new gas line and engine afterward, I just cluck-clucked sympathetically and acted like I knew nothing about it."

Meanwhile, Ophelia was pursuing her divorce action against him and seeking alimony and child support for their daughter, Eugenia. Lipscomb, for his part, was staying out all night and sleeping in the back of Younger's car on the way to Rams practices. Hungover, he often nodded off during team meetings; coaches would awaken him by pounding on a set of metal drawers with a canister of film. "I wasn't asleep!" he'd say, bolting up to a roomful of laughter. "I heard every word you said."

It was no wonder that the Rams gave up on him. "The coaches got fed up with his off-field behavior," Younger says. In September 1956, Los Angeles put Lipscomb on the waiver wire. The Colts picked him up for the going price: $100.

> Big Daddy Lipscomb, who used to help them up
> After he'd pulled them down, so that "the children
> Won't think Big Daddy's mean"; Big Daddy Lipscomb,
> Who stood unmoved among the blockers, like the Rock
> Of Gibraltar in a life insurance ad,
> Until the ball carrier came, and Daddy got him. . . .
>
> — SAY GOOD-BYE TO BIG DADDY

Lipscomb's arrival in Baltimore, like his coming to Camp Pendleton, placed him in a highly structured environment in which he flourished. For the first time he learned how to play football. He may have missed college drills, but he ended up studying at the University of Marchetti, Donovan, and Joyce. There was not much formal coaching on the line in those years, Marchetti says, so the players would gather on the field and share their tricks and techniques. "It was like an on-field seminar," Marchetti says. "What Big Daddy learned, he learned through watching us."

He complemented the other defensive linemen perfectly. As Donovan and Joyce mixed it up in the trenches, caving in pockets and warding off traps, and the great Marchetti hounded and crushed quarterbacks, Lipscomb was left to plug holes and chase the screens and sweeps. Pursuit, full bore, became his game. "From sideline to sideline, I don't think anybody ever did a better job than Big Daddy did," Marchetti says. Lipscomb blossomed in the '57 season, when he led the team in tackles with 137, a stat usually belonging to a linebacker.

In 1958, just two years after being waived by the Rams, Lipscomb was an All-Pro on Baltimore's first championship team, a marked man who was often double-teamed. John Bridgers, the Colts' defensive line coach back then, recalls Marchetti's telling him, "We can't win without Big Daddy. We've got to have him pursuing and making tackles."

"He just got better and better," said Ewbank. It was in Baltimore that Lipscomb felt free enough to develop his signature shtick: picking up all those sweet peas he had flattened on the field. "What the fuck are you doing?" Donovan asked after Lipscomb lifted a downed rival. "Let 'em get up themselves!"

"I don't want people thinking I'm mean," Big Daddy said.

In his lighter mood Lipscomb was among the funniest, most colorful players in the league. Winner remembers the day Lipscomb was bent over a table, about to have his prostate checked by a team doctor, when he looked around and saw that the doctor was slipping a rubber sheath on his finger. He asked the doc what that thing was.

"A prophylactic," said the doc.

"Take that thing off," the player deadpanned. "I'm a Catholic."

He was honey for the writers, who quoted him endlessly. On a fine point of interior line play, Lipscomb said, "If a player starts holding, I smack my hand flat against the earhole of his helmet. When he complains about dirty playing, I tell him to stop holding and I'll stop slapping. That's what I call working out a problem." On the art of tackling the ballcarrier, Lipscomb said, "I just reach out and grab an armful of players from the other team and peel them off until I find the one with the ball. I keep *him*."

He knew how to play to an all-white audience in a Southern town. At a banquet in Baltimore, asked what he was going to do with his money after he retired, he brought down the house: "I'm gonna go down to Texas and buy a cotton plantation and have nothing but white cotton pickers!"

Oh, they loved him on the Chesapeake. He had searched all his life for acceptance and respect, and in Baltimore he found it. Buddy Young, the old Illinois All-America, had become his mentor off the field, importuning him to control his temper, take charge of his life, stay disciplined and focused. Lipscomb went to formal dinners now, and the Youngs taught him how to use his silverware.

"You should have seen this raw man when he came to Baltimore," Geraldine says. "He talked about how raggedy his shoes were when he went to school and how his pants were always too short. Deep down, he felt, *There's more to life than what I've lived.* He was scared, and he didn't know why. People talked to him as if he were a child. They all thought he was this big lummox who had no brains. He saw this, and there was this real hurt. Here he saw rewards for fulfilling a commitment and following orders."

Lipscomb remained keenly sensitive about his lack of college schooling—he used to refer to his high school as Miller Tech—and whenever players started to talk about their alma maters, he would stop them short. "Cut out all that college bullshit!" he snapped at Moore one day. "I don't want to hear about that."

He seemed to resent especially the college-educated blacks. Marchetti recalls the time that Lipscomb, who had been drinking, approached Milt Davis, an erudite black halfback out of UCLA, and threw a handful of money in front of him, snarling, "Here, Milt, this is what you're after. That's all you need is moneymoneymoney!"

Then there was the day, Joyce says, when Lipscomb lunged in a rage at a white teammate, linebacker Bill Pellington. Ewbank used to have the players take classroom notes, and Pellington got his hands on Lipscomb's book and opened it. The pages were filled with meaningless scrawls. Pellington held up the book: "Look here! Big Daddy can't write!" Players had to step between them.

"You sonofabitch, I'll kill you!" Lipscomb screamed.

Baltimore won its second NFL title in 1959 but failed to make the championship game in 1960, and in July'61, to the shock of Colts fans, the 29-year-old Lipscomb was the key player in a five-man deal that sent him and center Buzz Nutter to the Steelers for Jimmy Orr, the promising flanker with the gifted hands, and two warm bodies. Ewbank said Baltimore had to deal Lipscomb to get Orr, but Winner says Lipscomb was dealt in part because so much trouble tracked him off the field. "It was always something," Winner says. "Money problems. Legal and personal problems." (Lipscomb was often served legal papers for failing to make child support payments. His top NFL salary was $14,000, which he supplemented with his off-season income from pro wrestling.)

He had intertwined his courtships like a braid. When Lipscomb joined the Colts in the fall of '56, he began courting Cecelia Williams, who would become his third wife. But on a California road trip that October, according to court documents, he sought a reconciliation with his first wife, Ophelia, to whom he was still legally married, and he got her pregnant. (Their second child, a son, Raymond, would be born the next July.) Big Daddy moved in with Ophelia at the end of that season but left her almost immediately, in December, the month their divorce went through. He called Cecelia in Baltimore and asked her, "Is it all right if I stay with you?"

Cecelia took him in, and they were married on May 19, 1957. She never knew about his attempt to reconcile with Ophelia, and he never told her of his earlier bigamy. ("Well, I'll be damned," she said when SI informed her of it recently.) She divorced him on June 10, 1960, on grounds of abandonment and "misconduct with other women," but she says he never physically harmed her. On the contrary, she says, "He was a good provider. He brought all his money home, and he was very generous. I wasn't denied anything." What she could not abide, she says, was his chronic infidelity, the phone calls from women asking for him.

"Who are you?" Cecelia would ask.

"Who are *you?*" the voice would ask back.

Sleepless in Pittsburgh, he sated his appetites with unbridled zeal. In quarterback Bobby Layne and other Steelers roughnecks, Lipscomb had new drinking pals. After practices they would repair to the South Park Inn, where Layne would buy everyone except Lipscomb a drink. "He would buy Big Daddy a whole bottle of VO," says Pat Livingston, who covered the team for the *Pittsburgh Press.*

Lipscomb's libidinous adventures in Pittsburgh became the stuff of lore. When defensive back Brady Keys drove by Big Daddy's place in the morning to pick him up for work, an orgy was often in progress. "There would be three or four women, and they would be half naked," Keys says. "Big Daddy had enough energy for them all. He was always drunk. And he always had cash lying all over the place. Big Daddy did three things: He drank, he screwed, and he dominated football games."

Big Daddy was as popular in Pittsburgh as he had been in Baltimore. He had two exceptional seasons with the Steelers, at the end of which, in the '63 Pro Bowl, he turned in one of the greatest performances of his career: 11 tackles, two forced fumbles and one blocked pass. Lions guard Harley Sewell faced him across the line, and for the first time in his career Sewell felt helpless. "Big Daddy was just running over me, throwing me around, coming and blowing snot, and anything I tried to do, he countered."

Four months later, still surfing the high of that performance, Big Daddy told Geraldine Young, "Know what, Sweetie Cakes? I'm becoming a *real* football player."

Lipscomb lived his offseasons in Baltimore, and by May '63 he had begun to renew his romance with Cecelia. They even talked about getting married again. On the night of Wednesday, May 8, they slept together at her place. He left her on Thursday morning and ran into her at a record shop that afternoon. He told her he was pitching in a softball game that night. That was the last time she ever saw him.

There is only one detailed account of where Lipscomb went and what he allegedly did from the time the softball game ended until he died in the ambulance on Friday morning. That story was told by one Timothy Black, an admitted heroin user with an extensive criminal record. Black's account, according to his testimony at the coroner's inquest and various published reports, is this: Lipscomb had been using heroin three times a week for about six months, since he first asked Black to buy it for him. Late on Thursday night Black climbed into Lipscomb's Cadillac on a street corner in Baltimore, and together they picked up two women. They partied until 3 A.M. at Black's apartment on North Brice Street. The women then

276 / My Turf

left. At Lipscomb's urging, the two men went out and bought a $12 bag of heroin. They returned to the apartment. Black cooked the heroin in a whiskey bottle top and drew the solution into an eyedropper connected to a crude syringe. Lipscomb shot the heroin into his arm. He started nodding off.

"Then I noted that he was making funny sounds and drooling at the mouth," Black testified at the inquest. "I slapped him in the face to try bringing him around, and he fell on the floor. I put some ice packs around his waist and on his face, but I couldn't bring him around. I then shot up the rest of the heroin that was left in the cooker."

A friend joined him, and together they tried to revive Lipscomb, injecting him with a saline solution. When this failed, they called the ambulance. Lipscomb never regained consciousness.

Rudiger Breitenecker, who did the autopsy, found four fresh needle marks on Lipscomb's body, accounting for the deadly heroin dose and the saline injections, and only one old one, which could have been left by "an old blood test," Breitenecker says.

What the medical examiner also found surprised no one: a fatty liver. "If he hadn't died from heroin, he would have died from liver disease due to chronic alcoholism," Breitenecker says.

Although the Lipscomb case has been closed for more than 35 years, the player's friends and teammates harbor a powerful skepticism about Black's version of events. While no one has provided evidence to sustain a plausible alternative to Black's story, these doubts—based not only on the results of Breitenecker's autopsy but also on what Lipscomb's friends and teammates knew of his behavior—linger. The theory most often advanced by the skeptics holds that Black administered the shot that killed Lipscomb, either accidentally or in order to steal his money; they also speculate that the Baltimore police helped cover up the circumstances of Big Daddy's death because Black had worked for them as an informant.

Black, who died last month of a cerebral hemorrhage, never said anything to support any of those theories. But the people who knew Lipscomb best, off and on the field, still don't believe he injected himself with heroin—or anything else, for that matter. Lipscomb lived in morbid fear of needles. The stories documenting this abound: how he swooned or broke into a sweat at the very sight of a needle, and how Cecelia had to sit on his lap to keep him in a dental chair when he took shots of novocaine for a tooth extraction. "He never acted weird, dopey or glassy-eyed," Buddy Young says. "There is no way in the world he used any kind of drug."

Lipscomb drank that last night, though not to excess. The autopsy revealed his blood alcohol level to be .09, barely high enough to make him legally drunk in most states today. Black told the *Saturday Evening Post* that he and Lipscomb had "bought a six-pack" of malt liquor before picking up the two women, though Lipscomb's friends insist that he was strictly a VO drinker.

Black did not appear to be the most reliable of witnesses. Not only was he a drug user and an ex-con, but he also changed the story he told the police. When first questioned on May 10, Black said that he and Lipscomb took the two women home about 3 A.M. after partying with them and then returned to Black's apartment. Leaving Lipscomb there, Black said, he then went to an all-night diner, ate some breakfast and returned home at 7 A.M.. He said he found Lipscomb slumped over the kitchen table. By May 11, Black had added the drug purchase to his account, and his trip to the diner had disappeared from the story.

Geraldine Young says that Lipscomb had about $700 in cash in his pocket when he went out that night. Police found $73 on him. For years, until he was killed in an automobile accident in 1983, Buddy Young insisted that the missing money held the secret to Lipscomb's fate. "Find out what happened to that, and you'll know why Daddy is dead," he said.

Lipscomb's supporters believe that the heroin found in his body has denied him what they think is rightfully his: a place in the Hall of Fame. "But I doubt he ever will get in," Marchetti says. "What they said about him with drugs may be held against him."

How good was he? "Big Daddy was in the same category as [Hall of Famers] Merlin Olsen and Bob Lilly," says John Wooten, the former guard with the Cleveland Browns and now assistant director of college and pro football personnel for the Baltimore Ravens. "He could devastate an offense by himself."

Compared with players today? "Big Daddy was better than Leon Lett when Lett is at his best," Wooten says, referring to the 6' 6", 300-pound Dallas Cowboys tackle. "Lett doesn't have the lateral movement Big Daddy had. And I don't think he's as mean."

Nor anywhere as earthy or evocative. One thousand people were at Lipscomb's funeral in Detroit, and symbols of the life he had led surrounded the gravesite in Lincoln Memorial Cemetery. There were those eight great football players—Erich Barnes, John Henry Johnson, Dick (Night Train) Lane, Moore, Owens, Jim Parker, Plunkett and Sample—carrying the coffin draped in the U.S. flag, a reminder of Lipscomb's service in the Marine Corps. There were his friends from Black Bottom. And there were all those honeys, at least one fiancée wearing a ring and two others claiming they were engaged to Big Daddy.

"They were around there screaming and hollering, 'What are we gonna do without him?'" says Geraldine Young.

Big Daddy Lipscomb, being carried down an aisle
Of Women by Night Train Lane, John Henry Johnson,
And Lenny Moore; Big Daddy, his three ex-wives,
His fiancée, and the grandfather who raised him
Going to his grave in five big Cadillacs . . .
                                                    —SAY GOOD-BYE TO BIG DADDY

The preacher said, "He did some good, he did some wrong . . ."
A spring wind rustled in the trees, whispering, Amen to that.

January 1999

In doing this story, I tried but failed to find anyone who knew or played with Big Daddy when he was knocking down opponents in Marine Corps football in the early 1950s. After the story ran in Sports Illustrated, I received several letters from people who knew the man and had stories corroborating and embellishing upon the tales told therein. One such correspondent was Roy Phillips, of Edgewood, Texas, a former member of the Camp Pendleton track team in Big Daddy's time, who wrote: "Now after forty-five years I understand why Lipscomb was a loner, always in a bad mood, and often flew into a rage. One such night he came in after a few drinks and challenged the entire boxing team. When they were afraid to fight, he threw them all out of the barracks. He would never prepare for inspections, make up his bunk, clean his uniforms. Across his locker he painted in large letters "black death." The officers in charge of inspection would ignore Lipscomb completely."

Ah, Big Daddy. Just another bad day.

A LIFE CUT SHORT

"ERNIE DAVIS HAS BEEN DEAD MORE YEARS THAN HE LIVED,
AND HERE YOU ARE CALLING ME ABOUT HIM NOW.
IT'S INCREDIBLE. PEOPLE STILL REMEMBER HIM AND TALK ABOUT
HIM. THE MAN TOUCHED EVERYONE HE KNEW. AS GREAT
AN ATHLETE AS HE WAS, HE WAS EVEN A BETTER PERSON."

—Jack Moore, a friend of Ernie Davis's

The last night she ever saw him, they were sitting together at a table with candlelight in an Italian restaurant just off the campus of Syracuse University, near the hangout for black students, a bar called the Tippin' Inn, where they had met almost two years before. It was Friday night, May 3, 1963, an evening that she still recalls with sadness.

Helen Gott was a 20-year-old senior who would be graduating from Syracuse in one month with degrees in political science and journalism, and Ernie Davis . . . well, he was a handsome, 23-year-old former Syracuse football star—the first black player to be voted the Heisman Trophy—who was two weeks away from dying of leukemia in a hospital in Cleveland. Of course, Ernie never let on to Helen how sick he was, never in all the Sunday phone calls or throughout the days they shared or in the letters he sent to her.

"He would have really, really hated for me to feel sorry for him," she says now. "He didn't know I knew how sick he was. He would never want me to worry." She understood by then how grave his condition was, as everyone who knew him understood. He had the rarest, deadliest form of the blood disease, but that night in Syracuse was the first time she contemplated a life without him. Seen through the candlelight, as she still sees him now, he seemed sadder and quieter than she had ever known him, and then the waiter appeared and Davis ordered chicken livers for dinner.

"Why are you ordering that?" Helen asked.

"The doctor told me to eat this because it's good for my blood," he said. Her eyes filled, but she averted her glance, and he did not notice.

"I had this feeling of overwhelming sadness," she says. "He was trying to do all the right things. He'd never ordered chicken livers before. I was just feeling sad at dinner because I knew the chicken livers were not going to help, but he was being so conscientious about doing what the doctor told him to do, with the hope that whatever he could do would help. He was always upbeat. He never talked about anything being terminal. He always sounded like everything would be cleared up. Sitting there with him, for the first time I was thinking there was the possibility that he was going to die. . . ."

Theirs had been a long, sweet romance, one in which they shared his final year of glory as a running back at Syracuse, when he was spinning and double-clutching through autumn's Saturday afternoons in Archbold Stadium, carrying the great Jim Brown's old number, 44, from one All-America team to the next, and breaking nearly all of Brown's school records on the way. Davis's final season in college, 1961, came in the first year of President John F. Kennedy's administration, as Martin Luther King Jr. was marching in the South and an inchoate civil rights movement was beginning to spread across the land.

On Dec. 4, the day Davis accepted the Heisman in ceremonies at the Downtown Athletic Club in New York City, President Kennedy happened to be visiting in Manhattan. Learning that Davis was in town, Kennedy asked to meet him. The two men shook hands outside the Grand Ballroom at the Waldorf-Astoria. Later that afternoon, a beaming Davis, seeing Syracuse coach Ben Schwartzwalder, went floating toward him through a crowd.

"Put 'er there, Coach," Davis said. "Shake the hand that shook hands with President Kennedy!"

Those were heady times for America's most celebrated college football player. At the end of the 1961 season the Cleveland Browns traded running back Bobby Mitchell and their No. 1 draft choice, halfback Leroy Jackson, to the Washington Redskins for Washington's first pick overall in the draft, Ernie Davis. The Browns would thus have two of the greatest running backs in college football history, Jim Brown and Ernie Davis, in the same backfield. Adding money to this magic, on Dec. 28, 1961, Cleveland owner Art Modell signed Davis to what was then the largest rookie contract in National Football League history—a three-year, $65,000, no-cut contract with a whopping $15,000 signing bonus.

Davis crowned his college career on June 2, 1962, when, having been chosen by the students as a marshal of his senior class at Syracuse, he led his classmates into graduation ceremonies.

"Some people would be boasting and bragging and loud about it," says Helen. "But he was grateful, humbled by it. It was just the beginning. . . . The most exciting things for him were yet to come. Playing pro ball. He looked forward to playing with Jim Brown. For Ernie, it was going to be a dream come true. He was on the threshold—the beginning of a long, exciting, wonderful life."

By the time Davis graduated, he had been Helen's steady beau for eight months. Helen had been to his hometown of Elmira, New York, to meet his mother, Marie, and he had spent weekends at her parents' home in East Orange, New Jersey. One day there, he gave Helen a 45-rpm record of Ruby and the Romantics singing "Our Day Will Come," a sanguine melody of the times. "That was his favorite record," Helen says, "and when he would come by my parents' house, we would go down to the basement and play that over and over and dance. Our day will come."

It never did. In the end, what came instead was May 3, 1963, that Friday night, in the lonely gloaming of his life, when Ernie Davis ordered chicken livers and made the only promise to her that he would not keep.

"Promise me that you will come to my graduation?" Helen asked.

"I promise," he said.

His grave lies hard by a four-foot hedge in Woodlawn Cemetery in Elmira under a headstone that reads ERNIE DAVIS. His epitaph was written by the Downtown Athletic Club: HEISMAN TROPHY 1961. Elmira natives remember his funeral, on May 22, as the grandest ever held in the history of the city. For 12 hours the day before, the lines had been two blocks long as mourners filed by his open coffin in the Neighborhood House, a recreation center where Davis had played as a kid. For one entire day that city of 50,000 stood still. "Why, there were thousands here for the funeral!" recalls Marty Harrigan, Davis's high school football coach. "They came from all over. Hey, the Cleveland Browns flew in here, too."

Indeed, practically the whole Cleveland team, for which Davis never played a down, flew in to bid him farewell. "He was everybody's son, big brother or kid brother," Cleveland placekicker Lou Groza said at the time. Davis is remembered in Elmira with the reverence accorded a patron saint. His old high school, Elmira Free Academy, is now Ernie Davis Junior High. A city park named after him lies across the street from the school, and last year, to commemorate the 25th anniversary of his death, a citizens' committee led by Harrigan unveiled a striking, life-sized bronze statue of Davis in front of the school that bears his name. Every year on May 18, the anniversary of Davis's death, Harrigan buys a bouquet of flowers and places it on the grave out of a kind of paternal love.

"The flowers don't last, but Ernie does," Harrigan says with a shrug. "Twenty-six years. Every day I miss him. Every day I think about him. Every day!"

Davis made his name in Elmira, dashing up sidelines with the mail under his arm. At Syracuse, he came to be known as the Elmira Express, but that was really only his adopted town. Davis spent most of his formative years in Pennsylvania. He was born in New Salem, Pennsylvania, on Dec. 14, 1939, and never knew his natural father. "Ernie's dad was killed in an accident before Ernie was born," says his mother, Marie.

Very young, out looking for a job and unable to care for Ernie, Marie Davis Fleming sent her only child, at the age of 14 months, into the care of her mother and father, Elizabeth and Willie Davis. They settled in Uniontown, Pennsylvania, where Ernie grew up. Willie was a coal miner, the father of 12 children of his own, and rattling around in that huge family, Ernie acquired his notions of discipline, faith and home.

"My father was a strong disciplinarian," says Chuck Davis, one of Willie's sons and Ernie's uncles. "We all had time schedules. We had lunch at the same time. We had dinner at the same time. Don't be late or you didn't eat. We all ate at a big table and talked about sports and world events. We all dressed up neat—my father was a clean, neat dresser—and we all went to church on Sunday together. We were a family."

Ernie was quiet, gentle and shy when, at the age of 12, he showed up in Elmira, where his mother had resettled and called for him, and he began playing small-fry football. Big for his age—at 13 he was a rock-solid 145 pounds—he could have been a punishing football player against the smaller kids his age, but that was never his style. Al Mallette, the retired sports editor of the Elmira Star-Gazette, coached a youth team against him and still remembers the way Ernie tackled the Lilliputians who bravely dropped their heads and ran into him. "Ernie would just grab those little running backs and hold them in the air until the whistle blew," Mallette says. "No slamming them to the ground. No ego trip. He could have hurt them, but he didn't."

As consummate a football player as he became in high school—he averaged 7.4 yards per carry throughout his varsity career—those who witnessed his career at Free Academy believe that basketball was really his game. "Ernie was a much better basketball player than football player," says his old Free Academy coach, Jim Flynn. "He was a great jumper and rebounder. And he could shoot, too." By the end of his senior year, Davis had set an All-Southern Tier Conference career scoring record of 1,605 points, averaging 18.4 points a game, and in his final two years he led the team to 52 straight victories.

"He was the greatest chips-are-down player I've known," Flynn says. "But if we were running away with a ball game, you couldn't find Ernie out there. He wouldn't shoot or rebound." In his last year, in a game against intracity rival Southside High School, Free Academy had the game in hand when the Southside forward whom Davis was guarding, Billy Morrell, got loose for five quick baskets. Free Academy won, but Flynn went to Davis afterward and said, "I thought you let that guy go at the end."

"I've played against Billy for years and I respect him," Davis said. "His teammates weren't giving him the ball. I laid off him a little bit, and they had to give it to him."

Such was Davis's style. At the beginning of his junior year in high school, a young boy who had never played football tried out for the team. In the locker room the boy got so tangled up in his shoulder pads that he ended up putting them on backward. He grew red-faced as the cruel taunting began. "Next thing you know, Ernie is walking over there," says Harrigan. "He says, 'Here, let me help you with this. Don't be embarrassed.' A little thing? Maybe. But not to me, as a coach. It was a big thing, and I'll never, ever forget it."

And Davis did not suffer bullies gladly. In fact, in all the years that his best and oldest friends knew him, the only two times they ever saw him fly into a rage was when his old friend Frankie Cox, an athlete almost Davis's size, provoked him beyond his patience. The first time was at the Green Pastures Bar and Restaurant, a haunt in the black section of Elmira, where Davis came upon Cox pounding on a helplessly beaten man. Davis was extremely powerful, with a strong, wide upper body and tree-trunk legs, and he picked Cox up, literally, and carried him out the door. "In front of the Green Pastures was a tree," recalls Mickey Jones, one of Davis's closest friends, "and he took the guy out and pinned him against the tree and told him, 'I told you about getting in trouble. I want you to cool it.'"

On the other occasion, Cox was not so lucky. He and Davis were outside the Green Pastures again, and a young kid walked by. Cox grabbed him and kicked him in the rear. "Just booted him," says Howard Coleman, the proprietor. "Boom, like that."

"What did you do that for?" Davis asked Cox.

"What the hell is it to you?" Cox snapped back.

Davis sprang on him like a cat out of a tree. "He hit him until Cox told him, 'I've had enough, I've had enough,'" says Coleman. "Just because he kicked this kid."

Children flocked to Davis. Over the years, he became a kind of Pied Piper for city kids. They followed him everywhere, clutches of them, wherever he walked across town. They watched him run for miles around Elmira in the summer heat, along the streets and stretches of park grass—his head up, shoulders straight, arms pumping.

Whenever Davis showed up at Green Pastures among the beer drinkers at the bar, Coleman would call out to the bartender, "Give the Reverend Davis a Coke," and Ernie would laugh with them. "He didn't smoke, he didn't swear, he didn't drink," Coleman says. At night, before going to sleep, Davis prayed in silence on his knees, his elbows resting on the bed. "We were all taught to do that," says Marie.

Davis was an ideal black football prospect at a time when racially skittish colleges were just beginning to integrate their teams. He was well suited to carry on at Syracuse, which Jim Brown had left three years before with these records behind him: 2,091 rushing yards in 361 carries, 5.8 yards per carry; 25 touchdowns; and 187 points scored. But Brown ran into more than tackling dummies and opposing linemen in his years at Syracuse. Shortly before he arrived, another black Syracuse football player, Avatus Stone, had scandalized the school by indulging in what was perceived at the time to be an unseemly social life. "He dated a blonde majorette," says Brown.

When Brown got to Syracuse, the caution light was on. "Don't be another Avatus Stone," he was warned. Brown toed the line, but in his way. He remained true to himself, an outspoken, strong and challenging personality, perhaps the only kind that could have survived the wary, uptight environment in which he found himself. Brown was watched as if he were an alien who had descended on the town in a pod from outer space.

"They didn't want me at the start. But they finally accepted me," Brown says now. "And we had some success. I set records. We went to the Cotton Bowl, got on national television, and I didn't mess with the white girls on campus. Then they gave me the privilege of helping them recruit Ernie Davis. That meant they had finally accepted black players and wanted black players. Here they had a chance to get a player that fit all the molds and parameters they had."

Indeed, Schwartzwalder recruited Davis tirelessly, with the help of Brown and an Elmira attorney and Syracuse alumnus, Tony DeFilippo, whose son, Ted, was a high school basketball teammate of Davis's.

Says Brown, "They got him: Ernie Davis. And Ernie made it beautiful for that new era of championship guys. Dynamite dudes, black guys, came to Syracuse after Ernie. Floyd Little and Jim Nance and others. It was fantastic. They could go there without losing their dignity. I was fighting every day at Syracuse to hold on to my dignity. I broke through, but Ernie created the new era. Ernie was Ben's man. Schwartzwalder loved him."

Indeed, they all did, from the moment he hit the campus and first suited up for freshman football. In all his 25 years as a college coach, Schwartzwalder says, he never met another player like him. "Ernie was just like a puppy dog, friendly and warm and kind," he says. "He had that spontaneous goodness about him. He radiated enthusiasm. His enthusiasm rubbed off on the kids. Oh, he'd knock you down, but then he'd run back and pick you up. We never had a kid so thoughtful and polite. Ernie would pat the guys on the back who had tackled him and help them up. And compliment them: 'Great tackle.' Even opponents had a kindly feeling for him. They'd come into the dressing room after the game to see him. Jim Brown, Floyd Little and Larry Csonka [another great Syracuse back of yesteryear] would knock you down and run over you because they didn't like you. You were enemy. Ernie didn't dislike anybody. He'd knock you down and run over you because of his enthusiasm. If there was ever a perfect kid, it was Ernie Davis. He was the best kid I ever had anything to do with."

And he could play, to be sure, as grindingly hard as any of them. In his sophomore year, Davis carried 98 times for 686 yards—seven yards a carry—and scored 10 touchdowns as Syracuse went undefeated in the regular season, 10–0, and won its only national championship. Davis pulled a hamstring several days before Syracuse was to meet Texas in the Cotton Bowl in the final game of the season, and there was some doubt as to whether he could even play. Yet play he did. On Syracuse's first possession, running back Ger Schwedes threw an option pass to Davis, who was running a deep pattern, and the young halfback, limping noticeably, took off down the sideline. Fearing that Davis would reinjure the hamstring, Schwartzwalder ran after him, screaming, "Slow down, Ernie! Don't pull it!"

Davis limped into the end zone, completing a 57-yard run and an 87-yard play from scrimmage that was then the longest touchdown pass in the history of any major bowl. And despite his tender leg, he kept on playing, both ways. It was a vicious, meanly played game, with Texas players baiting the Orangemen with racial slurs, but Davis played as if unfazed by it all. He scored one more touchdown, set up a third with an interception from his defensive back spot and scored twice on two-point conversions. Syracuse won 23–14.

Two years later, after junior and senior years as an All-America, Davis was awarded the Heisman, which confirmed that he was the finest running back in college football. Brown's Syracuse records were now his—2,386 rushing yards, a 6.6-yard average per carry, 35 touchdowns and 220 points. Of course, he would be the most sought-after player in the NFL draft.

Davis had dreamed of playing professional ball for as long as he could remember, since the days of small-fry football in Elmira. And now, in his senior year, he was almost there. Davis and his college roommate, tight end John Mackey, used to talk for hours about the prospect. "We used to lie in bed at night when we roomed together, talking about what life would be like in the National Football League," says Mackey, a former Baltimore Colt. "What it would be like making money; having kids; taking care of our families, our parents. We were just kids, lying in bed and talking, wondering if we'd be friends forever."

"Oh, yeah," Davis said. "We will be friends forever."

Mackey and Davis first met when Mackey came to campus as a high school recruit, a year behind him. Davis told Mackey that they could room together if he chose Syracuse. "I thought he was kind of lonely," Mackey says. "Ernie was kind of a rookie by himself." They grew extremely close over the next three years. Davis and Mackey touched each other's lives in different ways. "I was the brother that he didn't have," Mackey says. In two separate ways Davis altered the directions of Mackey's life. Schwartzwalder had recruited Mackey as a running back, but Davis was so dominant at the position that Mackey faced the prospect of playing behind him until he left. The coach promised Mackey that he would wear number 44 when Davis graduated.

"I don't want to be number 44," Mackey told him. "I don't want to play behind anyone."

"You can either be a second-string halfback or a first-string tight end," Schwartzwalder said.

So Mackey became a tight end.

Davis also became a voice in Mackey's ear, urging him to be a gentleman. One evening Mackey met an attractive black student named Sylvia Cole, who asked him, "Why is it that black guys don't date any black girls on campus?"

That was easy, Mackey told her: "You have to have a girl in town: a) there is no curfew, and b) we can always get something to eat. We don't have any money."

Cole persisted, and to end the discussion, Mackey asked her out for Friday night. She accepted. "I wasn't planning to take her out," Mackey recalls. "I was just getting rid of her."

Word spread that they were going out, and Davis was among the first to hear about it. He asked Mackey about it, but Mackey waved him away. "Ah, man, forget that," he said to Davis.

"Hey, she's a real nice girl," Ernie told him. "You ought to take her out."

"If you think she's so nice, why don't you take her out?"

"I didn't ask her out—you did. Remember?"

"I didn't ask her out either," Mackey lied.

"That's not what I heard."

Mackey was cornered. "I don't have any money! So I can't take her any-place. I don't have a car. You got the car. What am I going to do, take her for a walk?"

Davis handed his roommate five dollars and flipped him the keys to his gray-and-black Edsel. "Now take that girl out and have a nice time," he said. Sylvia and John were married nearly three years later and are living today in California.

Helen Gott and Davis first met in the spring of his junior year, but they did not start going out until the next fall. Shy, reserved and deeply religious, she had never even considered dating one of those loud, boisterous football jocks. "I wasn't into that fast act," she says. "I didn't drink. I was a good kid who had a dad who was an Army colonel, and I was pretty sheltered. Ernie was different from those other football players, and that's what I liked. Ernie was a gentleman. He had a good balance between being gentle and manly. He didn't feel he had to prove his manhood by being overtly macho. He was not afraid to be gentle and considerate and open the doors."

Not long after they started dating, Helen took him home to meet her parents. She was an only daughter, and in the colonel's mind no man she had ever brought home was good enough. Until he met Davis. "This was the only relationship that he tried to coddle along," Helen says. "But then Ernie knew how to talk to parents. He talked sports with Dad. I have a pretty mother, and Ernie could be a little bit of a flatterer. I remember he made some kind of slang expression that nobody would know now. He said, 'Your mother's really sayin' a little taste.' It was an expression meaning 'foxy' now. When I told mother, she was flattered to death."

So was most of Cleveland when Davis turned his back on a substantially larger offer from the Buffalo Bills of the old American Football League and signed that $80,000 contract with the Browns. The Bills reportedly offered Davis a three-year deal worth well over $100,000. The Browns' front office crowed. "No college halfback playing today has his combination of size and speed," Paul Bixler, the Browns' chief scout, said. "He is one of the greatest running backs I have seen."

How Davis would have played off Jim Brown in that Cleveland backfield is only to be imagined. "Ernie was an elusive Jim Brown," says former Cleveland lineman John Brown, who played with Davis at Syracuse and roomed with him during Ernie's year in Cleveland. "Today Marcus Allen reminds me of Ernie. He was not as strong as Jim Brown, but stronger than Marcus Allen. On a scale of 1 to 10, Ernie's strength was a 9, Brown's a 10. Ernie could glide, he could reverse field, he could double-clutch and bowl you over. As to whether Jim would have resented him, I doubt it. As great as Jim was, I think Ernie's presence would have pushed him to even greater heights."

No one knows for sure when the trouble began, but those who knew Davis said they first saw a change in him at the Coaches All-America Game, an East-West matchup in Buffalo on June 29, 1962. He appeared sluggish and slow on his feet. "Bix, what's wrong with him?" Modell asked Bixler, sitting at the game. "He looks terrible."

"He'll be all right," Bixler said.

In the locker room after the game, Davis told John Brown, "I'm tired, John."

"Man, it was hot out there," said Brown. "I'm tired, too."

Davis returned to Elmira after the game and went to a cookout at Harrigan's house. He was not hungry and did not eat. "I'm a little tired," he told Marty. "My legs are tired. And my gums are bleeding. I've got to get my gums checked."

The symptoms of acute monocytic leukemia can include persistent fatigue and bleeding gums, as the blood-forming tissues of the body begin producing extremely high numbers of abnormal white blood cells. These cells collect in the lymph glands, causing swelling in the neck, and crowd out both oxygen-bearing red cells and platelets vital to clotting. The decline in the red-cell count causes fatigue, and the fall in platelet levels permits bleeding in the nose and gums.

Davis flew to Chicago to begin practice for the Aug. 3 game between the College All-Stars and the NFL champion Green Bay Packers. Davis was listless during workouts, and the All-Stars coach, Otto Graham, recalls, "We all just looked at each other and someone said, 'He's an All-America?' He had no pep. He wasn't showing us anything." Davis's teeth were bothering him, and he spent a day in a Chicago hospital to stem the bleeding that followed the removal of two wisdom teeth.

On Saturday, July 28, Davis felt a swelling in his neck, and he was admitted to Evanston Hospital, near the practice site at Northwestern University, with the fear that he may have contracted the mumps or mononucleosis. Doctors ran a test on his blood and found something much worse. Modell was at home in Cleveland when the doctor called and said, "Mr. Modell, I have some dreadful news for you about Ernie Davis."

Modell bolted up, thinking there had been an accident. "We've ruled out trench mouth and the mumps," he said. "He has a dreadful blood disorder, the worst kind of leukemia."

Modell winces today as he recalls that message. "It was like someone had stuck a knife in me," he says. "I couldn't believe it." So he denied it.

"I don't believe you," he said. "There's something wrong with your tests."

"I'm sorry," the doctor said.

Modell flew to Chicago immediately, drove to Evanston, conferred with doctors and checked Davis out of the hospital. Before leaving, Modell announced that Davis would not be playing in the All-Star Game, adding, "Doctors at Evanston Hospital are still completing tests that have diagnosed his condition as a blood disorder requiring extended treatment and rest." Davis and Modell flew back to Cleveland, where the player entered Marymount Hospital.

"Let's have a new round of tests," Dr. Victor Ippolito, the Browns' team physician, suggested. "Make sure they didn't mix his slides with someone else's."

They were grasping. Dr. Edward Siegler, a pathologist at Marymount, tapped a sampling of marrow from Davis's breastbone. "There was no doubt," Siegler recalls. "It was a routine, clear-cut diagnosis. I expected him to live no longer than six months or a year."

No one told Davis what he had, and speculation was rampant as to what was wrong with him. In hopes of keeping the truth out of the news, where Davis might read it or hear about it, Modell and Dr. Austin Weisberger, Davis's hematologist, held a background meeting with the local press and wire service reporters, telling them the news and asking that they not write about it. No one did. On Aug. 8, Davis wrote a letter to Buz Stark, an old Elmira friend, reporting that he was feeling well in Marymount: "While I don't really have to be here for the treatments that they are giving me for my blood disorder, I am hoping and praying for a quick recovery that will enable me to rejoin the Browns that much quicker."

Davis underwent chemotherapy that fall, and by early October the leukemia had gone into remission. With Modell present, Weisberger called Davis into his office on Oct. 4, more than two months after the diagnosis, and finally told him exactly what disease he had. "Can it be cured?" asked Davis. Weisberger held out hope. Modell studied Davis's face. "Nothing," he says. "He sat there passively. No telling what was going on in his mind." Davis brightened when Weisberger told him that as long as the disease was in remission, he saw no reason why he shouldn't play pro ball.

In an article in the *Saturday Evening Post* shortly before his death, Davis wrote, "Now I knew what I was battling and that there was something to look forward to—football. That's what I thought when I was told I had leukemia."

His hope of playing football again proved illusory. After consulting Dr. James Hewlett, a hematologist at the Cleveland Clinic, Cleveland coach Paul Brown refused to allow Davis to suit up. The issue became a point of contention between Brown and Modell, with Modell's doctor advising that Davis could play, Brown's that he could not.

"Dr. Hewlett told me, 'Don't put him in; who knows what could take place,'" says Brown. "So I wouldn't do it. It would be difficult to put a guy in a game who you know doesn't have much time to live. It was one of the saddest things I experienced in all my years as a coach."

Davis never complained to anyone. Says John Brown, "My one regret is that I didn't have the clout, the insight or the maturity to speak up and say, 'Let him play.' That bothers me to this day."

Davis carried on, thinking that he would conquer his leukemia. "He may have been sick," says John Brown, "but he had pride and did not want to be pitied. He emphatically thought he could beat that disease. Riding that wave, I thought he could beat it, too."

Modell called specialists from all over, seeking help. "I was determined to save his life," he says. "I tried everything, even quackery." Even that. A TV commentator in Cleveland, knowing how desperate Modell was, told him of a European doctor working in the basement of a Cleveland city hospital on a cure for leukemia. Modell and Ippolito visited the place. The doctor was surrounded by pans, coils, test tubes, boiling liquids. "It was like something out of a Boris Karloff movie," Modell says. "The doctor was a hunchback and looked like Quasimodo. It about scared the crap out of me."

They gave the doctor the records, which he studied, and then Modell asked, "Can you help?" The doctor nodded.

"What are you using?" Modell asked. "This is a very tragic case. We're not going to make a human guinea pig out of him."

"Horse serum," the doctor said.

"Horse serum?" blurted Modell.

"Serum from horses. An extract."

That's all Modell had to hear: "Vic, let's get out of here! I can't take this. . . ."

Davis's leukemia remained in remission throughout the fall of 1962. In mid-December, in a snowstorm, Davis accompanied Schwartzwalder to the New Haven, Connecticut, home of Floyd Little, who had just finished his final, record-breaking season as a running back at Bordentown Military Institute in New Jersey. Little was wavering between Army and Notre Dame, until that night. "Boy, did Ernie make an impression on everybody in that house, my mom and sisters," he says. "I mean, 6' 2", 215! Wearing a camel-hair coat and a stingy-brimmed hat. He had this big smile on his face, and he shook my hand and said, 'I understand we play the same position.' "

Schwartzwalder and Davis took Little to dinner that night, and after Little had finished his lobster, Davis waved him into the bathroom for a private talk. For nearly an hour, face-to-face, Davis sold Syracuse to Little. "Let me explain one thing to you," Ernie said. "You go to Syracuse, you'll get a chance to carry the football. The coach hates to throw." Davis went through it all that night—the life Syracuse offered for blacks, the tutoring services, the dorms, the campus, the tradition of number 44. "Jim Brown recruited me," Davis told him. "Now I've got to recruit the guy who's going to replace me. It's traditional."

Little went home leaning toward the Orange. Davis called him once in January and asked him what he was going to do. "You know I'm going to Syracuse," Little said. "My mom wants me to grow up just like you." Weisberger had announced in October that Davis had a "form of leukemia," but Little had read nothing about it, and did not know how ill Davis was.

The disease recurred in March, and Davis resumed regular visits to the hospital. Each time, he would call Modell and say, "I'm sorry, but I have to go into the hospital again." Or, "I know this is costing you a lot of money, but they want me in for another treatment."

Jim Brown could see the problems that Davis was having at the end, trying to stick the cotton up his nose, fumbling with it, tipping back his head. "I remember him touching the cotton up his nose, quickly, so no one would notice it," Brown says, "taking care of the nosebleed while not drawing attention to it. When he had to go to the hospital, which he felt was going to be the last time, I remember him touching the cotton and saying, 'Hey, check you later.' I knew what he was doing. That he was really saying goodbye. And he went on in to die. To perform like an athlete and then face death without whimpering, to have great consideration of others and to know you're going to die and then to bow out with such grace—I've never seen anyone else do that."

Over the years, Brown had grown to respect Davis enormously, not just for his talent or his grace in parting but for what he represented, something that reminded him of Joe Louis.

"The greatest thing about Ernie Davis is that white people liked him and black people liked him," says Brown. "And I liked him, too, because I never thought of him as an Uncle Tom. I thought of him as a certain kind of spiritual individual, a true kind of spirit who had the ability to rise above things and deal more with the universe, so that white people would forget their racism with him and black people would never think he was acquiescing to white people. And, you know, you have to be a bad sucker to do that, because usually you either line up on one side or the other. So Ernie Davis transcended racism. That was his essence. That was his greatness."

Davis left the others as quietly as he left Jim Brown. On Thursday, May 16, he wrote John Brown a note on a yellow legal pad: "Going to the hospital for a few days. Don't tell anybody. See you around."

That day he went to Modell's office, instead of calling him on the telephone, and told the owner he was going into Lakeside Hospital.

"You don't have to come down to tell me that," said Modell. "Call me when you get out. I want you to get busy and start lifting weights." The two men chatted briefly, shook hands, and Davis left.

On Friday night, in Lakeside, Davis lapsed into a coma, and at 2 A.M. on Saturday, he coughed once and died. Modell got the call early that morning: "The first thing that went through my mind, and still does, was Ernie coming to my office to say goodbye."

Floyd Little was in Bordentown when a friend told him the news. He had not been sure what he was going to do when he told Davis in January that he was going to Syracuse. He was still thinking of West Point and Notre Dame. But remembering what he had told Davis the last time they had spoken, Little made up his mind. "I did not want to lie to him," he said. So he called Schwartzwalder. "I'm coming to Syracuse," Little said.

For years, Helen Gott would not and could not listen to "Our Day Will Come." And for years she could not talk about Ernie's death. Today, more than 26 years have passed and the pain is gone, if not the sadness. She is Helen Gray now, and she is the religion editor of the *Kansas City Times*. She is married and has a seven-year-old child.

She still has the mementos—Davis's letters to her, the photographs and the scarab bracelet and the gold cross and chain he gave her. And the memories of the two years they knew each other, the last dinner together and the Saturday he died. She was in her sorority house, Sigma Delta Tau, when two of her sisters came over and put their arms around her. She looked up and saw the university chaplain. And she knew.

"He's dead," she said.

She left the house to be alone. "I remember I went outside and sat under a tree. At that time, even with the faith that I had in God, it seemed unfair. It seemed like he had done all the right things. He had led a good life. He had overcome obstacles. He had excelled. He would be just a great role model. Not only for black youths, but for everybody. This was a truly good person. If he didn't ask the question—'Why me?'—I think I did. You know, 'Why him? Why Ernie?'"

September 1989

PART 5

BONUS PIECES

BLOOD MONEY

*In the rich, clubby world of horsemen,
some greedy owners have hired killers to murder
their animals for the insurance payoffs*

On the rainy night of Feb. 2, 1991, in despair over the prospect of causing the death of a horse by breaking its hind leg with a crowbar,
Tommy (the Sandman) Burns sat in a bar outside Gainesville, Florida, and
got drunk on gin and tonic. "Really wasted," Burns recalls. "I had never
done one like that before."

For a decade the cherubic 30-year-old had made a sporadic living as a hit
man hired to destroy expensive horses and ponies, usually so their owners
could collect on lucrative life-insurance policies. But no owner had ever
ordered Burns to dispose of a horse by breaking one of its legs—that is, by
causing a trauma so severe that a veterinarian would be forced to put the
animal down with a lethal injection.

Burns's preferred method of killing horses was electrocution. It had been
so ever since the day in 1982 when, he says, the late James Druck, an
Ocala, Florida, attorney who represented insurance companies, paid him to
kill the brilliant show jumper Henry the Hawk, on whose life Druck had
taken out a $150,000 life-insurance policy. In fact, says Burns, Druck per-
sonally taught him how to rig the wires to electrocute Henry the Hawk:
how to slice an extension cord down the middle into two strands of wire;
how to attach a pair of alligator clips to the bare end of each wire; and how
to attach the clips to the horse—one to its ear, the other to its rectum. All
he had to do then, says Burns, was plug the cord into a standard wall socket.
And step back.

"You better get out of the way," says Burns. "They go down immediately. One horse dropped so fast in the stall, he must have broken his neck when he hit the floor. It's a sick thing, I know, but it was quick and it was painless. They didn't suffer." And it was, for the collection of insurance claims, an ideal method of execution. According to doctors at the University of Pennsylvania's New Bolton Center, one of the nation's leading large-animal hospitals, even the most experienced pathologist would be unlikely to detect signs of death by electrocution—unless, perchance, the pathologist was looking for it and the clips happened to leave singe marks. Many of the horses Burns electrocuted were assumed to have died of colic.

So Tommy Burns (a.k.a. Timmy Robert Ray), who had worked around horses since he had run away from home in Connecticut at the age of 15, became a serial killer of horses and got away with it for 10 years. According to federal agents, Burns destroyed some 20 horses, mostly show jumpers and hunters, on the show-horse circuit from Florida to Vermont to Illinois. "In 1989 it got crazy," Burns says. "I killed three horses in one week." Indeed, toting the canvas athletic bag in which he hid his deadly wires, Burns became such a regular presence among the wealthy show-horse crowds that he earned a sobriquet of which he would remain, until recently, unaware. "People knew what was going on," says a prominent West Virginia horsewoman. "When Tommy arrived at a show, they would say the Sandman was around. They knew a horse would be put to sleep." In almost every case, something about a horse—its performance, its health, its age—had made the unthinkable occur to its owner.

By that night of Feb. 2, Burns had, by his own admission, run "hard and wild for 10 years." A few days earlier he and his associate, Harlow Arlie, had driven a vanload of show horses from their base in northern Illinois to Canterbury Farms in Florida. Among the equine passengers was Streetwise, a sporty chestnut jumper with a white stocking on each leg, a blaze on its face and a $25,000 insurance policy on its life. Burns has told federal investigators that the 7-year-old gelding's owner, Donna Brown, a prominent horsewoman on the clubby show-horse circuit, had hired him for $5,000 to arrange a fatal accident for Streetwise. According to Burns, the insurance policy did not cover death by colic—Streetwise had a history of colic, a life-threatening condition in a horse—so Brown insisted that he break the animal's leg.

"I don't *want* to break his leg," Burns, at the bar near Gainesville, sang to Arlie in his executioner's song. "I'm not into that."

"I'll do it," Burns says Arlie told him. "For half your fee."

The two men left the bar and returned to Canterbury. Burns figured the rain that night would make the perfect alibi: They were loading Streetwise into the van when the horse slipped, fell off the ramp and broke its leg. At about 10:10 P.M., after helping to load three other horses into the van for a trip south to West Palm Beach, Burns stood in the middle of a brightly lighted lot and held a lead shank tethered to Streetwise's halter.

Unbeknownst to Burns, investigators for the Florida Department of Agricultural and Consumer Services, acting on a tip, had been following his van ever since it had rolled into Florida, and on this night they were staking out the farm. One of the investigators, Harold Barry, lay flat and still on the top of a beat-up horse trailer less than 100 yards away, watching helplessly as the dark, rain-swept scene suddenly turned from eerie to macabre.

The powerfully built Arlie appeared behind Streetwise's right rear leg, a crowbar in his hand. Arlie swung the bar like a baseball bat, and agents across the highway could hear a crack. Neighing loudly, in a high, panicky scream, Streetwise began thrashing on his dangling leg, fell to the ground as a stunned Burns hung onto the lead—"I'd never seen anything like it; the horse went into shock," he says—and then scrambled back to his feet. The keening horse tore the shank from Burns's hand and took off around the stable, disappearing in the night, falling again, bellowing, only a sound now, an echo behind the barn now, in the dark now, in the quiet rain.

Tommy Burns punched numbers on a cellular phone, calling Donna Brown in West Palm Beach to inform her of events. Meanwhile Arlie informed Carlie Ferguson, president of Canterbury Farms, who summoned a vet. The vet phoned Brown, and on her instructions he called the insurance company on its 800 emergency number. Of course, the company authorized immediate euthanasia for the suffering animal. Moments after arriving on the scene, the vet put the horse down.

Burns and Arlie did not get far. After the death of Streetwise, Burns fired up the rig and took off. But two miles down Route 26, Florida Highway Patrol cars converged on the van from all directions. "They were even coming out of dirt roads," says Burns. He made a run for it, but he was quickly subdued, handcuffed and arrested at shotgun point. "What were you guys doing at the farm?" a cop yelled in Burns's ear.

They had him cold. Agricultural investigators found the crowbar and the electrocution wires in Burns's white pickup. An accomplice who had helped to load the horses at the scene, Chad Sondell, said in a sworn statement to state investigators that Burns and Arlie had told him they were to be paid $5,000 by Brown to kill Streetwise. Arlie confirmed Sondell's story, according to police reports, and admitted having struck Streetwise with the crowbar. Arlie soon pleaded guilty to charges of insurance fraud and cruelty to animals, and he eventually served six months of an 18-month sentence before being paroled.

Federal authorities had been investigating Burns for months—it was they who had tipped the Florida agricultural department that the Sandman was heading south with a potential victim in his van—and Burns's arrest turned out to be the major break in what had become a difficult collection of cases to crack.

Underscoring the importance of the arrest, an FBI agent and a top Justice Department prosecutor from Chicago, Steve Miller, descended on Gainesville only hours after Burns was taken into custody. Caught in the act, incriminated by Arlie and Sondell and facing certain conviction and a jail term on charges of insurance fraud and cruelty to animals, Burns decided to cooperate with federal prosecutors. He spent three weeks in jail, and after the Alachua County Circuit Court finally released him on $100,000 cash bail—under an order that he stay away from horses—he returned to Chicago, where he began cooperating with a grand jury that has been looking into the killing of horses for insurance money.

Burns quickly unraveled his sordid tale to law-enforcement officials, giving names, places and dates from his history as a professional horse-killer and a co-conspirator in cases of insurance fraud. Burns faces sentencing Dec. 14 in the case involving Streetwise, and he expects the feds to seek leniency on his behalf on grounds that he is a key government witness in what has become an investigation of stunning scope.

"Tommy Burns turns out to be the tip of the iceberg," one federal agent says. In the next few weeks, as agents from the FBI, the Internal Revenue Service and the Bureau of Alcohol, Tobacco and Firearms wind up their investigations, sources estimate that as many as 40 owners, trainers, veterinarians, and riders will be indicted on various charges related to the killing of horses for insurance payments. Law-enforcement officials are piecing together felony fraud cases against the owners and trainers who hired Burns, and they're tracking down itinerant stable hands and grooms who can confirm details of the killings that the Sandman carried out for their bosses. The inquiries have led agents on a long, circuitous trail from one scene of electrocution to the next, and along the way investigators have picked up leads on other insurance-related deaths not involving Burns and on still other crimes that include suspicious stable fires and the fraudulent sale of overvalued horses.

In the 21 months since Burns's arrest, investigators have developed hard evidence that such crimes have not been confined to the show-horse business and that Burns is not the only hit man working expensive stables. During that time the investigators have concluded that killing horses for insurance claims is business as usual at all levels in the world of show horses.

This phenomenon is hardly new, nor is it confined to jumpers and hunters. Twenty years ago, at some prominent thoroughbred racetrack barns, animals were dying at such an alarming rate that insurance companies were refusing to insure the trainers' horses. At one Belmont Park barn where horses were expiring mysteriously in the night, cynical grooms would show up in the morning and ask, "Anyone die last night?"

Veteran insurance adjusters say, however, that the number of suspicious claims by horse owners has increased dramatically in the years since the 1986 Tax Reform Act eliminated performance horses as depreciable assets. That "reform" and the anemic state of the economy cut the bottom out of the horse business, leaving a cash-starved industry with farms and stables struggling desperately to stay afloat.

Unlike paintings by Renoir or baseball cards bearing pictures of Honus Wagner, horses experience wild, often unforeseen fluctuations in value. Say, for instance, that a thoroughbred investor spends $500,000 for a well-built, well-bred yearling, insures him for that sum and sends him off, as a 2-year-old, to a racetrack trainer. And say that the trainer then informs the owner that the colt is so slow that he couldn't beat a $15,000 maiden claimer. Or that he is an ill-tempered, untrainable rogue. Or that he is about to bow a tendon and will never race. The humane sportsman might wince and take the loss, but more than a few others would make other arrangements. "The insurance is there, and it is very tempting," says one federal agent.

Over the last few years, says Harvey Feintuch, a New York lawyer who specializes in the investigation of equine insurance claims, "we have had a very, very significant increase in the number of claims that just don't look right."

Given the current economic climate, the sudden deaths of expensive, stall-bound horses tend to raise suspicions, even at the highest levels of the horse business. A widely respected freelance turf writer, Carol Flake, sent shudders through the thoroughbred industry when, in a meticulously reported article in the February 1992 issue of Connoisseur magazine, she raised the possibility that the death of Alydar—one of the most popular racehorses of modern times and one of the world's prepotent stallions—was not an accident.

In the investigation of thoroughbred fatalities, federal agents have found more than mere suspicions. In Brooklyn and South Florida, the feds say, they recently uncovered an insurance scheme that led to the death of one horse, a son of Seattle Slew named Fins, and nearly resulted in the death of another, Cutlass Reality, a New York stakes winner of $1.4 million. Prosecutors say that the scheme involved Victor Arena, the reputed head of the Colombo crime family; Howard Crash, a New York securities broker who is under indictment for bribery; and Larry Lombardo, a licensed owner and trainer of thoroughbreds who has been indicted on federal charges that he killed Fins "while making the death appear to be due to natural causes." Sources speculate that the horse was injected with parasitic bloodworms that brought on a case of thromboembolic colic, a fatal illness.

According to a 21-count indictment handed up in Miami on Aug. 4, Lombardo purchased Fins for $7,500, inflated the horse's value to $400,000 through a series of sales of phony shares, insured Fins for that amount and then collected on the policy after the horse died. Ron Rubinstein, Lombardo's defense attorney, claims that Fins died of natural causes and argues that the colt, at $400,000, was not overvalued as a breeding prospect. But Seth Hancock, the president of Claiborne Farm, which bred Fins, and who has been in the thoroughbred-breeding business for 80 years, said that Fins was a big, crooked-legged colt who couldn't run a lick.

Lombardo is also charged with conspiring to kill Cutlass Reality, the smashing winner of the 1988 Hollywood Gold Cup (and conqueror of the Horse of the Year, Alysheba), in an alleged insurance-fraud scheme. Crash and his former business associate Mark Hankoff—the two key government witnesses against Lombardo, according to sources close to the case—owned the horse in partnership with Lombardo and several others. What saved Cutlass Reality is unclear, but the hit was never made. "Somebody got scared and backed out," an FBI agent says. What is clear, according to the sworn testimony of an FBI agent involved in the case, is that Crash, Lombardo and Arena would have each received $1 million from the insurance settlement if the horse had been killed. Instead, Cutlass Reality will be standing stud in California next spring, servicing mares at $5,000 a pop—and that beats colic.

While the company that insured Fins had some doubts about the horse's stated value and was suspicious of the timing of the claim, which was made six months after the purchase of the policy, it nonetheless sent the $400,000 check to Lombardo and his cohorts. (Lombardo goes on trial next March 22; if convicted, he may be forced to make restitution to the insurance company.) Increasingly, however, insurance companies are balking at paying suspicious claims and are fighting them in court. The companies are also investigating suspicious claims more assiduously, looking for signs of fraud such as the bogus inflation of a horse's value and the concealing of ailments and infirmities. "We began to take more time and more care," says Feintuch, adding that Lloyds of London and other carriers have toughened their approach to paying claims.

Lloyds's increased vigilance dates back eight years to a case that rocked the highest levels of the thoroughbred breeding world and drove some of its biggest players to hide behind the woodshed in embarrassment. When, on March 25, 1984, an imported English horse named Pelerin died of vitamin D toxicosis shortly after ending his inconsistent career by finishing out of the money in a race in Louisiana, the underwriters of the insurance on the horse, all associated with Lloyds, had reason to be skeptical of the $1.45 million policy that Kentucky horseman Harold Snowden held on his half of the animal. Not only did Pelerin appear to have been poisoned, as the term *toxicosis* implies, but his value (Snowden and a partner had purchased him for $2 million) had dropped sharply in light of his less-than-stellar racing career.

Snowden, co-owner of the Stallion Station and breeder of two Kentucky Derby winners, Dust Commander (1970) and Bold Forbes (1976), had been one of the most active players in the business, the syndicator of more than 100 stallions and a prolific insurer of horses. In a gesture aimed at staying in Snowden's favor, the underwriters offered him $1 million—exactly what he had paid originally for half of the horse—to settle the claim. Snowden held out for $1.35 million. The carriers refused to budge, and Snowden took them to court. It was the first time that an equine insurance company had opposed someone of his stature.

Snowden came armed with 10 letters from fellow horsemen, all dated *before* Pelerin's death, in which each breeder expressed interest in buying a share in the horse for $75,000 upon his retirement to stud. At the 40 shares Snowden said he would have sold, Pelerin's claimed value now rose to $3 million. Among the nationally known breeders who sent letters were Warner Jones, then chairman of the board of Churchill Downs; J.T. Lundy, later head of Calumet Farm; and the late Leslie Combs II, then the aging pillar of Spendthrift Farm.

Snowden looked as if he would win in a gallop when—in a maneuver Perry Mason would have envied—Feintuch, acting on the underwriters' behalf, called two witnesses who destroyed Snowden's case and earned him the glowering wrath of the judge, Henry Wilhoit. One of the witnesses, a secretary for breeder Dwayne Rogers, testified that she had typed Rogers's letter to Snowden. The problem was that she had not begun working for Rogers until 14 months *after* Pelerin's death. She explained to the court that Rogers told her to backdate the letter to Jan. 5, 1984, two months before the horse's demise. The other witness, a receptionist at Spendthrift Farm, testified that she had typed Combs's letter to Snowden but that she did not go to work at Spendthrift until July 1984, by which time Pelerin had been dead four months. She testified that Combs had her type the backdated letter late one day, after everyone else had left the office.

Snowden was in trouble. His lawyers withdrew on him, leaving him to face a furious Wilhoit. Snowden hired F. Lee Bailey to put the toothpaste back in the tube, but that did no good. After a third horseman admitted that his letter was a fraud, Wilhoit concluded that "all 10 letters had been backdated." While never addressing the question of whether Pelerin was poisoned, Wilhoit charged that "a fraud had been practiced upon the court." Not only was Snowden out the $1 million that Lloyds had offered in the original settlement, but he was also left with a dead horse, a court-ordered judgment against him for $194,131.12 (to cover court costs and the amount Lloyds spent in legal fees fighting his claim) and bills from his own departed lawyers, not to mention from Bailey.

While the thoroughbred business has had its sorry share of cases involving insurance fraud, it has experienced nothing like the maelstrom that Burns is about to set spinning in the show-horse business. Sources say that, based on Burns's testimony, some of the most celebrated figures in the game are targets of the grand jury probe. They include Donna Brown and her husband, Buddy Brown, a member of the U.S. equestrian team at the 1976 Olympics and still one of the nation's leading performers in Grand Prix jumping. Not only does Donna face allegations in connection with the death of Streetwise, but she and Buddy are also under investigation for the death of Aramis, another show jumper. According to sources, insurance records show that Aramis, while insured for $1 million, died under suspicious circumstances. (No charge has been filed in either case.)

Asked about the federal investigations into the deaths of two of the Browns' horses, the couple's lawyer, Mark Arisohn, a Manhattan criminal defense specialist, says, "I wish I could give you a response. We will plead not guilty. Our defense will be established in the courtroom."

Another horseman who has attracted the attention of investigators is George Lindemann Jr. of Greenwich, Connecticut, who has emerged as one of the nation's most accomplished equestrians since graduating from Brown University in 1986. Lindemann has ridden his stable of gifted show jumpers to victory in some of the Grand Prix circuit's richest and most prestigious events, but federal investigators are more interested in what role, if any, he played in the December 1990 death of his champion hunter Charisma.

Tommy Burns has told authorities that Charisma was insured for $400,000 when Burns electrocuted him for Lindemann in a stall at the Lindemann family's Cellular Farms, in Armonk, New York. According to another source, Lindemann had purchased Charisma for $250,000 in 1989. Minus Burns's alleged $35,000 fee for the hit, the insurance payoff would have left Lindemann with a $115,000 profit. It also left investigators wondering why, if Burns's allegations are true, the enormously rich Lindemann—the name Cellular Farms refers to cellular phones, the source of the family's wealth—would take so big a risk for so small a sum.

Asked about the inquiry into Charisma's death, Lindemann referred all questions to his lawyer, Elaine Amendola, who said, "Why should I be talking about this when George has the FBI hanging all over his neck?" She added, however, that "George is completely innocent."

Additionally, federal agents are looking into the possible involvement of veterinarian Dana Tripp, also an accomplished equestrian, in the death of Streetwise. Florida investigators say that Tripp's red pickup truck—with DANA TRIPP, D.V.M. emblazoned on its doors—was part of Burns's caravan as it made its way toward Canterbury Farms. It was Tripp, according to sources cited in the police report, who recommended to Donna Brown that she hire Burns to stage Streetwise's accident. Prosecutors have phone records revealing Tripp's numerous conversations with both Brown and Burns in the two days leading up to the death of Streetwise. Tripp has refused to respond to SI's questions about the matter.

The Sandman's trail has led federal agents to stables in at least eight states. Sources say that Paul Valliere of North Smithfield, Rhode Island, one of the show circuit's leading trainers, is under federal investigation. Burns has told authorities that Valliere hired him to destroy Roseau Platiere, one of Valliere's own horses. Burns says he electrocuted the animal one night in its stall at a horse show in Sugarbush, Vermont. Reached at his Acres Wild Farm in Rhode Island, Valliere refused to answer any questions. Seeking corroboration of Burns's Sugarbush story, Sports Illustrated spoke to a woman who said that she had picked Burns up at the airport in Burlington, Vermont, and taken him to the horse show. (The woman said she had given this information to the FBI.) Sports Illustrated also spoke to others who described Roseau Platiere as vigorous and healthy in the hours before Burns's visit. Burns says he has told federal agents that Roseau Platiere was one of the three horses he destroyed in 1989 during the busiest week of his career as a contract killer.

Agents are also following up Burns's account of the death of a show horse named Rainman. His owner, Chicago businessman Allen Levinson, collected a $50,000 insurance policy on Rainman's death, but he denies any wrongdoing. "I have never heard of Tommy Burns," Levinson says. "I was trying to sell that horse. I had it sold for more money than the insurance policy. There was a complete autopsy."

For the agents, investigating horse killings has been a difficult, unfamiliar experience. Only rarely has there been a body on which to perform a necropsy, as there was in the case of Streetwise; the carcasses usually have been lost to the rendering plants. So this has been in good part a paper chase. In some cases agents have served subpoenas on claims adjusters who had long before paid the owners for their losses. But the owners' files and personal financial records have been valuable, frequently confirming details of Burns's story of a horse's death—including in some cases the exact barn and stall where it occurred.

In fact, investigators have been struck by the ease with which they were able to follow the paper trail that some of Burns's clients left behind. Burns's presence on the circuit and the things that tended to happen when he was around became so accepted that he was treated like the feedman or the farrier. His employers frequently paid him with personal checks and sometimes with cashier's checks purchased at their banks.

Even federal agents, who thought they had seen everything, were shocked by the insouciance of some of those who dealt with Burns. Burns recalls one woman's approach to him at a horse show: "She said, 'Do you think you could kill my horse for $10,000?' So I did. She bought another horse with the insurance money and came up to me two months later and asked me to kill her new horse. She didn't like it."

There is a troubling banality about the evil at work in these cases. "We are dealing with a way of life here," one investigator said. "These people thought they had some sort of right to do these things."

Largely because of the nature of the crime ("These animals are so vulnerable that I'd compare it almost to hurting children," says Florida agriculture commissioner Bob Crawford), some law-enforcement officials have pursued the investigation with an inspired intensity. "This is a case where you can lose your detachment," says one federal agent. "These were beautiful animals. They were standing there helpless in their stalls. Most of these people had plenty of money. So you get outraged. And you work a little harder."

Burns knows better than anyone how the horses were standing in their stalls, wearing their halters and alligator clips and watching him curiously, like deer in a clearing, as he stepped outside and moved for the socket. He wants it known, as he has been telling the feds, that he wasn't there on his own. "I was not alone in all of this," he says. "I feel terrible about what I did. But I did not advertise. I did not do any sales calls. People found me and came to me. Very important people. Very wealthy people. They came to me because they somehow knew that I might be willing to do something they wanted done. They wanted these horses dead."

What the clients wanted, the clients got. However well he warbles, Burns knows he will do some jail time, just as he knows there will be no escaping, ever, what he did for so long with his life. There's no escaping that night in Florida, in the dark, in the rain, and the sight of Arlie with the crowbar, and the crack and the screams, the horse falling and thrashing, rising and running. Burns can still hear the cops yelling at him after his arrest: "You killed all those horses, and we know you did!"

"They were right," says Tommy Burns.

They always will be. That is his sentence.

November 1992

At the close of his career as a horse killer, Tommy (The Sandman) Burns ended up singing more than the executioners' song. His cooperation with the FBI, the Illinois State Police, and the Bureau of Alcohol, Tobacco and Firearms led to to 27 indictments and 26 convictions and was vital in exposing widespread insurance fraud in the show-horse industry. A federal judge, Charles Norgle, Sr., sentenced Burns to six months in jail in 1996—the minimum under federal rules—for his part in the death of Streetwise and 19 other similar horse killings. George Lindemann, Jr. and Donna Brown were among those sentenced to prison terms as a result, in part, of Burns's singing. Paul Valliere also cooperated with authorities when he agreed to be "wired" with a recorder to gather evidence against Lindemann. For his cooperation and guilty plea, Valliere was sentenced to four years of probation and ordered to pay a $5000 fine. Allen Levinson, for his involvement in the death of Rainman, was sentenced to 12 months in prison and fined $20,000. Harold Snowden died in 2000 of a blood clot in one of his lungs. He was 77.

THE MUSCLE MURDERS

When Bertil Fox, a former Mr. Universe, was arrested for double homicide last year, he became only the latest accused murderer among hard-core bodybuilders, whose subculture is a volatile mix of fragile egos, economic hardship and anabolic steroid abuse

In a cell in the west wing of the Basseterre prison on the West Indies island of St. Kitts, behind lava-brick walls rimmed with coils of concertina wire, Bertil Fox is melting away in the Caribbean heat. Of the two-time Mr. Universe, a former bodybuilding prodigy who was once the Mozart of muscles, all that appear to retain their former size and shape are the mole below the right side of his lower lip and the gap between his two front teeth. Fox has lost his armor, the blood-filled sinew of those days during which he waged the battle for the perfect bulge—for the ribbed striations and popping vascularity that were his hallmarks. A sculptor bereft of his tools, he now wraps towels over the prison bars and pulls on them to exercise his once diamond-cut back.

He does push-ups for his arms. He lifts buckets filled with water for his triceps and his delts. But anabolic steroids, the Wheaties of most pro bodybuilders, aren't served in prison along with the chicken and the rice. So the 270-pound man they used to call Brutal Fox is just a 205-pound Bertil now.

He has even lost the timbre of his voice. Facing him behind a sheet of perforated Plexiglas in the narrow visiting room of the prison—a bastille built in 1840 to entertain captured pirates—one has to press an ear against the barrier to hear him speak. "Everybody here is lonely for freedom," Fox, 47, says. "So am I. I've never been in prison before. I'm locked up all day. I come out to shower in the morning and come out to shower at night. I work out in the cell. That's all there is to do. I've never been in trouble in my life. Overnight, I'm a monster."

In the last eight months Fox has gone from being the Arnold Schwarzenegger of St. Kitts to being the island's O.J. Simpson. On Sept. 30, 1997, he allegedly shot and killed his former girlfriend, model Leyoca Browne, and her mother, Violet, in Violet's dress shop on Cayon Street in downtown Basseterre. He was charged with double murder and imprisoned without bail. During a four-day trial in February, Fox, facing a possible sentence of death by hanging, testified that the shootings were an accident that occurred when he struggled with Violet over his pistol. His best friend, Edmund Tross, testified that Fox had admitted the killings to him and to an associate without making any claim of self-defense. "He said he had shot Leyoca and her mother," Tross told the court. "He said Leyoca's mother was pushing him out the door. At that point he pulled out the gun and started shooting." A seamstress at the dress shop also gave testimony incriminating Fox. Nevertheless, only the nine-member jury ended up hung. Fox faces a retrial in the near future.

While news of the killings and the subsequent proceedings riveted St. Kitts and Nevis, a two-island nation of 41,803 souls, it also sent chillingly familiar reverberations through the insular, narcissistic subculture of hardcore bodybuilding. It's a bizarre world of beetle-browed loners with eggshell egos who are engaged in an obsessive quest for self-mastery; of men posturing before wraparound mirrors, casting illusory reflections of strength, masculinity and virility from which hang, metaphorically, their steroid-shrunken testicles; of cartoonish characters chiseling and tanning and oiling their hairless bodies to camouflage impoverished self-esteem; of fat-free, high-protein starvation diets that can heighten the irritability and anxiety brought on by steroid abuse; and of all those needles and vials and pills—whole families of anabolic steroids, hormones and diuretics, insulin and speed. Not even Wrestlemania achieves such a triumph of illusion over substance.

This subculture offers unusually fertile soil for aggression and, in some cases, deadly violence. Now that bodybuilding is being considered for inclusion in the Olympics, it will come under increasing scrutiny by the international athletic community. Studies have shown that the ingestion of large quantities of anabolic steroids—many bodybuilders take up to 3,000 milligrams a week, 500 times more than the male body produces—can trigger episodes of violent rage in certain people. Researchers who have studied both bodybuilders and the effects of steriod abuse agree that these athletes seem more inclined to extremely violent behavior than performers in any of the more conventional sports, including college and pro football, where steroid abuse has also been widespread. Murder in muscledom isn't uncommon. Fox isn't the only bodybuilder doing reps in jail these days.

Former amateur bodybuilding champion Gordon Kimbrough, 35, trains clients by telephone from Mule Creek State Prison in Ione, California, outside Sacramento, where he's serving 27 years to life for the first-degree murder of his fiancée, Kristy Ramsey, with whom he won the 1991 USA pairs title. Meek and shy when not on steroids, Kimbrough, according to a family member, becomes short-tempered and violent when using them. On June 20, 1993, after Ramsey told him in their San Francisco apartment that she'd had sex with another man and that the wedding was off, the 250-pound Kimbrough struck his 137-pound fiancée on the chin, wrapped an electrical cord three times around her neck, tying it in a knot, and stabbed her twice in the throat with a paring knife. He spent the night with her corpse while trying to kill himself by injecting into his neck a prescription diuretic, Lasix, and a household cleanser, Lysol. When police found him the next morning, with Ramsey lying at the foot of their bed, Kimbrough was holding a large kitchen knife to his throat and muttering, "She found someone else, another guy." He surrendered quietly.

Kimbrough is one of two prominent former bodybuilders in the California prison system. John Alexander Riccardi of Venice, Calif., has been on death row in San Quentin since 1994, after a jury convicted him of the '83 murders of his estranged girlfriend, Connie Hopkins Navarro, and her best friend, Sue Marshall Jory.

It was in the gyms of Santa Monica that Riccardi built his quads and abs and started seeing Navarro, a former cheerleader at Santa Monica High. They dated for more than two years. But when Navarro ended the relationship, Riccardi's behavior toward her grew increasingly malicious and bizarre, according to prosecutors. Afraid to go home, Connie sometimes stayed with her former husband, James Navarro, who later testified that Connie said Riccardi once raped her at knifepoint and another time kidnapped her for a few hours. She also claimed, according to prosecutors, that on another occasion Riccardi handcuffed to a toilet the Navarros' 13-year-old son, David, who would later become a guitar player with the rock band Red Hot Chili Peppers. According to James, Connie was about to seek a restraining order against Riccardi when, on March 3, 1983, he broke into her West Los Angeles apartment and shot her and Jory (who just happened to be visiting) in what LAPD detective Lee Kingsford described as "a jealous rage."

Connie's body was found half-stuffed into a linen closet. Riccardi fled town. An L.A. homicide detective conducting the manhunt placed an ad in Muscle & Fitness magazine, appealing to readers for help in finding the missing gym rat. Riccardi wasn't captured until eight years later, in Houston, after a viewer spotted his mug on America's Most Wanted.

Not all the muscle murders have been committed by men against women. About 100 miles southeast of San Quentin, at the Valley State Prison for Women in Chowchilla, California, former strength champion Sally McNeil is serving 19 years to life for the murder of her 256-pound husband, pro bodybuilder Ray McNeil, three years ago. She had earned her prophetic nickname, Killer Sally, by making easy money wrestling schmoes—the word used for men who worship female bodybuilders—in the couple's tiny apartment in Oceanside. The McNeils used the 150-pound Sally's income as a so-called apartment wrestler to help support their appetite for bodybuilding chemicals.

When Ray came home late at night on Valentine's Day 1995, Sally suspected that he had been with another woman. They began to quarrel, and then, she told police, "he was beating on me." Later, as Ray was cooking some chicken, Sally appeared in the kitchen doorway and fired on him with a 12-gauge shotgun, ripping a hole in his abdomen. After reloading, she shot him in the face as he crawled toward the front door. She called 911. On the tape of that call, police could hear Ray moaning, "Why, oh God, why?" She had blown away a pound of his liver and parts of his tongue and lower jaw. The toxicology report on Ray's corpse revealed that he had been using five anabolic steroids. Sally tested positive for one. "Ray got the best steroids, and I got the leftovers," she complained later.

All of this occurred in the middle of a particularly volatile season of muscle mayhem. In the early morning of Jan. 16, 1995, just a month before Sally killed Ray, two competitive bodybuilders with a history of violence toward one another—former Mr. America and Mr. Universe Warren Frederick and his onetime training partner, Danny Flanagan—got into a fight after Flanagan cut off Frederick in a Tampa parking lot. The 260-pound Flanagan ended up sitting on Frederick and pummeling him. In the struggle, Frederick reached out and grabbed an undetermined sharp object from the ground and stabbed Flanagan in the chest with it, puncturing his aorta. Frederick fled, not knowing that the wound was fatal. (Later that morning he called police to file an assault complaint against Flanagan.) Flanagan, bleeding profusely, struggled to his blue pickup truck and drove away. He was found soon after on the side of a road, slumped over his steering wheel, disoriented and trying to speak. He died before he could tell what had happened. Three weeks later the local state's attorney's office, after reviewing the evidence, called the stabbing an act of self-defense and didn't press charges against Frederick.

No wonder that with two musclemen killed since Jan. 1, 1995, what actor and former pro bodybuilder Lou Ferrigno did on March 24 of that year was viewed as comic relief. Ferrigno, who had played the title role in the TV series *The Incredible Hulk*, began popping his buttons when he saw Bernadine Morgan, an L.A. meter maid, writing a parking ticket for his pickup. Just as he might have on television, Ferrigno came bounding out of his house. He screamed, "Don't cite that truck!" As Morgan slapped the ticket on the vehicle, Ferrigno ran up to her scooter, loosed a Hulkian growl and shattered its windshield with a single punch. Ferrigno, usually a gentle soul, quickly grew contrite. "I'm sorry," he told Morgan. "I didn't mean to break the window—just punch it." Ferrigno, who is hearing impaired, later said that he tends to express himself with his hands. Police charged him with vandalism, and he paid a fine.

News of homicidal violence in the hard-core bodybuilding world came again on July 6, 1995, when former bodybuilder James Batsel pleaded guilty to the Feb. 10, 1993, murder of the owner of an Atlanta all-nude club. Batsel shot his victim nine times during a botched robbery attempt. The bodybuilder had been taking 3,200 milligrams of steroids a week—he was a buff 298 pounds, with 2% body fat—and he blamed his rage on steroids.

In light of all that had happened in recent years, few people in bodybuilding were taken aback when word came from St. Kitts that Fox had been arrested on charges of murdering his ex-fiancée and her mother. Certainly the string of killings didn't startle the academics who have studied bodybuilding.

"On one level I'm not surprised," says Alan Klein, a sociology professor at Northeastern and the author of *Little Big Men*, the definitive work on the bodybuilding subculture. "But if these murders had happened among baseball players, I'd be speechless." Indeed, no sport in America creates a world more fertilized for deadly violence than bodybuilding. The irony is that its passive contests—in which performers do nothing more violent than strut and grunt and grimace and flex upon the stage—make synchronized swimming look as perilous as bullfighting.

"It is very interesting that the vast majority of these violent episodes have been with bodybuilders," says Chuck Yesalis, a professor of health and human development at Penn State and an expert on steroid abuse. "You almost never see these types of extreme behavior in other athletes. Yes, football players get into fights, but they don't kill people. But is it the drugs? Or is it the bizarre subculture in which these people are immersed? When you talk to them, they generally talk about their diets, drugs and lifting routines. And they hang around people who talk about their diets, drugs and lifting routines.

"When I heard that bodybuilding was being considered for an Olympic event, I was astounded. I wondered what the IOC was thinking. This is the only sport I know of where nearly everyone contends that, at the elite level, participation in the sport and illicit drug use are absolutely intertwined."

The performers at the highest levels are walking pharmacies, willing guinea pigs who ingest anything that promises to make them large. They are artisans commissioned by their own fragile egos to sculpt fortresses to protect them. Instead of working in marble, as Michelangelo did in chiseling his David, they use far more perishable stuff, engorging and shaping their sinew with pills and fluids, including dangerous growth hormones that enlarge everything from heart to bone to muscle; equally dangerous diuretics, which strip the body of water and help define the shape of muscles; insulin, which metabolizes carbohydrates into glucose, which in turn builds muscle mass; and a cornucopia of other drugs to ease the way: thyroid stimulants, amphetamines, appetite suppressants, painkillers, cocaine, marijuana, tranquilizers, sleeping pills, and antidepressants. Underlying all of this, of course, are the monstrous ingestions of anabolic steroids and testosterone to promote muscle growth.

Fueled by these substances that permit them to exercise more vigorously and recover more quickly, bodybuilders pump iron to make their visions of themselves come true. Through countless reps, they work on each muscle group. In the argot of bodybuilding, bulging arms are guns; lats spread into wings; legs become wheels. Bodybuilders want each muscle, distinct and defined, to impress the eye in its size and detail, and they exult in the onionskin look of dry hardness and in those infinitesimally striated fibers. This is called looking ripped and shredded and cut. As one builder, Samir Bannout, a former Mr. Olympia, liked to crow, "I was so cut, you could see my kidneys pumping."

"They want to take up as much space in the universe as possible," says Klein, who spent seven years in California gyms researching his book. "That's their reason for existing. The more space they can take up, the more worthy they feel they are."

The price they pay for this chemical sculpting is high. Not only are the drugs expensive—some bodybuilders spend as much as $5,000 a month on them—but the physical and psychic costs can be incalculable. No one knows the long-term effects of making all those weird molecules cavort together in the body, but there's no doubt that steroids alone, taken in such gargantuan doses, can turn some psyches into razors. "You take a couple of tabs of Anadrol and tell me you don't feel aggressive," says former serious bodybuilder John Romano, who writes a column called "Rage" for *Muscular Development* magazine. "If you thought you couldn't bench-press 405 pounds last week, you know you can press it this week. These murders don't surprise me at all. When I was using 1,000 milligrams a week, I dragged a guy out the window of his car for cutting me off in traffic, and I'm usually a calm man."

Many bodybuilders have experienced what Harrison Pope, an associate professor of psychiatry at Harvard Medical School and a student of anabolics, calls the "manic syndrome" that can attend steroid abuse. The symptoms, according to Pope, include "euphoria, expansiveness, grandiose feelings, decreased need for sleep, irritability, racing thoughts, pressured speech, reckless behavior and aggressiveness."

Joe Bucci, a former Mr. World, has felt the side effects of steroid and hormone abuse. "Testosterone gives you a more animalistic approach to training, and you start to take it out on people who get in your way," he says. "You're not looking to be violent, but if you already have that violent nature in you, testosterone will enhance it. Where normally you'd ask yourself, 'Should I smack this guy or shouldn't I?' now you just smack him because he's in your way."

Bucci recalls the day eight years ago when he was working with 485 pounds in weights and he saw a man dressed in "a little pink outfit" standing before him, watching him intently. "The pink was making me feel not strong," says Bucci. "It was somehow neutralizing my desire to lift the weight. So I politely asked him, 'Will you please move out of the way? I need to lift this heavy weight, and I wouldn't want it to fall on you.' He said, 'I'll stand anywhere I like.' So I do a set, and he still doesn't move. A friend of mine goes to him and tells him, 'You better move, because he's serious.' The guy still wouldn't move. In the middle of my set, in a 'roid rage, I jumped up and punched him in the jaw. Blood was all over the gym. The gym owner, being a fanatic bodybuilder, kicked the guy out and let me stay. So it's a sick sport, what can I tell ya?"

None of this, of course, is meant to suggest that all hard-core bodybuilders murder people. "What we are talking about here is the lunatic fringe," says Klein. But the violence has been prevalent enough at the sport's highest levels to raise questions about its causes. Domestic violence among bodybuilders is unusually widespread; the murders of Ramsey and McNeil represent merely the extremes of it. In a 1996 interview in *Flex* magazine, 1984 World Amateur Champion Mike Christian admitted to having physically abused his longtime girlfriend and blamed it on steroids. He said that anabolics affected 80% of his fellow muscleheads psychologically. "Ask their old ladies," Christian said. "They're the unsung heroes of this sport. Nobody really knows what they go through."

But abuse of steroids and testosterone alone doesn't explain the murders and the high levels of tension and aggression that suffuse serious bodybuilding. "A fundamental streak of antisociability also marks many of the bodybuilders," says Klein. "They lack a developed way of handling competitive failures." Their massive physiques may "broadcast invulnerability and confidence," Klein continues, but they "leave the internal psychological structure weak. Rather than admit to vulnerability, big men can almost believe in their images and hence avoid dealing with issues of insecurity, hurt and the like."

Since the early 1950s, studies focusing on why bodybuilding appeals to some people have revealed central themes. According to Klein, the majority of bodybuilders got into the sport as a reaction to feelings of weakness and inadequacy rooted in childhood. They might have had dyslexia or bad acne, or maybe they stuttered. Many were short or skinny. They had sand kicked in their faces at the beach. They emerged from adolescence feeling inferior and often came to adulthood as loners unable to socialize and make lasting friends. "Bodybuilding has a neurotic core," Klein says. "In all the cases I observed, there was some phenomenon, some perceived shortcoming—like shortness—that created this downward spiral of self-esteem."

In the gym and through the chemicals, bodybuilders can bury all those feelings of inadequacy under muscle, mounds upon bulging mounds of it. Every human being compensates for his weaknesses, but the building of hypermuscles is compensation in the extreme, and it provides a particularly weak cover. The old inadequacies still lurk close to the surface. Bodybuilders are easily deflated and angered by suggestions that they look "small" or "smooth." (In the weeks leading up to his death, Flanagan had taunted Frederick by saying he was "ugly" and "washed up.") Many builders suffer from what Pope calls muscle dysmorphia, a condition akin to anorexia nervosa. Looking in a mirror, an anorectic sees "large and fat." A dysmorphic bodybuilder sees "small and skinny." Thus telling a builder he looks small is as unsettling to him as telling an anorectic she looks fat is to her.

So builders try, through vial and error, to take up more and more space. "No matter how big they get, they're not big enough," says Klein. "Why? Because of the emaciated character of their egos."

This contradiction complicates a subculture already fraught with inordinate pressures and frustrations. There's little money to be made in bodybuilding, even at the top (first prize in the Mr. Olympia contest is $110,000) and some bodybuilders earn cash to live on and to buy their drugs by working as male prostitutes. For long periods they subject themselves to diets of agonizing deprivation: low-calorie, fat-free and sugarless. The drug use, meanwhile, has been out of control for more than 10 years—in the late 1980s, Christian said in the *Flex* interview, bodybuilders began growing bigger and more ripped—and today, according to one veteran, "it's chemical warfare out there." The war can be fatal. In '92, immediately following the Dutch Grand Prix bodybuilding event, competitor Mohammed Benaziza of France died of renal failure after overdosing on diuretics. Others have collapsed from dehydration.

Benaziza's death is one reason that competitors are tested for diuretics at a few pro events, including the Mr. Olympia contest and the Night of the Champions. Some entrants, however, have found an undetectable substitute for diuretics: an injectable starch that acts as a magnet for excess fluids and helps the body expel them. The International Federation of Body-Builders, the professional sport's governing body, does not test competitors for any substance other than diuretics, on grounds that random testing for steroids and other muscle-building drugs would be expensive and impractical.

"If you just do drug testing at the contest, it does not solve the steroid problem," says IFBB vice president Wayne DeMilia. "You'd need to test the athletes several times going into the contest, but, considering that our events include participants from all over the world, it's almost impossible to get official testers out to each athlete or get each athlete to specific testing sites." Perhaps so, but the IFBB and other event promoters can't be blind to the fact that steroids are essential to the kind of muscle development on display at pro competitions and that random in-contest testing would disqualify at least some of the participants.

The dangers of diuretics and steroids notwithstanding, this is the only world that bodybuilders care to know, and it involves them in an endless struggle for self-mastery and control. The gym is a monastery in which they live like giant monks. They have no control over the world outside the gym. They have no control over the men who judge the cut of their anatomical suits. But they have at least a sense of control over their drugs, their diets, their training regimens—and their mates. Bodybuilders, given their often troubled histories, have more than their share of problems with rejection.

"On the one hand they are masters of their destiny," says Klein. "They buy into their own mythology. Their bodies and their power and their being in control. It's false. They can't accept rejection. Their response often is rage. Women are particularly vulnerable to that rage. Bodybuilders buy into this hypermasculine lifestyle, and here they are with 23-inch biceps and they can't control a little woman? Deep inside they know they don't have the power. That's what makes it so devastating. Factor in the steroids and other drugs and the dieting and the competition, and you've got a tinderbox."

So Kimbrough, thrown over for another man, stabbed Ramsey. Riccardi shot Navarro after she rejected him. Killer Sally, as much the breadwinner in her household as her husband, killed him after his ill-timed return home on Valentine's Day. Then came Fox, who fit the bodybuilding profile perfectly. Born in St. Kitts, Fox moved to England with his family when he was five, and there he suffered what an old friend, Rick Wayne, calls "the belittling taunts of schoolmates who enjoyed nothing more than making his life miserable, who had targeted him for their worst practical jokes and bullied him mercilessly." Fox, who would grow no taller than 5' 7", found his refuge in the gym. There, says Wayne, "bodybuilding had turned Bertil into a man's man even before he'd turned 17."

Fox competed all over the world. In 1980 he won the Mr. Universe title, one of bodybuilding's highest honors, and during the next few years he was at the apex of his sport. "Bertil was probably the best bodybuilder on the planet," says Peter McGough, the editor-in-chief of *Flex*, "but he couldn't, or didn't care to, get his act together on contest day. He would sometimes self-destruct as the contest drew near." In '88 Fox flew from London to Chicago to compete in a pro invitational. Upon arriving at his hotel, he was informed that his room wasn't ready. "He turned on his heels, went back to the airport and caught the next flight back to London," says McGough. "No other champion bodybuilder has ever done such a thing. When he self-destructed it was always somebody else's fault; he was the victim."

He kept to himself. "Fox was a loner even among loners," McGough says. Tross, his best friend since 1991, describes him as having "an adult body but . . . the mind of a 13-year-old. A very simple mind. He has very low self-esteem." He also had a history of violent behavior toward women. Several friends of Fox's and relatives of Leyoca's told *Sports Illustrated* that Fox had abused his late lover.

Bertil and Leyoca had been going together for two years when she broke off the relationship last summer. In late August, the *Observer* of St. Kitts-

Nevis reported, Bertil had finished doing a cycle of injectable steroids when he took off for England, leaving Leyoca with the keys to his house. He reportedly called her twice from London, trying to win her back, but by the time he returned to St. Kitts, on Friday, Sept. 26, she had taken up with another man. Fox testified at his trial that he had discovered upon his return that his gun and bullets and the pouch in which he carried them were missing from his house. He said that on Monday, Sept. 29, he went to the dress shop to retrieve the items. (Contradicting that testimony, Tross later told *Sports Illustrated* that he saw Fox wearing the gun pouch on his waist on Saturday, Sunday, and Monday.)

Fox testified that when he arrived at the shop, Leyoca greeted him, led him inside and told him she had given the gun to Violet "for safekeeping." Fox said that Violet approached him with the pouch in one hand and the gun in the other, held them above her head and said, teasingly, "These what you want? These what you want?" As Violet approached him, Fox said, she pushed him with the hand carrying the gun, and he grabbed it. In the struggle, he said, the gun went off and Leyoca was shot. (Curiously, she was found lying outside on the veranda, shot in the back.) As he continued to struggle with Violet, Fox said, the gun went off a second time, and she fell. He then fled in his car to Tross's office, he says, where he told Tross, "Leyoca and her mother just got shot." Tross, sitting behind Fox while he was testifying, shook his head at that. Tross had testified that Fox had said to him, "I just shot Leyoca and Violet." A witness who heard the conversation, Leon Issac, Tross's assistant, corroborated Tross's version.

Amanda Matthews, a seamstress who was working in a room adjoining the dress shop's reception room, testified that Leyoca went out to the veranda to greet Bertil, and he followed her back in. They were arguing, and Violet stepped between them. Bertil pushed Violet back into Leyoca. Matthews said she heard Violet exclaim three times, "Don't come in here with that!" Matthews then heard a scream and a gunshot. She ran into the bathroom and then heard two more shots. When she came out a few minutes later, Violet was sprawled on the shop floor and Leyoca was lying outside the front door.

Tross says Fox had told him the previous Saturday that he had found in his house a wire-transfer slip for $1,500, made out to Leyoca, from a man named Jason. Fox also said that Leyoca and Violet had laughed at him in the shop, and Violet had said he was "too old" for her 20-year-old daughter. (The wire transfer was not allowed in evidence in Fox's trial.)

Based on trial testimony other than Fox's and on interviews with Tross, the most plausible account of events that day is this: A spurned and jealous

Fox discovered the wire transfer and confronted Leyoca with it in the dress shop. When Violet stepped between them, he pushed her back, drew his gun and shot her twice, once in the head. As Leyoca fled out the door, Fox shot her in the back. The prosecutor, Francis Bell, called it a crime of "jealousy and rage," but he failed to present evidence that it was either. He didn't elicit key testimony from Tross—for instance, that Tross had seen Fox with the gun pouch in the days leading up to the shootings.

Leyoca and Violet are buried in a single grave in Springfield Cemetery, on a hilltop with a view of Basseterre's blue harbor and of gleaming white cruise ships resting at anchor. It's a bright midafternoon in March, and Denise Williams, Violet's sister and Leyoca's aunt, is standing at the grave, with its dusty plastic flowers of red, purple and yellow. "Nobody in the family wants to come here," she says. "We are just trying to forget the day of the shootings. It was just terrible. Awful, awful, awful "

Down below the cemetery, on Cayon Street, behind the thick prison door with its sliding peephole, Bertil Fox is still alive but missing his life, the barbells and the dumbbells that anchored him in the only safe harbor he has ever known. "I miss bodybuilding," he says. "I miss training. I miss the weights. I miss pumping iron. I miss that world. I miss being big! I miss the stage."

They'll all have to wait. The only stage he faces now is the four-by-four-foot courtroom box known as the dock.

May 1998

In May of 1998, Bertil Fox, the poster boy for this story, was sentenced to death by hanging on the prison gallows after a nine-man jury in St. Kitts found him guilty of two counts of murder in the shooting deaths of Leyoca and Violet Browne. The prosecution had established jealousy as the motive, accusing him of going after his fiancée after learning she was involved with another man. The Privy Council later quashed Fox's sentence, and today he awaits re-sentencing by the St. Kitts High Court. He could still be sentenced to death.

FULL-COURT PRESSURE

The Kentucky Wildcats' relentless attack reflects the ferocious drive of their coach, Rick Pitino, who left the NBA to rescue the Roman Empire of college basketball

Joanne Pitino knew the time was upon her again. She had sensed it coming through those tinted evenings in Manhattan when the limo would fetch her and her husband, Rick, outside Madison Square Garden, and the crowds would cheer from the sidewalk as the couple climbed inside and began the long drive home to Bedford, New York, 35 miles north of the city. She felt it even after Rick had turned the New York Knicks around and had them trapping and pressing and running opponents out of the Garden. She saw it in the sleepless, raccoon hollows of Rick's eyes, in the long silences of those rides back home in the gloom.

It was the spring of 1989, and Rick Pitino, after two years as coach of the Knicks, was trapped once again in his own frantic press and was casing his office for exits. He had grown up in Queens, and coaching the Knicks had always been the job of his dreams, but he had been consumed by a front-office power struggle that had left him feeling isolated and exposed, and he had started to regret that he had ever come back to New York. Forget that he had taken just two years to disinter the cadaver in the Garden, reviving a Knicks team that had gone 24–58 the year before he had gotten there and now was racing through a 52–30 season on its way to the playoffs; forget that Knicks home games lifted off like rock concerts, rattling the girders in the arena.

"He would sit in the limo all the way home and would not talk," Joanne says. "The Garden was hopping, and he was winning all those games at home, and it should have been a happy time, but it wasn't. He was so sad. He really felt unwanted."

She sensed that he was gone already, and all that remained for her to do was to dread where he would be taking her next. By late April, as the Knicks were getting ready to face Charles Barkley and the Philadelphia 76ers in the playoffs, the new athletic director at Kentucky, C.M. Newton, had heard from mutual friends that Pitino might consider the coaching job in Lexington. The Wildcats basketball program, long suspected of corruption, had pushed the envelope so hard that, well, the envelope had popped open and $1,000 in cash—intended for the father of a Kentucky recruit— had spilled out. That was in March 1988, and in the scandal that ensued Kentucky basketball lay suddenly in ruins, facing NCAA probation. In April '89 Newton was hired to raise it from the ashes. Pitino had rescued every team he'd ever coached, from Boston University to Providence College to the Knicks, and none needed more rescuing than Kentucky. So Newton headed for Bedford, and Pitino turned to his wife.

Joanne has a New York sense of humor reminiscent of comedienne Joan Rivers's, but she saw nothing amusing in Newton's visit. She had been raised in suburban Long Island, and there was no way she was heading off for the wilds of Kentucky, like some settler in a Conestoga wagon, just so her shaman-husband could rattle his gourds among the true believers while most of her family remained back East.

Rick regaled her with tales of the long and storied tradition of Kentucky basketball. "I'm not going," Joanne said. "I don't even know where Kentucky is."

He told her tales of the white fences and the beauty of the bluegrass. "I'm not going," she said.

He added tales of the citadel of hoops built by the Baron himself, Adolph Rupp. "Don't you realize," Rick pleaded, "that this is the Roman Empire of college basketball?"

"So? Go yourself," she replied. She had been through all this before. Only two years earlier she had sat in her white Mercury Sable outside Alumni Hall at Providence and waited grimly as Pitino conferred with college officials about whether he should take an offer to coach the Knicks. He had just crowned one of the most surpassing coaching feats in college basketball by taking the Friars to the 1987 Final Four. The team had gone 11–20 in 1984–85, the year before Pitino arrived, and did not have a single dominant player. After that Final Four the Knicks had approached Pitino but had not made a formal offer. At one point, tired of waiting, Pitino had set a May 1 deadline for the offer, but it passed without a word from New York. So, on June 4, he signed a five-year contract with Providence.

He was 34, and in a city peopled largely by Italian-Americans, he had risen to the status of folk hero—the celebrated *paesano* who had turned basketball around at Providence, the closest thing Rhode Island has to a big-time franchise. He nearly owned the town. Joanne had been elated when he signed on again. After years of moving she saw Providence as their permanent home. They had built their first house there. "This was our Camelot," she says. They had filled the house with family and furniture and friends. Their six-month-old son, Daniel, born with a heart defect, had died in his crib in early March, four days before the Friars began their magical run to the Final Four, and he was buried in Providence.

The loss of the boy had driven Joanne to inconsolable grief, and it had bound her even closer to this place where she and Rick had settled with their three other children. Rick had told everyone, "This is my dream job. I'm gonna be here forever." And then the Garden called again.

It was early July '87, six weeks after he re-signed with Providence, and Joanne was sitting in the Sable with John Marinatto, the Friars' sports information director, as Rick met with Father John Cunningham, the university president. Joanne was so agitated that she distractedly pulled a safety razor from her purse and began to shave her legs.

"I can't believe he's doing this to me again," she said. "We just got here! How can he ask me to pick up and leave again? I've been through this too many times. I can't believe, after all I've been through this year, that he is asking me to do it again."

Two days later, as she and her husband headed south in a limo toward Manhattan, he tried to tell her that this was the best move for her, with her family in New York and all, but she was not buying it. "You're justifying it for yourself," she said. The last time she had been at Madison Square Garden was the first day she had ever spent away from Daniel. Rick had taken her there for the Big East tournament, and while they were gone, the boy had died. Now she was back for a press conference to announce that her husband was coming to New York. She had the final word on that, though. Stepping from the limo, she saw the Garden and threw up on the sidewalk.

And now here it was, two years later, and the dream job in New York had soured, and now another dream job, the whole Roman Empire, was beckoning. The night before Newton showed up at their Bedford estate, Rick promised Joanne, "He will paint a picture of Kentucky second to none!" Instead, Newton's pitch suggested the last days of Pompeii. Newton talked about the mess Kentucky was in—how the scandal and impending probation had scared off the best players and how the 1989–90 schedule was stacked with Louisville, Indiana, North Carolina and Kansas. "You're not going to win but three or four games," Newton said. "We have major problems."

The Pitinos were silent. Newton looked at Rick and said, "And we can't figure out why the head coach of the New York Knicks, on the threshold of winning a championship, would ever want to come into this mess." At which point Joanne glanced up and whispered, "Thank you, God!"

She rose and asked to see Rick alone. They walked to the front door. "Some Roman Empire!" she hissed. "Are you crazy? Are you *crazy?*"

She would ultimately give in, of course, just as she always had, surrendering to the forces that drive her husband, because of her love and respect for him. "I have accepted his ambition and his drive," she says. "I used to fight it, but I can't win, because it is a part of him."

That was more than six years ago, and today Rick is winding up his seventh season in Kentucky, in which he finds himself with the best college players he has ever had. "I don't know if this will be the best *team* I've ever had," he had said before the season, "but these are the best players."

They have proved to be an awe-inspiring collection. At week's end Kentucky had a 22–1 record and was ranked second in the AP poll. The Wildcats hadn't lost a game since Massachusetts beat them back on Nov. 28. And they have not just beaten opponents, they have humiliated them, winning by an average margin of 23.0 points, tops in the nation. "They annihilated us," said LSU coach Dale Brown, whose Tigers were beaten by the Wildcats 129–97 on Jan. 20.

"I told our guys we could play a perfect game and still not beat Kentucky," said Mississippi State coach Richard Williams, whose Bulldogs were far from perfect (with 28 turnovers) in a 74–56 loss to the Wildcats in Starkville on Jan. 9.

The testimonials have been pouring in all season. Pitino may already be the most celebrated college coach in the country who has never won a national championship, but this is the year the Kentucky faithful have been waiting for.

What the man pulled off in his first few seasons in the commonwealth is as much a part of Kentucky basketball lore as anything the Baron did in all his 42 years. By the second game of Pitino's first season, in which the Wildcats nearly beat 14th-ranked Indiana, dropping a 71–69 heartbreaker, the coach had turned a gang of role players, pine jockeys and walk-ons into the woolliest, grandest, damnedest basketball show that anyone had seen in

Kentucky in years. Through cajolery and flattery, praise and scorn, he had gotten his players to chase the ball like a hockey puck into all four corners, to run and to press just as his teams had done in Boston and Providence and New York. It was as though, in the darkest of days, a magic circus had come to town, and the enchantment culminated on the night of Feb. 15, 1990, when the Cats beat Shaquille O'Neal and ninth-ranked LSU 100–95, in a game that ended with a thunderous tribute from the fans in Rupp Arena.

"That first year the games ended with people just sitting there with tears running down their faces," says Anita Madden, Lexington's premier hostess and a longtime Cats watcher. "People were as proud of that team as of any that ever played for Kentucky. The coach and those boys were trying so hard that it was just touching to watch them." They ended up 14–14. A year later, with freshman Jamal Mashburn as an added starter, the Wildcats went 22–6; a year after that they were 29–7, and if Christian Laettner had missed that miraculous basket at the buzzer in the East Regional final, the shot that earned Duke a 104–103 overtime win and a trip to the Final Four, those Cats might have won Kentucky's first NCAA title since 1978 and ended up, like Secretariat, cast in bronze in a Lexington park. Instead, four of the no-name starters on Pitino's original team—Sean Woods, Deron Feldhaus, Richie Farmer and John Pelphrey—watched in wonder a week later as their jerseys rose to Rupp's rafters in retirement.

"It was unimaginable," says Pelphrey, who went from all-average to All-SEC in two years. "We won 65 games in three years! The NCAA put us on probation to make us suffer, but we never really did."

What Pitino brought to Lexington was the same unbounded passion to succeed that had always governed his life—that and an unearthly appetite for work that transformed him, as each season wore on, into a walking wraith. But even then he could take his own energy and instill it in his players till they ran at a pace that turned every game into Armageddon. And he still had that magical ability to get players to believe in themselves—in who they were and what they were doing and where they wanted to go. Where did his drive come from? And where did it all begin?

Pitino was born in Manhattan on Sept. 18, 1952, and his family moved to a house on Springfield Boulevard in Cambria Heights, Queens, when he was six. Rick was the third son of Rosario (Sal) Pitino, a building superintendent whose Sicilian-born parents owned a fruit stand in New York, and Charlotte Newman, an administrator at Bellevue Hospital. Rick's two brothers were so much older than he—Bob by 10 years, Ron by eight—that he hardly knew them. He was just a blur around their feet. "Always going 100 miles an hour," recalls Bob, a retired Long Island cop who lives in Florida.

Sal and Charlotte both commuted to work in Manhattan, leaving home early and returning late to avoid the traffic, and Rick vividly remembers his solitude as an eight-year-old. He was alone as he ate breakfast in the morning, alone as he walked to grade school in the winter, alone and frightened as he walked home in the dark to that empty house. "I had kind of a strange childhood," he says. "I got a lot of love from my family, but I was lonely. I remember being lonely. From age six on, I was coming home in the dark, and I had a little fear of the darkness, and I'd always be looking around, and I'd be by myself entering a dark house. It was scary for a kid."

He still recalls those Friday nights in the summers of his youth, just after he discovered sports, when he would lie awake in the dark in his second-floor room and listen to the rain on the roof. It thrummed out a message he could hardly bear to hear: that his Saturday-morning CYO baseball game would probably be called off, and there would be no gathering of friends and no crowds—none of the companionship for which he so keenly yearned. Of course, there was only one thing to do about that. He would go out and save the day.

So, on those rainy Saturday mornings he would rise and dress at six o'clock, while his parents were still asleep. He would scoop up an armful of his mother's towels and head out the door, grabbing a garden rake on the way. He would hike alone the seven blocks up 121st Avenue to the baseball diamonds at Colin Field. And there, in a scene right out of a Rockwell painting, the boy would race to beat the league officials who would come to check the grounds. He would swab and dry the bases with the towels. He would rake the water from the batter's box and the base paths. And finally, towels in hand, he would stoop over and sop up the last gray puddles that lay between him and his friends. Charlotte would wonder where all her linens disappeared. "I was always buying towels," she recalls. It wasn't until years later that she learned that Rick had been ditching them in the trash; bringing them home would have given away his early morning flights to Colin Field.

Many years later in Kentucky, after Joanne gave birth to their fifth son, Ryan, in June 1990, Rick pleaded with her to have a sixth child. All her pregnancies had been difficult, and she dreaded going through another. Daniel had died three years earlier, and his death had left almost eight years between Ryan and Richard, the next oldest boy, and Rick shivered at the thought of Ryan growing up alone. "He'll always have us," Joanne protested.

"You don't understand," Rick said. "You just do not understand." She yielded again, of course, and two years later they had Jaclyn, their only daughter.

As a boy, Rick had found in basketball his anodyne, his escape from loneliness, and he had spent hours on the courts of Queens, losing himself in the game. "I dreamt day and night about sports, almost in a fantasy league of my own," he says. By 1966 his family had moved out to Bayville, on Long Island's north shore, and Rick was a 14-year-old gym mouse for whom the game had evolved into an obsession. "A coach's dream," says Patrick McGunnigle, Rick's coach at St. Dominic's High School. "A 12–7–10 kid: 12 months a year, seven days a week, 10 hours a day."

Rick dreamed of playing pro ball and wanted desperately to win a basketball scholarship. He wouldn't be able to go to college any other way, so he dedicated himself to the game. By the time he was 16, when he started dating Joanne Minardi, the boy in him had all but vanished. "I always thought of him as a manchild," says Joanne. "It was like he was never a child. He was *sooo* responsible." She used to beg him to take her to Jones Beach, her favorite place, but he set the terms of the courtship.

So she often ended up watching him play pickup games on a playground or retrieving his free throws in the deserted gym at C.W. Post College. He promised her they would go to the beach if he hit 100 free throws in a row, telling her, "If I miss, we have to start all over again." They never made it to the beach. Second prize was the Carvel ice-cream stand. "Every day I would get my butterscotch sundae and Rick his double banana barge," she says. "Our whole courtship was not a courtship."

His whole life, by then, was a romance with basketball, his way to seize the future. He was not a naturally gifted athlete—only six feet tall and a tad slow—but in high school he made himself into a good player, wringing every scintilla of ability from his scrawny frame. "He was a one-on-one scoring machine with 176 moves," says Howard Garfinkel, Rick's coaching guru at the Five Star basketball camp in the Catskills. "He had a *game*." By his senior year he was known as Rifle Rick and was on the first team of the Long Island Catholic High School All-Stars. He averaged 28 points and 10 assists a game for St. Dominic's. "A phenomenal passer and ball handler," McGunnigle says. "He was responsible for 50 points a game."

UMass assistant coach Ray Wilson came to a St. Dominic's game to scout another player and saw Pitino on a night when he was on. "He was shooting the lights out yet moving the ball around," Wilson says. "He'd come down that center lane, and you could see he was watching the whole court. He was like a little coach out there."

So the man-child reached his goal and got a full ride at UMass. Before it ended, however, the ride would become one of the most painful experiences of Pitino's basketball life. Going into his sophomore year, the first year of varsity eligibility in those days, Pitino was chesty and full of himself, boasting that he would take the starting job at point guard from the team's captain, senior Mike Pagliara. "He was very vocal about that," recalls the other senior guard, John Betancourt. When head coach Jack Leaman chose to go with Pagliara, Pitino resented it, and the rivalry between the two players heated up through the fall and winter—until, at a practice in January, they got into a scrap in which Pagliara broke a finger. According to the next day's *Springfield Union*, Leaman announced that Pagliara had been injured and Pitino had been "dropped from the squad for the season."

Pitino thought about transferring, but Wilson talked him out of it and admonished him: "You need to grow up." When Pitino came back his junior year, he apologized to Leaman, who told him, "O.K., but you're the last man on the team. You've got to earn your way back." Amherst became Pitino's gulag for the next two months. Given his history, he could have suffered no worse a fate than to be treated as though he did not exist, and that is what he suffered under Leaman. Pitino was always last in line—to eat, to board the bus, to run the mile—and he was ignored by the coach.

"He didn't speak to me," Pitino recalls. "I felt like crying a hundred times." Behind Pitino, Wilson kept whispering, "He's testing you. Hang in there."

Pitino earned his way back into the starting lineup the week before the season's first game, and he felt euphoric after all he had endured. "My self-esteem was so high," he says. But 20 minutes before the game Leaman stuck it to Pitino one last time, announcing to the team, "I've decided to make a change. I'm not going to start Pitino." A wave of nausea came over Pitino, and he nearly got sick right there. Leaman had lifted him up so he could drop him again. On that night, Pitino says with a lingering touch of emotion, "I hated the son of a bitch." Just 45 seconds into the game, Leaman looked over at Pitino and said, "Slug, get in there."

Heading toward the scorer's table, Pitino passed Wilson, who winked and said, "It's over, kid."

Pitino's two years as a starter in Amherst had a reverberating impact on him as a player and as a coach. Leaman's disciplined, patterned style of play was as old-fashioned as a peach basket, and it required Pitino to turn his game inside out. For the point guard, shooting was verboten. His sole job was to run the offense—to set the tempo of the attack and distribute the ball. "It incorporated me into the world of 'we' and 'team,'" says Pitino. "And 'I' and 'my' kind of left. I became the ultimate team player."

He had practiced shooting all his life, and for two long years he was forced to check his jumper at the door. No wonder that, as if in rebellion, he has instilled a run-'em-ragged, aim-and-drain style in every team he has coached: a system of organized chaos in which players move in swarms, like bees, and everyone, from the tallest to the smallest, shoots the ball—even (and especially) the three-pointer.

Pitino became a bold innovator. When the three-point shot was introduced in 1986, he was the first college coach to exploit its potential, the first to understand the game's new math: Shooting 40% from outside the arc produces more points than shooting 59% from inside it. And he turned upside down the fundamental notion that teams must "work the ball" close to the basket on offense and drop back on defense. His teams held *back* on offense to fire from afar and swarmed *forward* on defense.

His experience at UMass ultimately taught Pitino lessons in button-pushing that he would draw upon time and again to motivate players. Bill Reynolds, a sports columnist at the *Providence Journal-Bulletin* and a biographer of Pitino, says Pitino manipulated players all the time at Providence. "They'd play on Tuesday night," says Reynolds, "and on Wednesday he would kill them: 'You're horrible. . . . You suck. . . . You're the worst.' By Friday, when they were ready to play again, Rick would say, 'You're the greatest. . . . You're the best shooter . . . the best rebounder.' They believed it."

And Pitino had the seductive spiel of a Chautauqua orator. When he arrived in Providence in 1985, he gave a speech at a booster luncheon that had the audience in a trance. "Forget about your bills!" Pitino declared. "Buy those season tickets now. When you go to sleep tonight, I want you to dream about cutting down those nets!"

Reynolds sat transfixed. "I thought, Who could possibly believe this nonsense?" he says. "Does *he* believe it? He was like a tent revivalist. Brother Ricky's Traveling Salvation Show." Two years later there was Reynolds in Freedom Hall in Louisville just moments after Providence beat Georgetown in the Southeast Regional final. "They were cutting down the nets," he recalls. "It was unbelievable."

Wherever Pitino went, he could not get there fast enough. He wanted to be a head coach by the time was 25, and he nearly self-destructed trying to get there. In 1976, after he had been an assistant at Hawaii for two years, the school came under investigation by the NCAA, which later nailed the Rainbows' basketball program for 68 rules violations, citing Pitino by name in eight of them. Among other things, according to the NCAA, Pitino had arranged a deal in which a Honolulu Ford dealer would receive two season tickets in return for giving cars to two players. Pitino was also accused of providing three players with airline tickets between New York and Honolulu. Pitino denies these charges. "I had absolutely nothing to do with any of that," he says.

Hawaii coach Bruce O'Neil lost his job in the scandal, and he asserts that Pitino betrayed him by going to the university president, Fujio Matsuda, and angling for the head coaching job while the investigation was still going on. "He said he wanted to be a head coach at age 25," says O'Neil. "Maybe he had to do whatever it would take to further his career, but what he chose to do, I thought at the time, was at my expense. I thought I deserved some loyalty." O'Neil worked out a deal with the university under which he resigned as head coach and became an assistant athletic director—on one condition: "Rick didn't get the job," O'Neil says.

Says Matsuda, "I remember that Rick brought with him a couple of graduate assistants from the team. They said they were not involved in any [misdeeds]. They said it was others who were responsible. After that discussion Rick expressed his interest in the job. I thought it was odd. It seemed to me at that time that Rick Pitino was a very ambitious, aggressive young man."

So Pitino bid aloha to the ruins of Rainbows basketball and winged back to New York—if not triumphant, at least relatively unscathed. He and Joanne were married shortly thereafter, on April 3, 1976, but even the honeymoon had to wait on his ambition.

No sooner had they arrived at their Manhattan hotel room on their wedding night than the phone rang. It was Jim Boeheim, the new Syracuse coach, offering Rick an interview for an assistant coaching job. Right then. "I'm downstairs in the lobby," Boeheim said. "Can you come down now?" Halfway out the door, Rick told his bride, "I'll be right back." He called every 20 minutes from the lobby. "Just a few more minutes," he would say. Three hours later she was watching television and thinking, Oh, my goodness, this is *awfully* strange. What have I gotten myself into?

He finally returned—after taking the job, of course. But that night was an omen for Joanne. "A rude awakening to what my life was gonna be like," she says. Two years later, at age 26, Rick became head coach at Boston University, missing his target by a year.

He was on his way. And each of his moves up the ladder would be the result of hard work. They laugh about it now, but men who have worked for Pitino make the experience sound like laboring in a cross between a madhouse and a sweatshop.

Pitino has always been highly organized and compulsively neat (his walk-in closet at home, for instance, has more than a hundred shirts, all of them hung facing in the same direction and all arranged by color and designer, e.g., all his blue Calvin Klein shirts with stripes hang together). His subordinates have all found in time that control is very important to Pitino.

When Ralph Willard was Pitino's assistant coach with the Knicks, he was in charge of videotaping the games of upcoming opponents. Willard used a series of VCRs linked to a satellite dish at the Knicks' training complex in Purchase, New York. One morning, he says, he arrived to discover that lightning had struck the dish and shorted the VCRs, leaving no tapes of games from the night before. When Pitino showed up at 9 A.M. to watch the film and Willard told him what had happened, Pitino launched into a tirade.

"How can lightning hit the satellite, Ralph?" he demanded. "It was your responsibility! How can we prepare for this game?" Pitino ordered Willard to rent an apartment near the training complex, because he lived more than an hour away, but Willard refused. Instead, he bought an air mattress, blew it up and slept on it in the video room, among the blinking lights, for two weeks. An alarm clock roused him in the middle of the night so he could make sure the system was working. Pitino ignored Willard before he finally saw the assistant lying on the floor one day and blurted out, "All right, you've made your point!"

"I was so pissed off," says Willard, who is now the coach at Pitt. "He's very difficult to work for." Yet in the next breath, Willard says he loves Pitino and owes him a great deal.

When Stu Jackson—now the president of the Vancouver Grizzlies—was an assistant to Pitino at Providence, his phone would sometimes ring at 2 A.M., and he would hear Pitino's voice rousing him: "We're meeting." Jackson would pull on his sweats and head for Alumni Hall, where he would find the coach and two other assistants waiting to play two-on-two. After an hour of that they would repair to the sauna and literally sweat over a magnetized board on which the coach, pushing little metal figures through droplets of water, diagrammed plays. "It was crazy," Jackson says.

No more so than Pitino's scoring system in those 15-point games. "If we were ahead 14–13," says Jackson, "he would say they were up 12–9. We got in an argument about it. But how can you argue with the boss? I stopped playing with him. He couldn't stand to lose."

Jackson endured harsher trials than that with Pitino. He followed Pitino to the Knicks, and on the eve of the '89 playoff series with the 76ers, Jackson returned to Purchase following a 2 1/2-week road trip that ended with a red-eye from California. He was drained and looking forward to an evening with his wife and one-year-old child. Knicks assistant Jim O'Brien had just taken the coaching job at Dayton, leaving the staff a man short, so Pitino told Jackson that he wanted him in Philly that night to scout the Sixers—a team New York had already played six times and knew as cold as Barkley's shiny pate. Jackson choked up when Pitino told him to go. "Rick, I just can't do it," he said. "I haven't seen my wife. I'm exhausted." He started to cry.

Pitino bristled. "Will you knock off the fucking crying!" he said. "Get your ass down to Philly. This is the goddam playoffs!" As Jackson left, Pitino turned to Willard and said, "Is he *really* that upset?"

Pitino recalls the episode with remorse. "I don't know what made me do it," he says. "Afterward I felt terrible, but I didn't blink."

Jackson is among scores of former assistants and players who have felt the sting of Pitino's wrath and danced like marionettes at the end of his wires, and the remarkable thing is that so many of them feel affection for him and gratitude for his willingness to have shared what he knows. Today, after a year as head coach of the Knicks and two more as top man at Wisconsin, Jackson has reached the top management ranks of the NBA. Working for Pitino required "great sacrifice personally," Jackson says, but then, "I am where I am today because of him. He taught me the trade."

No one has felt the heat of Pitino's ambition more than his wife, a captive from Gotham, living in exile in Kentucky. For years, whenever the Pitinos went out in Lexington, Rick had to plead with Joanne to be more diplomatic with folks who approached their table. Inevitably someone would ask her how she liked Kentucky. "Oh, I don't like it," she would say. He would kick her under the table. "*Oww!*" she would yell. Feigning surprise, he would mutter, "I'm sorry. Did I step on your foot?"

She had nothing against Lexington, Joanne says, but New York was her home, and that was where she wanted to be. Rick had ripped her out of Providence and then out of New York. "I was so furious with him that I wanted to aggravate him," she says. "I was deliberately not nice to people." She is more comfortable in Kentucky now that Rick has bought her a home in New York's Westchester County, which she visits once a month. "It's my New York fix," she says.

Joanne has seen a softening in her husband. It began when Daniel died. Even today, eight years later, Rick gets a catch in his voice when he remembers Joanne cradling the child in the emergency room in Providence. "There's no easy way to handle that," he says. And eight months after Daniel died, Rick's father died of cancer.

But now the family has a sense of place and permanence that it never knew before. Joanne spends most of her time raising the five children, and the simple geometry of Rick's life confines him mostly to the four miles between Memorial Coliseum and his house off Tates Creek Road. He has no idea when his time in Kentucky might end. "Nobody thought I'd be here seven years," he says. "I thought I'd be here five. If I last 10 years and haven't won a championship, I'll be the first to say, 'You've got to make a change.' That's what people here want. If we won that, I might be here forever. But I won't be consumed by that."

He is in a place he has never been as a coach. His team is so rich in talent that at times it resembles a semipro operation in some covert NBA farm system. Of course, part of Pitino's reputation is that he always takes players further than their talent should allow. "As a rescuer, you have no place to go but up," he says. "But now I think we have a legitimate shot at being a dominating team. I've never had that before."

Skeptics suggest that Pitino is merely a rebuilder, the handyman you hire to swing a place around but not the one to finish the job. And so the line on him goes like this: *We know that he can get you out of the wilderness, but can he take you to the promised land?*

He is already there himself. Where else could a man of his drive and needs be happier than in Lexington—where he is fawned over and feted like Caesar in the Roman Empire of college basketball?

But with this position comes constant scrutiny. Pitino's favorite teacher at St. Dominic's High, Sister Clarita Maloney, was recently sitting in the reading room of the Marian Convent in Scranton, Pennsylvania, where she supervises the care of 150 retired nuns. The 73-year-old sister had seen the often frantic and confused Wildcats lose 74–61 to North Carolina last spring in the Southeast Regional final of the NCAAs, and the performance raised a question in her mind.

"Why hasn't Rick won anything?" she asked, leaning forward. "You know what I mean, the NCAAs."

"Do you have an idea?" Sister Clarita was asked.

She nodded. "If what he tells them isn't working," she said, "he should tell them to just play. They're too tense. He should call them all over and say, 'Just have fun. . . . *Just play!*'"

February 1996

Pitino's Kentucky Wildcats won the NCAA championship in 1996, but there was no keeping him where he belonged. The Boston Celtics offered him zillions to run and coach the club, and off he went to Beantown in 1998. For the first time in his life, Pitino simply failed. He never got the Celtics in the hunt. In January of 2001, after losing to the Heat in Miami, Pitino stayed at his home in Florida while the team flew home. With three years and more than $20 million on his contract, Pitino had clearly had enough of the pros. He was gone. He ended up signing on that year as head coach at the University of Louisville, of all places—Kentucky's most despised rival, right down the road—returning as though to haunt the folks he had taken to the title only five years before.

BOBBY FISCHER

While conducting a search that turned into an obsession,
the author discovers a great deal about the chess genius
who drifted into seclusion after winning the world title

A *bout six years ago, sportscaster Dick Schaap was visiting Wilt Chamberlain*
in Wilt's celebrated California mansion when Schaap got the idea of trying
to get in touch with his old friend Bobby Fischer. Schaap had known him since the
1950s, when Fischer was a rising chess star in New York and Schaap was a
young magazine reporter assigned to cover him.

So Schaap called Fischer's closest friend and confidante, Claudia Mokarow of
Pasadena, and asked her to tell Bobby to contact him at Chamberlain's home.

Soon afterward, Bobby rang back.

"Are you really at Wilt's house?" an astonished Bobby asked. Schaap assured
him he was.

"I'd really like to see that house!"

"Would you like to join us for dinner?" Schaap asked.

"I'd like to," Bobby Fischer said, "but I'm not seeing people."

At 7:51 P.M. on the evening of Wednesday, April 3, this year, as I was walking out of the history department of the main branch of the Los Angeles
Public Library, I stopped for a moment by the card-catalog files in the
library's second-floor rotunda. Suddenly, and unexpectedly, I had one of
the most extraordinary experiences of my life.

The library was closing in nine minutes, and for about the last half hour
I had experienced that hollow sensation I had grown to know so well, the
one that always accompanied the awareness of another day lost in Palo
Alto, another afternoon misspent in Pasadena, another evening busted and

shot in Los Angeles. Off and on for almost two years, I had been to all those places and more looking in vain for Robert James (Bobby) Fischer.

To find him, to see him, had become a kind of crazy and delirious obsession, the kind of insanity that has hounded other men in search of, say, the Loch Ness monster. Fischer was the most gifted prodigy in chess, the game's equivalent of Mozart. At age 15, in 1958, he became the youngest player in history to become a grandmaster, and his performance at the Interzonal and Candidates' matches in 1970 and 1971—in which he won an unprecedented 20 straight games against some of the strongest players in the world, without playing a single game to a draw—remains today the most enduring signature of his art and skill. When, in the summer of 1972, he overwhelmed Soviet world champion Boris Spassky in Iceland to win the world title, he merely reaffirmed what most chess masters already believed and still believe today. By a consensus of grandmasters, he had become the strongest chess player in history. "The greatest genius to have descended from the chess heavens," Mikhail Tal of Latvia, the former world champion, once said.

During those two months in Iceland, Fischer attained a folkloric celebrity that attracted millions of Americans to a game they had long associated with the relative obscurity of park benches and coffeehouses. Looking out from the cover of national magazines that wild summer, he was depicted as a gallant cold warrior, a solitary American genius taking on and crushing the Soviet chess juggernaut, with its Moscow computers and its small army of grandmasters arrayed against him.

The 29-year-old Fischer emerged a hero, of course, but he promptly rejected scores of offers, worth millions of dollars, to capitalize on his fame. In fact, though promising to be a fighting champion, he turned back every offer to play chess again. To this day, since Spassky resigned in the 21st and final game on Sept. 1, 1972, Fischer has not played a single game of chess in public. He forfeited his world title in 1975, turning down a multimillion-dollar offer to play challenger Anatoly Karpov in the Philippines when the world chess federation refused to meet all his conditions for the match.

So Bobby Fischer was gone. Ever since he won the championship, Fischer had been drifting quietly into seclusion, finding refuge in Herbert W. Armstrong's Worldwide Church of God in Pasadena, a fundamentalist cult that observes Saturday as the Sabbath and believes in the Second Coming. After several years of serving as what is called a coworker—Fischer hadn't been baptized—he left the church, too, and since then has retreated even further into his own private world. It is one in which journalists are not permitted. Indeed, his closest friends are sworn not to speak about him to the press, under the threat of Bobby banishing them forever from his life.

After Fischer relinquished the title, Karpov was named champion. Karpov still holds the title, but his crown has not been without a singularly painful thorn, for Fischer is still alive, out there somewhere in Southern California. No longer merely a former world chess champion, he has grown to almost mythic size, leaving behind him a trail of rumors and a chess world that is still reaching out for him in the void.

Much the same kind of effect was created in the 1850s when Paul Morphy, a New Orleans chess prodigy then recognized as the world champion, returned in triumph from Europe and soon simply stopped playing. Morphy was regarded as one of the game's true innovators. Fischer revered him. They are the only two Americans ever acclaimed as world chess champions, and there remains that striking parallel in their careers. "Fischer's like Morphy," says international master Igor Ivanov, a Soviet defector. "What's the story with you Americans? You win the title, go home and don't play any more."

Later in his life, after abandoning chess altogether, Morphy suffered from delusions of persecution and withdrew into his own private world. Occasionally he strolled the streets of New Orleans, muttering, in French, "He will plant the banner of Castille upon the walls of Madrid, amidst the cries of the conquered city, and the little king will go away looking very sheepish." He died of apoplexy, at age 47.

But Fischer is still alive, and still very much on many minds. Until recently Robert J. Fisher lived in Pasadena, just about a mile east of where Bobby was arrested in 1981 for allegedly holding up a bank. Fisher installs cable television and spells his name without the "c," but over the years he has received telephone calls from all over the world, often at three in the morning, awakening to hear:

"This is the international operator, Mr. Fisher. You have a telephone call from Yugoslavia." Or the Soviet Union, or Czechoslovakia, or Bulgaria, or Germany.

Almost invariably, the voices speak broken English and cry out, "Boooby! Are you Booby Fischer, the chess player?"

To which Bob Fisher will sing back, "Wrong number! This is Bob Fisher, the cable-television guy."

Fischer is out there, to be sure, but so elusive as to be almost a figment of the imagination. "It's like this god of chess hanging over everybody's head," says American grandmaster Larry Christiansen.

Yasser Seirawan, one of the world's strongest players, speaks for all young U.S. chess masters when he says, "It's a tragedy. Imagine: The greatest chess player who ever lived is living in our time, and he's not even playing. I've never even met him. It's very frustrating."

Grandmaster Lubomir Kavalek, a 41-year-old Czechoslovakian expatriate living in Reston, Virginia, says, "Players Bobby's age, like myself, are a lost generation. We always lived in the shadow of Bobby. We had him as an idol. He was someone to follow. When he stopped playing, I somehow got lost. We lost our inspiration. The last decade belonged to me in the United States. I was always ahead in ratings, but I can't say I was first because, in the back of my mind, there was always Bobby. He was still alive. He is still alive."

That he was out there, still lurking around, was what had drawn me to the second-floor rotunda of the Los Angeles Public Library at 7:51 P.M. on the night of April 3. Desperately looking for a lead earlier that day, I had visited the chambers of Madame Lola, a clairvoyant working in Westminster, California, and sought her help in ferreting out Fischer.

"Have you ever thought he might want to be left alone?" Madame Lola asked.

"Look, Madame Lola, a lot of people are wondering what has happened to him," I said.

"A lot of celebrities want to be left alone," she said.

In my own paranoia, the thought suddenly occurred to me: Maybe she knows Bobby and is trying to protect him.

"Do you know Fischer or something?" I blurted.

There was no doubt that I had become slightly wiggy. I had been prowling the catacombs of the main branch of the Los Angeles Public Library for months because Fischer had often been sighted there—as recently as a few weeks earlier—but he had never appeared when I was there. I had begun to think that perhaps he had contacts at the library who would tip him off whenever I showed up. After all, I had a source working at the library, Gordon Brooks, who had promised to call me if Fischer ever showed. In fact, over the last few weeks, I had developed a network of librarians who had agreed to call Brooks, who in turn would ring me, if they spotted him.

The day before, on April 2, I had gone to a Goodwill store in the city of Orange and purchased a disguise, clothes that would have suited any bum wandering around nearby MacArthur Park or the broken-bottle district of downtown L.A.: a $5 pair of baggy brown pants, marked down to $2.50, whose cuffs scraped the floor; a large gold shirt for $3; a white tie, with a bright yellow stain, for 15 cents; a pair of brown shoes, which I wore without socks or laces, for $5; and the ugliest sports coat in the store, a black number with red and white flecks, for $2.50. An accommodating friend stained the coat and pants with grease and glue to match the sorry tie. At a magic shop, I bought a pair of wire-rimmed spectacles and a can of gray makeup paint with which I liberally doused what was left of my hair.

Thus disguised on April 3, on my way to the library I stopped off to see Madame Lola. It was a sweltering day, about 85°, but the disguise and the promise of finding Fischer had buoyed me with a new sense of mission. I strode into her storefront chambers, apologized for my wardrobe, and within 10 minutes we were ensconced in a backroom cubicle adorned with religious paintings and statues. At Lola's request, I had brought several pictures of Fischer that I had been showing around restaurants and stores in Pasadena, hoping someone might recognize him. I also brought copies of papers bearing Fischer's handwriting, including the pseudonym Robert D. James, which appeared at the end of his 14-page pamphlet, *I Was Tortured in the Pasadena Jailhouse*.

Fischer had written it in 1981 after he was arrested in Pasadena—he was mistaken for a bank robber—and jailed for two days. In this remarkable document, Fischer described his arrest and then detailed what happened to him in two days of incarceration, during which, he says, he was ordered to strip and was threatened with confinement in a mental hospital. The chapter headings include: Brutally Handcuffed, False Arrest, Insulted, Choked, Stark Naked, No Phone Call, Horror Cell, Isolation & Torture.

Madame Lola placed her hands on the papers and the photographs, tipped her head forward and closed her eyes. "He has been hurt in many ways by people in business," she began. "He feels that people are going to take advantage of him. . . . Have you tried looking toward the desert?"

"The desert?" I said. "No . . . what about Pasadena?"

Madame Lola opened and closed her eyes. "He's not there now," she said. "I feel him towards some place hot, very hot. Very, very warm. I feel a lot of sun. . . ." Outside, it felt hot enough to roast a duck, but that was not what Lola meant. "It could be Nevada," she said. "This is what I'm picking up. . . . He is a very confused person. . . . He feels everyone is going to recognize him. . . . I feel you will find him when you least expect him."

Madame Lola looked up, fixed me with her eyes and said finally, "He's always one step ahead of you. I'd give up on the whole idea."

Moments later I was heading for the library in Los Angeles. Time was getting short. By now, the office was restless, and more than one editor had told me to write the story whether I had found him or not, but I was having trouble letting it go.

So what was I doing here, dressed up like an abject bum and looking for a man who would bolt the instant he knew who I was? And what on earth might he be doing now in the desert? Pumping gas in Reno? Riding a burro from dune to dune in the Mojave, looking over his shoulder as the sun boiled the brain that once ate Moscow? And what of his teeth? I had been thinking a lot lately about Fischer's teeth.

In the spring of 1982, one of Fischer's oldest chess-playing friends, Ron Gross of Cerritos, Calif., suggested to him that the two men take a fishing trip into Mexico. Gross, now 49, had first met Fischer in the mid-'50s, back in the days before Bobby had become a world-class player, and the two had kept in irregular touch over the years. In 1980, at a time when Fischer was leaving most of his old friends behind, he had contacted Gross, and they had gotten together. At the time, Fischer was living in a dive near downtown Los Angeles.

"It was a real seedy hotel," Gross recalls. "Broken bottles. Weird people."

At one point, Gross made the mistake of calling Karpov the world champion. "I'm still the world champion," snapped Fischer. "Karpov isn't. My friends still consider me champion. They took my title from me."

By 1982, Fischer was living in a nicer neighborhood in Los Angeles. Gross began picking him up and letting him off at a bus stop at Wilshire Boulevard and Fairfax, near an East Indian store where Bobby bought herbal medicines.

That March, on the fishing trip to Ensenada, Fischer got seasick, and he treated himself by sniffing a eucalyptus-based medicine below deck. Fischer astonished Gross with the news about his teeth. Fischer talked about a friend who had a steel plate in his head that picked up radio signals.

"If somebody took a filling out and put in an electronic device, he could influence your thinking," Fischer said. "I don't want anything artificial in my head."

"Does that include dental work?" asked Gross.

"Yeah," said Bobby. "I had all my fillings taken out some time ago."

"There's nothing in your cavities to protect your teeth?"

"No, nothing."

Gross dropped the subject for the moment, but later he got to thinking about it and, while taking a steam bath in a health spa in Cerritos, he asked Fischer if he knew how bacteria worked, warning him that his teeth could rot away. "As much as you like to eat, what are you going to do when your teeth fall out?" asked Gross.

"I'll gum it if I have to," Fischer said. "I'll gum it."

Their relationship ended that summer, after Gross gave an interview to the chess writer for the *Register* of Orange County, for an innocuous but informative piece about the fishing trip. There was no mention of the teeth, and nothing about the anti-Semitic tirades that for years had laced Fischer's conversations. Though his mother, Regina Pustan, a Palo Alto physician, is a Jew, Fischer had long ago rejected Judaism. In restaurants, says Gross, it was embarrassing how Fischer sometimes ranted on loudly about "kikes" and "Jew bastards." Nor was there anything in the *Register* about how tiresome it had become for Gross to hear Fischer lecture about how everything was controlled by "the hidden hand, the satanical secret world government," to listen to him lecture on *The Protocols of the Elders of Zion*, an anti-Semitic work, and to hear his version of the Holocaust and the "myth" of six million dead: "maybe 100,000 trouble-makers and criminals."

When Fischer heard about the *Register's* story, he called up Gross, furious, though he admitted not having read the piece. "But I don't have to," he told Gross. "I know what it's about."

"How can you feel that way?" Gross asked. "I didn't say anything bad about you."

"It doesn't matter," said Bobby. "You're not supposed to talk to these guys. Do you realize I don't let my friends talk to the press?" Gross tried to mollify him, but it was no use. That was their last conversation.

Lina Grumette, for years a Los Angeles chess organizer and promoter, had been Fischer's West Coast "chess mother," beginning in the early 1960s. When Fischer, who was raised in Brooklyn, went to California, he lived at her home, at times for weeks on end. She recalls Fischer sitting down at the bridge table after dinner and analyzing chess games. His hand would snap pieces rapidly off the board, and he would shake his head.

"This move is no good," he would say to Grumette. "He should have done this. What do you think?"

"What are you asking me for?" she would say.

"Well, everybody's opinion helps," he would answer.

That is how she remembers him best, sitting at the board and having fun playing games. "Whatever people say about him, he has a very kind heart," Grumette says. "He always impressed me as a normal, kind, decent human being. He visited my husband in the hospital when he was dying of cancer, and walked my dog every night. Bobby was part of the family."

Until, that is, Grumette talked innocently about him to a reporter from the *Los Angeles Times* following his defeat of Spassky in 1972. "He dropped me, too," she says.

Lina took me to the second-floor room which Fischer had used when he lived there, and showed me a box of possessions that he had left behind: a warranty for a Zenith television set given to him after a tournament in 1966, a few religious books and stacks of letters from children asking him about chess.

She last spoke to him around 1979, when she was trying to arrange an exhibition match for him at Caesars Palace in Las Vegas. Caesars offered him $250,000 in appearance money. After he had agreed to the terms and all the arrangements had been made, Fischer called her. "I've been thinking," he began.

The minute he said that, she knew the deal was off. "I'm risking my title," Fischer said. "I should get $1 million."

The last time Grumette tried to reach him, she called Claudia Mokarow to ask for her assistance. It was just after the appearance of another *Los Angeles Times* article in which Grumette was quoted. "That'll cost you $1,000," Mokarow told her.

Actually that figure was cheap. Not long after inviting Fischer to Chamberlain's house for dinner, Schaap got in touch with Mokarow and told her he wanted to interview Fischer for *Games Magazine*.

"Bobby will be perfectly happy to interview with you," Mokarow said. "He's charging $25,000 per interview. Since he didn't charge you for the last interview, it will be $50,000."

None of his old chess friends have seen or spoken to him in years. Grandmaster Robert Byrne, now the chess editor of the *New York Times*, knew him well as a fellow American player for years, but he lost touch with him in the 1970s. "He does not return my messages," says Byrne. "I'm a journalist now."

Grandmaster William Lombardy, who was Fischer's second when he won the world title, has not talked to Fischer since 1978 in Pasadena, when the U.S. championships were held at the Worldwide Church's Ambassador College.

"I worry about him, but I can't worry about him night and day," Lombardy says. "I've made efforts to get in touch with him. I've tried to get his phone number, but he doesn't like his number given out. I can't be chasing him around, just to get hold of him to talk to him. In L.A., I've tried to find him. I've asked people where he might live, where you might see him. My door is always open. If he wants to get in touch with me, he can."

Bernard Zuckerman, a New York chess theoretician and one of Fischer's friends, also last saw him at the '78 championships. In fact, he went to dinner with Fischer at a restaurant in Chinatown in L.A.—Fischer and Zuckerman are avid eaters of Chinese food—and they brought along young Larry Christiansen, who was meeting Fischer for the first time.

"We talked about chess," Christiansen says. "He didn't have much respect for Karpov's play. . . . He launched into a tirade against the Jews, the world conspiracy. He seemed like a nice guy, then he launched into that tirade. I felt kind of sorry for him. I could see Zuckerman in the back seat, masking laughter."

For most of those who knew him well, though, Fischer's flights into such fantasies were no laughing matter. Perhaps his oldest friends in the world are Jack Collins and his sister, Ethel. Jack was Fischer's principal chess teacher, and Fischer spent hours at the Collinses' Brooklyn home, playing endless games of chess with Jack and eating food prepared by Ethel.

"He began to visit us when he was just 13," says Jack. "We played thousands and thousands of speed games. You can't predict what a boy that age will be. The next thing I knew, he went up like a Roman candle. It's hard to believe he's not the Bobby Fischer we knew. I still think of him as the little prodigy who lived with us years ago. We had a lot of fun together. They're one thing as boys; they're another as men."

The question of whether he would ever come back remains open in his teacher's mind.

"Chess players don't get better as they get older, they get worse," Collins says. "Their careers roughly parallel those of big league pitchers. It's hard to know why. Maybe it's nerves. Maybe it's the will to win. But Bobby always admired players who competed into old age, such as Wilhelm Steinitz, a world champion who played till he died. Bobby always told me he'd do that. He loved chess. That's the strange part, that he should drop it. Everyone asks me why. I don't know."

Fischer has not been in touch with the Collinses for five years. They don't know how to reach him. He used to call once a month. Now there is nothing.

"His view of the world is completely incompatible with mine," Collins says. "He wants to talk about that all the time. What do you do with a person who insists the Holocaust didn't happen?"

His oldest friends are not the only ones who have become alienated from him. Harry Sneider, once Fischer's personal fitness trainer and confidant, had been almost like a brother to him for seven years. In the late '70s, Sneider sensed he had to back off.

As Sneider drifted away from Fischer, Bobby found a set of surrogate parents in Mokarow and her husband, Arthur, then members of the Worldwide Church. Sneider had sensed early in Fischer a desire for a world utterly apart from chess. "He would really like to be just left alone," Snei-der says. "He's trying to live a normal life, with regular hours. He is saying, 'I want my own space.'" When Sneider encouraged him to play chess, Fis-cher would say, "That's none of your business. Just be my friend."

In Claudia, Fischer found someone to screen his calls and otherwise pro-tect him from the inquiring world. When I phoned her, here's the way the conversation went:

"Hello?" answered the female voice.

"Is Claudia Mokarow there?" I asked.

"Yes, this is she." I told her who I was, that I wanted to speak to Bobby, and asked her to help.

"No, I really can't," she said.

I pressed gently, asking her if Bobby was in town. "No, I'm not able to help you," she said.

"May I come and see you?" I asked. Silence.

More frantic now, my voice rising as I thought of Schaap: "Is he seeing people?" Again, silence. More desperate now, almost a whinny: "Is he in town? Is he anywhere in Southern California?"

"I think I'd better hang up," Claudia said.

Again: "Is he in Southern California?"

"Bye," she said sweetly. Click.

I paid a call on Mokarow on March 9, Fischer's 42nd birthday, knocking on her door on San Remo Road in Pasadena. I knew the house well, for I had staked it out on several occasions in the past months, hoping to see Fis-cher come or go. A woman's voice answered from behind the door.

"Who is it?" Claudia asked, in her telephone voice. I told her who I was. "It's Bobby Fischer's 42nd birthday, and I would like to talk to you, please!"

"I'm not interested in talking to you," she said.

So it was with Claudia and all of those still known to be in touch with Fischer. I ran into Miguel Quinteros one day at a chess tournament in New York, and Fischer's closest friend among the grandmasters only smiled and said, "We have a deal. The only thing I can tell you is he is in very good shape. He hasn't lost anything."

So, too, came the word one day from Joan Fischer Targ, Bobby's older sister, who lives in Palo Alto. Asked for help, she replied very politely, "Sorry, I can't."

"Have you seen him lately?" I asked.

"I guess what you're asking are personal questions," Joan said.

"I'm in Palo Alto," I said. "Could I see you?"

"There wouldn't be much point in it," she said.

Nor was there much point in asking to see Jim Buff, Fischer's good friend living in the Bay Area.

"Sir!" shouted Buff. "You're calling me on an unlisted number! I have nothing to say to you! If you call me again, I'll call the chairman of the board of SPORTS ILLUSTRATED!"

Bobby had been known to like San Francisco. In 1981 he had lived at the apartment of Greek-born grandmaster Peter Biyiasas and his wife, Ruth Haring. Through Buff, Biyiasas had invited Fischer to live with them.

One day Buff called. "Peter, he's coming up. Bobby's coming up on the bus to stay with you!"

Fischer arrived one early March morning with his suitcase of clothes and vitamins and a large orange-juice squeezer that he had bought in Mexico. He stayed for two months, returned to Los Angeles in the summer, then came back in the fall to stay two more months. They swam in the ocean, played pinball machines, bowled, went to movies, squeezed oranges and played baseball in Golden Gate Park. Fischer shagged Buff's fly balls and pegged them back to the plate as hard as he could.

"How was it coming in?" asked Bobby.

He was more overpowering at the chessboard with Biyiasas. During his four months in San Francisco, he beat Biyiasas 17 straight speed games before Biyiasas finally surrendered. "He was too good," Biyiasas says. "There was no use in playing him. It wasn't interesting. I was getting beaten, and it wasn't clear to me why. It wasn't like I made this mistake or that mistake. It was like I was being gradually outplayed, from the start. He wasn't taking any time to think. The most depressing thing about it is that I wasn't even getting out of the middle game to an endgame. I don't ever remember an endgame. He honestly believes there is no one for him to play, no one worthy of him. I played him, and I can attest to that. It's not interesting."

As time passed, Fischer's taste for the eccentric and his preoccupation with Jews became evident to Biyiasas. Biyiasas says Fischer referred to Jews as "Yids," telling him that one controlled the fluctuating price of the world's gold. "He is fascinated by who this might be," Biyiasas says. Fischer had what he called Chinese healthy brain pills ("Good for headaches," Fischer told him) and Mexican rattlesnake pills ("Good for general health"). He had vitamins in a suitcase, and he invited Biyiasas to help himself to them.

One day, Biyiasas tried to open the suitcase but found it locked. Later, Biyiasas asked him about this. "It's not locked for you," Fischer said. "If the Commies come to poison me, I don't want to make it easy for them."

Now Fischer was moving in a vacuum. A reporter had checked all public records in the San Francisco and Los Angeles areas for a clue to Fischer's whereabouts, and he had found none. No telephone, no driver's license, no vehicle registration, no real property and no records of him in an array of courts.

Nonetheless, I sensed that I was closing in, if only I could get more time to prowl the library in my disguise. I knew he had been seen there, which meant he wasn't in Brazil. That he had gone to Brazil had been the big rumor in December.

The scent seemed to be fresh. There was the tale told by Ben Lewis, a truck driver who had spent part of a late February lunch hour attending George Putnam's radio talk show in a studio right across the street from the library. As the show ended at 2 P.M., Lewis turned and saw Bobby right behind him. A chess player, Lewis said he recognized him immediately, even though Fischer had a short beard.

"Bobby, hello," Lewis said. Fischer reeled backward. "About 10 feet," Lewis later recalled. The first thing Fischer said was, "How do I know you're not a journalist?"

Lewis thought that was pretty funny. "Bobby, I'm in my uniform, I drive a truck," Lewis said.

"Show me some ID," Fischer demanded.

Assured that he was, indeed, a truck driver, Fischer talked to Lewis for about a half hour. At one point, Lewis told him, "Bobby, you were the greatest!" To which Fischer sternly replied, "What do you mean, were?"

They chatted amiably, Lewis telling him that he had two sons and asking Fischer how he could make them better players.

"Don't try to make them child prodigies," Fischer said. "Forget about all that. Just let them play."

Lewis had a fine time talking to Bobby and, looking back, he has but one regret.

"If I had had a chess set, Bobby would have played me," Lewis said. "That's the thing that hurts more than anything else. I didn't have a doggone chess set."

So he was probably here somewhere, and there I was, dressed like a derelict and making my way up the steps of the library's Hope Street entrance at 4:35 P.M. I did a quick circuit of all the rooms and at once found Gordon Brooks standing in the social sciences department. I approached him from behind and gruffly asked him for a cigarette. He turned: "I'm sorry, I. . . . Oh, it's you."

I told him to keep his eyes peeled, that I was on the prowl. Gordon nodded. An expert chess player, Brooks had once lost to Fischer in a simultaneous exhibition.

He had seen Fischer several times at the library in the last four years. The first time he spotted him, Fischer had a beard and was standing in front of the card-catalog files. Brooks approached him. "He mumbled something and turned and walked away," Brooks said.

They spoke on another occasion and, according to Brooks, Fischer said, "I'm bothered by a lot of weirdos."

Leaving Brooks, I swung through the history department and I thought I saw Fischer crouching by a stack of books along a wall. I could not see his face, so I sat down at the nearest desk and waited. He looked tall—Fischer is 6' 2"—and he had a balding spot on the back of his head. Vintage Bobby. Suddenly the man stood up. I breathed deeply, and looked. Ohhh! Not him.

I got up, caught my breath and was about to head out the door when someone tapped me on the shoulder. Startled, I jumped and blurted, "Ahhh!" It was Brooks. He whispered to me, "He was here yesterday."

"What?" I breathed. "Are you sure?"

"The lady in Social Sciences said she saw him in there," he said.

Brooks and I swept through History into Social Sciences. "Are you positive it was Fischer?"

Pat Spencer looked me up and down, smiled demurely and said, "Yesterday, he was definitely here. It was late, between seven and eight o'clock. I know, because I didn't come out to the desk until then. He asked for the big dictionary over there. He had on a suit, real baggy pants."

"How do you know it was Fischer?" I asked. Spencer pulled out an old newspaper photo of Fischer and flashed it from behind the counter. "I know him," she said. "I see him a lot in here."

Turning to Brooks, I said, "A day! I missed him by a lousy day!"

But he was here! He was in town, certainly in the neighborhood. I left the library, went to a deli and bought a Diet Sunkist and a bag of cheese corns and sat on the stoop of The Church of the Open Door, thinking Bobby might stroll past any time now and look at me and figure I was O.K., just a bum feeding the pigeons. Ha! So I flipped some cheese corns to the birds strutting past and waited in the gathering dusk. Where is he? At 6:10 P.M., I walked up the stairs and into the library and began my regular tour of the place, like a night watchman with a key.

Nothing in Philosophy and Religion, nor in the Newspaper Room, where Fischer used to go last fall to read Harry Golombek's commentaries on the Karpov-Kasparov world title match in the *Times* of London. Nor in the downstairs head. It was 6:30 P.M., then 7:15.

Another quick swing through the rooms revealed nothing. It was 7:30 P.M., then 7:45. Suddenly the bell rang, signaling 15 minutes left before closing. The man reading the trigonometry book looked up in the back of History. A bum dressed even worse than I, with holes in his pants and a torn coat, sauntered toward the door. At 7:51, I got up from a table and walked out of History and into the rotunda.

Passing the card catalogs, I glanced up and stopped—jerked to a stop and froze. There he was. Bobby Fischer was standing about 15 feet away, and for an instant he looked right at me, so I could see his face straight on, and I think my mouth dropped open but I can't be sure, because all I can remember is how it suddenly went dry and how I ducked behind the card catalogs and leaned my head against the files and said, in a suppressed whisper, "Oh my God! I found him. I don't believe this. Now what the hell do I do?"

I had never seen him in my life, except in dated photographs, but I knew it was Fischer, just plain knew it the instant I saw him. The long face. The brown eyes. The half-inch beard. The brown hair revealing a slightly balding patch at the back of his pate. About 6' 2". He was carrying a plastic bag—Ben Lewis said Fischer was carrying a bag when he met him—and as I emerged from behind the files, he was already ducking into the telephone booth, as he had when Brooks first saw him. He had materialized out of nowhere at closing time, as if he had descended from the dome to use the phone. After watching him disappear into the booth, I dashed downstairs to watch the exits.

At almost eight sharp, as the guards were seeing patrons out the door, Fischer came down the winding staircase and walked quickly past me to the Hope Street exit. He went through the door, took a left, then moved fast down the stairs to the street. I followed him, about 30 feet behind. Halfway down the stairs, he turned his head and saw me again. Does he think I'm following him? He never turned back again. Nearing the corner of Sixth and Hope, Fischer suddenly stopped and picked up a public telephone. Of course, I thought, an old trick to lose a tail! Head down, I swept past him, crossed Sixth Street to a row of hedges at the Lincoln Savings and Loan and crouched down to hide. Looking around, he appeared not to have noticed me.

He was on the phone about five minutes. Not sure what he was going to do, I crossed Hope, doubled back across Sixth to his side of the street and lurked about in wait. Fischer hung up the phone, crossed Sixth, passed the hedges of the Lincoln Savings and Loan and strode quickly into the night. I followed him at a distance of 50 yards, at times having to break into a trot to keep up. Ron Gross had been right. "Fischer is a fast walker," Gross had said. "With those long, fast strides he takes, he's hard to keep up with."

Half-jogging, I watched him as he disappeared in shadows and reappeared in the light, his bag twirling and swinging at his side. Everywhere he went, I trailed just behind him on the other side of the street. I could not hear him whistling, but he moved as if he were.

For some 21 months I had wondered what I'd say to Fischer upon meeting him face to face. Dressed as I was this night, I knew I could have affected a foreign accent, stuck out my hand and said, "Boooby Fischer! You ah zee greatess chiss playah uff all zee time!" But I had decided long ago I could not do that. Were I to confront him, I would have to do so on his terms, which meant I would have to be scrupulously honest. No lies, no evasions, no deceptions. He detests all such things. So, confronting him, I would have to tell him who I was and why I was there, whereupon he would either flee in horror or lash out.

After spending weeks of my life looking for this man, in a journey that had led me to countless homes, libraries, bookshops, chess tournaments, stakeouts, police stations, restaurants, bowling alleys and health spas, I finally had him in my sights, and I simply could not bring myself to reach out a hand to shake his. Fischer had chosen this life of privacy and seclusion, for whatever reason, and to breach it now seemed a pointless intrusion. I was certain enough in my own mind that the man was Bobby Fischer. I chased him for block after block through the streets of Los Angeles, thinking he might lead me to his home, for I was curious to know for myself just where he lived after hearing all the rumors.

In the end, even that didn't really matter. He stopped on one street corner for a while, waiting for a light to change, and then crossed the street and stopped at another. There were bums and winos all around, but he appeared to pay them no mind. I watched him for a long while from across the street. Fourteen years ago, he had stormed the chess world by winning those 20 straight games, and he was on his way to Iceland to do battle with Spassky. What seemed like only the beginning then was really the end.

Now here he was, momentarily sharing a street corner with winos in downtown Los Angeles. The last time I saw him, he was standing there under a large clock hung upon the corner of a building. Fittingly enough, the clock was broken, its hands motionless on the dial. Then he disappeared into a group of people climbing on Bus 483, bound for Pasadena.

July 1985

In September of 1992, on the 20th anniversary of their world championship match in Iceland, Bobby Fischer astounded the chess world by surfacing in the little Montenegrin village of Sveti Stefan, on the Adriatic coast, to do battle against the aging Boris Spassky. Fischer won the match and most of the $5 million purse, $3.5 million to Spassky's $1.65 million, but it was not without a price. In playing, he defied an executive order imposing economic sanctions against Serbia and Montenegro, and at a press conference before the match, in an unsanitary show of defiance, he held up the Treasury Department's letter warning him of fines and imprisonment if he played. Dangling it in front of the crowd, he spit on it. He left for Budapest after the match, and over the ensuing ten years there have since been sightings of him in Brazil, England, Japan, and the Phillipines. The U.S. government issued a warrant for his arrest on Dec. 15, 1992, but the millionaire expatriate remains abroad, the warrant still unserved.

FOYT

Three laps to go, floating out there in the middle of the high bank of Turn 3, Bobby Unser lost it.

Flat lost it. Swung low and, sweet chariot, suddenly lost control of his car while trying to get the lead underneath A.J. Foyt. All afternoon long, for nearly 200 miles around the two-mile stretch of Michigan International Speedway in Cambridge Junction, Unser and Foyt had been charging at each other, in a pair of USAC stock cars, like the hammers of hell, Foyt in a Ford and Unser in a Dodge. Into Turn 3, Unser was drafting right behind Foyt when, knowing he had the faster car and deciding to wait no longer, he dipped down and stomped on it. At once he was racing under Foyt, and now they were side by side.

"I'm trying to pass Foyt for the lead and I started losing my car in his draft," Unser recalls. "I let my car get loose; my rear end started coming around. The air from his car is sucking mine up toward him. My car is going to spin. And I'm going to hit him because we're so dang close together. I made a mistake and I knew better. I'm going to have a wreck. I'm going to wreck him, too, and it's going to be my fault. Just as simple as A-B-C. At about, oh, 165 miles an hour."

Foyt glanced over and saw the trouble Unser was in, saw he was out of control and about to spin into him. "He saw it," says Unser. "Saw I'd lost it. You know what the guys does? This'll show you how smart he is. Most drivers would have shied away. Not A.J. Foyt. Instead of trying to run away, or pulling to the right to get away from me—and maybe he can get away and leave me to hit the wall, but maybe I hit him, too—no, no . . . he guaranteed the outcome. Guaranteed it. And he did it out of instinct. There wasn't time to think about it. He pulled *down* on me. *On me!* He backed off and came down and cut the draft between us. *Let* my car bump his. It was a very gentle thing. And he put my race car straight. We quivered a little bit but he got me straight."

Roaring out of Turn 3, Unser found himself on the lead with those few laps to go, and down the front straight he acknowledged the debt to Foyt in the only way that he knew how, as one race car driver to another. "I had to wave him by," recalls Unser. "The man saved me from a wreck, and I owed it to him." That done, they went at each other furiously through the final three laps, with Foyt eventually winning a squeaker. Climbing from his car, Foyt spotted Unser.

"Saved your ass, didn't I?" said Foyt.

This was 18 years ago, back in the days when Foyt was still building the legend that he would come to be known by, as the greatest American race car driver in history. Those were the days when his father, Tony, was still alive and the son, craving his approval, fanned with his yearnings the inextinguishable fire that burned in his still-flat belly. Back when he and Unser were still going at it on oilstained tracks across the land, when their memories were still fresh of raising rooster tails deep in the corners of dirt ovals like the one at Langhorne, Pennsylvania, where Foyt once spun like a dervish through the D-shaped circuit's most difficult and dangerous stretch, a dip that the drivers called Puke Hollow. That was back when, at California's Ascot Park, Foyt's keenest rival, Parnelli Jones, once stood in the middle of the racetrack, with cars broadsliding past him, so Foyt couldn't miss the finger that Jones was giving him. And it was when Foyt and Unser had still more Indy 500 victories in them (Foyt's fourth and Unser's second and third), and Foyt had this reputation as a profane, rude, swaggering, mesquite-tough, hot-tempered Texan who ate chili by the quart and flew a red bandanna around his neck. His driving style, paradoxically, belied that image and was, in fact, a sort of model of its kind: cool and clean, patient and precise, free of mistakes.

"That's the key to Foyt's greatness," says Chris Economaki, the editor and publisher emeritus of *National Speed Sport News*, who has watched Foyt since the 1950s. "He almost never made mistakes. Never put a wheel wrong. He never overdrove into a corner, or when conditions were bad. Never spun out, to speak of. Never overshot his pit. He judged his equipment. He won so many races with the canvas showing through a right rear tire that would have blown in another lap. He *really* understood the business he was in. Just never made mistakes."

It was the only style that could have suited the survivor he was to become and remains today. He is a dinosaur from another age, lumbering toward some inevitable extinction, the last of his species, the ultimate driver-mechanic, wearing on his shirts the grease stains from a thousand cars and on his face and neck the faint burn scars from Milwaukee and

DuQuoin, Illinois. Foyt still bears the limp he got last year in Elkhart Lake, Wisconsin, where his brake pedal broke and he flew off the course and plunged into an embankment, burying the nose of his car four feet deep in the dirt, crushing his feet and driving a broken tibia bone, like a dagger, 12 inches up into his thigh. The wounds were so painful that he begged attending medics to knock him out with a hammer as he sat for 40 minutes while being cut out of the remains of the car. At age 56, A.J. Foyt is in his last year as a full-time race car driver, taking his bows as he does the Indy Car circuit a final time. Unless he decides to take one more turn at the Indy 500 next May—it would be his 35th straight appearance in the race, and those who know him believe he will be there—he will drive his last race on Oct. 6 in the Bosch Spark Plug Grand Prix in Nazareth, Pennsylvania.

In this age of complex, time-consuming specialization, when drivers rarely stray for long from their corners of the sport, Foyt leaves behind a career so diverse it may never be matched. Certainly no other man in the history of motor sports has done what he has over the last 35 years, winning not only those four Indy 500s, a record at the time, but also all those races in the sport's other disciplines, in radically different cars: the Daytona 500 stock car race; and the 24 Hours of Le Mans, the 24 Hours of Daytona (twice) and the 12 Hours of Sebring, all sports car races.

"A.J. Foyt is the greatest driver that I ever knew," says NASCAR's own enduring legend, Junior Johnson. "The best all-around. He could drive anything, anywhere, anytime. Won in about everything he ever sat down in."

Bobby Unser is retired from driving, doing television commentary on racing, and he knows all the fine younger drivers—his nephew, Al Unser Jr., and Michael Andretti and Arie Luyendyk—and he wonders just how to tell them about A.J. Foyt, about how he used to drive a race car, this paunchy old crock who walks around with the limp and the scars and the bald spot on the back of his pate. Bobby Unser can close his eyes and see Ascot and Langhorne and Milwaukee and Springfield, Illinois, and the Indianapolis Motor Speedway, and he can see the high bank of Turn 3 in Michigan, where Foyt came down on him, instantly but oh so gently at 165 mph, and nudged him straight.

"And that, my friend, is talent," says Unser. "That a person can do that, from instinct, so fast! You don't find that nowadays. Who would have that kind of experience? How could the young drivers, like my nephew or Arie Luyendyk, know how good A.J. Foyt was? He was *really* talented. But how in the hell could they know? They have no idea. They say, 'Oh, he won four Indys and Daytona and Le Mans. . . .' But they don't *really* know. None of them saw the old A.J. The real A.J. The great A.J. Foyt."

Midafternoon, and the old A.J., the real A.J., is holding the wheel of his black Honda Accord and tooling along a country road northwest of Houston, beyond the White Oak Bayou toward a setting sun. It is June 25, and the real A.J. Foyt hasn't won an Indy Car race in 10 years, since the Pocono 500 on June 21, 1981—the longest day of the year, of course, and the perfect omen to usher in the longest twilight in the annals of the sport. His mother, Evelyn, had died of heart failure that spring of 1981—on the night, in fact, that A.J. qualified for the Indy 500—and two years later, in 1983, he would lose his father to cancer, also on the night he qualified at Indy.

"Weird, isn't it?" Foyt says as his hands make almost imperceptible corrections on the steering wheel. "The way they both passed away. They lived to see me make the race, and that was it. I came home, talked to them, they closed their eyes. They died about the same time, 10 minutes till 10."

Foyt is driving out to his ranch, the 1,500-acre spread where he raises cattle for market and thoroughbred horses for racing and breeding. Where, above the workshop door, untouched, Foyt keeps the symbol of his father's hold on him. If the loss of his mother devastated the man—"A.J. was a momma's boy," says his wife, Lucy. "She just idolized him"—the death of his father left him adrift, benumbed by a grief that perhaps he will never shake. "It took a long time," says Lucy. "It took a long time to sink in. He'll never get over the loss."

Even today, Foyt often speaks of his father, at times eerily, in the present tense, as if Tony were waiting for him out at the ranch. "My daddy's a pretty good-sized guy," he is saying as the Honda rolls along. "Not that big, but stout. His damn fingers are"—A.J. holds up a thumb and index finger touching in a circle at their tips—"that big around. Daddy'd give you the shirt off his back. If he didn't like you, don't mess with him. He believes in talking straight, not that phony stuff. He's just that type of guy."

So, of course, A.J. likes to spin those tales about the old man. About how tough and honest and ornery he was . . . about how loyal he was to those he counted as family and friends . . . about how hard he had worked up through the Depression and how no one had ever pushed him around . . . about the afternoon in the pits at Indianapolis when, angered by a persistent TV reporter, Tony dropped his wrenches and went after him, leaping over tires and fuel hoses, with A.J. leaping right behind him, chasing him chasing the reporter and yelling, "No, Daddy! No. Don't hit him, Daddy! No, Daddy. No. No. No" . . . about how the old man rarely spared the rod with the boy when he was growing up: "I never got that many whippings, but, whew, when I did, my daddy tore my ass up" . . . about the race where Tony, an automobile mechanic by trade, was doing tech inspection and he caught his son cheating: "He saw what I did, which I didn't think he would, and I won the race but he disqualified the car. I was mad as hell. . . . He didn't care if I was his son or not."

About how the old man never, but never, praised the son for anything he ever did in a race car, not even after A.J. won that record fourth Indy 500, in 1977 . . . and about how he and the old man could barely speak, after all they had been through together, when Tony was on his deathbed in the hospital and the doctor left them alone and A.J. bit his lip and said, "Well, Daddy, you know everything about me. . . ."

Foyt swings the Honda off the road and through the gates to the ranch, slowing as he reaches the asphalt drive, pointing here left and there right as he cruises past the wooden fences, clean and painted white, and the neatly tended pastures. "You're looking at the guy who dug all those postholes," he says. "I dug every hole. You're looking at the guy who painted all this white fence, by himself. You're looking at the guy who built that training track. I built this all up. You're looking at the guy who planted this pasture . . . who cleared all this land, with a bulldozer. And burned it. You're looking at the man who laid this road after he won at Phoenix, '65 . . . put up all these running sheds for the mares and these cattle pens over here. I cleared it all. You're looking at him right now."

He edges the Honda down the road that lines the fields, where bands of broodmares, some with suckling foals at their sides, are grazing with the cattle. Past the watering troughs and the hay barn, up past the oaks and the pond with a jetty reaching out almost to the middle of it. "My father wired all this, ran the lights," Foyt says, his arm sweeping the pens and sheds. "I dug the pond. See that strip of land? I built that so my mother could drive her little motor home out there and fish off it. I got it stocked with bass. Call it Nanny's Lake. . . ."

Up beyond Nanny's Lake, Foyt pulls off the road and parks the car next to the large, orange workshed. Stepping inside the shed, he points straight up, to the runners on which the sliding doors operated. "This was the last building that Daddy wired before he died," says Foyt. "I closed the door one day and looked up and there it was. I thought, 'I'll be goddamned! There's that hammer I've been looking for for over a year.' I said to one of the workers, 'You're not going to believe where the old man left that hammer. Look right above your head.' Daddy left it up there and I ain't never taking it down."

Because the ranch was where he and his father worked side by side, A.J. moving the earth, Tony doing the plumbing and the wiring, today it serves as a kind of monument to their work—the hedges trimmed and the lawns edged and clipped around a spacious brick house that sits on a circular drive behind stone gates crowned with concrete horses' heads. The ranch is Foyt's personal dig. He is out there, on the seat of that chuffing bulldozer, trying to unearth what he still surely longs for, as if father-love were some lost city and he will find it if he just keeps digging. So, to be sure, the place represents, for him, an unending search for the missing and inexpressible. Five years ago, a friend of Foyt's, commentator Jack Arute of ABC and ESPN, asked him to define "love, love of your family."

Foyt replied: "It's hard for me to. . . . I probably don't show partiality to nobody. No individual that much. I've had a lot of people say, 'You just don't love nobody.' I guess I do, but I guess I'm kind of like my father. It's hard for me to show. . . . But I don't know. I've worked all my life. And I guess what I have love for more than anything is work. I love to get on my bulldozer. I love to take land and clear it and try to make it pretty. I also love the challenges of business."

Anthony Joseph Foyt Jr. may have been his mother's boy, but he is his father's son. He has been challenging his corner of the world, largely on his own terms, since he first crawled into the little red open-wheel racer, with the Briggs-Stratton engine, that his father gave him to patrol the yard in when he was three. When he wore that out, Tony built him a midget-type racer that could hit 50 mph, and one night, at the old Houston Speed Bowl, Tony arranged for A.J. to challenge one of the leading adult drivers, Doc Cossey, to a three-lap duel. Little A.J. led Cossey into the first turn, to the cheering of the crowds, threw it sideways into the dirt corners, to even louder roars, and came charging home in front, to an ovation.

He was five. And, for then and forever, a race car driver.

The family lived in the Heights, a working-class section in north Houston, across the street from a pickle factory and not far from the garage where Tony worked on other people's cars. (He kept his own race cars at home.) A.J. spent hours at his father's knee, poking under hoods and chassis, learning how things all worked. "When I was a little bitty kid, I'd do anything, just to be with him," A.J. says. Just as his mother embraced him, so his father disciplined him. "A.J. was definitely very afraid of his dad," says Lucy. When A.J. was 11, with the help of friends he took his father's midget race car off the trailer, fired up the flathead Ford V–8 and rode it around the yard like a cowboy on a bull, nearly tearing off a corner of the house and turning the yard into a plowed field. The ride ended when the engine burst into flames, bubbling the paint on the hood.

Waiting for the whipping, A.J. was in bed when his parents came home that night, and he could hear his father roaring toward the bedroom. Tony snatched him out of bed, and the boy could hear his mother pleading, "Please don't whip him, please don't whip him," and above that his father yelling, "You do something like that again, I'll beat you to death!"

Five years later, A.J. committed that most unpardonable of all sins in the eyes of his father. The boy and some friends were hot-rodding around Houston in A.J.'s 1950 Ford when the police spotted them and gave chase. A friend was doing the driving, A.J. says, and he asked him to pull over. When the other boy kept gunning it, Foyt says, "I jumped out of the car." The boys eventually ditched the Ford, and the police picked it up. When the old man asked his son about the car—Tony had bought it for him and was still making payments on it—that was when A.J. did it. He lied to his father. "It was stolen," A.J. said. Of course, the police soon found out what had happened, called the boys in and advised them that their fathers had been summoned.

Given a choice, A.J. would have opted for the gallows. "Just put me in the reform school," he said. "I don't want to see my daddy. I lied to him. He always said he'd beat me to death for lying. *Unmercifully!* Please, just let me go. . . ."

Tony arrived at the station house with a face of stone. He listened as the officer explained that they were not filing charges against A.J., and they were going to release him. "He's a good boy," the officer said. "Even though he lied to you."

Tony glanced over at his frozen son. "That's right," Tony said. "He lied to me."

A.J. began to say his prayers and the police answered. They were releasing him, they told Tony, on one condition: "That you will not lay a hand on him."

The old man thought about that a moment but finally agreed. Recalls A.J.: "I thought, '*Thank you, Lord!*' We got in his car. I can still remember it, '49 Mercury, metallic-green convertible with a Cadillac motor. I got in the right side. I thought, 'Any minute, I'm going to spit all my teeth out. He's going to bust me upside my head.'" Tony never laid a hand on his son. What he did, if you were 16 years old and you loved cars, was worse.

"You know that car you've got?" Tony said.

"Yessir. . . ."

"It's going to sit in the driveway for *one* year."

"Daddy. . . ."

"Shut up! One year. Every day after school, you catch that bus and be at my shop at 3:30."

And there the Ford stayed, idle in the driveway while the old man worked to pay it off, and nothing could persuade him to reduce the sentence. Tony Foyt was old school, a quiet, strong, stubborn Texan who brooked no nonsense and catered no small talk. Says Tim Delrose, a long-time family friend, "If Tony said something and A.J. asked him, 'What did you say?' Tony would say, 'You heard me.'" The old man worked obsessively. One evening he was laying a septic field at the ranch. A.J.'s crew had the cars all set to drive to a race up in Bryan, Texas. They were getting anxious. Tony wouldn't be rushed.

"It's getting too dark, Daddy," said A.J. "We're not leaving till it's done," the old man said. "Get the cars, A.J., and bring' em around and shine the lights on me." They all worked into the night, in the glinting headlights. "We finished it," says Delrose.

The old man's extended family adored him. A.J. and Lucy raised three children, all of them grown up now—Anthony Joseph III (Tony), 35, who trains a barnful of racehorses in Kentucky; Terry, 33, a housewife in Houston whose first child, Larry, from an earlier marriage, was adopted by Lucy and A.J.; and Jerry, 28, a graduate of the University of Texas, who is vice-president of his father's Honda dealership near Houston. "My grandfather didn't raise us, but he took care of us if we ever needed anything," young Tony says of his namesake. "They really don't make 'em like him anymore. If he liked you, he would absolutely go out of his way for you."

Foyt viewed himself and his parents as a kind of team, bonded by the hardscrabble life they had endured together in the Heights, in the days they had to scratch to make things go. Early in Foyt's career, when he was out there racing from one bullring to another, sleeping in his car and washing at gasoline stations, he found himself stranded and penniless with a midget car in Florida. He called his parents in the Heights, and they broke the piggy bank and went down to Western Union. "My parents rolled 50 dollars' worth of pennies and sent me the money to get home," A.J. says.

Foyt always had this vision of how he would claw his way to the top, earning fame and fortune on the way, and then set his parents up in easy retirement—his mother fishing forever in Nanny's Lake and his father running the lights and hammering the nails. And the fame came fast enough to A.J. Foyt—first in the dirt cars, the midgets and the sprint cars, and then the Indy Cars and the stockers and, finally, the sports cars. Foyt was 26 years old when he won his first Indy, in 1961, but by then he was known throughout the sport as this hard-charging, bandanna-flying, damn-the-torpedoes kid who could drive the paint off the midgets and the sprint cars.

"He was the best midget car racer ever," says George Bignotti, Foyt's chief mechanic when he won at Indy in 1961 and '64, who raced midgets with A.J. beginning in '59. "Start him in the back of 12 cars and drop the flag, and in five or ten laps he'd be leading the race. He *wanted* to win. Very aggressive. He was fantastic in the midgets."

Those were the days when dirt-track racing was a major element in motor sports, when even the big Indy-type cars raced over the dirt and shot out rooster tails of dirt and stone behind them. Says Foyt: "Some of the hardest races I ever had—been so tired and beat up with blood running out of my eye and all—have been sprint races on the dirt. Got out of there many a time and there'd be just solid blood on my shoulder and around my face. They'd run those big old knobby tires, and they just dug and throwed stones and dirt, just like a guy shot you with a shotgun. Hands as raw as hamburger. Now that hurt. God, I'd like to see some of the Indy Car drivers today get in a sprint car and I have a set of knobs and I'd just sweep by 'em. I guarantee you. I have had my face shield and my goggles knocked clean off my face, sheared right off my helmet—*tat-tat-tat-tat*—just like a machine gun."

"Watching Foyt on the dirt was like watching a concert," says Cecil Taylor, a car owner and mechanic who first saw him race in 1956. "Artistry in motion. It was a beautiful thing to watch. He'd be running fast and be sitting back in the car like in a rocking chair, all relaxed and everything under control, with those clods flying up. Those were *men* who drove those cars, in those days; they weren't boys. And A.J., he was the Man."

He was the Man through two decades, the 1960s and into the '70s, the years he developed a constituency of racing fans who saw him then, as they still see him today, as a folk hero and pioneer, a kind of throwback. The perception is central to his enduring appeal as the tough, rugged individualist building his cars and driving them himself; the mean, self-reliant loner doing battle against the Organization Men, the Roger Penskes and the Carl Haases; the aging, outspoken guy taking on the aerodynamicists and engineers and pale little men with computers.

They saw him when he was the Man. They saw him in Langhorne that day when he was racing on the lead with three or four laps to run and a bolt fell out of the radius rod—a part of the car's suspension—and the rod flew right up next to him. "And Foyt sticks his hand out," Bignotti recalls, "and gets the radius rod in one hand, and he comes by and has his knee on the steering wheel to keep it straight. The sonofagun drove that car and won the race, holding the radius rod with one hand and driving the car with the other. The people all saw that."

They watched him, with a touch of awe, when he raced his dirt car on the pavement against all those Indy pavement cars in Milwaukee, in 1965, just a day after he'd won a dirt race with it in Springfield, Illinois. "He went out and put the dirt car on the pole," says driver Johnny Rutherford. "That was unheard of. Over cars designed *specifically* for pavement. It endeared him to the masses." Particularly when the masses saw him nearly pull it off: "Come the start," says Foyt, "and I'm sitting waaaay up here and everybody else is sittin' waaaay down there. After every yellow flag I'd take the lead. Accelerate past everybody. Then they'd run me down. Finally blistered a right rear tire. Damn near won the race. Ran second."

And they saw him crush his bones at Elkhart Lake and remember him saying, "Fire can make a dead man move." They stood in horror in DuQuoin in 1972, the day he was leading the dirt track race by a lap, with only five to go, and he pitted for a squirt of fuel and the fuel hose broke loose and doused his head with two gallons of alcohol-nitro mixture. "I figured it would evaporate," Foyt says. "The exhaust pipes coming out the side, sometimes they burp fire, and when they did, I went up in flames like a Buddhist monk. I'd already left the pits, and I tried to jump from the car because I was burning, goddam, and when I jumped out of the car, I didn't have it stopped, and I fell in front of my left rear wheel, so it run over my left foot and it twisted and flipped me in the air, and I was still burning. I knew the infield had a lake in it, and so I'm trying to run for the lake, in a panic, and I'm limping on my ankle, like a horse with a broken leg, and my daddy was running after me with a fire extinguisher, and as I hit the inside guardrail, I fell over it, and my daddy squirted me with the extinguisher and put the fire out. Whew! My face was burned, and the docs told me, 'You won't have no beard.' And I said, 'Who gives a shit?'"

They saw him beat on his cars with hammers, in a rage, and snarl at the press and stomp through the pits. They heard him say whatever came to mind. He was trying to qualify a March chassis in 1983 at Indy and going nowhere. The public address announcer asked him what the problem was, and Foyt blurted, "This car I'm driving is just a tub a shit." Robin Miller, a sportswriter for *The Indianapolis Star*, recalls looking over and seeing the reaction of Robin Herd, a co-founder of March Engineering: "Herd is sitting on the pit wall with his head in his hands. The Great American Legend just called his car a tub of shit." They all knew how Foyt and Bignotti used to carry on, fighting and shouting at one another. They sometimes fought so much that they forgot to celebrate. Rutherford recalls a time when Foyt, after winning a feature race in a sprint car that Bignotti had built, pulled into the pits, took off his helmet, threw it in the seat and yelled, "Goddammit, George, I'm getting tired of driving my ass off to make you look good. . . ."

For years Foyt has been the most intimidating presence in motor racing, and there are few drivers out there who have not felt at least a gust of his passing heat. In 1982, in his rookie year at Indy, Bobby Rahal was coming out of a turn with Foyt right behind him. "I didn't cut him off," says Rahal, "but I think he expected me to move out of his way, and I didn't. And he shook his fist at me as he went by. But, you know, you're nobody unless you've had a fist shaken at you by A.J. Foyt."

As volatile as he can be outside a race car, no driver has ever seen him lose the handle on himself in a race car. "He tried to be, and was, very intimidating," says Mario Andretti, 51, Foyt's most enduring rival. "And I've had my run-ins with him. A lot of them. But I'll tell you one thing: I've never, ever, *ever* seen him do anything foolish out on a racetrack. Never. I've seen occasions in a race where he could have gotten carried away, but I have never seen his emotions get the best of him."

To be sure, most drivers who have known him long do not buy into the man's image as a distant, fearsome, unapproachable presence in the garages. Like his father before him, Foyt chooses his friends sparingly, but he will do most anything for those he chooses. All these years later, Al Unser Sr. still can't figure why Foyt picked him. It was 1965, Unser's rookie year at Indy, and the last of his cars had blown up and he was resigned to not making the show. And there, in Unser's garage, appeared Foyt, who had already won Indy twice and had two fast cars ready for the race.

"You want to run my backup car?" A.J. asked. "Think it over and come to my garage."

Unser followed him like a puppy through clapboard rows of garages that made up Gasoline Alley. He finished ninth that year in Foyt's car, and he went on to win the 500 four times in the next 22 years, tying Foyt for most Indy victories. "I've often wondered why the man did a thing like that," Unser says. "It has meant a lot to me over the years. I wasn't anything, and there were experienced drivers standing in line to get in that backup car. For some reason he picked me. I still don't know why. He's just like that. He looks at somebody and likes them."

Rutherford was another. He was running an Indy Car in Phoenix in 1968, and he hit an oil slick and then a fence and spun to a stop. Andretti and Roger McCluskey hit the slick, too. McCluskey's car spun Rutherford's sideways, and Andretti's slammed into the right side of Rutherford's. It burst into flames. Rutherford put his hands on the sides of the cockpit to push himself out, and the leather glove on his right hand shrunk instantly in the ferocious heat of the burning fuel. He pulled the glove from his hand. Much of the skin on his fingers slid off with the glove, the skin turning inside out and hanging like tubes from his hand. Foyt came running from the pits and looked at Rutherford and hollered, "Goddamn!"

"A.J., my feet are burning," Rutherford screamed. The laces on his shoes were smoldering like wicks. Foyt dropped to his knees and, with a fingernail, raked down the burning laces until they popped open. Turning, he saw McCluskey lying on a stretcher, slightly dazed. Foyt, an immensely strong man, picked McCluskey up off the litter and handed him to a medic. "You're not hurt that bad, Roger," A.J. said. He laid Rutherford on the empty stretcher and followed the ambulance to the hospital. When the doctor finally showed up, Foyt bellowed, "Where the hell you been?"

"I was mowing my yard," the doctor said.

Rutherford thought Foyt might lay the doctor out right there. "If looks could kill . . . ," he said.

Foyt never left Rutherford that day. He helped wheel him out of the hospital after Rutherford's burns had been treated. He helped him into the car. And he was driving him back to the hotel when Rutherford, nauseated from medication, started to get sick. Foyt pulled over, jumped out, whipped open the passenger door, and then held Rutherford's forehead as he vomited into a ditch. "That O.K.?" Foyt kept asking. "You feeling better?"

That was nearly 25 years ago, but Rutherford still thinks about Phoenix. "I'll never forget that, ever," he says. "Lot of people classify him as an S.O.B., but he's far from it. He's a pussy cat. With people he knows who are in need or in trouble. . . ."

As Tony Foyt was. He was dying in the winter of '83. For nearly 20 years, since A.J. and Bignotti had gone their separate ways, the old man had been his son's chief mechanic. Together, with cars they built back in Houston, they had won the Indy 500 twice, in 1967 and '77. "They fought with each other, they cussed each other, and they went everywhere together," says Delrose. "They drove down all the roads. How many times do you see a thing like that between a father and son? But they had that."

Through the years, Tony was the only figure of authority who could command his son's undivided respect, the only man who ever demanded and set limits for him, the only man who could ever stand up to him. A.J. has a galactic ego—"It swelled up too many years ago and stayed there," says Bobby Unser—and at times it is suggested that the way he carries on is like a prolonged case of the Terrible Twos. Taylor, who works frequently on Foyt's pit crew, recalls the aftermath of a frustrating practice session at Indy in the late '60s. When the car was rolled back into the garage, A.J.

threw a tantrum that stunned even his crew to silence. Tony came forward and grabbed his son and slammed him up against a wall. "What the hell's wrong with you, boy?" he demanded. "You gone crazy?"

Only Tony could have gotten away with that. "He was the only guy I ever saw that could really deal with A.J.," says Taylor. "What A.J. probably didn't realize is that Tony was not only his father, but probably his best friend, his mentor, his team and financial manager, just a whole lot of people rolled into one." "Tony was the rock," says Delrose. "His dad controlled him. He'd fire at the drop of a hat if anybody said anything against A.J. They loved each other. But they just didn't show it."

Tony never told A.J. how proud he was of his son's race car driving. Not one word of praise in all the years they were together. Not once in all the victory lanes they ever visited. Not even after that final victory at the Brickyard. Says A.J., "After I won, the crew was drinking and blowing their horns on how they did this and how they did that, and I said, 'Well, Daddy, what do you think? Did I do a pretty good job today?'"

Tony turned and grinned. "I don't know about good," the old man said. "You did fair. . . ."

"That's the best words I ever heard from you," said his son.

In the winter of 1983, Foyt resisted all entreaties that he run in the 24-hour race at Daytona. He hadn't driven an endurance race since he and Dan Gurney had taken Le Mans in 1967. He did not want to leave his dying father, but Tony had insisted. "There ain't a damn thing you can do sitting around here," the old man said. "Go down there and have some fun. Get out of here."

Reluctantly, A.J. left. When the car he was supposed to drive broke down, another car owner, Preston Henn, urged him to jump in his Porsche 935. "I've never driven a Porsche," A.J. protested. "I don't even know the shift pattern."

There was a derelict Porsche sitting nearby, and Henn persuaded Foyt to sit behind the wheel and learn the pattern. With Bob Wollek as his co-driver, Foyt raced to victory at Daytona. After the grueling event Foyt remembers thinking what he had never thought before: *If I never won another race, I wouldn't care.*

It all seemed so quick and unfair. So quick that Tony forgot to put away the hammer, the one he left above A.J.'s head, and so unfair that it would grieve and trouble the son for years. "And a lot of times I get tears in my eyes," A.J. would say. "I know it's silly. But it's like I lost something that I never really had. You know, it's kind of like a dream. Am I in a dream? Am

I going to wake up or what? I guess I lost it all so quick. . . . We all worked our butts off, and when my parents can finally turn around and have life easy, everything was just swept out from under 'em."

It left A.J. trapped in an unending search. . . .

Not long before the old man died, in a hospital room in Houston, Tony's doctor, Gary Friedman, gave two generations of Foyts his final notice at bedside: "If you have anything to say to each other, or you're holding back, I think maybe you ought to say it. I'll wait outside."

Friedman left and A.J. began to bite his lip.

"I've assigned the accounts over to you," Tony said. "You know everything. You know what I want you to do. What do you think?"

A.J. could hardly speak. "Well, Daddy, things aren't working like we hoped."

"I know it," said Tony.

"You have anything you want to talk about?"

"No, not really," Tony said.

"Well, I don't really have much to say. If anything ever happens, I'll do what I can to try to carry on."

"I know that," Tony said, "But don't worry about things."

"Are you *sure* you ain't got something to tell me?"

"No," the old man said. "I've told you everything."

August 1991

———————————

Foyt drove his last Indy 500 in 1992, a record 35th straight, and took his final lap at the Brickyard a year later, when everyone thought he was set to try to qualify for No. 36. Climbing from his car, teary-eyed, he said, "There comes a time . . ." Foyt did not retire on his chuffing bulldozer. He joined the new Indy Racing League in 1996 as a race-car owner, and already twice has won the IRL championship—with drivers Scott Sharp in 1996 and Kenny Brack in 1998. Brack then won the Indy 500 for Foyt in '99. A year later, A.J. formed a NASCAR Winston Cup team out of Moorseville, North Carolina, and enlisted his youngest son, Larry, to drive the cars and manage the team.

THE LONESOME END

By standing apart, Bill Carpenter became an All-America at West Point and one of the country's finest soldiers

DEAR COLERIDGE — DID YOU SEIZE THE OPPORTUNITY
OF SEEING KOSCIUSKO WHILE HE WAS AT BRISTOL?
I NEVER SAW A HERO; I WONDER HOW THEY LOOK.
— *Charles Lamb, in a letter to Samuel Taylor Coleridge,*
June 24, 1797

At about half past three on the afternoon of June 9, 1966, on an exploding finger of land in a dense bamboo jungle of South Vietnam's Central Highlands, Capt. Bill Carpenter barked into his radio-telephone the message that would echo through his life as a combat soldier. "We're being overrun!" Carpenter called to the air spotter circling above the battlefield. "Bring it right on top of me. Put it right on my smoke."

From the east an Air Force fighter, laden with napalm, swept over the treetops toward Carpenter's position.

So it was there—with his company trapped on that ridgeline, pinned down among the raking machine guns and exploding hand grenades, and now nearly surrounded by North Vietnamese soldiers—that William Stanley Carpenter arrived at the defining moment of his professional life. A 28-year-old company commander, he was seven years and half a world removed from West Point, where he had captained the Army football team of 1959, his second and final season as the Black Knights' storied Lonesome End, that remote, hauntingly romantic figure who stood apart from Army huddles, out near the sidelines, facing his teammates with his arms akimbo, picking up signals from the footwork of quarterback Joe Caldwell.

Suddenly, there he was again, surfacing this day on a far more perilous field and surely more alone than he had ever been and ever would be—as only a combat infantry leader can know the meaning of alone—caught in the jungle with a brave but crippled company of soldiers. Enemy mortars were so close that he could hear the rounds scraping as they dropped down the tubes, and through the bamboo he could hear the North Vietnamese chattering. This fight was but a small piece of a larger engagement known as the Battle of Toumorong, the brunt of which had been carried one bloody day after another by the First Battalion, 327th Airborne Infantry Regiment, 101st Airborne Division. Led by Maj. David Hackworth, who would soon become the most decorated soldier in the U.S. Army, that battalion was in terrier pursuit of the 24th North Vietnamese Regiment.

On the late morning of June 9, the Screaming Eagles of Carpenter's Charlie Company, Second Battalion, 502nd Airborne Infantry Regiment, were ordered north to set up a blocking position ahead of Hackworth's advance. One of Carpenter's four platoons had been detached the day before on another mission, leaving Carpenter with only three platoons, or about 90 men. By early afternoon, as Charlie Company moved up a slight rise, the head of the lead platoon, Lieut. William Jordan, radioed to Carpenter that he could hear Vietnamese voices 200 meters away, down along a streambed below the rise.

At around 2:30 P.M. Carpenter called his platoon leaders together. Using the name by which enemy soldiers were known, Jordan asked him, "Do you want to establish the blocking position or do you want to hunt Charlie?"

"Let's hunt Charlie," Carpenter replied. Turning to Lieut. Jim Baker, one of the two other platoon leaders, Carpenter told him what to do if Jordan needed help: "Bring your platoon around to the left of Jordan." He ordered Lieut. Bryan Robbins, the leader of the other platoon, to wait to move wherever he was needed.

Returning to his platoon, Jordan set out for the voices down toward the creek. His lead squad was approaching the creek bed when several North Vietnamese soldiers materialized out of the bamboo growth along the bank. One of them, carrying a roll of toilet paper, turned his back on the creek and squatted to relieve himself. The others were bathing, or scrubbing clothes and utensils. The Americans opened fire, instantly killing the squatter and either wounding or killing the rest, the survivors scrambling up into the bush.

So the battle began. Carpenter would learn soon enough that he had roused a terrible beast. "We had surprised them, and for the first 15 or 20 minutes it was a cakewalk," he recalls. "Most of the fire was ours. As the fire built up, I knew I had found more than stragglers on the tail end of a regiment. I could hear 50-caliber machine-gun fire, and I didn't have any 50-caliber machine guns. Then, when the mortars kicked in, I knew we were in the middle of a regiment. I didn't have any mortars, either."

North Vietnamese soldiers were soon swarming around the narrow mountain finger on which Charlie Company had deployed to do battle. Robbins heard Jordan on the radio: "I'm taking fire. I'm pinned down. I can't move." Carpenter ordered Baker to swing his platoon around Jordan's left in an attempt to flank the fire that was pinning down Jordan's men from the front. Baker had just wheeled his men around Jordan's left when they were flattened under murderous automatic-weapons fire from their own left. Crippled and bloodied, Baker's platoon was now pinned down itself.

Then, suddenly, intersecting fire from several heavy and light machine guns began raking Carpenter's command position. He ordered Robbins and his platoon up the ridge, hoping to relieve the pressure from over there, but, recalls Robbins, "all of a sudden we got hit. We couldn't maneuver. Carpenter was pinned down on our left. They were really getting hit over there."

All three platoons had wounded men, so withdrawal was unimaginable to Carpenter. "When you've got a bunch of guys wounded, you're not going anyplace," Carpenter says. "At least I'm not going anyplace, leaving wounded kids around, and that was the crux of the whole thing."

So Carpenter stuck. From Baker's left the North Vietnamese had just launched their first assault, lobbing grenades and attacking behind bursts of automatic-weapons fire, one of which killed Baker instantly. Seconds later Baker's platoon sergeant died when two grenades exploded near him. The platoon was leaderless. "There was no way to figure out what was happening over there," says Carpenter. "They were only 30 meters away, but you couldn't see anything in the bamboo."

Then came a chilling, nameless voice calling Carpenter on Baker's radio: "We're all dead. We've been completely overrun. I'm the only one alive. We're all dead." The voice broke off.

"I thought I'd lost one whole platoon," Carpenter recalls. Enemy soldiers now made a second assault, this one against Jordan's front. Carpenter began to see the North Vietnamese in and among Jordan and his men, some of whom dropped back to form a tight defensive perimeter around the command post. No one experienced the surreal terror and chaos of the unfolding drama more vividly than Mike Baldinger, a medic, who was dashing frantically around the position answering cries for help.

"I knew we were surrounded, because everywhere I went on the perimeter, I could hear [Vietnamese] voices," Baldinger recalls. "You could see them running past you in the bamboo. I remember working on a wounded soldier named Marcus Hurley. I was lying next to him and trying to put albumin in his arm with a needle. I was holding the bottle up in the air when it got shot out of my hand. I started to reach back for another when this sergeant yelled, 'Doc, look out! Grenade!'"

Baldinger glanced back and saw a potato masher bouncing toward him, and a North Vietnamese soldier about 100 feet away. Baldinger pushed himself up against Hurley's body to shield him from the blast. The grenade exploded, driving shrapnel into Baldinger's back. Glancing around, he saw the sergeant and the North Vietnamese soldier lying dead. He returned to Hurley. "I was trying to stick the needle into a vein when I heard some firing right on top of me," Baldinger says. "I turned around again, and an NVA soldier was about 30 feet away. He was walking backward and spraying an AK-47. I didn't have my rifle with me—I needed both hands to work—so I took my .45 out of the holster and shot him twice in the back. They were running around all over. They were like ghosts."

There was really only one thing left to do. About a mile and a half away, Carpenter's battalion commander, Lieut. Col. Hank (the Gunfighter) Emerson, listened anxiously on his radio-telephone as the circumference of Carpenter's world grew smaller and more violent. Emerson had been Carpenter's tactical officer at West Point, and he had come to admire the young captain so much as a soldier that when Carpenter returned to Vietnam for a second tour of combat duty, Emerson asked for him. Yet the Gunfighter never thought more of him than he did at that hour, when he heard Carpenter talking coolly to the aerial spotter.

Carpenter: "They're in real close to us. They're in among us."

Spotter: "I have two birds on station. If you have a target, we can bring it in."

Carpenter did not know what kind of ordnance the planes were carrying, but he reacted instinctively, popping a yellow smoke grenade and heaving it 15 meters to his front. He dropped to the ground and watched the cloud as it curled up through the canopy of trees. "Put it right on my smoke!" Carpenter said.

Listening, Emerson was stunned. "I said, 'Holy crap! He's called it in on himself,'" recalls Emerson, now a retired three-star general. "Mind-blowing."

Emerson's voice broke over the radio: "If I don't see you again, I'm going to put you in for the Medal of Honor!"

"That's bullshit!" Carpenter yelled back.

The napalm canister tumbled end over end from the jet into the bamboo thickets, into the yellow smoke, exploding in one apocalyptic roar of wind and fire—whoosh!—as flames sucked the breath out of the jungle and crackled through the burning bamboo tops. "The world turned orange," says Baldinger. "Hot and orange."

And the battlefield, of an instant, turned eerily quiet. "A lot of NVA got caught in it," says Robbins, now a retired lieutenant colonel. "I saw NVA running up the ridge, on fire. That napalm strike, I'm convinced, saved our lives."

Not another shot was fired at Charlie Company for 30 minutes, giving Carpenter time to gather his wounded and dig in around a tighter perimeter. By the time relief arrived late that night, his company had lost only eight men, none to napalm. Of course, the instant the Saigon press corps got word of Carpenter's act—with Emerson, true to his word, immediately putting him in for the nation's highest award for bravery—reporters winged north to Dak To, the city nearest to the scene, and feted him in a rush of dispatches.

What made the story so compelling, to be sure, was less the act itself than the man who had performed it. Over a June 9 article that began on page 1, the *New York Times* ran a headline that set the tone for all the lavish coverage that followed: A DARING CAPTAIN SAVES A COMPANY. The subhead made the telling connection: EX-ARMY FOOTBALL STAR, IN VIETNAM, CALLS FOR AN AIR STRIKE ON OWN POSITION.

At military bases like Fort Benning, in Georgia, the home of the Army Infantry School, where Carpenter had earned his patches as an airborne Ranger, he became not only the object of admiring colloquies but also the source of debates on all the implications, from the tactical to the moral, of calling one's own fire on one's own self. If he had always had a commanding presence, with that mystique spun from his exploits as the Lonesome End—that blue-eyed, flattopped All-America who on one Saturday, with one arm strapped to his side to protect a dislocated shoulder, ran around catching passes one-handed—he was now thrust into a domain so rare as to be quite exclusively his own. The classic American football hero had become, in a stroke, an even more triumphant figure in the real-world business of infantry combat, with which football, in its wildest institutional fantasies, most identifies. Carpenter never talked about his days as the

Lonesome End or of that desperate afternoon outside Dak To, but together they gave him an aura, as some would call it, that made him about as close to untouchable as a military man can be.

Carpenter knew early on where he wanted to go, and his life as a soldier grew out of the most wounding trauma of his childhood years. He was born in Woodbury, New Jersey, in 1937, the only child of a semipro football player and car salesman, William Sr., and his wife, Helen. "I never got up during the night with that child," says Helen. "His daddy always did: 'You have him all day; he's mine at night.'"

After the Army drafted William in 1944, at age 36, he and the boy exchanged letters frequently. On April 11, 1945, one month before the war ended in Europe, Carpenter was killed by a German artillery round. The boy was 7 1/2. "I was worried about him," says Helen. "I knew he was griev-ing inwardly. He wasn't eating like he should, he wasn't playing like he should, he wasn't himself."

Helen remarried in 1947—gentle Clifford Dunn would soon become the comptroller at the Philadelphia Navy Yard—and the man and the boy became like father and son. Carpenter recalls listening to Army football games on the radio in the days of Blanchard and Davis, and those games drew him toward football and the Point. At Springfield High, outside Philadelphia, he was a sprinter with 9.9 speed in the 100-yard dash and, at 6' 2", 200 pounds, a halfback in football with strength and sure hands.

A score of colleges pursued him as a player, but all it took was one visit to West Point and the issue was settled. Those were still glory days for Army football, when the Army-Navy game was treated like Armageddon and Army football heroes glowed in the dark. In the season of 1958, Car-penter's junior year, no player glowed brighter than halfback Pete Dawkins—captain of the corps of cadets, captain of an undefeated team (8–0–1) and winner of the Heisman Trophy. Carpenter, not a man to mince words, says, "I think Pete was vastly overrated. There were seven or eight players who were better. Bill Rowe and Bob Novogratz were great linemen, and Bob Anderson was a better halfback." End Don Usry, he says, was the team's best all-around player.

Army was ranked third nationally in '58. Pittsburgh held the Black Knights to a 14–14 tie, but Army whipped Penn State 26–0 and Notre Dame 14–2. That year coach Earl (Red) Blaik introduced him as the Lonely End. Sportswriter Stanley Woodward was the first to use the term in print, and it gradually evolved into the Lonesome End over Blaik's protestations.

Blaik decided to keep Carpenter out in the flat during huddles because he was lining up as a "far flanker," and Blaik feared the young man would wear out dashing back and forth between plays. In '58 Carpenter tied the Army record for receptions in a season, with 22. He gained 453 yards and scored two touchdowns, and on the train ride home after Army had licked Navy 22–6 in the year's final game, the Cadets elected Carpenter their captain for 1959.

It is not a season fondly remembered. Cursed by one injury after another, Army went 4–4–1 under Dale Hall, who had replaced the retired Blaik. Carpenter was everyone's All-America that season, catching 43 passes for 591 yards, both single-season Army records that would last until 1970. His finest hour came against Oklahoma when he grabbed six passes for 67 yards and ran back four kickoffs for 65 yards, playing with one arm strapped down so that he couldn't raise it above his dislocated shoulder. Carpenter's remarkable athletic career at the Point did not end until the spring of 1960, when he was voted an All-America defenseman in lacrosse a year after he first picked up a stick. "He was like a gazelle," says Ace Adams, his coach. "Probably the best pure athlete that I ever coached. Just plain, rawboned athletic ability."

What Anderson recalls most fondly about Carpenter, his best friend at the Point, has nothing to do with sports. He and Carpenter had made a pact to raise some hell after graduation, but Anderson realized before their senior year even began that those days were not to be. One balmy night the two were sitting on the porch of the boathouse at Camp Buckner, where cadets train during the summer. "Andy, see that girl over there?" Carpenter said. An attractive young woman was passing in review. "I'm going to marry her someday." Toni Vigliotti, a model from nearby Central Valley, was dating a plebe at the time.

"He pursued me," she says. "He really did. He pursued me."

She got her first glimpse of Carpenter's nature when she visited his home in Springfield a few months later. "After we had dinner, the town fire alarm went off," says Toni. "Bill dashed out the door. The next day in the paper was a picture of Bill on the roof of a house with an ax in his hands, ready to break out this second-floor window. The caption said something about 'the Lonesome End working to save someone's life.'"

She married him anyway. In fact, they got engaged the night before he graduated, in 1960, and made plans to marry in June of the following year. But one night in the summer of '60, Toni received a moony phone call from him while he was training at Fort Benning, beseeching her to move up the date. "I'm really lonely," he said. "I need a wife."

They were wed on Jan. 2, 1961. A month later the young second lieutenant became a platoon leader at Fort Campbell, in Kentucky, and set about to make himself a troop commander. Even as a young officer Carpenter began resisting the brass. That fall, when the division commander at Fort Campbell, a two-star general, told him he had to play football for the base team, Carpenter refused. The general was leaving the command, and he did not force the issue. However, the two-star who followed him did. In the fall of 1962 Carpenter was ordered to give up his company command and play football. He became furious. "Football for me was over with and done," he says. "I wanted to go on and be something else."

He ultimately yielded to the brass and played that year, but he vowed never to do it again. Sure enough, the following spring he was ordered to give up his new command and rejoin the team. Playing football for the base team was cushy duty, but Carpenter wanted no part of it. He had been drafted by the Baltimore Colts, and he was thinking that he would rather leave the service than play service ball. He called his assignment officer at the infantry branch, in Washington, D.C., and said, "Look, if I am going to be forced to play football, I'm going to do it for a hell of a lot more than $200 a month." That was lieutenant's pay.

"Where do you want to go?" the officer asked.

"Anywhere I'm not forced to play football," he said.

"How would you like to go to Vietnam?"

So in the spring of 1963 he went to Southeast Asia as the adviser to a South Vietnamese army unit. On that first tour he was twice wounded—once by shrapnel and earlier by a VC bullet; as he was setting fire to a stand of sugarcane, he surprised a Viet Cong soldier, who shot him in the right arm. "I threw three grenades at him lefthanded, emptied my carbine into his foxhole and then emptied my pistol," he says. "Jesus, I was mad."

Home by June 1964, Carpenter returned two years later, just in time to climb that finger near Dak To. For his extraordinary gambit there he did not receive the Medal of Honor—he got the nation's second-highest award for valor, the Distinguished Service Cross—and he lost his company command. Gen. William Westmoreland, the commander of all U.S. forces in Vietnam, pulled him out of the field and made him his aide-de-camp. "I thought he was going to get himself killed," Westmoreland recalls. "It was kind of a reckless affair. I'm not saying it critically. It was a battlefield decision that had to be made. I was a little shocked by it."

Carpenter liked Westy well enough, but not the job. Most rising young captains would have considered being named an aide to Westmoreland a plum assignment, but within a week of joining the staff Carpenter began urging Westmoreland to release him. After a few weeks of this steady pestering, Westmoreland said to him, "Only ask me once a week from now on." So Carpenter set aside every Tuesday morning to spring the question.

"Can I leave yet, sir?"

"No."

Yet only four months into his supposed six-month stretch, Westmoreland let him leave. Carpenter never did get his command back, but he did not stop making news. On Feb. 1, 1967, a C–123 transport plane in which he was flying made a belly landing at Tan Son Nhut airport in Saigon. A major suffered a broken ankle in the crash, and Carpenter carried him on his shoulders from the plane. CARPENTER HERO AGAIN AS HE RESCUES MAJOR read the headline in the *New York Times*. As much as he wished to, Carpenter never made it back to Vietnam after leaving in the spring of '67, and only years later did he discover in his file a directive issued by the Army Chief of Staff, stating that he never be assigned there again. Westmoreland's fear—that Carpenter was going to get himself killed—had ultimately resonated at the highest levels of the U.S. Army.

If by his instincts Carpenter had always been a troop commander, then his experience at Dak To clearly enriched and deepened them. Throughout his next 26 years in the service, all the way up to his retirement last year as a three-star general, Carpenter worked strenuously at ducking assignments that would take him to the Pentagon and fought to train and command troops for as long as he could. "I've never met a senior officer who did not say, 'The soldier has to come first,'" says Terry Roche, a retired full colonel who was one of Carpenter's garrison commanders at Fort Drum, in upstate New York. "But a lot of that's only rhetoric. Bill felt it in the marrow of his bones. He never, never strayed from that."

Indeed, if there is a single cord that runs through Carpenter's career, it is his affection for foot soldiers. "I like what they stand for," Carpenter says. "I like what they do. I like to listen to them talk and laugh. I like to listen to their tales. I like to be around them. I just like them."

Ultimately what he left behind when he retired was the belief, shared by a number of senior officers who knew him, that the Army had lost a leader virtually without peer. "He is, in my view, the finest soldier-leader that America has produced since the Korean War," says Hackworth, now a writer on military affairs. "And the fact that he didn't get a fourth star tells me about the sickness we have in the Army. He was the Lonesome End throughout his military career, and the reason he didn't get a fourth star was that he didn't schmooze with the brass. Carpenter is the kind of guy who cared about the guys down below and didn't really give a rat's ass about the guys at the top. He's a national treasure. The big, quiet American. Gary Cooper. We just don't make those kind anymore."

During his entire career Carpenter had only one tour in the Pentagon, from 1976 to '78, as the senior military assistant to Clifford Alexander, Secretary of the Army under Jimmy Carter. The bureaucratic wheel-spinning, the egos, and the infighting left him cold. The Pentagon is where fast-track officers routinely stop on their way up, but Carpenter wanted no part of it.

When the job of director for operations of the Joint Chiefs of Staff was due to come open in early '88, one of Carpenter's mentors, Gen. Robert RisCassi, ordered him to go and be interviewed. Carpenter was a two-star general at the time, and this was a three-star job. So Carpenter walked into the office of the Chairman of the Joint Chiefs, Adm. William Crowe, whose celebrated collection of hats lined the shelves of one wall. Carpenter had a reputation for saying precisely what was on his mind, and Crowe learned this quickly enough. "I don't want the job," he told Crowe right off. "I'm not interested in working in Washington. I'm not interested in a promotion if it means coming to Washington. If you say I have to come, I'll come, but I won't be a happy camper."

"Thank you very much," the admiral said. Then, gesturing toward those shelves, he asked, "How do you like my hat collection?" End of interview.

Carpenter had been just as blunt in refusing to get a master's degree, another accustomed step for officers on the ascent. In 1970, fresh out of Command and General Staff College, at Fort Leavenworth, in Kansas, Carpenter had received a call from an aide to Sam Walker, who at the time was a brigadier general and the commandant at West Point. "We're sending you to Purdue for a year to get your master's," said the aide. "Then you're coming to West Point to teach."

To Carpenter, the cloistered world of West Point had about as much to do with the real Army as did the Pentagon. "I'm not going to West Point," said Carpenter, then a young major. "And you can send me to Purdue, but at the end of the year I won't have a master's degree, because I'm not going to class."

Carpenter saw himself as a soldier, not a scholar. He never did go to Purdue, and he never got a master's. In 1975, when as a lieutenant colonel he took command of a battalion in Korea, he found a unit in chaos and a new brigade commander, Col. Andrew Cooley, who told him simply, "Take charge and straighten it out."

This was the new volunteer Army, and the straightening took some doing. "No vehicles worked," Carpenter recalls. "There were fights in the officers' club every night. There was a whole generation of lieutenants who thought that it was O.K. to throw their buddies through plate-glass windows. Half the platoon leaders were shacked up in town."

Soldiers were running around with little silver patches on their coveralls. "What do those mean?" Carpenter asked a soldier.

"Each bullet is a case of VD," replied the soldier.

By the time Carpenter left a year later, he had brought order and discipline to the ranks, and Cooley ultimately saw a rare gift at work during tactical maneuvers—the athlete's sense of timing and anticipation, of seeing the whole field and what everybody was doing on it. "It all blended together in a natural way," says Cooley, now a retired two-star. Upon Carpenter's departure Cooley wrote on his efficiency report: "He has the potential to be one of the great battle captains in history."

The Lonesome End finally became a general in 1982. He could have moved up from full colonel to one-star general earlier. That, however, would have required him to give up his brigade command, a post normally held for two years but which he clung to for 33 months. He chose to stay at the lower rank.

Indeed, Carpenter's life as an American soldier stands in vivid contrast to that of his more celebrated teammate, Dawkins, whose career seemed preordained to lead him straight to the White House by way of the desk of the Army Chief of Staff. Dawkins was a Rhodes scholar at Oxford, received a doctorate in international relations from Princeton and served three tours in the Pentagon, six years in all, including one as a White House Fellow. While Carpenter spent his career shunning life in the limelight, Dawkins was not so inclined.

Says Cooley, who served with both men, "Bill was always the quiet man who didn't blow his own horn. Dawkins was just the opposite. Here was Bill, who went through the system as a leader, taking all the assignments and not doing the stuff that Dawkins did—the advanced degrees and all—and I think there was a difference in how they eventually came out."

Dawkins left the Army as a one-star general in 1983, joined the Wall Street investment-banking firm of Lehman Brothers and had a brief dalliance with politics when, as a Republican, he lost the race for a U.S. Senate seat in New Jersey in 1988.

Meanwhile, Carpenter went soldiering on. And nothing he ever did in his three decades in the Army compares with his work at Fort Drum, 25 miles south of the Canadian border, outside Watertown, New York. As a major general, with two stars, Carpenter oversaw the $1.3 billion construction of a state-of-the-art military post, the largest Army building

374 / My Turf

project since World War II, and at the same time built from scratch a reactivated 10th Mountain Division. The division brought 30,000 soldiers and their dependents into the area around Fort Drum, nearly doubling the population. Most of the citizenry had never seen a general, but everyone knew who Carpenter was on the day he first showed up in Watertown, in late 1984, to advise a packed room of businessmen on how to deal with the federal government.

"Everyone knew about the Lonesome End and the hero of Dak To," says Terry Roche. "He walked in the back of the room with his fatigue uniform on, and this silence fell across the room. Everybody turned around. I'll never forget it. There was such an aura about him."

What he built at Fort Drum, not surprisingly, was a soldier's fort—a vast city of homes and buildings and barracks that were designed not only for the soldier but also by the soldier. Maj. Gen. Jack Keane, one of Carpenter's brigade commanders, recalls that he entered a room one day where architects and engineers were standing over designs for the barracks, and he started studying them, looking for things to improve. He could find nothing. "Who has seen these barracks?" Keane asked a young architect.

"Sir," the architect replied, "we've had soldiers of all ranks looking at these designs. General Carpenter sends all the people down here who have to live in them, and they tell us what to fix."

When it came time to design a youth center, Carpenter told the architects to sit down with teenagers and build it around their ideas. "The people who had the most to say about family housing were not engineers," Keane says. "He said, 'Let the wives tell us how to build it.' That's his thumbprint on the place."

That and the division he and his staff built from nothing. "It ended up the best division in the Army," says Hackworth. "No doubt about it—in terms of the quality, of the depth, of the brains and leaders he collected."

Carpenter left Fort Drum in April 1988, and a month later he was the assistant chief of staff for operations in the U.S.–Republic of Korea combined command. In September 1989 he finally got that third star as a lieutenant general and assumed command of the combined field army, potentially one of the hottest combat posts in the U.S. Army. With 240,000 troops under him, most of them forces of the Republic of Korea, Carpenter's mission was to guard the main invasion routes leading south across the DMZ toward Seoul. After four years in Korea, Carpenter resigned on Aug. 31, 1992.

For nearly two decades he had invested his life in helping to build the all-volunteer Army that triumphed in Desert Storm, and he did not want to be around when the budget ax began to fall. "Why should I sit and preside over the demise of something that I struggled for 20 years to crank up?" he says. "I left with a pretty good taste in my mouth. It was time to go. It felt right."

It is late morning of a day in August, and Carpenter is bearing north and east along the shore of Kintla Lake in Montana, sitting in the back of his canoe and digging his paddle into the water with deep, powerful strokes. The lake lies in a bowl of rock in the far northwest corner of Glacier National Park—above the rushing north fork of the Flathead River, up along a winding dirt road that cuts through charred forests, up at the end of the last twisting elbow of road that curls around the campsite at the water's edge.

"You should come up here in June," Carpenter says, "when the snow is melting and waterfalls are all over that mountain. I come up here by myself on occasion. You can go out in a place like this for a week and not see anybody. If I were living back east, the last thing I'd do on Memorial Day is say, 'Let's go for a drive.' But Toni and I did that this year. We drove up to the Yaak Valley, at the Idaho-Canadian border, and were gone all day. We saw 17 cars. We had lunch at the Dirty Shame Saloon. Can you beat that?"

Not by any measure known to Carpenter. The fact that he left the Army with three stars instead of four troubles him not at all. It is clearly a point that distracts him even less these days than the deer that sneak onto his property to nibble at the flowering crab apple bush that he planted. Far weightier than any other issue bearing on his life are the railroad ties he has been struggling to lay for a walkway leading to the backyard deck, a wrap-around porch with a commanding view of a stand of larch pines and several cords of wood he has been cutting and stacking for the winter.

Bill and Toni are home at last. They live in a two-story log house whose design he sketched for the builder on the back of an envelope. "If I had it to do over again," he says, "I'd have retired after military school, bought two acres out here somewhere and lived off the land. And not worked for anybody."

In the year since his retirement, he has settled into a life of ease. The couple's three boys are on their own. Bill Jr., 31, is a high school football coach in Colville, Washington; Ken, 29, a former end at the Air Force Academy, is an F–15 fighter pilot; and Steve, 28, sells outdoor equipment in Southern California.

The 56-year-old Carpenter rises every morning at 5:30 and spends his days drifting casually between working on his house and backpacking through the endless woods or canoeing some pristine lake or river. "I always said I wasn't going to hang around the military when I retired," he says. "I was thinking of all those ex-military guys with their suits and briefcases, trying to get the Army to buy something."

Carpenter holds tightly to his new freedom. He is cultivating a beard, and he is letting his subscriptions to military publications expire. Here is a man who never made a sentimental journey to any of his old posts, though this year he has returned twice to South Korea to help an American firm, Titan Applications Group, evaluate the Korean high command in computer-simulated exercises. The money is excellent, and he is selling not hardware but a singular expertise, the consoling point in a venture for which he seems almost apologetic: "No one knows the personalities of the Korean high command better than I do."

In a few years, as that command turns over and his expertise grows obsolete, he will retire as a consultant, too, and do something far earthier if he needs the extra work. His unaffected humility, his utter lack of pretense, is his fourth star. "I'd drive a delivery truck," he says. "Or work in a hardware store. Or pump gas. What I'd really like to do is go to work for my builder. I can do almost anything. I can put in bathrooms. I can lay tile. I can wallpaper. I can paint. I'm finishing my basement right now. I'd go to work for my builder. In a heartbeat."

As for now, far richer in space and time than he has ever been, Carpenter is making his last stand way out there in the wild, way up along the nation's northern sideline, about as far away as he can get from the world's work. Toni is holding a large painted sign with mountains in purple and lettering that says LONESOME END. Carpenter shakes his head. "It should be an apostrophe—Lonesome's End," he says. "I'm not hanging the sign on me. I'm going to hang it on the house."

Toni tips her head. She had it right. "No," she says. "Lonesome End. That's what we're calling our place. I thought of it. What else could ours be other than the Lonesome End?"

October 1993

Carpenter still lives with his wife in that two-story log house in northwestern Montana not far from the Canadian border, near Kalispell. He is still canoeing on its lakes and rivers. As remote as they are, Carpenter is thinking now that they might move even farther north. "It's getting too crowded around here," he says. "We're thinking of moving closer to Canada."